Korean
Dictionary & Phrasebook

Korean-English
English- Korean

CONTENTS

INTRODUCTION
What Kind of Language Is Korean?

Korean is the native language of 67 million people living on the Korean peninsula, as well as the heritage language of 5.6 million Diaspora Koreans.

The Korean language consists of seven geographically based dialects. Despite the differences in dialects, Korean is relatively homogeneous, with strong mutual intelligibility among speakers from different areas. This is because the mass media and formal education are based on standard speech and strongly contribute to the standardization of the language.

The closest sister language of Korean is Japanese. However, they are not mutually intelligible and their relationship is very weak. Some scholars claim that Korean and Japanese are remotely related to the Altaic languages, such as native Manchu, Mongolian, and the Turkic languages.

Although Korean and Japanese are geographically, historically, and culturally close to China, Korean and Japanese are not part of the same language family as Chinese, and therefore are not grammatically similar. However, both Korean and Japanese have borrowed a large number of Chinese words and characters throughout the course of their long historical contact with various Chinese dynasties, and those borrowed Chinese words and characters have become an integral part of the Korean and Japanese vocabularies.

Since the end of World War II, Korean people have been in contact with many foreign countries and have borrowed thousands of words, the majority from English. During the 35-year occupation of Korea by Japan, a considerable number of Japanese words were also borrowed.

The Korean vocabulary has three components: native words and affixes (approx. 35 percent), Sino-Korean words (approx. 60 percent), and loanwords (approx. 5 percent). Native words denote daily necessities (food, clothing, and shelter), locations, basic actions, activities, states of being, lower-level numbers, body parts, natural objects, animals, and so forth.

Due to their ideographic and monosyllabic nature, Chinese characters are easily combined and recombined to coin new terms as new cultural objects and concepts are created. Most institutional terms, traditional cultural terms, personal names, and place names are Sino-Korean words. There are 14,000 loanwords in Korean, almost 9 percent from English. Most of those loanwords are commonly used, facilitating, to a certain extent, cross-cultural communication.

Korean is often called a situation-oriented language in that contextually or situationally understood elements, including subject and object, are omitted more frequently than not. Therefore, inserting the pronoun "you" or "I" in expressions such as 안녕하세요? (an-nyeong-ha-se-yo?) / "How are you?," or 고맙습니다 (go-map-sum-ni-da) / "Thank you," would sound awkward in normal contexts.

Korean is a "macro-to-micro" language. The larger context of something is presented first, followed by gradually smaller contexts, ending with the individual context. For example, when referring to someone by name, Koreans say or write the family name first and the given name second, which may be followed by a title. An address is given by first indicating the country, followed by, in descending order, the province, city, street, house number, and, finally, the name of the addressee. Koreans indicate a date with the year first, the month second, and the day last.

Korean may be called an honorific language in that one uses different words and phrases depending on the status of the person being discussed or to whom one is speaking. Differences such as age, family relationship, and social status are systematically encoded in the structure and use of Korean. A small number of commonly used words have two forms, one plain and one honorific. The honorific forms are used with an adult of equal or greater status, such as an elder, whereas the plain forms are reserved for another of lesser status. There are also humble verbs used to express deference to an elder or one of greater position.

Korean has an extensive set of address and reference terms that are sensitive to degrees of social stratification and distance between the speaker and addressee and between the speaker and referent. The most frequently used terms for a social superior or an adult distant equal are composed of an occupational title followed by the gender-neutral honorific suffix –님 (nim), such as 교수님 (gyo-su-nim) / Professor.

This may be preceded by the full or family name. There are several titles. The most frequently used among younger co-workers or when speaking to a child or adolescent is the gender-neutral noun –씨 (ssi). This noun is affixed to one's full or given name. When speaking or referring to child, use either the given name alone or the full name without a title. When addressing a child by a given name, the name is followed by a particle. When the name ends with a consonant, the particle is 아 (a). When it ends with a vowel, the particle is 야 (ya).

In Korean, first person pronouns—the English "I" and "we"—have both plain and humble forms. The plain singular form is 나 (na) and the plain plural is 우리 (u-ri), while the humble singular is 저 (jeo) and the humble plural is 저희 (jeo-hui). The humble forms are used when speaking with an elder or an adult of higher social status. Second person pronouns, the equivalent of the English "you", are used only when speaking with children. The singular form is 너 (neo) and the plural is 너희 (neo-hui). When speaking with an adult, one must address them with their name and title. For example: 김선생님 (gim-seon-saeng-nim) / "you, teacher Kim".

Korean is currently written using both Chinese characters and the Korean phonetic alphabet known as 한글 (hanguel/hangul). Chinese characters were used exclusively in written Korean until 1443, when King Sejong the Great, the fourth king of the 조선 (jo-seon) Dynasty, created 한글 with his court scholars. 한글 has continued to enjoy increasing favor over Chinese characters. The latter's contemporary usage is largely restricted to newspapers and scholarly books, and even there it is limited. Chinese characters, however, are very useful in differentiating between words with identical pronunciation and 한글 spelling.

There are considerable differences between the Korean and English languages. Such differences range from pronunciation and grammar to vocabulary principles and writing systems to underlying traditions and culture. These differences make Korean one of the most challenging languages for a native English speaker to learn. We hope this book will help to make it one of the most rewarding.

KOREAN ALPHABET & PRONUNCIATION GUIDE

The Letters of the 한글 (Hangul/han-geul) Alphabet and Their Pronunciation

The current 한글 alphabet has 40 characters: 19 consonants, 8 vowels, and 13 diphthongs. A diphthong combines two separate vowel sounds. In English, examples include the "ou" sound in the word "out" and the "eo" sound in the word "people".

Korean allows a three-way voiceless contrast (plain, aspirate, and tense) in plosive consonants, and a two-way (plain and tense) or no contrast in fricative consonants. In addition to these consonants, Korean has the liquid consonant *l*, which is pronounced as *r* in initial position or between vowels, and three nasal consonants.

There are four kinds of consonants in Korean: plosive, fricative, liquid, and nasal. Plosive consonants have three kinds of contrasts: plain, aspirate, and tense. Twelve consonants are plosive, with four in each contrast. There are 3 fricative consonants, two using the plain contrast and the other using the tense contrast. The one liquid consonant is *l*, although it is pronounced as *r* when it begins a word or appears between two vowels. There are three nasal consonants, but they are not distinguished by contrasts.

This pronunciation chart, which also indicates the proper tongue position when making the consonant sounds, illustrates the various differences:

	Lips	Gum Ridge	Hard Palatal	Soft Palatal	Throat
PLOSIVE					
Plain	ㅂ [p/b] baby	ㄷ [t/d] day	ㅈ [ch/j] angel	ㄱ [k/g] begin	
Aspirate	ㅍ [p'] public	ㅌ [t'] atomic	ㅊ [ch'] achieve	ㅋ [k'] akin	
Tense	ㅃ [pp] spoon	ㄸ [tt] state	ㅉ [tch] pizza	ㄲ [kk] skate	
FRICATIVE					
Plain		ㅅ [s/sh] sheep			ㅎ [h] home
Tense		ㅆ [ss] assign			
LIQUID		ㄹ [l/r] leaf radio			
NASAL	ㅁ [m] me	ㄴ [n] now		ㅇ [ng] song	

Consonants change sounds depending on their position in a word. The 한글 spellings, however, do not change.

In standard Korean, there are 8 vowels and 13 diphthongs. The vowels are grouped into categories of front and back. Back vowels are further categorized as round and unround. (All front vowels are unround.) The Korean vowel chart, which indicates both these divisions and the tongue position during pronunciation, is below:

Tongue Position	Front		Back	
	Unround	Round	Unround	Round
High Mid Low	] [i] beet ᅦ [e] bet ᅢ [ae] at		― [û] good ᅥ [ô] mother ᅡ [a] father	ㅜ [u] buoy ㅗ [o] awkward

There are two semi-vowels, *y* and *w*, and they combine with 8 vowels to make 13 diphthongs. The Korean diphthong chart is represented below.

	ᅡ	ᅥ	ㅗ	ㅜ	―	]	ᅦ	ᅢ
y	ᅣ[ya] yacht	ᅧ[yô] young	ㅛ[yo] yawn	ㅠ[yu] yukon	ᅴ[ûi]		ᅨ[ye] yet	ᅤ[yae] yak
w	ᅪ[wa] wander	ᅯ[wô] wonder			ᅱ[wi] win	ᅬ[we] west	ᅰ[we] west	ᅫ[wae] wangle

Syllable Blocks in Korean

한글 (han-geul) letters are combined into syllable blocks. The syllable blocks are constructed out of what is referred to as consonant, vowel, and dipthong positions. A square syllable block has the initial consonant position followed by a vowel or diphthong position. In the final consonant position, one or two consonants may occur. If a syllable does not begin with a consonant, the syllable block must have the letter ○ in the initial consonant position. The letter ○ is silent and functions as a zero consonant in the initial position of a syllable block.

If the vowel letter in the syllable block contains one or two long vertical strokes, it is written to the right of the initial consonant letter (e.g. 나 [na] , 계 [gye]). If the vowel letter in the syllable block contains only a long horizontal stroke, the vowel letter is written below the initial consonant letter (e.g. 무 [mu], 교 [gyo]). If a diphthong letter contains a long horizontal stroke and a long vertical stroke, the initial consonant letter occurs in the upper left corner (e.g. 귀 [gwi], 놔 [nwa]). When a syllable ends with consonants, they occur beneath the vowel letter (e.g. 밧 [bwat], 김 [gim], 흙 [heuk, heulk]). Final consonants can be all single consonant letters and the following two-letter combinations: ㄲ (kk), ㅆ (ss), ㄳ (ks), ㄵ (nj), ㄶ (nh), ㄺ (lk), ㄻ (lm), ㄼ (lp), ㄽ (ls), ㄾ (lt'), ㄿ (lp'), ㅀ (lh), ㅄ (ps). When writing the letters in syllable blocks, they should be balanced to fill the space.

To demonstrate the construction of a word in written Korean, let us consider the word 한글 (han-geul). It has two syllable blocks, 한 (han) and 글(geul). In the first syllable block, ㅎ(h), ㅏ (a), and ㄴ(n) combine like this:

한 (han)

In the second syllable block, the letters ㄱ(g), ㅡ(eu), and ㄹ(l) combine to form:

글 (gul)

Note how, in accordance with the rules outlined above, the initial consonant ㅎ(h) in 한 (han) appears with ㅏ (a) to its right and the final consonant ㄴ(n) below. With the syllable block 글(geul), note how the initial consonant ㄱ(g) is placed first, with the vowel ㅡ(eu), which is written as a horizontal stroke, below it, and the final consonant ㄹ(l) appearing below the vowel.

The Romanization of Korean (according to the Korean Ministry of Culture and Tourism proclamation No. 2000-8)

1. Basic principles of romanization

(1) Romanization is based on standard Korean pronunciation.
(2) Symbols other than Roman letters are avoided to the greatest extent possible.

2. Summary of the romanization system

(1) Vowels are transcribed as follows:

Simple Vowels ㅏ *a* / ㅓ *eo* / ㅗ *o* / ㅜ *u* / ㅡ *eu* / ㅣ *i* /
ㅐ *ae* / ㅔ *e* / ㅚ *oe* / ㅟ *wi*

Diphthongs ㅑ *ya* / ㅕ *yeo* / ㅛ *yo* / ㅠ *yu* / ㅒ *yae* /
ㅖ *ye* / ㅘ *wa* / ㅙ *wae* / ㅝ *wo*
ㅞ *we* / ㅢ *ui*

> Note 1: ㅢ is transcribed as *ui*, even when pronounced as ㅣ.
>
> Note 2: Long vowels are not reflected in romanization.

(2) Consonants are transcribed as follows:

Plosives (Stops) ㄱ *g, k* / ㄲ *kk* / ㅋ *k* / ㄷ *d, t* / ㄸ *tt* / ㅌ *t* /
ㅂ *b, p* / ㅃ *pp* / ㅍ *p*

Affricates and Fricatives ㅈ *j* / ㅉ *jj* / ㅊ *ch* / ㅅ *s* / ㅆ *ss* /
ㅎ *h*

Nasals and Liquids ㄴ *n* / ㅁ *m* / ㅇ *ng* / ㄹ *r, l*

> Note 1: The sounds ㄱ, ㄷ, and ㅂ are transcribed respectively as *g*, *d*, and *b* when they appear before a vowel; They are transcribed as *k*, *t*, and *p* when followed by another consonant or forming the final sound of a word.
>
> Note 2: ㄹ is transcribed as *r* when followed by a vowel, and *l* when followed by a consonant or when appearing at the end of a word. ㄹㄹ is transcribed as *ll*.

3. Special provisions for romanization

(1) When Korean sound values change as in the following cases, the results of those changes are romanized.

    1) The case of assimilation of adjacent consonants
    2) The case of the epenthetic [inserted within the body of a word] ㄴ and ㄹ
    3) Cases of palatalization
    4) Cases where ㄱ, ㄷ, ㅂ and ㅈ are adjacent to ㅎ. However, aspirated sounds are not reflected in case of nouns where ㅎ follows ㄱ, ㄷ, and ㅂ.
    Note: Tense (or glottalized) sounds are not reflected in cases where morphemes [the smallest part of a word that has meaning] are compounded.

(2) When there is the possibility of confusion in pronunciation, a hyphen "-" may be used.

(3) The first letter is capitalized in proper names.

(4) Personal names are written by family name first, followed by a space and the given name. In principle, syllables in given names are not separated by hyphen, but the use of a hyphen between syllables is permitted.

    1) Assimilated sound changes between syllables in given names are not transcribed.
    2) Romanization of family names will be determined separately.

(5) Administrative units, such as 도 *do*, 시 *si*, 군 *gun*, 구 *gu*, 읍 *eup*, 면 *myeon*, 리 *ri*, 동 *dong*, and 가 *ga* are transcribed respectively as *do, si, gun, gu, eup, myeon, ri, dong,* and *ga,* and are preceded by a hyphen. Assimilated sound changes before and after the hyphen are not reflected in romanization.
    Note: Terms for administrative units such as 시 *si*, 군 *gun*, 읍 *eup* may be omitted.

(6) Names of geographic features, cultural properties, and manmade structures may be written without hyphens.

(7) Proper names such as personal names and those of companies may continue to be written as they have been previously.

(8) When it is necessary to convert romanized Korean back to 한글 in special cases such as in academic articles, romanization is done according to 한글 spelling and not pronunciation. Each 한글 letter is romanized as explained in section 2 except that ㄱ, ㄷ, ㅂ and ㄹ are always written as *g, d, b* and *l*. When ㅇ has no sound value, it is replaced by a hyphen. It may also be used when it is necessary to distinguish between syllables.

Pronunciation Rules

Rule 1. Resyllabification

When a syllable in a word ends with a consonant and the next syllable begins with a vowel, the consonant, when pronounced, is part of the latter syllable. For example, 한글은 (han-geul-eun) is pronounced han-geu-reun. In this case, the sound of ㄹ changes from *l* to *r* because ㄹ now appears between two vowels. Similarly, when a syllable block ends in a double consonant, the second consonant is pronounced before the vowel as part of the latter syllable, so the Korean word for "read," 읽어요 (ilk-eo-yo), is pronounced il-geo-yo.

Rule 2. Final closure in syllable pronunciation

At the end of a word or before a consonant, all Korean consonants are pronounced without releasing air. As a result, consonants at the end of words or preceding other consonants change sounds. For example, 꽃 (kkoch) is pronounced kkot and 꽃도 (kkoch-do) is pronounced kkot-do. The change of ㅊ to ㄷ happens here because the speech organs responsible for the articulation of the word-final and pre-consonantal ㅊ are not released. The sound of ㅊ (ch') becomes *t* because one does not release air when pronouncing it in these and similar words. The only consonant sounds that occur at the end of a word or before another consonant are the seven simple consonants: ㅂ (p/b), ㄷ (t/d), ㄱ (k/g), ㅁ (m), ㄴ (n), ㅇ (ng), and ㄹ (l/r).

The sound changes are illustrated in the chart below.

ㅂ, ㅃ, ㅍ → ㅂ

ㄷ, ㄸ, ㅌ, ㅅ, ㅆ, ㅈ, ㅉ, ㅊ, ㅎ → ㄷ

ㄱ, ㄲ, ㅋ → ㄱ

ㅁ → ㅁ

ㄴ → ㄴ

ㅇ → ㅇ

ㄹ → ㄹ

Rule 3. *Nasal assimilation*

All plosive and fricative consonants become corresponding nasal consonants when preceding a nasal consonant. For example, the word 앞문 (ap-mun) is pronounced am-mun and 일학년 (il-hak-nyeon) is pronounced il-hang-nyeon. The chart below fully illustrates the changes.

ㅂ, ㅃ, ㅍ → ㅁ

ㄷ, ㄸ, ㅌ, ㅅ, ㅆ, ㅈ, ㅉ, ㅊ, ㅎ → ㄴ

ㄱ, ㄲ, ㅋ → ㅇ

Rule 4. ㄴ *to* ㄹ *assimilation*

When ㄹ (l/r) and ㄴ (n) appear together in a word, the *n* sound is usually replaced by the *l/r* sound, as in the Korean word 칠년 (chil-lyeon). When *l/r* is followed by the vowel ㅣ (i) or the semivowel ㅑ (ya) in certain compound words, another *l/r* is inserted between them, as in the Korean word 물약 (mul-lyak).

Rule 5. *Tensification*

When a plain plosive consonant (ㅂ (p/b), ㄷ (t/d), ㅈ (ch/j), ㄱ (k/g)) or the fricative consonant ㅅ (s/sh) is preceded by a plosive or fricative consonant (ㅂ, ㄷ, ㅈ, ㄱ, ㅅ, ㅍ[p'], ㅌ[t'], ㅊ[ch'], ㅋ[k'], ㅎ[h], ㅃ[pp], ㄸ[tt], ㅉ[tch], ㄲ[kk], ㅆ[ss]) it becomes a corresponding tense consonant, as in the words for "students" 학생 (hak-ssaeng), "non-existent" 없다 (eop-tta), and "school" 학교 (hak-kkyo).

Rule 6. Aspiration and the weakening of ㅎ

When the fricative consonant ㅎ (h) is preceded or followed by a plain plosive consonant (ㅂ [p/b], ㄷ [t/d], ㅈ [ch/j], ㄱ [k/g]), it merges with the consonant to produce a corresponding aspirate consonant (ㅍ [p'], ㅌ [t'], ㅊ [ch'], ㅋ [k']), as in the words for 좋다 (jo-ta) "to be good", 입학 (i-pak) "entering school", and 착하다 (cha-ka-da) "to be kind".

Rule 7. Double consonant reduction

As indicated in Rule 1, the second of the two consonants at the end of a syllable is, when pronounced, carried over to the following syllable if the latter syllable does not begin with a consonant. However, one of the two consonants becomes silent at the end of a word or before a consonant, as in the words 값 (gap) and 값도 (gap-tto). In English, up to three consonants may be combined in a syllable, but not even two may be combined in Korean. It is difficult to predict which of two consonants will become silent. The silent consonant is usually the second one, but there are exceptions.

Rule 8. Palatalization

When a word ending in ㄷ (t/d) or ㅌ (t') is followed by a suffix beginning with the vowel ㅣ (i) or the semi-vowel ㅕ (yeo), the ㄷ and ㅌ are pronounced, respectively, *ch/j* and *ch'*, as in the words for "to be closed," 닫혀요 (da-chyeo-yo), and "to attach," 붙이다 (bu-chi-da). This change is technically called "palatalization" because the original consonants, which are pronounced using the gum-ridge, are articulated with the hard palate.

ABBREVIATIONS

abbr.	abbreviation
adj.	adjective (including noun-modifier in Korean)
adv.	adverb
coll.	colloquial
conj.	conjunction
cop.	copula, i.e., linking verb
count.	counter
dat.	dative/indirect object particle
dir.	direction
e.g.	for example
fut.	future tense
hon.	honorific
loc.	location
n.	noun
num.	number
obj.	object/object particle
part.	particle
pl.	plural
pren.	pre-noun/noun modifier
pres.	present tense
pron.	pronoun
pst.	past tense
sing.	singular
subj.	subject/subject particle
top.	topic/topic particle
v.	verb (including both active verb and descriptive verb in Korean)
v. stem	verb stem
v. intr.	intransitive verb, i.e., cannot have an object
v. tr.	transitive verb, i.e., can have an object

KOREAN-ENGLISH DICTIONARY

ㄱ

가게 (ga-ge) *n.* store

가격 (ga-gyeok) *n.* price

가구 (ga-gu) *n.* furniture

가구점 (ga-gu-jeom) *n.* furniture store

가깝다 (ga-kkap-da) *v.* to be close; **가까운** (ga-kka-un) *adj.* close

가끔 (ga-kkeum) *adv.* once in a while, sometimes

가늘다 (ga-neul-da) *v.* to be thin; **가는** (ga-neun) *adj.* thin

가능하다 (ga-neung-ha-da) *v.* to be possible; **가능한** (ga-neung-han) *adj.* possible

가다 (ga-da) *v.* to go

가르쳐주다 (ga-reu-chyeo-ju-da) *v.* to teach

가르치다 (ga-reu-chi-da) *v.* to teach

가방 (ga-bang) *n.* bag

가볍다 (ga-byeop-da) *v.* to be light; **가벼운** (ga-byeo-un) *adj.* light

가수 (ga-su) *n.* singer

가슴 (ga-seum) *n.* chest

가운데 (ga-un-de) *n.* middle, center

가위 (ga-wi) *n.* scissors

가을 (ga-eul) *n.* autumn, fall

가장 (ga-jang) *adv.* the most, head of a family

가정교사 (ga-jeong-gyo-sa) *n.* tutor

가족 (ga-jok) *n.* family

가죽 (ga-juk) *n.* leather

가지고 가다 (ga-ji-go ga-da) *v.* to take

가지고 오다 (ga-ji-go o-da) *v.* to bring

가지다 (ga-ji-da) *v.* to have

간단하다 (gan-dan-ha-da) *v.* to be simple; **간단한** (gan-dan-han) *adj.* simple

간장 (gan-jang) *n.* soy sauce

간판 (gan-pan) *n.* store sign

간호사 (gan-ho-sa) *n.* nurse

갈비 (gal-bi) *n.* sparerib

갈비구이 (gal-bi-gu-i) *n.* barbecued spareribs

갈비탕 (gal-bi-tang) *n.* sparerib soup

갈색 (gal-saek) *n.,adj.* light brown

갈아입다 (gal-a-ip-da) *v.* to change (clothes)

갈아타는 곳 (gal-a-ta-neun got) *n.* place to change vehicles

갈아타다 (gal-a-ta-da) *v.* to change (vehicles)

감기 (gam-gi) *n.* a cold

감기약 (gam-gi-yak) *n.* cold medicine

감기에 걸리다 (gam-gi-e geol-li-da) to catch a cold

감사하다 (gam-sa-ha-da) *v.* to be thankful

감색 (gam-saek) *n.* navy blue

감자 (gam-ja) *n.* potato

갑자기 (gap-ja-gi) *adv.* suddenly

값 (gap) *n.* price

갔다오다 (gat-da-o-da) *v.* to go and come back

강 (gang) *n.* river

강아지 (gang-a-ji) *n.* puppy

강하다 (gang-ha-da) *v.* to be strong; **강한** (gang-han) *adj.* strong

갖다놓다 (gat-da-no-ta) *v.* to bring and put

같다 (gat-da) *v.* to be the same; **같은** (gat-eun) *adj.* same

같이 (ga-chi) *adv.* together

개 (gae) *n.* dog

개그맨 (gae-geu-man) *n.* comedian

개미 (gae-mi) *n.* ant

개방적이다 (gae-bang-jeog-i-da) *v.* to be open-hearted, to have empathy; **개방적인** (gae-bang-jeog-in) *adj.* open-hearted, empathetic

개장 (gae-jang) *n.* opening

개장하다 (gae-jang-ha-da) *v.* to open

거기 (geo-gi) *n.* there

거나 (geo-na) *conj.* or (with verb)

거리 (geo-ri) *n.* street, road

거북하다 (geo-bu-ka-da) *v.* to be uncomfortable; **거북한** (geo-bu-kan) *adj.* uncomfortable

거스름돈 (geo-seu-reum-don) *n.* change

거실 (geo-sil) *n.* living room

거울 (geo-ul) *n.* mirror

거의 (geo-ui) *adv.* almost

거짓말 (geo-jin-mal) *n.* lie

거짓말을 하다 (geo-jin-mal-eul ha-da) to tell a lie

걱정 (geok-jeong) *n.* worry

걱정을 하다 (geok-jeong-eul ha-da) to worry

걱정이 되다 (geok-jeong-i doe-da) to be worried

건강 (geon-gang) *n.* health

건강하다 (geon-gang-ha-da) *v.* to be healthy; **건강한** (geon-gang-han) *adj.* healthy

건강해지다 (geon-gang-hae-ji-da) *v.* to become healthy

건강히 (geon-gang-hi) *adv.* healthily

건너다 (geon-neo-da) *v.* to cross (the road)

건너방 (geon-neo-bang) *n.* second bedroom

건너편 (geon-neo-pyeon) *n.* other side of the street

건물 (geon-mul) *n.* building

건전지 (geon-jeon-ji) *n.* battery

건조기 (geon-jo-gi) *n.* drier

건조하다 (geon-jo-ha-da) *v.* to be dry; **건조한** (geon-jo-han) *adj.* dry

건축가 (geon-chuk-ga) *n.* architect

걷다 (geot-da) *v.* to walk

걸레 (geol-le) *n.* duster, mop

걸리다 (geol-li-da) *v.* to take (time)

걸어가다 (geol-eo-ga-da) *v.* to walk (to a place)

걸어오다 (geol-eo-o-da) *v.* to come on foot

검사 (geom-sa) *n.* prosecutor

검은색 (geom-eun-saek) *n., adj.* black

검정색 (geom-jeong-saek) *n., adj.* black

겁나다 (geom-na-da) *v.* to be scared; **겁먹은** (geom-meog-eun) *adj.* scared

겉 (geot) *n.* surface

게임 (ge-im) *n.* game

겨우 (gyeo-u) *adv.* barely

겨울 (gyeo-ul) *n.* winter

결정하다 (gyeol-jeong-ha-da) *v.* to decide

결혼 (gyeol-hon) *n.* marriage

결혼식 (gyeol-hon-sik) *n.* wedding, marriage ceremony

결혼식장 (gyeol-hon-sik-jang) *n.* wedding hall

결혼하다 (gyeol-hon-ha-da) *v.* to get married

겹치다 (gyeop-chi-da) *adj.* to overlap

경기 (gyeong-gi) *n.* game

경쟁 (gyeong-jaeng) *n.* competition

경쟁률 (gyeong-jaeng-nyul) *n.* competition rate

경제 (gyeong-je) *n.* economy

경찰 (gyeong-chal) *n.* police

경찰서 (gyeong-chal-seo) *n.* police station

경찰차 (gyeong-chal-cha) *n.* police car

경험 (gyeong-heom) *n.* experience

경험자 (gyeong-heom-ja) *n.* experienced person

계단 (gye-dan) *n.* stairs

계란 (gye-ran) *n.* egg

계산서 (gye-san-seo) *n.* check, bill

계속 (gye-sok) *adv.* continuously

계속되다 (gye-sok-doe-da) *v.* to continue

계시다 (gye-si-da) *v.* to exist, stay (*hon.*)

계절 (gye-jeol) *n.* season

계획 (gye-hoek) *n.* plan

계획을 짜다 (gye-hoeg-eul jja-da) to make plans

계획하다 (gye-hoe-ka-da) *v.* to plan

고기 (go-gi) *n.* meat

고등학교 (go-deung-hak-go) *n.* high school

고등학생 (go-deung-hak-saeng) *n.* high school student

고래 (go-rae) *n.* whale

고르다 (go-reu-da) *v.* to choose

고맙다 (go-map-da) *v.* to be thankful

고모 (go-mo) *n.* aunt

고모부 (go-mo-bu) *n.* uncle

고민하다 (go-min-ha-da) *v.* to worry

고상하다 (go-sang-ha-da) *v.* to be elegant; **고상한** (go-sang-han) *adj.* elegant

고생하다 (go-saeng-ha-da) *v.* to suffer, to have a hard time

고속도로 (go-sok-do-ro) *n.* highway, expressway

고속버스 (go-sok-beo-seu) *n.* express bus

고속버스터미널 (go-sok-beo-seu-teo-mi-neol) *n.* express bus terminal

고양이 (go-yang-i) *n.* cat

고장나다 (go-jang-na-da) *v.* to be out of order, to be broken; **고장난** (go-jang-nan) *adj.* out of order, broken

고추 (go-chu) *n.* red pepper

고추장 (go-chu-jang) *n.* red-pepper paste

고춧가루 (go-chut-ga-ru) *n.* red-pepper powder

고층아파트 (go-cheung-a-pa-teu) *n.* high-rise apartment

고치다 (go-chi-da) *v.* to fix, to repair, to cure

고향 (go-hyang) *n.* hometown

곧 (got) *adv.* immediately, soon

골프 (gol-peu) *n.* golf

골프를 치다 (gol-peu-reul chi-da) *v.* to play golf

곰 (gom) *n.* bear

곰인형 (gom-in-hyeong) *n.* teddy bear

공 (gong) *n.* ball

공기 (gong-gi) *n.* air

공부방 (gong-bu-ppang) *n.* study room

공부하다 (gong-bu-ha-da) *v.* to study

공사 (gong-sa) *n.* construction

공사중이다 (gong-sa-jung-i-da) *v.* to be under construction; **공사중** (gong-sa-jung) *adj.* under construction

공연 (gong-yeon) *n.* performance

공원 (gong-won) *n.* park

공장 (gong-jang) *n.* factory

공중목욕탕 (gong-jung-mog-yok-tang) *n.* public bath

공짜 (gong-jja) *n.* free

공짜로 (gong-jja-ro) *adv.* for free

공책 (gong-chaek) *n.* notebook

공항 (gong-hang) *n.* airport

과식하다 (gwa-si-ka-da) *v.* to overeat

과외비 (gwa-oe-bi) *n.* tuition fees

과일 (gwa-il) *n.* fruit

과일가게 (gwa-il-ga-ge) *n.* fruit store

과자 (gwa-ja) *n.* chip, cookie

관계 (gwan-gye) *n.* relation

관광객 (gwan-gwang-gaek) *n.* tourist, traveler

관광지 (gwan-gwang-ji) *n.* place to tour, tourist attraction

광고 (gwang-go) *n.* advertisement

광고지 (gwang-go-ji) *n.* ad flyer

광장 (gwang-jang) *n.* plaza

괜찮다 (gwaen-chan-ta) *v.* to be all right, to be okay

괴롭다 (goe-rop-da) *v.* to be troublesome, to be distressing; **괴로운** (goe-ro-un) *adj.* troublesome

굉장히 (goeng-jang-hi) *adv.* very much

교수님 (gyo-su-nim) *n.* professor

교육 (gyo-yuk) *n.* education

교육자 (gyo-yuk-ja) *n.* educator

교제하다 (gyo-je-ha-da) *v.* to date

교차로 (gyo-cha-ro) *n.* intersection

교통 (gyo-tong) *n.* traffic

교통 표지판 (gyo-tong pyo-ji-pan) *n.* traffic sign

교통위반 (gyo-tong-wi-ban) *n.* traffic violation

교통편 (gyo-tong-pyeon) *n.* transportation

교포 (gyo-po) *n.* an ethnic Korean living abroad

교환하다 (gyo-hwan-ha-da) *v.* to exchange

교회 (gyo-hoe) *n.* church

구 (gu) *n.* nine

구경하다 (gu-gyeong-ha-da) *v.* to sight-see

구두 (gu-du) *n.* dress shoes

구두를 신다 (gu-du-reul sin-tta) to wear a shoe

구둣가게 (gu-dut-ga-ge) *n.* dress-shoe store

구름 (gu-reum) *n.* cloud

구름이 끼다 (gu-reum-i kki-da) to get cloudy

구멍 (gu-meong) *n.* hole

구멍가게 (gu-meong-kka-ge) *n.* convenience store

구월 (gu-wol) *n.* September

국 (guk) *n.* soup

국경일 (guk-gyeong-il) *n.* national holiday

국그릇 (guk-geu-reut) *n.* soup bowl

국내선 (gung-nae-seon) *n.* domestic flight

국립 (gung-nip) *n.*, *adj.* national, government-established

국수 (guk-su) *n.* noodle

국제선 (guk-je-seon) *n.* international flight

국제전화 (guk-je-jeon-hwa) *n.* international call

국화 (gu-kwa) *n.* chrysanthemum

국회 (gu-koe) *n.* Congress, the National Assembly

굵다 (gulk-da) *v.* to be thick; 굵은 (gulg-eun) *adj.* thick

궁금하다 (gung-geum-ha-da) *v.* to be curious about, to
    wonder; 궁금한 (gung-geum-han) *adj.* curious

권투 (gwon-tu) *n.* boxing

귀 (gwi) *n.* ear

귀걸이 (gwi-geol-i) *n.* earring(s)

귀엽다 (gwi-yeop-da) *v.* to be cute; 귀여운 (gwi-yeo-un)
    adj. cute

귀이개 (gwi-i-gae) *n.* ear swab

귀찮다 (gwi-chan-ta) *v.* to be bothersome; 귀찮은 (gwi-
    chan-eun) *adj.* bothersome

귀찮아하다 (gwi-chan-a-ha-da) *v.* to feel bothered

규칙적이다 (gyu-chik-jeog-i-da) *v.* to be regular;
    규칙적인 (gyu-chik-jeog-in) *adj.* regular

그냥 (geu-nyang) *adv.* just, without any special reason

그래서 (geu-rae-seo) *conj.* so, therefore

그러면 (geu-reo-myeon) *conj.* if so, then

그런데 (geu-reon-de) *conj.* by the way, but then

그렇지만 (geu-reo-chi-man) *conj.* but, however

그릇 (geu-reut) *n.* container, vessel, dish

그리고 (geu-ri-go) *conj.* and

그리고 나서 (geu-ri-go-na-seo) *conj.* and then

그리다 (geu-ri-da) *v.* to draw

그림 (geu-rim) *n.* picture

그림을 그리다 (geu-rim-eul geu-ri-da) to draw a picture

그립다 (geu-rip-da) *v.* to be missed; 그리운 (geu-ri-un)
   adj. missed

그만 (geu-man) *adv.* without doing any further

그만두다 (geu-man-du-da) *v.* to quit, to stop

그만이다 (geu-man-i-da) *v.* to be enough, to be good

그만큼 (geu-man-keum) *adv.* that much

그저 그렇다 (geu-jeo geu-reo-ta) *v.* to be only so-so; 그저
   그런 (geu-jeo geu-reon) *adj.* so-so

그저께 (geu-jeo-kke) *n.* the day before yesterday

그제 (geu-je) *n.* the day before yesterday

그쪽 (geu-jjok) *n.* that side

극장 (geuk-jang) *n.* movie theater

근교 (geun-gyo) *n.* the suburbs

근처 (geun-cheo) *n.* neighborhood, nearby

글씨 (geul-ssi) *n.* handwriting

금년 (geum-nyeon) *n.* this year

금방 (geum-bang) *adv.* soon, immediately, in a short time

금붕어 (geum-bung-eo) *n.* goldfish

금연 (geum-yeon) *n.* no smoking

금요일 (geum-yo-il) *n.* Friday

급하다 (geu-pa-da) *v.* to be in a hurry, to be urgent; 급한
   (geu-pan) *adj.* urgent

급히 (geu-pi) *adv.* in a hurry

기다리다 (gi-da-ri-da) *v.* to wait

기르다 (gi-reu-da) *v.* to raise, to grow

기름 (gi-reum) *n.* oil, fat, gasoline

기린 (gi-rin) *n.* giraffe

기분 (gi-bun) *n.* feeling

기분이 나쁘다 (gi-bun-i na-ppeu-da) *v.* to feel bad

기분이 좋다 (gi-bun-i jo-ta) *v.* to feel good

기뻐하다 (gi-ppeo-ha-da) *v.* to be happy

기쁘다 (gi-ppeu-da) *v.* to be happy; 기쁜 (gi-ppeun) *adj.*
   happy

기사 (gi-sa) *n.* newspaper article, driver

기숙사 (gi-suk-sa) *n.* dormitory

기억 (gi-eok) *n.* memory

기억나다 (gi-eong-na-da) *v.* to remember

기억에 남다 (gi-eog-e nam-tta) to remain in one's memory

기억하다 (gi-eo-ka-da) *v.* to remember

기온 (gi-on) *n.* temperature

기온이 낮다 (gi-on-i nat-da) the temperature is low

기온이 낮아지다 (gi-on-i naj-a-ji-da) the temperature goes down

기온이 높다 (gi-on-i nop-da) the temperature is high

기온이 높아지다 (gi-on-i no-pa-ji-da) the temperature goes up

기자 (gi-ja) *n.* reporter

기차 (gi-cha) *n.* train

기차역 (gi-cha-yeok) *n.* train station

기차표 (gi-cha-pyo) *n.* train ticket

기찻길 (gi-chat-gil) *n.* railroad

기침 (gi-chim) *n.* cough

기침약 (gi-chim-nyak) *n.* cough medicine

기침을 하다 (gi-chim-eul ha-da) to cough

기침이 나오다 (gi-chim-i na-o-da) to cough

기타 (gi-ta) *n.* guitar

기타를 치다 (gi-ta-reul chi-da) to play guitar

기회 (gi-hoe) *n.* chance

길 (gil) *n.* street, road

길다 (gil-da) *v.* to be long; 긴 (gin) *adj.* long

김치 (gim-chi) *n.* Korean pickled cabbage

김치찌개 (gim-chi-jji-gae) *n. kimchi* stew

깊다 (gip-da) *v.* to be deep; 깊은 (gi-peun) *adj.* deep

까마귀 (kka-ma-gwi) *n.* craw

까만색 (kka-man-saek) *n.* black

까맣다 (kka-ma-ta) *v.* to be black; 까만 (kka-man) *adj.* black

까치 (kka-chi) *n.* magpie

깎다 (kkak-da) *v.* to cut a man's hair, to discount a price

깔다 (kkal-da) *v.* to spread, to pave

깜깜하다 (kkam-kkam-ha-da) *v.* to be dark; 깜깜한 (kkam-kkam-han) *adj.* dark

깜빡 잊어버리다 (kkam-ppak ij-eo-beo-ri-da) *v.* to completely forget

깜짝 놀라다 (kkam-jjak nol-la-da) *v.* to startle

깡통따개 (kkang-tong-tta-gae) *n.* can opener

깨끗이 (kkae-kkeus-i) *adv.* cleanly

깨끗하다 (kkae-kkeu-ta-da) *v.* to be clean; 깨끗한 (kkae-kkeu-tan) *adj.* clean

깨우다 (kkae-u-da) *v.* to wake someone up

깨지다 (kkae-ji-da) *v.* to be broken; 깨진 (kkae-jin) *adj.* broken

껌 (kkeom) *n.* chewing gum

꼭 (kkok) *adv.* without fail, for sure, exactly

꼭대기 (kkok-dae-gi) *n.* the top

꽃 (kkot) *n.* flower

꽃을 기르다 (kkoch-eul gi-reu-da) to grow flowers

꽃집 (kkot-jip) *n.* flower shop, florist

꽤 (kkwae) *adv.* quite, fairly, pretty much

꿈꾸다 (kkum-kku-da) *v.* to dream

끄다 (kkeu-da) *v.* to turn off

끈 (kkeun) *n.* cord

끊다 (kkeun-ta) *v.* to quit (smoking), to hang up

끓다 (kkeul-ta) *v. intr.* to boil

끓이다 (kkeul-i-da) *v. tr.* to boil

끝 (kkeut) *n.* end

끝나다 (kkeun-na-da) *v. intr.* to be over, to finish

끝내다 (kkeun-nae-da) *v. tr.* to finish

끝마치다 (kkeun-ma-chi-da) *v.* to finish

끼니를 거르다 (kki-ni-reul geo-reu-da) to skip a meal

끼다 (kki-da) *v.* to put on, to wear (glasses)

끼리끼리 (kki-ri-kki-ri) *adv.* among in-group people

ㄴ

나 (na) *pron.* I

나가는 곳 (na-ga-neun got) *n.* exit

나가다 (na-ga-da) *v.* to go out

나다 (na-da) *v.* to break out

나들이 (na-deul-i) *n.* outing

나라 (na-ra) *n.* country, nation

나무 (na-mu) *n.* tree

나뭇가지 (na-mut-ga-ji) *n.* tree branch

나뭇잎 (na-mun-nip) *n.* leaves

나쁘다 (na-ppeu-da) *v.* to be bad; 나쁜 (na-ppeun) *adj.* bad

나오다 (na-o-da) *v.* to come out

나이 (na-i) *n.* age
나이프 (na-i-peu) *n.* knife
나중에 (na-jung-e) *adv.* later
나홀 (na-heul) *n.* four days
낚시 (nak-si) *n.* fishing
낚시를 가다 (nak-si ga-da) *v.* to go fishing
낚시하다 (nak-si ha-da) *v.* to fish
난초 (nan-cho) *n.* orchard
날 (nal) *n.* day
날마다 (nal-ma-da) *adv.* every day
날씨 (nal-ssi) *n.* weather
날씬하다 (nal-ssin-ha-da) *v.* to be slim, to be thin; 날씬한
    (nal-ssin-han) *adj.* slim, thin
남기다 (nam-gi-da) *v.* to leave behind
남녀노소 (nam-nyeo-no-so) *n.* men and women in all ages
남다 (nam-tta) *v.* to remain, to be left; 남은 (nam-eun) *adj.*
    remaining, left behind
남동생 (nam-dong-saeng) *n.* younger brother
남미 (nam-mi) *n.* South America
남방 (nam-bang) *n.* golf shirt, tennis shirt
남부 (nam-bu) *n.* the southern part
남성 (nam-seong) *n.* male
남성용품 (nam-seong-yong-pum) *n.* goods for a male
남자 (nam-ja) *n.* male
남자친구 (nam-ja-chin-gu) *n.* boyfriend
남쪽 (nam-jjok) *n.* south side
남편 (nam-pyeon) *n.* husband
남학생 (nam-hak-saeng) *n.* male student
남한 (nam-han) *n.* South Korea
낫다 (nat-da) *v.* to recover from an illness, to be better
낮 (nat) *n.* daytime, day
낮다 (nat-da) *v.* to be low; 낮은 (na-jeun) *adj.* low
내 (nae) *pron.* my
내년 (nae-nyeon) *n., adv.* next year
내다 (nae-da) *v.* to turn in, to hand in, to pay
내려가다 (nae-ryeo-ga-da) *v.* to go down
내려오다 (nae-ryeo-o-da) *v.* to come down
내려주다 (nae-ryeo-ju-da) *v.* to drop off someone
내리다 (nae-ri-da) *v.* to get off
내성적이다 (nae-seong-jeog-i-da) *v.* to be introspective;
    내성적인 (nae-seong-jeog-in) *adj.* introspective

내일 (nae-il) *n., adv.* tomorrow

내후년 (nae-hu-nyeon) *n., adv.* the year after next year

냄비 (naem-bi) *n.* pot

냄새 (naem-sae) *n.* smell

냄새가 나다 (naem-sae-ga na-da) *v.* to smell

냄새를 맡다 (naem-sae-reul mat-da) *v.* to smell

냅킨 (naep-kin) *n.* napkin

냉수 (naeng-su) *n.* cold water

냉장고 (naeng-jang-go) *n.* refrigerator

너무 (neo-mu) *adv.* too much

넓다 (neol-tta) *v.* to be spacious, to be wide; 넓은 (neolb-eun) *adj.* spacious, wide

넘어지다 (neom-eo-ji-da) *v.* to fall down

넥타이 (nek-ta-i) *n.* necktie

넷 (net) *n.* four

노란불 (no-ran-bul) *n.* yellow light

노란색 (no-ran-saek) *n.* yellow

노랗다 (no-ra-ta) *v.* to be yellow; 노란 (no-ran) *adj.* yellow

노래 (no-rae) *n.* song

노래를 부르다 (no-rae bu-reu-da) to sing a song

노래방 (no-rae-bang) *n.* karaoke room

노래하다 (no-rae-ha-da) *v.* to sing a song

노을 (no-eul) *n.* sunset

노을이 지다 (no-eul-i ji-da) to have a sunset

녹다 (nok-da) *v.* to melt

녹음 (nog-eum) *n.* audio recording

녹음하다 (nog-eum-ha-da) *v.* to record (audio)

녹화 (no-kwa) *n.* video recording

녹화하다 (no-kwa-ha-da) *v.* to record (video)

놀다 (nol-da) *v.* to play, to enjoy oneself, to not work

놀라다 (nol-la-da) *v.* to be surprised

놀러가다 (nol-leo-ga-da) *v.* to go out to play

놀이공원 (nol-i-gong-won) *n.* amusement park

농구 (nong-gu) *n.* basketball

농구선수 (nong-gu-seon-su) *n.* basketball player

농구하다 (nong-gu-ha-da) *v.* to play basketball

높다 (nop-da) *v.* to be high up; 높은 (no-peun) *adj.* high

놓다 (no-ta) *v.* to put down

놓아주다 (no-a-ju-da) *v.* to release

놓치다 (no-chi-da) *v.* to miss

누구나 (nu-gu-na) *pron.* anyone
누구든지 (nu-gu-deun-ji) *pron.* whoever
누군가 (nu-gun-ga) *n.* somebody
누나 (nu-na) *n.* male's older sister
누르다 (nu-reu-da) *v.* to press
눈 (nun) *n.* snow, eye
눈꺼풀 (nun-kkeo-pul) *n.* eyelid
눈썹 (nun-sseop) *n.* eyelash
눈이 오다 (nun-i o-da) it snows
눕다 (nup-da) *v. intr.* to lie down
눕히다 (nu-pi-da) *v. tr.* to make someone lie down
뉴스 (nyu-seu) *n.* news
느끼다 (neu-kki-da) *v.* to feel, to realize
느리다 (neu-ri-da) *v.* to be slow; 느린 (neu-rin) *adj.* slow
늘 (neul) *adv.* always
늘다 (neul-da) *v.* to improve, to increase
늙다 (neulk-da) *v.* to be old, to get old; 늙은 (neulg-eun) *adj.* old
늦게 (neut-ge) *adv.* late
늦다 (neut-da) *v.* to become late, to be late; 늦은 (neuj-eun) *adj.* late

ㄷ

다 (da) *adv.* all
다니다 (da-ni-da) *v.* to attend
다듬다 (da-deum-tta) *v.* to trim
다람쥐 (da-ram-jwi) *n.* squirrel
다르다 (da-reu-da) *v.* to be different; 다른 (da-reun) *adj.* different
다리 (da-ri) *n.* leg, bridge
다리미질하다 (da-ri-mi-jil-ha-da) *v.* to iron
다섯 (da-seot) *n.* five
다소 (da-so) *adv.* more or less, to some degree
다시 (da-si) *adv.* again
다음 (da-eum) *adv.* next, following
다음부터 (da-eum-bu-teo) *adv.* from next time
다이어트 (da-i-eo-teu) *n.* diet
다이어트 중이다 (da-i-eo-teu jung-i-da) *v.* to be on a diet
다이어트하다 (da-i-eo-teu-ha-da) *v.* to be on a diet
다치다 (da-chi-da) *v.* to be injured, to hurt

다행이다 (da-haeng-i-da) *v.* to be lucky, to be fortunate

다행히 (da-haeng-hi) *adv.* fortunately

단기간 (dan-gi-gan) *n.* short period

단독주택 (dan-dok-ju-taek) *n.* single-family house

단순하다 (dan-sun-ha-da) *v.* to be simple; 단순한 (dan-sun-han) *adj.* simple

단어 (dan-eo) *n.* word, vocabulary

단층집 (dan-cheung-jjip) *n.* one-story house

닫다 (dat-da) *v. tr.* to close

닫히다 (da-chi-da) *v. intr.* to be closed

달 (dal) *n.* month, moon

달다 (dal-da) *v.* to hang (something), to taste sweet

달러 (dal-leo) *n.* dollar

달력 (dal-lyeok) *n.* calendar

달리다 (dal-li-da) *v.* to run

닭 (dak) *n.* chicken

닭고기 (dak-go-gi) *n.* chicken (meat)

닮다 (dam-tta) *v.* to resemble; 닮은 (dalm-eun) *adj.* resembling

담다 (dam-tta) *v.* to put into, to fill

담배 (dam-bae) *n.* cigarette

담배를 끊다 (dam-bae-reul kkeun-ta) to stop smoking

담배를 피우다 (dam-bae-reul pi-u-da) to smoke

담요 (dam-nyo) *n.* blanket

답답하다 (dap-da-pa-da) *v.* to be stuffy, to be frustrated; 답답한 (dap-da-pan) *adj.* stuffy, frustrated

답장 (dap-jang) *n.* reply letter

답장을 보내다 (dap-jang-eul bo-nae-da) to send a reply letter

답장을 쓰다 (dap-jang-eul sseu-da) to write a reply letter

닷새 (dat-sae) *n.* five days

당근 (dang-geun) *n.* carrot

당분간 (dang-bun-gan) *adv.* for the time being

당황하다 (dang-hwang-ha-da) *v.* to be embarrassed; 당황한 (dang-hwang-han) *adj.* embarrassing

대 (dae) *n.* large size

대단하다 (dae-dan-ha-da) *v.* to be wonderful, to be great; 대단한 (dae-dan-han) *adj.* wonderful, great

대단히 (dae-dan-hi) *adv.* very much

대답 (dae-dap) *n.* answer

대답하다 (dae-da-pa-da) *v.* to answer

대부분 (dae-bu-bun) *adv.* mostly

대신 (dae-sin) *adv.* instead of

대인 (dae-in) *n.* adult

대일밴드 (dae-il-baen-deu) *n.* bandage

대중 (dae-jung) *adj.* public, popular

대중교통 (dae-jung-gyo-tong) *n.* public transportation

대중음악 (dae-jung-eum-ak) *n.* pop music

대체로 (dae-che-ro) *adv.* generally

대통령 (dae-tong-nyeong) *n.* president of a country

대학교 (dae-hak-go) *n.* university, college

대학생 (dae-hak-saeng) *n.* college student

대학생활 (dae-hak-saeng-hwal) *n.* college life

대학원 (dae-hak-won) *n.* graduate school

대학원생 (dae-hak-won-saeng) *n.* graduate student

댁 (daek) *n.* home, house (hon.)

더 (deo) *adv.* more

더러워지다 (deo-reo-wo-ji-da) *v.* to get dirty

더럽다 (deo-reop-da) *v.* to be dirty; 더러운 (deo-reo-un) *adj.* dirty

던지다 (deon-ji-da) *v.* to throw

덜 (deol) *adv.* less

덥다 (deop-da) *v.* to be hot; 더운 (deo-un) *adj.* hot

데이트하다 (de-i-teu-ha-da) *v.* to date

도 (do) *n.* degree (temperature, angle)

도구 (do-gu) *n.* tool

도둑 (do-duk) *n.* thief

도로 (do-ro) *n.* road

도로공사 (do-ro-gong-sa) *n.* road construction

도마 (do-ma) *n.* chopping board

도서관 (do-seo-gwan) *n.* library

도시 (do-si) *n.* city

도와주다 (do-wa-ju-da) *v.* to help

도저히 (do-jeo-hi) *adv.* never, not at all

도착 (do-chak) *n.* arrival

도착하다 (do-cha-ka-da) *v.* to arrive

독방 (dok-bang) *n.* single room

독서 (dok-seo) *n.* reading

독서하다 (dok-seo-ha-da) *v.* to read

돈 (don) *n.* money

돈을 내다 (don-eul nae-da) to pay money

돈을 벌다 (don-eul beol-da) to earn money

돈이 들다 (don-i deul-da) to cost money

돌 (dol) *n.* rock, stone

돌고래 (dol-go-rae) *n.* dolphin

돌다 (dol-da) *v.* to turn

돌려드리다 (dol-lyeo-deu-ri-da) *v.* to return (hon.)

돌려주다 (dol-lyeo-ju-da) *v.* to return

돌리다 (dol-li-da) *v.* to spin

돌아가다 (dol-a-ga-da) *v.* to go back

돌아가시다 (dol-a-ga-si-da) *v.* to die, to pass away

돌아오다 (dol-a-o-da) *v.* to come back, to return

돌에 걸리다 (dol-e geol-li-da) *v.* to trip over a rock

돕다 (dop-da) *v.* to help

동남아 (dong-nam-a) *n.* Southeast Asia

동네 (dong-ne) *n.* neighborhood

동료 (dong-nyo) *n.* colleague

동물 (dong-mul) *n.* animal

동물원 (dong-mul-won) *n.* zoo

동부 (dong-bu) *n.* the eastern part

동생 (dong-saeng) *n.* younger sibling

동안 (dong-an) *prep.* during

동전 (dong-jeon) *n.* coin

동쪽 (dong-jjok) *n.* east side

동포 (dong-po) *n.* an ethnic Korean living abroad

돼지 (dwae-ji) *n.* pig

돼지고기 (dwae-ji-go-gi) *n.* pork

되게 (doe-ge) *adv.* extremely, very much

되다 (doe-da) *v.* to become, to get, to turn into

되도록 (doe-do-rok) *adv.* as much as possible

된장 (doen-jang) *n.* soybean paste

된장찌개 (doen-jang-jji-gae) *n.* soybean paste stew

두껍다 (du-kkeop-da) *v.* to be thick; 두꺼운 (du-kkeo-un)
     adj. thick

두다 (du-da) *v.* to put

두통 (du-tong) *n.* headache

두통이 있다 (du-tong-i it-da) to have a headache

둘 (dul) *n.* two

뒤 (dwi) *n.* back, behind

뒤따라 (dwi-tta-ra) *adv.* following

뒷문 (dwin-mun) *n.* back door

드라이 (deu-ra-i) *n.* hair dryer

드라이클리닝 (deu-ra-i-keul-li-ning) *n.* dry-cleaning

드라이클리닝하다 (deu-ra-i-keul-li-ning-ha-da) *v.* to dry clean

드라이하다 (deu-ra-i-ha-da) *v.* to use a hair dryer

드리다 (deu-ri-da) *v.* to give (hon.)

드시다 (deu-si-da) *v.* to eat (hon.)

듣다 (det-da) *v.* to listen

들다 (deul-da) *v.* to hold up, to be included, to be among

들르다 (deul-leu-da) *v.* to stop by

들리다 (deul-li-da) *v.* to be heard, to be audible

들어가다 (deul-eo-ga-da) *v.* to enter

들어오다 (deul-eo-o-da) *v.* to come in

등 (deung) *n.* back

등기우편 (deung-gi-u-pyeon) *n.* registered mail

등산 (deung-san) *n.* hiking, mountain climbing

등산가다 (deung-san-ga-da) *v.* to go hiking

등산하다 (deung-san-ha-da) *v.* to go hiking

디자이너 (di-ja-i-neo) *n.* designer

따님 (tta-nim) *n.* daughter (hon.)

따다 (ttak-da) *v.* to pick up, to pluck

따뜻하다 (tta-tteu-ta-da) *v.* to be warm; **따뜻한** (tta-tteu-tan) *adj.* warm

따로 (tta-ro) *adv.* separately

따르다 (tta-reu-da) *v.* to follow

딱지를 떼다 (ttak-ji-reul tte-da) to get a traffic ticket

딸 (ttal) *n.* daughter

딸기 (ttal-gi) *n.* strawberry

땀 (ttam) *n.* sweat

땀을 흘리다 (ttam-eul heul-li-da) to sweat

때 (ttae) *n.* time, dirt

떠나다 (tteo-na-da) *v.* to leave

떠들다 (tteo-deul-da) *v.* to make a noise

떡 (tteok) *n.* rice cake

떡국 (tteok-guk) *n.* rice-cake soup

떨어뜨리다 (tteol-eo-tteu-ri-da) *v.* to drop something

또 (tto) *adv.* too, also, and

똑같다 (ttok-gat-da) *v.* to be the same; **똑 같은** (ttok gat-eun) *adj.* same

뚜껑 (ttu-kkeong) *n.* lid, cap, cover

뚱뚱하다 (ttung-ttung-ha-da) *v.* to be chubby; **뚱뚱한** (ttung-ttung-han) *adj.* chubby

뛰다 (ttwi-da) *v.* to run

뛰어가다 (ttwi-eo-ga-da) *v.* to run to somewhere
뛰어오다 (ttwi-eo-o-da) *v.* to come running
뜨겁다 (tteu-geop-da) *v.* to be hot; **뜨거운** (tteu-geo-un) *adj.* hot
뜯어지다 (tteud-eo-ji-da) *v.* to be torn, to be ripped

ㄹ

라디오 (ra-di-o) *n.* radio
라면 (ra-myeon) *n.* ramen, instant noodles
램프 (raem-peu) *n.* lamp
러시아워 (reo-si-a-wo) *n.* rush hour
레모네이드 (re-mo-ne-i-deu) *n.* lemonade
레몬 (re-mon) *n.* lemon
레슬링 (re-seul-ling) *n.* wrestling
렌트카 (ren-teu-ka) *n.* rental car
로션 (ro-syeon) *n.* lotion
롤러스케이트 (rol-leo seu-ke-i-teu) *n.* roller blade
린스 (rin-seu) *n.* conditioner

ㅁ

마 (ma) *n.* linen
마늘 (ma-neul) *n.* garlic
마당 (ma-dang) *n.* yard
마루 (ma-ru) *n.* floor
마르다 (ma-reu-da) *v.* to be thin, to be skinny, to be thirsty, to be dried; **마른** (ma-reun) *adj.* thin, skinny, thirsty, dried
마리 (ma-ri) *counter for animals*
마시다 (ma-si-da) *v.* to drink
마우스 (ma-u-seu) *n.* mouse (computer)
마음 (ma-eum) *n.* heart, mind, nature
마음에 들다 (ma-eum-e deul-da) *v.* to like
마이크 (ma-i-keu) *n.* microphone
마일 (ma-il) *counter for mile*
마중 나가다 (ma-jung na-ga-da) to come out to greet someone
마중 나오다 (ma-jung-na-o-da) to come out to greet someone
마지막 (ma-ji-mak) *adv.* last

마지막으로 (ma-ji-mag-eu-ro) *adv.* finally, last

마치 (ma-chi) *conj.* as if

마치다 (ma-chi-da) *v.* to finish

마침 (ma-chim) *adv.* coincidentally

마흔 (ma-heun) *n.* forty

막내 (mang-nae) *n.* younger child

막다 (mak-da) *n.* to block

막히다 (ma-ki-da) *n.* to be blocked, congested

만 (man) *n.* ten thousand; *part.* only

만나다 (man-na-da) *v.* to meet

만드는 법 (man-deu-neun-beop) *n.* recipe

만들다 (man-deul-da) *v.* to make

만화 (man-hwa) *n.* cartoon, animation

많다 (man-ta) *v.* to be many/much; **많은** (man-eun) *adj.* many

많아야 (man-a-ya) *adv.* at most

많이 (man-i) *adv.* many, much

말 (mal) *n.* language, words, end

말다 (mal-da) *v.* to stop, to cease

말씀 (mal-sseum) *n.* words (hon.)

맑다 (malk-da) *v.* to be clear, to be sunny; **맑은** (malg-eun) *adj.* clear, sunny

맛 (mat) *n.* taste

맛이 없다 (mas-i eop-da) to be flavorless

맛이 있다 (mas-i it-da) *v.* to taste good, to be tasty, to be delicious

맞다 (mat-da) *v.* to be correct, to fit, to meet; **맞은** (maj-eun) *adj.* correct, fitting, appropriate

맡기다 (mat-gi-da) *v.* to entrust

매년 (mae-nyeon) *adv.* every year

매달 (mae-dal) *adv.* every month

매미 (mae-mi) *n.* locust

매일 (mae-il) *adv.* every day

매주 (mae-ju) *adv.* every week

매표소 (mae-pyo-so) *n.* ticket booth

맥주 (maek-ju) *n.* beer

맵다 (maep-da) *v.* to taste spicy; **매운** (mae-un) *adj.* spicy

머리 (meo-ri) *n.* head, hair

머리가 무겁다 (meo-ri-ga mu-geop-da) to have a heavy feeling in the head

머리가 아프다 (meo-ri-ga a-peu-da) to have a headache

머리를 감다 (meo-ri-reul gam-tta) to wash one's hair

머리를 깎다 (meo-ri-reul kkak-da) to get a haircut (man)

머리를 다듬다 (meo-ri-reul da-deum-tta) to trim

머리를 말리다 (meo-ri-reul mal-li-da) to dry one's hair

머리를 자르다 (meo-ri-reul ja-reu-da) to get a haircut (woman)

머리방 (meo-ri-bang) *n.* hair salon

머리카락 (meo-ri-ka-rak) *n.* hair

머리하다 (meo-ri-ha-da) *v.* to get one's hair done (woman)

머플러 (meo-peul-leo) *n.* scarf, muffler

먹다 (meok-da) *v.* to eat

먹이다 (meog-i-da) *v.* to feed

먼지 (meon-ji) *n.* dust

멀다 (meol-da) *v.* to be far; 먼 (meon) *adj.* far

멈추다 (meom-chu-da) *v.* to stop

멋없다 (meot-eop-da) *v.* to be unattractive; 멋없는 (meod-eom-neun) *adj.* unattractive

멋있다 (meos-it-da) *v.* to be attractive, to be stylish; 멋있는 (meos-in-neun) *adj.* attractive, stylish

메뉴 (me-nyu) *n.* menu

메뉴를 짜다 (me-nyu-reul jja-da) to plan a meal

메세지 (me-sse-ji) *n.* message

며칠 (myeo-chil) several days, what day of the month?

면 (myeon) *n.* cotton, noodles

면접 (myeon-jeop) *n.* interview

면접하다 (myeon-jeo-pa-da) *v.* to interview

명 (myeong) *counter for persons*

명절 (myeong-jeol) *n.* traditional holiday

몇 (myeot) *adv.* how many?, what?

모 (mo) *n.* wool

모기 (mo-gi) *n.* mosquito

모두 (mo-du) *adv.* all

모레 (mo-re) *n., adv.* the day after tomorrow

모르다 (mo-reu-da) *v.* to not know, to be unaware of, to not understand

모시다 (mo-si-da) *v.* to accompany a senior citizen, to treat a senior citizen (well/to a meal)

모으다 (mo-eu-da) *v.* to collect

모이다 (mo-i-da) *v.* to get together

모자 (mo-ja) *n.* hat, cap, helmet

모자라다 (mo-ja-ra-da) *v.* to not be enough, to be insufficient

모자를 쓰다 (mo-ja-reul sseu-da) to wear a hat

모집하다 (mo-ji-pa-da) *v.* to recruit

목 (mok) *n.* neck

목걸이 (mok-geol-i) *n.* necklace

목도리 (mok-do-ri) *n.* muffler

목사님 (mok-sa-nim) *n.* pastor

목소리 (mok-so-ri) *n.* voice

목숨 (mok-sum) *n.* life

목요일 (mog-yo-il) *n.* Thursday

목욕타올 (mog-yok-ta-ol) *n.* bath towel

목욕탕 (mog-yok-tang) *n.* bathroom

목욕하다 (mog-yo-ka-da) *v.* to bathe

몰라보다 (mol-la-bo-da) *v.* not to recognize

몰래 (mol-lae) *adv.* secretly

몰리다 (mol-li-da) *v.* to flock, to swarm

몸 (mom) *n.* body

몸무게 (mom-mu-ge) *n.* body weight

몸무게가 늘다 (mom-mu-ge-ga neul-da) to gain weight

몸무게가 줄다 (mom-mu-ge-ga jul-da) to lose weight

몸살 (mom-sal) *n.* body ache

몸조리하다 (mom-jo-ri-ha-da) *v.* to take care of one's health

못 (mot) *adv.* not possible, incapable of; *n.* nail

못생기다 (mot-saeng-gi-da) *v.* to be ugly; **못생긴** (mot-saeng-gin) *adj.* ugly

못하다 (mo-ta-da) *v.* to be unable to do, cannot do

무 (mu) *n.* radish

무겁다 (mu-geop-da) *v.* to be heavy; **무거운** (mu-geo-un) *adj.* heavy

무경험자 (mu-gyeong-heom-ja) *n.* inexperienced person, novice

무늬 (mu-nui) *n.* pattern

무덥다 (mu-deop-da) *v.* to be hot and humid; **무더운** (mu-deo-un) *adj.* hot and humid, muggy

무료 (mu-ryo) *n.* free of charge

무섭다 (mu-seop-da) *v.* to be scared, to be afraid; **무서운** (mu-seo-un) *adj.* scared, afraid

무스 (mu-sseu) *n.* mousse

무스를 바르다 (mu-sseu-reul ba-reu-da) to apply mousse

무슨 (mu-seun) *adv.* what?, what kind of?

무시하다 (mu-si-ha-da) *v.* to ignore

무엇 (mu-eot) *adv.* what?

무용가 (mu-yong-ga) *n.* dancer

무지개 (mu-ji-gae) *n.* rainbow

무척 (mu-cheok) *adv.* very much

문 (mun) *n.* door

문방구 (mun-bang-gu) *n.* stationery store

문병가다 (mun-byeong-ga-da) *v.* to visit a sick person

문제 (mun-je) *n.* problem

문학 (mun-hak) *n.* literature

문화 (mun-hwa) *n.* culture

물 (mul) *n.* water

물가 (mul-kka) *n.* cost of living, water-side

물건 (mul-geon) *n.* merchandise

물고기 (mul-kko-gi) *n.* fish (living)

물다 (mul-da) *v.* to bite

물들다 (mul-deul-da) *v.* to be dyed

물들이다 (mul-deul-i-da) *v.* to dye

물리다 (mul-li-da) *v.* to be bitten

물리치료사 (mul-li-chi-ryo-sa) *n.* physical therapist

물어보다 (mul-eo-bo-da) *v.* to ask, to inquire

뭐 (mwo) *adv.* what? (contraction of 무엇)

뭐든지 (mwo-deun-ji) *adv.* whatever

뭔가 (mwon-ga) *adv.* somewhat

뮤지컬 (myu-ji-keol) *n.* musical

미국 (mi-guk) *n.* America

미국사람 (mi-guk-sa-ram) *n.* American person

미끄럽다 (mi-kkeu-reop-da) *v.* to be slippery; 미끄러운 (mi-kkeu-reo-un) *adj.* slippery

미성년자 (mi-seong-nyeon-ja) *n.* underage person, minor

미술 (mi-sul) *n.* fine art

미술가 (mi-sul-ga) *n.* painter, fine artist

미식축구 (mi-sik-chuk-gu) *n.* football

미안하다 (mi-an-ha-da) *v.* to be sorry; 미안한 (mi-an-han) *adj.* sorry

미역국 (mi-yeok-guk) *n.* seaweed soup

미용사 (mi-yong-sa) *n.* hair stylist

미인 (mi-in) *n.* beautiful woman

미장원 (mi-jang-won) *n.* hair salon, beauty salon

미터 (mi-teo) *counter for meter*

믹서 (mik-seo) *n.* blender

민속촌 (min-sok-chon) *n.* folk village, rural village
민족 (min-jok) *n.* people, ethnic group
믿다 (mit-da) *v.* to trust, to believe
밀리다 (mil-li-da) *v.* to be delayed, to be unfinished
밉다 (mip-da) *v.* to be ugly; 미운 (mi-un) *adj.* ugly
밑 (mit) *n.* below, beneath, under

ㅂ

바겐세일 (ba-gen-sse-il) *n.* bargain sale
바꾸다 (ba-kku-da) *v.* to exchange, to change, to switch
바뀌다 (ba-kkwi-da) *v.* to be changed
바나나 (ba-na-na) *n.* banana
바다 (ba-da) *n.* ocean
바닷가 (ba-dat-ga) *n.* beach
바라다 (ba-ra-da) *v.* to desire, to wish
바람 (ba-ram) *n.* wind
바람이 불다 (ba-ram-i bul-da) the wind is blowing
바로 (ba-ro) *adv.* right away, exactly
바르다 (ba-reu-da) *v.* to apply (of a creamy substance)
바빠지다 (ba-ppa-ji-da) *v.* to become busy
바쁘다 (ba-ppeu-da) *v.* to be busy; 바쁜 (ba-ppeun) *adj.*
    busy
바위 (ba-wi) *n.* rock
바이올린 (ba-i-ol-lin) *n.* violin
바지 (ba-ji) *n.* pants
박물관 (bang-mul-gwan) *n.* museum
밖 (bak) *n.* outside
반 (ban) *n.* half
반가워하다 (ban-ga-wo-ha-da) *v.* to be glad
반갑다 (ban-gap-da) *v.* to be glad, to be happy; 반가운
    (ban-ga-un) *adj.* glad, happy
반값 (ban-kkap) *adj.* half-price
반대 (ban-dae) *n.* opposite
반드시 (ban-deu-si) *adv.* by all means, without fail
반면에 (ban-myeon-e) *adv.* on the other hand, in contrast
반바지 (ban-ba-ji) *n.* short pants, shorts
반지 (ban-ji) *n.* ring
반짝이다 (ban-jjag-i-da) *v.* to glitter
반찬 (ban-chan) *n.* side dish
반창고 (ban-chang-go, ban-chang-kko) *n.* sticking plaster

반팔 (ban-pal) *n. adj.* short-sleeved

받다 (bat-da) *v.* to receive

발 (bal) *n.* foot

발바닥 (bal-ppa-dak) *n.* the sole of the foot

발음 (bal-eum) *n.* pronunciation

발표 (bal-pyo) *n.* announcement

발표하다 (bal-pyo-ha-da) *v.* to announce

밝다 (balk-da) *v.* to be bright; **밝은** (balg-eun) *adj.* bright

밤 (bam) *n.* night, walnut

밤새도록 (bam-sae-do-rok) *adv.* all night through

밤새우다 (bam-sae-u-da) *v.* to stay up all night

밤색 (bam-saek) *n., adj.* brown

밥 (bap) *n.* meal, cooked rice

밥그릇 (bap-geu-reut) *n.* rice bowl

방 (bang) *n.* room

방금 (bang-geum) *adv.* just now

방문하다 (bang-mun-ha-da) *v.* to visit

방법 (bang-beop) *n.* method, way

방세 (bang-sse) *n.* rent

방송 (bang-song) *n.* broadcasting

방송국 (bang-song-guk) *n.* broadcasting station

방송중이다 (bang-song-jung-i-da) *v.* to be on the air

방학 (bang-hak) *n.* school vacation

방향 (bang-hyang) *n.* direction(s)

배 (bae) *n.* stomach, ship, boat, pear

배가 고프다 (bae-ga go-peu-da) to be hungry

배가 부르다 (bae-ga bu-reu-da) to be full

배가 아프다 (bae-ga a-peu-da) to have a stomachache

배구 (bae-gu) *n.* volleyball

배달 (bae-dal) *n.* delivery

배달하다 (bae-dal-ha-da) *v.* to deliver

배우 (bae-u) *n.* actor, actress

배우다 (bae-u-da) *v.* to learn

배추 (bae-chu) *n.* Asian cabbage

백 (baek) *n.* one hundred

백화점 (bae-kwa-jeom) *n.* department store

뱀 (baem) *n.* snake

버리다 (beo-ri-da) *v.* to throw way

버섯 (beo-seot) *n.* mushroom

버스 (beo-seu) *n.* bus

버스 정류장 (beo-seu jeong-nyu-jang) *n.* bus stop

버스 터미널 (beo-seu teo-mi-neol) *n.* bus station

버스를 놓치다 (beo-seu-reul no-chi-da) to miss the bus

버스를 타다 (beo-seu-reul ta-da) to ride a bus

번 (beon) *counter for number of times*

번호 (beon-ho) *n.* number

벌 (beol) *counter for clothes*; *n.* punishment

범죄 (beom-joe) *n.* crime

범죄자 (beom-joe-ja) *n.* criminal

법대 (beop-dae) *n.* law school

벗다 (beot-da) *v.* to take off (clothes)

베개 (be-gae) *n.* pillow

벤치 (ben-chi) *n.* bench

벨트 (bel-teu) *n.* belt

벽 (byeok) *n.* wall

변덕꾸러기 (byeon-deok-kku-reo-gi) *n.* capricious person

변하다 (byeon-ha-da) *v.* to change

변호사 (byeon-ho-sa) *n.* lawyer

별 (byeol) *n.* star

별로 (byeol-lo) *adv.* not really, not particularly

별일 (byeol-lil) *n.* special event

병 (byeong) *n.* bottle, illness

병따개 (byeong-tta-gae) *n.* bottle opener

병에 걸리다 (byeong-e geol-li-da) *v.* to catch a disease

병원 (byeong-won) *n.* hospital

병이 생기다 (byeong-i saeng-gi-da) *v.* to develop an illness

보고하다 (bo-go-ha-da) *v.* to report

보관하다 (bo-gwan-ha-da) *v.* to keep

보내다 (bo-nae-da) *v.* to send mail, to spend time

보내주다 (bo-nae-ju-da) *v.* to send

보다 (bo-da) *v.* to see, to look, to watch

보도 (bo-do) *n.* sidewalk, report

보라색 (bo-ra-saek) *n.*, *adj.* purple, violet

보름 (bo-reum) *n.* fifteen days

보리차 (bo-ri-cha) *n.* barley tea

보물 (bo-mul) *n.* treasure

보물섬 (bo-mul-sseom) *n.* treasure island

보수적이다 (bo-su-jeog-i-da) *v.* to be conservative; 보수적인 (bo-su-jeog-in) *adj.* conservative

보여주다 (bo-yeo-ju-da) *v.* to show

보이다 (bo-i-da) *v.* to be seen, to be visible

보장하다 (bo-jang-ha-da) *v.* to guarantee

보통 (bo-tong) *adv.* usually, medium, commonly

보험 (bo-heom) *n.* insurance

보험을 들다 (bo-heom-eul deul-da) to insure an item

보험이 있다 (bo-heom-i it-da) to be covered by insurance

복 (bok) *n.* blessing

복권 (bok-gwon) *n.* lottery

복도 (bok-do) *n.* hallway, aisle

복사기 (bok-sa-gi) *n.* copy machine

복용하다 (bog-yong-ha-da) *v.* to take medicine

복잡하다 (bok-ja-pa-da) *v.* to be complicated, to be crowded; 복잡한 (bok-ja-pan) *adj.* complicated, crowded

볶다 (bok-da) *v.* to stir-fry

본업 (bon-eop) *n.* main occupation

볼링 (bol-ling) *n.* bowling

볼링을 치다 (bol-ling-eul chi-da) *v.* to bowl

볼링장 (bol-ling-jang) *n.* bowling alley

볼펜 (bol-pen) *n.* ballpoint pen

봄 (bom) *n.* spring

봉투 (bong-tu) *n.* envelope

뵙다 (boep-da) *v.* to see, to meet (hon.)

부드럽다 (bu-deu-reop-da) *v.* to be soft; 부드러운 (bu-deu-reo-un) *adj.* soft

부러지다 (bu-reo-ji-da) *v.* to be broken

부럽다 (bu-reop-da) *v.* to be jealous; 부러운 (bu-reo-un) *adj.* jealous

부모님 (bu-mo-nim) *n.* parents

부부 (bu-bu) *n.* husband and wife

부사장 (bu-sa-jang) *n.* vice-president of a company

부업 (bu-eop) *n.* second job, sideline

부엌 (bu-eok) *n.* kitchen

부인 (bu-in) *n.* wife (hon.)

부전공 (bu-jeon-gong) *n.* minor, second major

부족하다 (bu-jo-ka-da) *v.* to be lacking, to not be good enough; 부족한 (bu-jo-kan) *adj.* lacking, inadequate

부채 (bu-chae) *n.* fan

부치다 (bu-chi-da) *v.* to send a post

부탁하다 (bu-ta-ka-da) *v.* to ask a favor

부통령 (bu-tong-nyeong) *n.* vice-president of a country

북부 (buk-bu) *n.* the northern part

북쪽 (buk-jjok) *n.* north side

북한 (bu-kan) *n.* North Korea

분 (bun) *counter for people* (hon.), *counter for minute*

분야 (bun-ya) *n.* area

분위기 (bun-wi-gi) *n.* atmosphere

분홍색 (bun-hong-saek) *n., adj.* pink

불 (bul) *counter for dollar*; *n.* fire

불가능하다 (bul-ga-neung-ha-da) *v.* to be impossible; **불가능한** (bul-ga-neung-han) *adj.* impossible

불고기 (bul-go-gi) *n.* marinated beef

불고기감 (bul-go-gi-kkam) *n.* beef for bulgogi recipe

불다 (bul-da) *v.* to blow

불리하다 (bul-li-ha-da) *v.* to be disadvantageous; **불리한** (bul-li-han) *adj.* disadvantageous

불어 (bul-eo) *n.* French language

불충분하다 (bul-chung-bun-ha-da) *v.* to not be enough; **불충분한** (bul-chung-bun-han) *adj.* not enough, inadequate

불친절하다 (bul-chin-jeol-ha-da) *v.* to be unkind; **불친절한** (bul-chin-jeol-han) *adj.* unkind

불편하다 (bul-pyeon-ha-da) *v.* to be uncomfortable, to be inconvenient; **불편한** (bul-pyeon-han) *adj.* uncomfortable, inconvenient

불합격하다 (bul-hap-gyeo-ka-da) *v.* to fail the exam

불행 중 다행 (bul-haeng-jung da-haeng) a stroke of good luck in the midst of disaster

불행하다 (bul-haeng-ha-da) *v.* to be unhappy; **불행한** (bul-haeng-han) *adj.* unhappy

붐비다 (bum-bi-da) *v.* to be crowded

붓글씨 (but-geul-ssi) *n.* calligraphy

붓다 (but-da) *v.* to swell; **부은** (bu-eun) *adj.* swollen

붙다 (but-da) *v.* to stick, to pass

붙이다 (bu-chi-da) *v.* to stick, to affix

붙잡다 (but-jap-da) *v.* to catch, to hold

블라우스 (beul-la-u-seu) *n.* blouse

비 (bi) *n.* rain, broom

비가 오다 (bi-ga o-da) to rain

비교적 (bi-gyo-jeok) *adv.* relatively

비교하다 (bi-gyo-ha-da) *v.* to compare

비누 (bi-nu) *n.* soap

비디오 (bi-di-o) *n.* video

비디오게임 (bi-di-o-ge-im) *n.* video game

비디오를 보다 (bi-di-o-reul bo-da) to watch a video

비를 맞다 (bi-reul mat-da) to be caught in the rain

비밀 (bi-mil) *n.* secret

비빔밥 (bi-bim-ppap) *n.* rice with mixed vegetables

비서 (bi-seo) *n.* secretary

비슷하다 (bi-seu-ta-da) *v.* to be similar; 비슷한 (bi-seu-tan) *adj.* similar

비싸다 (bi-ssa-da) *v.* to be expensive; 비싼 (bi-ssan) *adj.* expensive

비올라 (bi-ol-la) *n.* viola

비옷 (bi-ot) *n.* raincoat

비용 (bi-yong) *n.* expenses

비자 (bi-ja) *n.* visa

비타민 (bi-ta-min) *n.* vitamin

비행기 (bi-haeng-gi) *n.* airplane

비행기값 (bi-haeng-gi-kkap) *n.* airfare

비행기표 (bi-haeng-gi-pyo) *n.* airline ticket

비행장 (bi-haeong-jang) *n.* airport

빌딩 (bil-ding) *n.* building

빌려가다 (bil-lyeo-ga-da) *v.* to borrow and go

빌려드리다 (bil-lyeo-deu-ri-da) *v.* to lend, to rent (humble)

빌려주다 (bil-lyeo-ju-da) *v.* to lend, to rent

빌리다 (bil-li-da) *v.* to borrow

빗 (bit) *n.* comb

빗길 (bit-gil) *n.* rain-covered road

빗다 (bit-da) *v.* to comb

빗자루 (bit-ja-ru) *n.* broom

빠르다 (ppa-reu-da) *v.* to be fast; 빠른 (ppa-reun) *adj.* fast

빠지다 (ppa-ji-da) *v.* to fall into

빨간불 (ppal-gan-bul) *n.* red light

빨간색 (ppal-gan-saek) *n.* red

빨갛다 (ppal-ga-ta) *v.* to be red; 빨간 (ppal-gan) *adj.* red

빨래 (ppal-lae) *n.* laundry

빨래비누 (ppal-lae-ppi-nu) *n.* detergent

빨래하다 (ppal-lae-ha-da) *v.* to do laundry

빨리 (ppal-li) *adv.* fast, quickly

빵 (ppang) *n.* bread

빵집 (ppang-jjip) *n.* bakery

빼다 (ppae-da) *v.* to exclude

빼앗기다 (ppaet-gi-da) *v.* to be taken away

뺏다 (ppaet-da) *v.* to take away
뺨 (ppyam) *n.* cheek
뽑다 (ppop-da) *v.* to select, to pick out

ㅅ

사 (sa) *n.* four
사가다 (sa-ga-da) *v.* to go carrying something bought
사거리 (sa-geo-ri) *n.* four-way intersection
사건 (sa-kkeon) *n.* event
사고 (sa-go) *n.* accident
사고가 나다 (sa-go-ga na-da) an accident happens
사고를 내다 (sa-go-reul nae-da) to cause an accident
사과 (sa-gwa) *n.* apple, apology
사교적이다 (sa-gyo-jeog-i-da) *v.* to be social, to be
   sociable; 사교적인 (sa-gyo-jeog-in) *adj.* social,
   sociable
사귀다 (sa-gwi-da) *v.* to date, to make friends
사다 (sa-da) *v.* to buy
사랑하다 (sa-rang-ha-da) *v.* to love
사모님 (sa-mo-nim) *n.* male senior citizen's wife
사슴 (sa-seum) *n.* deer
사실 (sa-sil) *n.* fact
사실은 (sa-sil-eun) *adv.* in fact, to tell you the truth
사업 (sa-eop) *n.* business
사업을 하다 (sa-eob-eul ha-da) *v.* to run a business
사오다 (sa-o-da) *v.* to come carrying something bought
사용하다 (sa-yong-ha-da) *v.* to use
사우나 (ssa-u-na) *n.* sauna
사월 (sa-wol) *n.* April
사이 (sa-i) *n.* relationship, between
사이다 (sa-i-da) *n.* 7-Up™ (soft drink)
사이즈 (ssa-i-jeu) *n.* size
사자 (sa-ja) *n.* lion
사장 (sa-jang) *n.* president of a company
사전 (sa-jeon) *n.* dictionary
사진 (sa-jin) *n.* picture, photograph
사진기 (sa-jin-gi) *n.* camera
사진을 찍다 (sa-jin-eul jjik-da) to take a picture
사진틀 (sa-jin-teul) *n.* photo frame
사촌 (sa-chon) *n.* cousin

사탕 (sa-tang) *n.* candy

사투리 (sa-tu-ri) *n.* dialect

사항 (sa-hang) *n.* item

사회 (sa-hoe) *n.* society

사흘 (sa-heul) *n.* three days

산 (san) *n.* mountain

산꼭대기 (san-kkok-dae-gi) *n.* mountain top

살 (sal) *counter for age*; *n.* flesh

살다 (sal-da) *v.* to live

살리다 (sal-li-da) *v.* to save one's life, to make good use of

살림 (sal-lim) *n.* household

살을 빼다 (sal-eul ppae-da) to lose weight

살이 빠지다 (sal-i ppa-ji-da) to lose weight

살이 찌다 (sal-i jji-da) to gain weight

살펴보다 (sal-pyeo-bo-da) *v.* to look over carefully

삶 (salm, sam) *n.* life, living

삼 (sam) *n.* three

삼거리 (sam-geo-ri) *n.* three-way intersection

삼월 (sam-wol) *n.* March

삼촌 (sam-chon) *n.* uncle

상 (sang) *n.* prize, table

상가 (sang-ga) *n.* mall, shopping district

상냥하다 (sang-nyang-ha-da) *v.* to be nice, to be kind;
　　상냥한 (sang-nyang-han) *adj.* nice, kind

상다리 (sang-tta-ri) *n.* table legs

상대편 (san-dae-pyeon) *n.* opponent

상어 (san-eo) *n.* shark

상의하다 (sang-ui-ha-da) *v.* to consult

상자 (sang-ja) *n.* box

상점 (sang-jeom) *n.* store

상추 (sang-chu) *n.* lettuce

상쾌하다 (sang-kwae-ha-da) *v.* to be refreshing, to freshen;
　　상쾌한 (sang-kwae-han) *adj.* fresh, refreshing

상품 (sang-pum) *n.* prize

상품을 타다 (sang-pum-eul ta-da) to win a prize

상하다 (sang-ha-da) *v.* to be damaged, to be spoiled; **상한**
　　(sang-han) *adj.* damaged, spoiled

새 (sae) *adj.* new, *n.* bird

새로 (sae-ro) *adv.* newly

새벽 (sae-byeok) *n.* dawn

새해 (sae-hae) *n.* new year

색 (saek) *n.* color

색깔 (saek-kkal) *n.* color

샌달 (ssaen-dal) *n.* sandals

샌드위치 (ssaen-deu-wi-chi) *n.* sandwich

생각 (saeng-gak) *n.* thought, idea

생각하다 (saeng-ga-ka-da) *v.* to think

생기다 (saeng-gi-da) *v.* to come into existence, to look

생명 (saeng-myeong) *n.* life

생선 (saeng-seon) *n.* fish (killed; for a meal)

생신 (saeng-sin) *n.* birthday (hon.)

생일 (saeng-il) *n.* birthday

생활 (saeng-hwal) *n.* living

샤워하다 (sya-wo-ha-da) *v.* to take a shower

샴푸 (syam-pu) *n.* shampoo

서다 (seo-da) *v.* to stand, to stop

서둘러 (seo-dul-leo) *adv.* in a hurry

서랍 (seo-rap) *n.* drawer

서로 (seo-ro) *pron.* each other

서른 (seo-reun) *n.* thirty

서부 (seo-bu) *n.* the western part

서비스(sseo-bi-seu) *n.* service

서울 (seo-ul) *n.* Seoul

서울역 (seo-ul-lyeok) *n.* Seoul Railroad Station

서재 (seo-jae) *n.* study room

서점 (seo-jeom) *n.* bookstore

서쪽 (seo-jjok) *n.* west side

선글라스 (sseon-geul-la-seu) *n.* sunglasses

선물 (seon-mul) *n.* present, gift

선생님 (seon-saeng-nim) *n.* teacher

선인장 (seon-in-jang) *n.* cactus

선전 (seon-jeon) *n.* advertisement

선택하다 (seon-tae-ka-da) *v.* to choose

선풍기 (seon-pung-gi) *n.* electric fan

설거지하다 (seol-geo-ji-ha-da) *v.* to wash dishes

설날 (seol-lal) *n.* New Year's Day

설명하다 (seol-myeong-ha-da) *v.* to explain

설사하다 (seol-ssa-ha-da) *v.* to have diarrhea

설탕 (seol-tang) *n.* sugar

섭섭하다 (seop-seo-pa-da) *v.* to be sorry, to be sad;
　　섭섭한 (seop-seo-pan) *adj.* sad

섭씨 (seop-ssi) *adj.* Celsius

성격 (seong-kkeok) *n.* personality

성실하다 (seong-sil-ha-da) *v.* to be sincere; 성실한 (seong-sil-han) *adj.* sincere

성인 (seong-in) *n.* adult

성적 (seong-jeok) *n.* grade

성함 (seong-ham) *n.* name (hon.)

세 (se) *counter for age* (hon.)

세면대 (se-myeon-dae) *n.* washstand, washbowl

세배 (se-bae) *n.* formal bow on New Year's Day

세배하다 (se-bae-ha-da) *v.* to bow on New Year's Day

세뱃돈 (se-baet-don) *n.* gift of money for New Year's bows

세상 (se-sang) *n.* world

세수하다 (se-su-ha-da) *v.* to wash one's face

세숫비누 (se-sut-bi-nu) *n.* bathroom soap, facial soap

세우다 (se-u-da) *v.* to stop, to park (a vehicle)

세일 (sse-il) *n.* sale

세탁기 (se-tak-gi) *n.* washing machine

세탁소 (se-tak-so) *n.* laundromat

센트 (ssen-teu) *counter for cents*

셋 (set) *n.* three

셔츠 (syeo-cheu) *n.* shirt

소 (so) *n.* ox, cow, small size

소개하다 (so-gae-ha-da) *v.* to introduce

소고기 (so-go-gi) *n.* beef

소극적이다 (so-geuk-jeog-i-da) *v.* to be passive; 소극적인 (so-geuk-jeog-in) *adj.* passive

소금 (so-geum) *n.* salt

소나기 (so-na-gi) *n.* rain shower

소리 (so-ri) *n.* sound, noise

소리가 나다 (so-ri-ga na-da) *v.* to sound

소매 (so-mae) *n.* sleeves

소문 (so-mun) *n.* rumor

소방서 (so-bang-seo) *n.* fire station

소방차 (so-bang-cha) *n.* fire truck

소설 (so-seol) *n.* novel

소설가 (so-seol-ga) *n.* writer

소식 (so-sik) *n.* news

소식을 듣다 (so-sig-eul deut-da) to hear the news

소용없다 (so-yong-eop-da) *v.* to be useless; 소용없는 (so-yong-eom-neun) *adj.* useless

소원 (so-won) *n.* wish, desire

소인 (so-in) *n.* child

소파 (sso-pa) *n.* sofa

소포 (so-po) *n.* parcel, package

소포를 부치다 (so-po-reul bu-chi-da) to send a package

소풍 (so-pung) *n.* picnic

소풍가다 (so-pung-ga-da) *v.* to go on a picnic

소화 (so-hwa) *n.* digestion

소화가 되다 (so-hwa-ga doe-da) to be digested

소화제 (so-hwa-je) *n.* digestive medicine

속 (sok) *n.* inside, interior

속눈썹 (song-nun-sseop) *n.* eyelash

속달우편 (sok-dal-u-pyeon) *n.* express mail

속도제한 (sok-do-je-han) *n.* speed limit

속상하다 (sok-sang-ha-da) *v.* to be distressed; 속상한 (sok-sang-han) *adj.* distressed, upset

속옷 (sog-ot) *n.* underwear

속을 썩이다 (sog-eul sseog-i-da) to annoy someone

속이 거북하다 (sog-i geo-bu-ka-da) to have indigestion

속이 답답하다 (sog-i dap-da-pa-da) to have indigestion

손 (son) *n.* hand

손녀 (son-nyeo) *n.* granddaughter

손님 (son-nim) *n.* guest, customer

손목시계 (son-mok-si-gye) *n.* watch

손바닥 (son-ppa-dak) *n.* palm (hand)

손수건 (son-ssu-geon) *n.* handkerchief

손을 씻다 (son-eul ssit-da) to wash one's hands

손을 흔들다 (son-eul heun-deul-da) to wave

손자 (son-ja) *n.* grandson

손잡이 (son-jab-i) *n.* handle

손질하다 (son-jil-ha-da) *v.* to take care of (hair, a garden, furniture)

손톱깎기 (son-top-kkak-gi) *n.* nail clipper

솜 (som) *n.* cotton

솜씨 (som-ssi) *n.* skill

송편 (song-pyeon) *n.* a rice cake on Chuseok

쇠고기 (soe-go-gi) *n.* beef

쇼핑센터 (syo-ping-ssen-teo) *n.* shopping center

쇼핑하다 (syo-ping-ha-da) *v.* to shop

수건 (su-geon) *n.* towel

수고하다 (su-go-ha-da) *v.* to put forth effort, take trouble

수도 (su-do) *n.* capital city, waterworks
수도꼭지 (su-do-kkok-ji) *n.* tap, hydrant
수돗물 (su-don-mul) *n.* running water
수면제 (su-myeon-je) *n.* sleeping pills
수박 (su-bak) *n.* watermelon
수술 (su-sul) *n.* operation
수술하다 (su-sul-ha-da) *v.* to have surgery
수업 (su-eop) *n.* class
수영 (su-yeong) *n.* swimming
수영복 (su-yeong-bok) *n.* swimsuit
수영장 (su-yeong-jang) *n.* swimming pool
수영하다 (su-yeong-ha-da) *v.* to swim
수요일 (su-yo-il) *n.* Wednesday
수저 (su-jeo) *n.* spoon and chopstick
수프 (su-peu) *n.* soup
숙모 (sung-mo) *n.* aunt
술 (sul) *n.* liquor
술을 마시다 (sul-eul ma-si-da) to drink an alcoholic
    beverage
술집 (sul-jjip) *n.* pub, bar
숨 (sum) *n.* breath
숨을 내쉬다 (sum-eul nae-swi-da) to exhale
숨을 들이쉬다 (sum-eul deul-i-swi-da) to inhale
숨을 쉬다 (sum-eul swi-da) to breathe
숨이 차다 (sum-i cha-da) to be out of breath
숟가락 (sut-ga-rak) *n.* spoon
숫자 (sut-ja) *n.* number
쉬다 (swi-da) *v.* to rest
쉰 (swin) *n.* fifty
쉽다 (swip-da) *v.* to be easy; 쉬운 (swi-un) *adj.* easy
슈퍼 (syu-peo) *n.* supermarket, store
슈퍼마켓 (syu-peo-ma-ket) *n.* supermarket, store
스물 (seu-mul) *n.* twenty
스웨터 (seu-we-teo) *n.* sweater
스웨터를 짜다 (seu-we-teo-reul jja-da) to knit a sweater
스위치 (seu-wi-chi) *n.* switch
스카프 (seu-ka-peu) *n.* scarf
스커트 (seu-keo-teu) *n.* skirt
스케이트 (seu-ke-i-teu) *n.* skating
스케이트를 타다 (seu-ke-i-teu-reul ta-da) to skate
스케이트장 (seu-ke-i-teu-jang) *n.* skating rink

스키 (seu-ki) *n.* skiing, a ski

스키를 타다 (seu-ki-reul ta-da) to ski

스키장 (seu-ki-jang) *n.* ski resort

스킨 (seu-kin) *n.* skin lotion

스타일 (seu-ta-il) *n.* style

스트레스 (seu-teu-re-seu) *n.* stress

스트레스가 쌓이다 (seu-teu-re-seu-ga ssa-i-da) stress
    accumulates

스트레스가 풀리다 (seu-teu-re-seu-ga pul-li-da) stress is
    relieved

스트레스를 받다 (seu-teu-re-seu-reul bat-da) to feel stress

스트레스를 풀다 (seu-teu-re-seu-reul pul-da) to relieve
    stress

스팀 (seu-tim) *n.* steam, heating, heat

스페인 (seu-pe-in) *n.* Spain

스페인어 (seu-pe-in-eo) *n.* Spanish language

스포츠 (seu-po-cheu) *n.* sports

스포츠카 (seu-po-cheu-ka) *n.* sports car

스프레이 (seu-peu-re-i) *n.* hair spray

스피커 (seu-pi-keo) *n.* speaker

슬리퍼 (seul-li-peo) *n.* slippers

슬프다 (seul-peu-da) *v.* to be sad; 슬픈 (seul-peun) *adj.*
    sad

습기 (seup-gi) *n.* humidity

습하다 (seu-pa-da) *v.* to be humid; 습한 (seu-pan) *adj.*
    humid

승차하다 (seung-cha-ha-da) *v.* to get in (a vehicle)

시 (si) *counter for the hour,* o'clock; *n.* city, poem

시간 (si-gan) *counter for time, hours*

시계 (si-gye) *n.* clock, watch

시계방 (si-gye-ppang) *n.* watchmaker

시골 (si-gol) *n.* country

시금치 (si-geum-chi) *n.* spinach

시끄럽다 (si-kkeu-reop-da) *v.* to be noisy; 시끄러운 (si-
    kkeu-reo-un) *adj.* noisy

시내 (si-nae) *n.* downtown

시다 (si-da) *v.* to taste sour; 신 (sin) *adj.* sour

시외 (si-oe) *n.* suburb

시외버스 (si-oe-ppeo-seu) *n.* suburban bus

시원하다 (si-won-ha-da) *v.* to be cool; 시원한 (si-won-
    han) *adj.* cool

시월 (si-wol) *n.* October

시인 (si-in) *n.* poet

시작하다 (si-ja-ka-da) *v.* to start

시장 (si-jang) *n.* market

시장을 보다 (si-jang-eul bo-da) to go grocery shopping

시집가다 (si-jip-ga-da) *v.* to marry (you are a woman)

시청 (si-cheong) *n.* city hall

시커멓다 (si-keo-meo-ta) *v.* to be dark, to be black;
시커먼 (si-kkeo-meon) *adj.* dark, black

시키다 (si-ki-da) *v.* to order (food in a restaurant), to make
someone do something

시합 (si-hap) *n.* sports game, match

시험 (si-heom) *n.* test, exam

시험을 보다 (si-heom-eul bo-da) to take an exam

식구 (sik-gu) *n.* family

식다 (sik-da) *v.* to cool off, to be cool; 식은 (sig-eun) *adj.*
cool

식당 (sik-dang) *n.* restaurant

식사 (sik-sa) *n.* meal

식성 (sik-seong) *n.* appetite

식전 (sik-jeon) *n.* the time before a meal

식초 (sik-cho) *n.* vinegar

식탁 (sik-tak) *n.* dining table

식품 (sik-pum) *n.* food

식품부 (sik-pum-bu) *n.* food section

식후 (si-ku) *n.* the time after a meal

신 (sin) *n.* shoe

신(발)을 신다 (sin-(bal)-eul sin-tta) to put on shoes, to
wear shoes

신기다 (sin-gi-da) *v.* to put shoes on

신기하다 (sin-gi-ha-da) *v.* to be marvelous, to be
supernatural; 신기한 (sin-gi-han) *adj.* marvelous,
supernatural

신나다 (sin-na-da) *v.* to be excited, to be exciting; 신나는
(sin-na-neun) *adj.* exciting, 신난 (sin-nan) *adj.* excited

신다 (sin-tta) *v.* to put on (shoes, socks)

신랑 (sil-lang) *v.* groom

신랑감 (sil-lang-kkam) *n.* groom candidate

신문 (sin-mun) *v.* newspaper

신문사 (sin-mun-sa) *v.* newspaper publisher

신발 (sin-bal) *v.* shoe

신부 (sin-bu) *n.* bride

신부감 (sin-bu-kkam) *n.* bride candidate

신중하다 (sin-jung-ha-da) *v.* to be discreet, to be prudent; **신중한** (sin-jung-han) *adj.* prudent, discreet

신체검사 (sin-che-geom-sa) *n.* a medical check-up, a physical

신호등 (sin-ho-deung) *n.* traffic light

신혼 (sin-hon) *n.* newlywed; *adj.* newly married

신혼부부 (sin-hon-bu-bu) *n.* the newlyweds

신혼여행 (sin-hon-nyeo-haeng) *n.* honeymoon

실내장식 (sil-lae-jang-sik) *n.* interior design

실력 (sil-lyeok) *n.* skill, ability

실례하다 (sil-lye-ha-da) *v.* to be excused

실수 (sil-ssu) *n.* mistake

실수하다 (sil-ssu-ha-da) *v.* to make a mistake

실크 (ssil-keu) *n.* silk

싫다 (sil-ta) *v.* to be not likable, to dislike; **싫은** (sil-eun) *adj.* dislikable

싫어하다 (sil-eo-ha-da) *v.* to dislike, to hate

심심하다 (sim-sim-ha-da) *v.* to be bored; **심심한** (sim-sim-han) *adj.* bored

심포니 (ssim-po-ni) *n.* symphony

심하게 (sim-ha-ge) *adv.* seriously

심하다 (sim-ha-da) *v.* to be severe, to be keen; **심한** (sim-han) *adj.* severe, keen

십이월 (sib-i-wol) *n.* December

십일월 (sib-il-wol) *n.* November

싱겁다 (sing-geop-da) *v.* to taste bland; **싱거운** (sing-geo-un) *adj.* bland-tasting

싱싱하다 (sing-sing-ha-da) *v.* to be fresh; **싱싱한** (sing-sing-han) *adj.* fresh

싸다 (ssa-da) *v.* to be inexpensive, to be cheap, to wrap; **싼** (ssan) *adj.* inexpensive, miserly, wrapped

싸우다 (ssa-u-da) *v.* to fight, to argue

쌀쌀하다 (ssal-ssal-ha-da) *v.* to be chilly, to be cold; **쌀쌀한** (ssal-ssal-han) *adj.* chilly, cold

쌓이다 (ssa-i-da) *v.* to pile up

썰다 (sseol-da) *v.* to cut into small pieces

쓰다 (sseu-da) *v.* to use, to write, to put on, to wear, to taste bitter

쓰러지다 (sseu-reo-ji-da) *v.* to collapse from exhaustion

쓰레기 (sseu-re-gi) *n.* garbage

쓰레기통 (sseu-re-gi-tong) *n.* dumpster

쓰레받기 (sseu-re-bat-gi) *n.* dustpan

쓸쓸하다 (sseul-sseul-ha-da) *v.* to feel lonely; 쓸쓸한 (sseul-sseul-han) *adj.* lonely

씨름 (ssi-reum) *n.* traditional Korean wrestling

씻다 (ssit-da) *v.* to wash

씽크 (ssing-keu) *n.* kitchen sink, kitchen cabinet

ㅇ

아기 (a-gi) *n.* baby

아까 (a-kka) *adv.* a while ago

아내 (a-nae) *n.* wife

아니다 (a-ni-da) *cop.* to not be

아드님 (a-deu-nim) *n.* son (hon.)

아들 (a-deul) *n.* son

아래 (a-rae) *n.* down, below, under

아래층 (a-rae-cheung) *n.* downstairs

아르바이트 (a-reu-ba-i-teu) *n.* part-time job

아르바이트를 하다 (a-reu-ba-i-teu-reul ha-da) to work part-time

아름답다 (a-reum-dap-da) *v.* to be beautiful; 아름다운 (a-reum-da-un) *adj.* beautiful

아마 (a-ma) *adv.* probably, perhaps

아무나 (a-mu-na) *n.* anyone

아무도 (a-mu-do) *n.* no one

아무렇지도 않게 (a-mu-reo-chi-do an-ke) *adv.* with no fuss, casually

아무리 (a-mu-ri) *adv.* no matter how

아버님 (a-beo-nim) *n.* father (hon.)

아버지 (a-beo-ji) *n.* father

아빠 (a-ppa) *n.* dad

아이 (a-i) *n.* child

아주 (a-ju) *adv.* very much

아직 (a-jik) *adv.* still, yet

아침 (a-chim) *n.* morning, breakfast

아파트 (a-pa-teu) *n.* apartment complex

아프다 (a-peu-da) *v.* to be sick; 아픈 (a-peun) *adj.* sick

아프리카 (a-peu-ri-ka) *n.* Africa

아홉 (a-hop) *n.* nine

아흐레 (a-heu-re) *n.* nine days

아흔 (a-heun) *n.* ninety

악기 (ak-gi) *n.* musical instrument

악어 (ag-eo) *n.* crocodile

안 (an) *adv.* not; *n.* inside, in,

안개 (an-gae) *n.* fog

안개가 끼다 (an-gae-ga kki-da) to be foggy

안경 (an-gyeong) *n.* eyeglasses

안경점 (an-gyeong-jeom) *n.* optician

안기다 (an-gi-da) *v.* to be held, to nestle in one's arms, to hug

안내 (an-nae) *n.* information

안내원 (an-nae-won) *n.* guide

안내책자 (an-nae-chaek-ja) *n.* brochure

안내하다 (an-nae-ha-da) *v.* to guide

안녕하다 (an-nyeong-ha-da) *v.* to be well, to feel well

안녕히 (an-nyeong-hi) *adv.* peacefully, safely

안다 (an-tta) *v.* to hold, to hug

안방 (an-ppang) *n.* master bedroom

안부 (an-bu) *n.* regards

안부를 전하다 (an-bu-reul jeon-ha-da) to give regards to someone

안전 (an-jeon) *n.* safety

안전하다 (an-jeon-ha-da) *v.* to be safe; **안전한** (an-jeon-han) *adj.* safe

안테나 (an-te-na) *n.* antenna

앉다 (an-tta) *v. intr.* to sit down

앉히다 (an-chi-da) *v. tr.* to make someone sit down

알다 (al-da) *v.* to know, to understand

알려주다 (al-lyeo-ju-da) *v.* to inform

알아듣다 (al-a-deut-da) *v.* to understand

알아보다 (al-a-bo-da) *v.* to find out, to check, to recognize

앞 (ap) *n.* front

앞문 (am-mun) *n.* front door

앞으로(는) (ap-eu-ro [-neun]) *adv.* from now on, in the future

앞치마 (ap-chi-ma) *n.* apron

애인 (ae-in) *n.* boyfriend, girlfriend

액자 (aek-ja) *n.* picture frame

야간 (ya-gan) *n.* night

야구 (ya-gu) *n.* baseball

야구장 (ya-gu-jang) *n.* baseball stadium

야구하다 (ya-gu-ha-da) *v.* to play baseball

야채 (ya-chae) *n.* vegetable

야채가게 (ya-chae-ga-ge) *n.* vegetable store

약 (yak) *n.* medicine, drug; *adv.* about, approximately

약간 (yak-gan) *adv.* a little

약국 (yak-guk) *n.* pharmacy

약도 (yak-do) *n.* sketch map

약방 (yak-bang) *n.* pharmacy

약속 (yak-sok) *n.* appointment, promise

약속하다 (yak-so-ka-da) *v.* to promise

약을 먹다 (yag-eul meok-da) to take medicine

약하다 (ya-ka-da) *v.* to be weak; **약한** (ya-kan) *adj.* weak

약혼하다 (ya-kon-ha-da) *v.* to engage

얇다 (yalp-da) *v.* to be thin; **얇은** (yalb-eun) *adj.* thin

양 (yang) *n.* sheep, amount, quantity

양념 (yang-nyeom) *n.* seasoning

양념하다 (yang-nyeom-ha-da) *v.* to season

양동이 (yang-dong-i) *n.* bucket

양말 (yang-mal) *n.* socks, stocking

양말을 신다 (yang-mal-eul sin-tta) *v.* to wear socks

양복 (yang-bok) *n.* man's dress suit

양식집 (yang-sik-jip) *n.* Western-style restaurant

양초 (yang-cho) *n.* candle

양치질하다 (yang-chi-jil-ha-da) *v.* to brush one's teeth

양파 (yang-pa) *n.* onion

어깨 (eo-kkae) *n.* shoulder

어느 (eo-neu) *adv.* which?

어둡다 (eo-dup-da) *v.* to be dark; **어두운** (eo-du-un) *adj.* dark

어디 (eo-di) *adv.* where?

어디든지 (eo-di-deun-ji) *adv.* wherever

어딘가 (eo-din-ga) *adv.* somewhere

어떤 (eo-tteon) *adv.* which?, what kind of?

어떻게 (eo-tteo-ke) *adv.* how?

어떻게든지 (eo-tteo-ke-deun-ji) *adv.* anyhow

어렵다 (eo-ryeop-da) *v.* to be difficult; **어려운** (eo-ryeo-un) *adj.* difficult

어른 (eo-reun) *n.* adult

어리다 (eo-ri-da) *v.* to be young; **어린** (eo-rin) *adj.* young

어린이 (eo-rin-i) *n.* child

어머니 (eo-meo-ni) *n.* mother

어머님 (eo-meo-nim) *n.* mother (hon.)

어서 (eo-seo) *adv.* please

어울리다 (eo-ul-li-da) *v.* to look good, to go well

어제 (eo-je) *n.* yesterday

어쩔 줄 모르다 (eo-jjeol jjul mo-reu-da) to not know what to do

언니 (eon-ni) *n.* woman or girl's older sister

언제 (eon-je) *adv.* when?

언제든지 (eon-je-deun-ji) *adv.* whenever

언젠가 (eon-jeon-ga) *adv.* someday

얹다 (eon-tta) *v.* to put

얼굴 (eol-gul) *n.* face

얼마 (eol-ma) *adv.* how much?

얼마 전에 (eol-ma jeon-e) *adv.* sometime ago

얼마 후에 (eol-ma hu-e) *adv.* sometime after

얼마나 (eol-ma-na) *adv.* how long?, how much?

얼만큼 (eol-man-keum) *adv.* how much?

엄마 (eom-ma) *n.* mom

엄청나다 (eom-cheong-na-da) *v.* to be huge, to be enormous; **엄청난** (eom-cheong-nan) *adj.* huge, enormous

없다 (eop-da) *v.* to not exist, to not have, to not own; **없는** (eom-neun) *adj.* nonexistent, unpossessed by oneself, unowned

에스컬레이터 (e-seu-keol-le-i-teo) *n.* escalator

에어컨 (e-eo-keon) *n.* air conditioner

엑스레이 (ek-seu-re-i) *n.* x-ray

엑스레이를 찍다 (ek-seu-re-i-reul jjik-da) to take an x-ray

엔지니어 (en-ji-ni-eo) *n.* engineer

엘리베이터 (el-li-be-i-teo) *n.* elevator

여관 (yeo-gwan) *n.* inn

여기 (yeo-gi) *n.* here

여덟 (yeo-deol) *n.* eight

여동생 (yeo-dong-saeng) *n.* younger sister

여드레 (yeo-deu-re) *n.* eight days

여든 (yeo-deun) *n.* eighty

여러 (yeo-reo) *adj.* several, many

여러분 (yeo-reo-bun) *n.* all of you; ladies and gentlemen

여름 (yeo-reum) *n.* summer

여보 (yeo-bo) *pron.* Honey (in addressing one's spouse)

여섯 (yeo-seot) *n.* six

여성 (yeo-seong) *n.* woman

여성용품 (yeo-seong-yong-pum) *n.* feminine products

여자 (yeo-ja) *n.* female

여자친구 (yeo-ja-chin-gu) *n.* girlfriend

여태 (yeo-tae) *adv.* until now

여행 (yeo-haeng) *n.* travel, trip

여행객 (yeo-haeng-gaek) *n.* traveler

여행사 (yeo-haeng-sa) *n.* travel agency

여행을 가다 (yeo-haeng-eul ga-da) to travel

여행하다 (yeo-haeng-ha-da) *v.* to travel, to take a trip

역 (yeok) *n.* subway, railroad station

역사 (yeok-sa) *n.* history

연극 (yeon-geuk) *n.* play

연극배우 (yeon-geuk-bae-u) *n.* actor, actress in a play

연날리기 (yeon-nal-li-gi) *n.* kite-flying

연두색 (yeon-du-saek) *n., adj.* light green

연락 (yeol-lak) *n.* contact

연락처 (yeol-lak-cheo) *n.* contact information

연락하다 (yeol-la-ka-da) *v.* to keep in touch

연립주택 (yeol-lip-ju-taek) *n.* attached house

연세 (yeon-se) *n.* age (hon.)

연습 (yeon-seup) *n.* practice

연습하다 (yeon-seu-pa-da) *v.* to practice

연애결혼 (yeon-ae-gyeol-hon) *n.* love marriage

연애하다 (yeon-ae-ha-da) *v.* to date, to go out with

연출하다 (yeon-chul-ha-da) *v.* to show, to stage

연필 (yeon-pil) *n.* pencil

연하다 (yeon-ha-da) *v.* to be tender; **연한** (yeon-han) *adj.* tender

연휴 (yeon-hyu) *n.* long weekend, extended holiday

열 (yeol) *n.* ten, fever

열다 (yeol-da) *v.* to open

열리다 (yeol-li-da) *v.* to be opened

열쇠 (yeol-ssoe) *n.* key

열심히 (yeol-ssim-hi) *adv.* diligently

열이 나다 (yeol-i na-da) *v.* to have a fever

열흘 (yeol-heul) *n.* ten days

염색약 (yeom-saeng-nyak) *n.* hair dye

염색하다 (yeom-sae-ka-da) *v.* to dye

엽서 (yeop-seo) *n.* postcard

엿새 (yeot-sae) *n.* six days

영국 (yeong-guk) *n.* England

영상 (yeong-sang) *n*. above zero

영어 (yeong-eo) *n*. English language

영하 (yeong-ha) *adj*. below zero

영화 (yeong-hwa) *n*. movie

영화관 (yeong-hwa-gwan) *n*. movie theater

영화를 보다 (yeong-hwa-reul bo-da) to see a movie

영화배우 (yeong-hwa-bae-u) *n*. actor, actress in a movie

옆 (yeop) *n*. side

옆문 (yeom-mun) *n*. side door

옆집 (yeop-jip) *n*. next door

예방하다 (ye-bang-ha-da) *v*. to prevent

예쁘다 (ye-ppeu-da) *v*. to be pretty; **예쁜** (ye-ppeun) *adj*.
   pretty

예순 (ye-sun) *n*. sixty

예술가 (ye-sul-ga) *n*. artist

예약 (ye-yak) *n*. reservation

예약하다 (ye-ya-ka-da) *v*. to reserve

옛날 (yen-nal) *n*. old days

옛날에 (yen-nal-e) *adv*. a long time ago

오 (o) *n*. five

오늘 (o-neul) *n*. today

오다 (o-da) *v*. to come

오디오 (o-di-o) *n*. audio

오락 (o-rak) *n*. computer game, recreation, pastime

오래간만 (o-rae-gan-man) *adv*. for the first time in a while

오래되다 (o-rae-doe-da) *v*. to be old, to stale; *adj*. **오래된**
   (o-rae-doen) old

오랜만에 (o-raen-man-e) *adv*. after a long time

오랫동안 (o-raet-dong-an) *adv*. for a long time

오렌지 (o-ren-ji) *n*. orange

오렌지 주스 (o-ren-ji ju-seu) *n*. orange juice

오른쪽 (o-reun-jjok) *n*. right side

오븐 (o-beun) *n*. oven

오빠 (o-ppa) *n*. female's older brother

오월 (o-wol) *n*. May

오이 (o-i) *n*. cucumber

오전 (o-jeon) *n*. a.m.

오케스트라 (o-ke-seu-teu-ra) *n*. orchestra

오토바이 (o-to-ba-i) *n*. motorcycle

오페라 (o-pe-ra) *n*. opera

오후 (o-hu) *n*. p.m.

오히려 (o-hi-ryeo) *adv.* rather, unexpectedly

옥수수 (ok-su-su) *n.* corn

온돌 (on-dol) *n.* under-floor heating

온돌방 (on-dol-ppang) *n.* room with under-floor heating

올라오다 (ol-la-o-da) *v.* to come up

올리다 (ol-li-da) *v.* to raise

올해 (ol-hae) *n.*, *adv.* this year

옮기다 (om-gi-da) *v.* to move

옷 (ot) *n.* clothes

옷가게 (ot-ga-ge) *n.* clothing store

옷감 (ot-gam) *n.* cloth

옷걸이 (ot-geol-i) *n.* hanger

옷이 맞다 (os-i mat-da) the clothes fit

옷장 (ot-jang) *n.* wardrobe, closet

옷집 (ot-jip) *n.* clothing store

와이셔츠 (wa-i-syeo-cheu) *n.* man's dress shirt

왕복 (wang-bok) *n.* round trip

왕복표 (wang-bok-pyo) *n.* round-trip ticket

왜 (wae) *adv.* why?

왜냐하면 (wae-nya-ha-nyeon) *conj.* because

외국 (oe-guk) *n.* foreign country

외국어 (oe-gug-eo) *n.* foreign language

외롭다 (oe-rop-da) *v.* to feel lonely; 외로운 (oe-ro-un) *adj.*
    lonely

외모 (oe-mo) *n.* appearance, look

외삼촌 (oe-sam-chon) *n.* uncle

외숙모 (oe-sung-mo) *n.* aunt

외우다 (oe-u-da) *v.* to memorize

외향적이다 (oe-hyang-jeog-i-da) *v.* to be extroverted;
    외향적인 (oe-hyang-jeog-in) *adj.* extroverted

왼쪽 (oen-jjok) *n.* left side

요 (yo) *n.* quilted mattress

요금 (yo-geum) *n.* fare

요금을 내다 (yo-geum-eul nae-da) to pay the fare

요리 (yo-ri) *n.* dish, cuisine

요리하다 (yo-ri-ha-da) *v.* to cook

요망하다 (yo-mang-ha-da) *v.* to request

요즘 (yo-jeum) *adv.* these days

요트 (yo-teu) *n.* yacht

욕조 (yok-jo) *n.* bathtub

용기 (yong-gi) *n.* container, courage

용량 (yong-nyang) *n.* amount

용모단정 (yong-mo-dan-jeong) *n.* neat appearance, having neat features

용법 (yong-ppeop) *n.* usage

우대하다 (u-dae-ha-da) *v.* to treat specially

우리 (u-ri) *pron.* we, us, ours

우산 (u-san) *n.* umbrella

우선 (u-seon) *adv.* first of all

우습다 (u-seup-da) *v.* to be funny; **우스운** (u-seu-un) *adj.* funny

우연히 (u-yeon-hi) *adv.* by chance

우유 (u-yu) *n.* milk

우체국 (u-che-guk) *n.* post office

우체부 (u-che-bu) *n.* postal worker

우체통 (u-che-tong) *n.* mailbox

우편번호 (u-pyeon-beon-ho) *n.* zip code

우편요금 (u-pyeon-yo-geum) *n.* postage

우표 (u-pyo) *n.* stamp

우표를 붙이다 (u-pyo-reul bu-chi-da) to put a stamp on

우회전하다 (u-hoe-jeon-ha-da) *v.* to turn right

운동 (un-dong) *n.* exercise

운동복 (un-dong-bok) *n.* exercise wear

운동선수 (un-dong-seon-su) *n.* athlete, player

운동장 (un-dong-jang) *n.* field, playground

운동하다 (un-dong-ha-da) *v.* to exercise

운동화 (un-dong-hwa) *n.* athletic shoes, sneakers

운전하다 (un-jeon-ha-da) *v.* to drive

울다 (ul-da) *v.* to cry

울리다 (ul-li-da) *v.* to make someone cry

웃기다 (ut-gi-da) *v.* to make someone laugh

웃다 (ut-da) *v.* to laugh

워크맨 (wo-keu-maen) *n.* portable cassette/CD player, Walkman™

원 (won) *counter for Korean currency*

원래 (wol-lae) *adv.* originally

원숭이 (won-sung-i) *n.* monkey

원인 (won-in) *n.* reason

원피스 (won-pi-seu) *n.* dress

원하다 (won-ha-da) *v.* to want

월 (wol) *counter for month*

월급 (wol-geup) *n.* salary

월급을 받다 (wol-geub-eul bat-da) to receive a paycheck

월급을 타다 (wol-geub-eul ta-da) to receive a paycheck

월요일 (wol-yo-il) *n.* Monday

웨딩 드레스 (we-ding-deu-re-seu) *n.* wedding gown

웬일 (wen-il) *adv.* what matter?

웬지 (wen-ji) *adv.* somehow

위 (wi) *n.* up, stomach

위층 (wi-cheung) *n.* upstairs

위치 (wi-chi) *n.* location

위하다 (wi-ha-da) *v.* to do for the sake of

위험하다 (wi-heom-ha-da) *v.* to be dangerous; 위험한 (wi-heom-han) *adj.* dangerous

유경험자 (yu-gyeong-heom-ja) *n.* experienced person

유럽 (yu-reop) *n.* Europe

유리하다 (yu-ri-ha-da) *v.* to be advantageous; 유리한 (yu-ri-han) *adj.* advantageous

유물 (yu-mul) *n.* relic

유아 (yu-a) *n.* infant

유아용품 (yu-a-yong-pum) *n.* infant products

유월 (yu-wol) *n.* June

유자차 (yu-ja-cha) *n.* citron tea

유치원 (yu-chi-won) *n.* kindergarten

유행 (yu-haeng) *n.* fashion, fad

유행하다 (yu-haeng-ha-da) *v.* to be fashionable, to be popular

육 (yuk) *n.* six

육개장 (yuk-gae-jang) *n.* shredded beef soup

육교 (yuk-gyo) *n.* pedestrian overpass

윤기 (yun-kki) *n.* luster, shine, gloss

윤기있다 (yun-kki-it-da) *v.* to be glossy; 윤기있는 (yun-kki-in-neun) *adj.* glossy

윷놀이 (yun-nol-i) *n.* traditional Korean four-stick game

은행 (eun-haeng) *n.* bank, ginkgo

음료수 (eum-nyo-su) *n.* beverage

음식 (eum-sik) *n.* food

음식을 차리다 (eum-sig-eul cha-ri-da) to prepare food

음식점 (eum-sik-jeom) *n.* restaurant

음악 (eum-ak) *n.* music

음악가 (eum-ak-ga) *n.* musician

음악을 감상하다 (eum-ag-eul gam-sang-ha-da) to listen to music

음악을 듣다 (eum-ag-eul deut-da) to listen to music

음악회 (eum-a-kwoe) *n.* concert

응급실 (eung-geup-sil) *n.* emergency room

의대 (ui-dae) *n.* medical school

의사 (ui-sa) *n.* doctor

의자 (ui-ja) *n.* chair

이 (i) *adj.* this; *n.* two, tooth

이가 썩다 (i-ga sseok-da) to have a cavity

이가 아프다 (i-ga a-peu-da) to have a toothache

이기다 (i-gi-da) *v.* to win over

이기적이다 (i-gi-jeog-i-da) *v.* to be selfish; **이기적인** (i-gi-jeog-in) *adj.* selfish

이나 (i-na) *conj.* or (used with noun only)

이따가 (i-tta-ga) *adv.* a little later, shortly thereafter

이레 (i-re) *n.* seven days

이르다 (i-reu-da) *v.* to be early; **이른** (i-reun) *adj.* early

이를 닦다 (i-reul dak-da) to brush one's teeth

이름 (i-reum) *n.* name

이만 (i-man) *adv.* this much, this many

이만큼 (i-man-keum) *adv.* this much

이메일 (i-me-il) *n.* e-mail

이메일을 받다 (i-me-il-eul bat-da) to receive an e-mail

이메일을 보내다 (i-me-il-eul bo-nae-da) to send an e-mail

이모 (i-mo) *n.* aunt (mother's sister)

이모부 (i-mo-bu) *n.* uncle (mother's sister's husband)

이민 (i-min) *n.* emigration, immigration

이민가다 (i-min-ga-da) *v.* to emigrate

이민오다 (i-min-o-da) *v.* to immigrate

이발사 (i-bal-sa) *n.* barber

이발소 (i-bal-so) *n.* barbershop

이발하다 (i-bal-ha-da) *v.* to get a haircut (men)

이불 (i-bul) *n.* quilted blanket

이사가다 (i-sa-ga-da) *v.* to move out

이사오다 (i-sa-o-da) *v.* to move in

이사하다 (i-sa-ha-da) *v.* to change residence, to move

이상 (i-sang) *n.* abnormal

이상이 없다 (i-sang-i eop-da) to be normal; **정상의** (jeong-sang-ui) *adj.* normal

이상이 있다 (i-sang-i it-da) to be abnormal; **비정상의** (bi-jeong-sang-ui) *adj.* abnormal

이상하다 (i-sang-ha-da) *v.* to be strange; 이상한 (i-sang-han) *adj.* strange

이야기 (i-ya-gi) *n.* story, talk

이야기를 걸다 (i-ya-gi-reul geol-da) to initiate a conversation

이야기하다 (i-ya-gi-ha-da) *v.* to talk

이용하다 (i-yong-ha-da) *v.* to utilize

이월 (i-wol) *n.* February

이유 (i-yu) *n.* reason

이제 (i-je) *adv.* now

이중언어구사자 (i-jung-eon-eo-gu-sa-ja) *n.* bilingual

이쪽 (i-jjok) *n.* this side

이층집 (i-cheung-jjip) *n.* two-story house

이틀 (i-teul) *n.* two days

이해 (i-hae) *n.* understanding

이해하다 (i-hae-ha-da) *v.* to understand

이혼 (i-hon) *n.* divorce

이혼하다 (i-hon-ha-da) *v.* to divorce

익숙하다 (ik-su-ka-da) *v.* to be familiar, to be good at; 익숙한 (ik-su-kan) *adj.* familiar, skilled, good at

익숙해지다 (ik-su-kae-ji-da) *v.* to get used to, to become familiar with

인구 (in-gu) *n.* population

인기 (in-kki) *n.* popularity

인도 (in-do) *n.* sidewalk, India

인사 (in-sa) *n.* greeting

인사하다 (in-sa-ha-da) *v.* to greet

인삼차 (in-sam-cha) *n.* ginseng tea

인상 (in-sang) *n.* impression

인상적이다 (in-sang-jeog-i-da) *v.* to be impressive; 인상적인 (in-sang-jeog-in) *adj.* impressive

인생 (in-saeng) *n.* life

인정 (in-jeong) *n.* human heart, sympathy

인터넷 (in-teo-net) *n.* Internet

인형 (in-hyeong) *n.* doll, puppet

일 (il) *n.* one, date, event, thing, work

일곱 (il-gop) *n.* seven

일기 (il-gi) *n.* journal

일기예보 (il-gi-ye-bo) *n.* weather forecast

일등석 (il-tteung-seok) *n.* first-class seat

일반석 (il-ban-seok) *n.* economy-class seat

일벌레 (il-beol-lae) *n.* workaholic

일부러 (il-bu-reo) *adv.* on purpose

일식집 (il-ssik-jip) *n.* Japanese-style restaurant

일어나다 (il-eo-na-da) *v.* to wake up, to stand up, to get up

일어서다 (il-eo-seo-da) *v.* to stand up

일요일 (il-yo-il) *n.* Sunday

일월 (il-wol) *n.* January

일을 시키다 (il-eul si-ki-da) to make someone work

일자리 (il-jja-ri) *n.* job

일자리를 구하다 (il-jja-ri-reul gu-ha-da) to look for a job

일찍 (il-jjik) *adv.* early

일하다 (il-ha-da) *v.* to work

일흔 (il-heun) *n.* seventy

읽다 (ilk-da) *v.* to read

잃다 (il-ta) *v.* to lose

잃어버리다 (il-eo-beo-ri-da) *v.* to lose

입 (ip) *n.* mouth

입고 가다 (ip-go ga-da) *v.* to wear something

입고 다니다 (ip-go da-ni-da) *v.* to wear something regularly

입고 오다 (ip-go o-da) *v.* to come wearing something

입구 (ip-gu) *n.* entrance

입다 (ip-da) *n.* to wear (clothes)

입맛 (im-mat) *n.* appetite

입술 (ip-sul) *n.* lips

입원하다 (ib-won-ha-da) *v.* to be hospitalized

입장 (ip-jang) *n.* entering, entrance

입장객 (ip-jang-gaek) *n.* ticket holder, visitor in public places

입장권 (ip-jang-kkwon) *n.* admission ticket

입장료 (ip-jang-nyo) *n.* admission fee

입장하다 (ip-jang-ha-da) *v.* to enter

입학하다 (i-pa-ka-da) *v.* to enter school

입히다 (i-pi-da) *v.* to dress someone

잇몸 (in-mom) *n.* the gum

있다 (it-da) *v.* to exist, to have, to own; **있는** (in-neun) *adj.* existing, possessed, owned

잊다 (it-da) *v.* to forget

잊어버리다 (ij-eo-beo-ri-da) *v.* to forget

ㅈ

자기 (ja-gi) *pron.* self
자기소개서 (ja-gi so-gae-seo) *n.* self-introduction
자다 (ja-da) *v.* to sleep
자동 (ja-dong) *n.* automatic
자동발매기 (ja-dong-bal-mae-gi) *n.* automatic ticket vendor
자동차 (ja-dong-cha) *n.* vehicle
자동칫솔 (ja-dong-chit-sol) *n.* automatic toothbrush
자동판매기 (ja-dong-pan-mae-gi) *n.* vending machine
자라다 (ja-ra-da) *v.* to grow up
자르다 (ja-reu-da) *v.* to cut
자리 (ja-ri) *n.* seat
자명종 (ja-myeong-jong) *n.* alarm clock
자세히 (ja-se-hi) *adv.* closely, in detail
자연 (ja-yeon) *n.* nature
자연식품 (ja-yeon-sik-pum) *n.* organic food
자연적이다 (ja-yeon-jeog-i-da) *v.* to be natural; **자연적인** (ja-yeon-jeog-in) *adj.* natural
자연히 (ja-yeon-hi) *adv.* naturally
자유 (ja-yu) *n.* freedom; *adj.* free
자전거 (ja-jeon-geo) *n.* bicycle
자전거를 타다 (ja-jeon-geo-reul ta-da) to ride a bicycle
자주 (ja-ju) *adv.* frequently, often
자주색 (ja-ju-saek) *n., adj.* purple
자켓 (ja-ket) *n.* jacket
작가 (jak-ga) *n.* writer
작곡가 (jak-gok-ga) *n.* music composer
작년 (jang-nyeon) *n.* last year
작다 (jak-da) *v.* to be small; **작은** (jag-eun) *adj.* small
작은술 (jag-eun-sul) *n.* teaspoon
작은아버지 (jag-eun a-beo-ji) *n.* uncle
작은어머니 (jag-eun eo-meo-ni) *n.* aunt
잔 (jan) *n.* glass, cup, counter for glass or cup
잔잔하다 (jan-jan-ha-da) *v.* to be calm; **잔잔한** (jan-jan-han) *adj.* calm
잔치 (jan-chi) *n.* party
잘 (jal) *adv.* well
잘되다 (jal-doe-da) *v.* to be going well

잘라 드리다 (jal-la deu-ri-da) *v.* to cut something for someone (hon.)

잘라 주다 (jal-la ju-da) *v.* to cut something for someone

잘못하다 (jal-mo-ta-da) *v.* to make a mistake, to not do well

잘생기다 (jal-saeng-gi-da) *v.* to be handsome; **잘생긴** (jal-saeng-gin) *adj.* handsome

잠 (jam) *n.* sleep

잠바 (jam-ba) *n.* jumper, jacket

잠시 (jam-si) *adv.* for a while

잠을 자다 (jam-eul ja-da) to sleep

잠이 깨다 (jam-i kkae-da) to wake up

잡다 (jap-da) *v.* to catch, to grab

잡담하다 (jap-dam-ha-da) *v.* to chat

잡수시다 (jap-su-si-da) *v.* to eat (hon.)

잡지 (jap-ji) *n.* magazine

잡채 (jap-chae) *n.* a mixed dish of vegetables and beef, fried noodle

장 (jang) *counter for sheet*; *n.* market

장가가다 (jang-ga-ga-da) *v.* to marry (male)

장갑 (jang-gap) *n.* glove

장거리전화 (jang-geo-ri-jeon-hwa) *n.* long-distance call

장기간 (jang-gi-gan) *n.* extended period

장난감 (jang-nan-kkam) *n.* toy

장남 (jang-nam) *n.* eldest son

장녀 (jang-nyeo) *n.* eldest daughter

장롱 (jang-nong) *n.* wardrobe, closet

장미 (jang-mi) *n.* rose

장사 (jang-sa) *n.* small business

장사를 하다 (jang-sa-reul ha-da) to run a small business

장소 (jang-so) *n.* place

장을 보다 (jang-eul bo-da) *v.* to go grocery shopping

장학금 (jang-hak-geum) *n.* scholarship

장학금을 받다 (jang-hak-geum-eul bat-da) to receive a scholarship

재미교포 (jae-mi-gyo-po) *n.* an ethnic Korean living in the United States

재미없다 (jae-mi-eop-da) *v.* to be no fun, to be boring; **재미없는** (jae-mi-eom-neun) *adj.* no fun, boring

재미있다 (jae-mi-it-da) *v.* to be fun; **재미있는** (jae-mi-in-neun) *adj.* fun

재일교포 (jae-il-gyo-po) *n.* an ethnic Korean living in
    Japan

재작년 (jae-jang-nyeon) *n., adv.* the year before last year

재학하다 (jae-ha-ka-da) *v.* to attend school

저 (jeo) *pron.* I (humble); *adv.* that over there

저기 (jeo-gi) *n., adv.* over there

저녁 (jeo-nyeok) *n.* evening, dinner

저울 (jeo-ul) *n.* scale

저쪽 (jeo-jjok) *n., adv.* that side over there

적극적이다 (jeok-geuk-jeog-i-da) *v.* to be active;
    적극적인 (jeok-geuk-jeog-in) *adj.* active

적다 (jeok-da) *v.* to be few; 적은 (jeog-eun) *adj.* few

적당하다 (jeok-dang-ha-da) *v.* to be appropriate, to be
    proper; 적당한 (jeok-dang-han) *adj.* appropriate,
    proper

적성 (jeok-seong) *n.* aptitude

적성에 맞다 (jeok-seong-e mat-da) to be appropriate to
    one's aptitude

적어도 (jeog-eo-do) *adv.* at least

전 (jeon) *n.* before

전공 (jeon-gong) *n.* major

전공하다 (jeon-gong-ha-da) *v.* to major in

전구 (jeon-gu) *v.* bulb

전국 (jeon-guk) *n., adv.* nationwide, the whole country

전기 (jeon-gi) *n.* electricity

전기밥솥 (jeon-gi-bap-sot) *n.* electric rice cooker

전등 (jeon-deung) *n.* light, lamp

전망 (jeon-mang) *n.* view

전망이 좋다 (jeon-mang-i jo-ta) *v.* to have a good view

전문 (jeon-mun) *n.* specialty

전부 (jeon-bu) *adv.* all together, total

전에 (jeon-e) *adv.* before

전철 (jeon-cheol) *n.* subway

전철역 (jeon-cheol-lyeok) *n.* subway station

전통 (jeon-tong) *n.* tradition

전통적이다 (jeon-tong-jeog-i-da) *v.* to be traditional;
    전통적인 (jeon-tong-jeog-in) *adj.* traditional

전하다 (jeon-ha-da) *v.* to pass, to convey

전화 (jeon-hwa) *n.* telephone

전화국 (jeon-hwa-guk) *n.* telephone company

전화기 (jeon-hwa-gi) *n.* telephone set

전화를 걸다 (jeon-hwa-reul geol-da) *v.* to make a call

전화를 끊다 (jeon-hwa-reul kkeun-ta) *v.* to hang up

전화를 받다 (jeon-hwa-reul bat-da) *v.* to receive a call

전화번호 (jeon-hwa-beon-ho) *n.* telephone number

전화비 (jeon-hwa-bi) *n.* telephone bill

전화하다 (jeon-hwa-ha-da) *v.* to make a phone call

젊다 (jeom-tta) *v.* to be young; 젊은 (jeolm-eun) *adj.* young

점 (jeom) *n.* spot, point, thing

점심 (jeom-sim) *n.* afternoon, lunch

점원 (jeom-won) *n.* clerk, salesperson

접시 (jeop-si) *n.* plate

젓가락 (jeot-ga-rak) *n.* chopstick

정가 (jeong-kka) *n.* regular price

정말 (jeong-mal) *adv.* indeed, really

정말로 (jeong-mal-lo) *adv.* indeed, really

정반대 (jeong-ban-dae) *n.* exact opposite

정신없이 (jeong-sin-eops-i) *adv.* mindlessly

정원 (jeong-won) *n.* yard, garden, quorum

정장 (jeong-jang) *n.* formal outfit

정직하다 (jeong-ji-ka-da) *v.* to be honest; 정직한 (jeong-ji-kan) *adj.* honest

정치 (jeong-chi) *n.* politics

정하다 (jeong-ha-da) *v.* to decide

젖다 (jeot-da) *v.* to get wet, to be wet

제 (je) *pron.* my (humble)

제공하다 (je-gong-ha-da) *v.* to offer

제과점 (je-gwa-jeom) *n.* bakery

제대로 (je-dae-ro) *adv.* appropriately, properly

제비 (je-bi) *n.* swallow

제시간 (je-si-gan) *n., adv.* the scheduled time

제일 (je-il) *adv.* the first, the most

젤 (jel) *n.* gel

조각 (jo-gak) *n.* sculpture, a piece

조건 (jo-kkeon) *n.* condition

조그맣다 (jo-geu-ma-ta) *v.* to be small; 조그만 (jo-geu-man) *adj.* small

조금 (jo-geum) *adv.* a little

조깅하다 (jo-ging-ha-da) *v.* to jog

조끼 (jo-kki) *n.* vest

조상 (jo-sang) *n.* ancestor

조심하다 (jo-sim-ha-da) *v.* to be careful

조용하다 (jo-yong-ha-da) *v.* to be quiet; 조용한 (jo-yong-han) *adj.* quiet

졸다 (jol-da) *v.* to doze off

졸리다 (jol-li-da) *v.* to feel sleepy

졸업 (jol-eop) *n.* graduation

졸업반 (jol-eop-ban) *n.* graduating class

졸업식 (jol-eop-sik) *n.* graduation ceremony

졸업하다 (jol-eo-pa-da) *v.* to graduate

좀 (jom) *adv.* a little, please

좁다 (jop-da) *v.* to be narrow; 좁은 (job-eun) *adj.* narrow

종류 (jong-nyu) *n.* kind, type

종업원 (jong-eob-won) *n.* waiter, waitress, employee

종이 (jong-i) *n.* paper

종이접시 (jong-i-jeop-si) *n.* paper plate

종이컵 (jong-i-keop) *n.* paper cup

좋다 (jo-ta) *v.* to be likable, to like, to be good; 좋은 (jo-eun) *adj.* likable, good

좋아하다 (jo-a-ha-da) *v.* to like, to be fond of

좌석 (jwa-seok) *n.* seat

좌회전하다 (jwa-hoe-jeon-ha-da) *v.* to turn left

죄송하다 (joe-song-ha-da) *v.* to be sorry (hon.); 죄송한 (joe-song-han) *adj.* sorry

주다 (ju-da) *v.* to give

주로 (ju-ro) *adv.* mainly

주말 (ju-mal) *n.* weekend

주머니 (ju-meo-ni) *n.* pocket

주무시다 (ju-mu-si-da) *v.* to sleep (hon.)

주문하다 (ju-mun-ha-da) *v.* to order

주방 (ju-bang) *n.* kitchen

주방용품 (ju-bang-young-pum) *n.* kitchen utensils

주부 (ju-bu) *n.* housewife

주사 (ju-sa) *n.* injection, shot

주사를 맞다 (ju-sa-reul mat-da) to get a shot

주소 (ju-so) *n.* address

주스 (ju-seu) *n.* juice

주유소 (ju-yu-so) *n.* gas station

주의사항 (ju-ui-sa-hang) *n.* warning

주제 (ju-je) *n.* topic, theme

주중 (ju-jung) *n.* during the week

주차금지 (ju-cha-geum-ji) *n.* no parking

주차장 (ju-cha-jang) *n.* parking lot
주차하다 (ju-cha-ha-da) *v.* to park
주황색 (ju-hwang-saek) *n.*, *adj.* orange (color)
죽다 (juk-da) *v.* to die
죽음 (jug-eum) *n.* death
죽이다 (jug-i-da) *v.* to kill
준비하다 (jun-bi-ha-da) *v.* to prepare
줄 (jul) *n.* row, line
줄넘기 (jul-leom-kki) *n.* jumping rope
줄다 (jul-da) *v.* to be reduced
줄무늬 (jul-mu-nui) *n.* stripe pattern
줄을 서다 (jul-eul seo-da) to stand in a line
줄이다 (jul-i-da) *v.* to reduce
중 (jung) *n.* monk, a medium size
중간 (jung-gan) *n.* middle
중고 (jung-go) *n.* used
중고차 (jung-go-cha) *n.* used car
중고품 (jung-go-pum) *n.* used merchandise
중국 (jung-guk) *n.* China
중국사람 (jung-guk-sa-ram) *n.* Chinese
중국집 (jung-guk-jip) *n.* Chinese-style restaurant
중매 (jung-mae) *n.* matchmaking
중매결혼 (jung-mae-gyeol-hon) *n.* arranged marriage
중매쟁이 (jung-mae-jaeng-i) *n.* matchmaker
중부 (jung-bu) *n.* central districts
중앙우체국 (jung-ang-u-che-guk) *n.* central post office
중요하다 (jung-yo-ha-da) *v.* to be important; 중요한
    (jung-yo-han) *adj.* important
중지하다 (jung-ji-ha-da) *v.* to discontinue
중학교 (jung-hak-gyo) *n.* middle school
중학생 (jung-hak-saeng) *n.* middle school student
쥐 (jwi) *n.* mouse
즐겁다 (jeul-geop-da) *v.* to be pleasant, to be enjoyable, to
    be joyful; 즐거운 (jeul-geo-un) *adj.* pleasant,
    enjoyable, joyful
즐기다 (jeul-gi-da) *v.* to enjoy
증상 (jeung-sang) *n.* symptom
지각하다 (ji-ga-ka-da) *v.* to be late
지갑 (ji-gap) *n.* wallet
지금 (ji-geum) *n.* now
지나가는 사람 (ji-na-ga-neun sa-ram) *n.* passerby

지난 (ji-nan) *adj.* last

지내다 (ji-nae-da) *v.* to spend days

지다 (ji-da) *v.* to be defeated

지도 (ji-do) *n.* map

지루하다 (ji-ru-ha-da) *v.* to be boring; 지루한 (ji-ru-han) *adj.* boring

지방 (ji-bang) *n.* local area, region, fat

지붕 (ji-bung) *n.* roof

지우개 (ji-u-gae) *n.* eraser

지우다 (ji-u-da) *v.* to erase

지원하다 (ji-won-ha-da) *v.* to apply for

지저분하다 (ji-jeo-bun-ha-da) *v.* to be messy; 지저분한 (ji-jeo-bun-han) *adj.* messy

지진 (ji-jin) *n.* earthquake

지진이 나다 (ji-jin-i na-da) an earthquake occurs

지키다 (ji-ki-da) *v.* to keep, to maintain

지폐 (ji-pye) *n.* bill

지하도 (ji-ha-do) *n.* pedestrian underpass

지하상가 (ji-ha-sang-ga) *n.* underground mall, mall below ground

지하철 (ji-ha-cheol) *n.* subway

지하철역 (ji-ha-cheol-lyeok) *n.* subway station

직사광선 (jik-sa-gwang-seon) *n.* direct sunshine

직업 (jig-eop) *n.* job, occupation

직장 (jik-jang) *n.* place to work, job

직장에 다니다 (jik-jang-e da-ni-da) to go to work

직장을 얻다 (jik-jang-eul eot-da) to get a job

직접 (jik-jeop) *adv.* directly

진보적이다 (jin-bo-jeog-i-da) *v.* to be progressive; 진보적인 (jin-bo-jeog-in) *adj.* progressive

진지 (jin-ji) *n.* meal, cooked rice (hon.)

진지를 드시다 (jin-ji-reul deu-si-da) to eat (hon.)

진지를 잡수시다 (jin-ji-reul jap-su-si-da) to eat (hon.)

진찰 (jin-chal) *n.* medical examination

진찰을 받다 (jin-chal-eul bat-da) to consult a doctor

진통제 (jin-tong-je) *n.* painkiller

질기다 (jil-gi-da) *v.* to be chewy (in a bad way); 질긴 (jil-gin) *adj.* chewy (in a bad way)

질문 (jil-mun) *n.* question

질문하다 (jil-mun-ha-da) *v.* to ask

집 (jip) *n.* house, home

집다 (jip-da) *v.* to pick up

집들이 (jip-deul-i) *n.* housewarming party

집안 (jib-an) *n.* house interior, family background

집주인 (jip-ju-in) *n.* owner of a house, landlord

짜다 (jja-da) *v.* to taste salty, to plan; 짠 (jjan) *adj.* salty, planned

짧다 (jjalp-da) *v.* to be short; 짧은 (jjalb-eun) *adj.* short

쪽 (jjok) *n.* side, direction

쫄깃쫄깃하다 (jjol-git-jjol-git-ta-da) *v.* to be chewy (in a good way); 쫄깃쫄깃한 (jjol-git-jjol-git-tan) *adj.* chewy (in a good way)

쫓기다 (jjot-gi-da) *v.* to be chased

쫓다 (jjot-da) *v.* to chase

쯤 (jjeum) *part.* about, around

찍다 (jjik-da) *v.* to take a photograph, to dip, to dot

ㅊ

차 (cha) *n.* car, automobile, tea

차고 (cha-go) *n.* garage

차남 (cha-nam) *n.* second son

차녀 (cha-nyeo) *n.* second daughter

차다 (cha-da) *v.* to put on, to wear. to be cold, 찬 (chan) *adj.* cold

차도 (cha-do) *n.* road

차라리 (cha-ra-ri) *adv.* rather, had better

차례 (cha-rye) *n.* turn, rites honoring ancestors

차례를 기다리다 (cha-rye-reul gi-da-ri-da) to wait one's turn

차례를 지내다 (cha-rye-reul ji-nae-da) to observe an ancestor worshipping

차리다 (cha-ri-da) *v.* to prepare for

차분하다 (cha-bun-ha-da) *v.* to be calm; 차분한 (cha-bun-han) *adj.* calm

차사고 (cha-sa-go) *n.* car accident

차에 치이다 (cha-e chi-i-da) to be hit by a car

차이 (cha-i) *n.* difference

차차 (cha-cha) *adv.* gradually

참 (cham) *adv.* very, really, by the way

참기름 (cham-gi-reum) *n.* sesame oil

참새 (cham-sae) *n.* sparrow

참석하다 (cham-seo-ka-da) *v.* to participate, to attend

찻길 (chat-gil) *n.* street, road

창고 (chang-go) *n.* storage

창문 (chang-mun) *n.* window

창피하다 (chang-pi-ha-da) *v.* to be shameful, to be embarrassing; **창피한** (chang-pi-han) *adj.* shameful, embarrassing

찾다 (chat-da) *v.* to withdraw money, to look for, to find, to search

채널 (chae-neol) *n.* TV channel

채소 (chae-so) *n.* vegetable

채소가게 (chae-so-ga-ge) *n.* vegetable market

책 (chaek) *n.* book

책방 (chaek-bang) *n.* bookstore

책상 (chaek-sang) *n.* desk

책임 (chaeg-im) *n.* responsibility

책임감이 강하다 (chaeg-im-gam-i gang-ha-da) to be responsible

책장 (chaek-jang) *n.* bookshelves, bookcase

챙기다 (chaeng-gi-da) *v.* to remember to take something, to take care of

처음 (cheo-eum) *n.* for the first time

천 (cheon) *n.* thousand

천천히 (cheon-cheon-hi) *adv.* slowly

첫사랑 (cheot-sa-rang) *n.* first love

청바지 (cheong-ba-ji) *n.* jean

청소기 (cheong-so-gi) *n.* vacuum cleaner

청소하다 (cheong-so-ha-da) *v.* to clean

체중계 (che-jung-gye) *v.* put a weight on a scale

체하다 (che-ha-da) *v.* to be nauseous, to have an upset stomach

첼로 (chel-lo) *n.* cello

쳐다보다 (chyeo-da-bo-da) *v.* to look at

초 (cho) *counter for seconds (time)*, *n.* candle

초대받다 (cho-dae-bat-da) *v.* to be invited

초대장 (cho-dae-jjang) *n.* invitation card

초대하다 (cho-dae-ha-da) *v.* to invite

초등학교 (cho-deung-hak-gyo) *n.* elementary school

초등학생 (cho-deung-hak-saeng) *n.* elementary school student

초록색 (cho-rok-saek) *n.*, *adj.* green

초인종 (cho-in-jong) *n.* doorbell

초콜릿 (cho-kol-lit) *n.* chocolate

최고 (choe-go) *n., adj.* highest

최고급 (choe-go-geup) *n.* the best quality

최근 (choe-geun) *adv.* lately

최선 (choe-seon) *n., adj.* best

최악 (choe-ak) *n., adj.* worst

최저 (choe-jeo) *n., adj.* lowest

추리소설 (chu-ri-so-seol) *n.* mystery novel

추리하다 (chu-ri-ha-da) *v.* to reason

추석 (chu-seok) *n.* traditional Korean Thanksgiving

추워지다 (chu-wo-ji-da) *v.* to become cold

추천 (chu-cheon) *n.* recommendation

추천서 (chu-cheon-seo) *n.* recommendation letter

추천하다 (chu-cheon-ha-da) *v.* to recommend

축구 (chuk-gu) *n.* soccer

축구하다 (chuk-gu-ha-da) *v.* to play soccer

축축하다 (chuk-chu-ka-da) *v.* to be wet, to be muggy; **축축한** (chuk-chu-kan) *adj.* wet, muggy

축하하다 (chu-ka-ha-da) *v.* to congratulate

출구 (chul-gu) *n.* exit

출근하다 (chul-geun-ha-da) *v.* to go to work

출발 (chul-bal) *n.* departure

출발하다 (chul-bal-ha-da) *n.* to depart, to leave

춤 (chum) *n.* dance

춤을 추다 (chum-eul-chu-da) *v.* to dance

춥다 (chup-da) *v.* to be cold; **추운** (chu-un) *adj.* cold

충분하다 (chung-bun-ha-da) *v.* to be enough; **충분한** (chung-bun-han) *adj.* enough

취미 (chwi-mi) *n.* hobby

취미생활 (chwi-mi-saeng-hwal) *n.* hobbies

취직 (chwi-jik) *n.* getting a job

취직하다 (chwi-ji-ka-da) *v.* to get a job

층 (cheung) *counter for floor*; *n.* layer

치과 (chi-kkwa) *n.* dentistry

치과의사 (chi-kkwa-ui-sa) *n.* dentist

치다 (chi-da) *n.* to play

치료받다 (chi-ryo-bat-da) *v.* to receive treatment

치료하다 (chi-ryo-ha-da) *v.* to treat a patient

치마 (chi-ma) *n.* skirt

치약 (chi-yak) *n.* toothpaste

치이다 (chi-i-da) *v.* to be hit by a car

친구 (chin-gu) *n.* friend

친절 (chin-jeol) *n.* kindness

친절하다 (chin-jeol-ha-da) v. to be kind; 친절한 (chin-jeol-han) *adj.* kind, nice

친척 (chin-cheok) *n.* relatives

친하다 (chin-ha-da) *v.* to be close, to be friendly; 친한 (chin-han) *adj.* close, friendly

칠 (chil) *n.* seven

칠월 (chil-wol) *n.* July

칠판 (chil-pan) *n.* blackboard

침대 (chim-dae) *n.* bed

칫솔 (chit-sol) *n.* toothbrush

ㅋ

카네이션 (ka-ne-i-syeon) *n.* carnation

카드 (ka-deu) *n.* card, credit card

카드로 내다 (ka-deu-ro nae-da) to pay by credit card

카드를 받다 (ka-deu-reul bat-da) to accept a credit card, to receive a card

카메라 (ka-me-ra) *n.* camera

카운슬러 (ka-un-seul-leo) *n.* counselor

카운터 (ka-un-teo) *n.* cash register, counter

카페 (ka-pe) *n.* café, coffee shop

칼 (kal) *n.* knife, sword

캐나다 (kae-na-da) *n.* Canada

캔디 (kaen-di) *n.* candy

캠코더 (kaem-ko-deo) *n.* movie camera

캠페인 (kaem-pe-in) *n.* campaign

커다랗다 (keo-da-ra-ta) *v.* to be big; 커다란 (keo-da-ran) *adj.* big

커피 (keo-pi) *n.* coffee

컴퓨터 (keom-pu-teo) *n.* computer

컵 (keop) *counter for cup*, *n.* cup

케이크 (ke-i-keu) *n.* cake

켜다 (kyeo-da) *v.* to turn on

켤레 (kyeol-le) *counter for a pair of shoes or socks*

코 (ko) *n.* nose

코가 막히다 (ko-ga ma-ki-da) to be congested, to be stuffed up

코감기 (ko-gam-gi) *n.* nasal congestion

코끼리 (ko-kki-ri) *n.* elephant

코미디 (ko-mi-di) *n.* comedy

코뿔소 (ko-ppul-so) *n.* rhino

코트 (ko-teu) *n.* coat

콘서트 (kon-seo-teu) *n.* concert

콘택트렌즈 (kon-taek-teu-ren-jeu) *n.* contact lens

콘택트렌즈를 끼다 (kon-taek-teu-ren-jeu-reul kki-da) to
    wear contact lenses

콜라 (kol-la) *n.* cola

콧물 (kon-mul) *n.* runny nose

콧물이 나오다 (kon-mul-i na-o-da) to have a runny nose

콩나물 (kong-na-mul) *n.* bean sprouts

퀴즈 (kwi-jeu) *n.* quiz

퀴즈를 보다 (kwi-jeu-reul bo-da) to take a quiz

크다 (keu-da) *v.* to be big; 큰 (keun) *adj.* big

크리스마스 (keu-ri-seu-ma-seu) *n.* Christmas

큰술 (keun-sul) *n.* tablespoon

큰아버지 (keun-a-beo-ji) *n.* uncle

큰어머니 (keun-eo-meo-ni) *n.* aunt

큰일나다 (keun-il-na-da) *v.* to be in big trouble

클라리넷 (keul-la-ri-net) *n.* clarinet

클래식 (keul-lae-sik) *n.* classical music

키 (ki) *n.* height

키가 작다 (ki-ga jak-da) to be short

키가 크다 (ki-ga keu-da) to be tall

키보드 (ki-bo-deu) *n.* keyboard, electric piano

ㅌ

타고 가다 (ta-go ga-da) *v.* to go riding

타고 다니다 (to-go da-ni-da) *v.* to ride regularly

타고 오다 (to-go o-da) *v.* to come riding

타다 (ta-da) *v.* to be burned, to ride, to get on, to get in;
    탄 (tan) *adj.* burnt

탁구 (tak-gu) *n.* ping-pong

탁자 (tak-ja) *n.* table

탈렌트 (tal-len-teu) *n.* TV actor or actress

탈춤 (tal-chum) *n.* traditional Korean mask dance

태권도 (tae-kkwon-do) *n.* traditional Korean martial art

태어나다 (tae-eo-na-da) *v.* to be born

태우다 (tae-u-da) *v.* to burn, to give a ride
태워주다 (tae-wo-ju-da) *v.* to give a ride
택시 (taek-si) *n.* taxi
택시비 (taek-si-bi) *n.* taxi fare
택시승차장 (taek-si-seung-cha-jang) *n.* taxi stop
턱 (teok) *n.* chin
테니스 (te-ni-seu) *n.* tennis
테니스장 (te-ni-seu-jang) *n.* tennis court
테이프 (te-i-peu) *n.* videocassette/videotape, tape
텔레비전 (tel-le-bi-jeon) *n.* television
텔레비전을 보다 (tel-le-bi-jeon-eul bo-da) to watch
    television
토끼 (to-kki) *n.* rabbit
토마토 (to-ma-to) *n.* tomato
토스터 (to-seu-teo) *n.* toaster
토요일 (to-yo-il) *n.* Saturday
토하다 (to-ha-da) *v.* to vomit
통 (tong) *adv.* not at all
통계 (tong-gye) *n.* statistics
통조림 (tong-jo-rim) *n.* canned food
통화중이다 (tong-hwa-jung-i-da) the line is busy
퇴근 (toe-geun) *n.* going home from work
퇴근하다 (toe-geun-ha-da) *v.* to go home from work
퇴원하다 (toe-won-ha-da) *v.* to be released from hospital
퇴장하다 (toe-jang-ha-da) *v.* to leave
투피스 (tu-pi-seu) *n.* two-piece women's suit
트럭 (teu-reok) *n.* truck
특별하다 (teuk-beol-ha-da) *v.* to be special; 특별한 (teuk-
    byel-han) *adj.* special
특히 (teu-ki) *adv.* particularly, especially
티셔츠 (ti-syeo-cheu) *n.* T-shirt
티슈 (ti-syu) *n.* tissue paper

ㅍ

파 (pa) *n.* scallion
파란불 (pa-ran-bul) *n.* green light
파란색 (pa-ran-saek) *n., adj.* blue
파랗다 (pa-ra-ta) *v.* to be blue; 파란 (pa-ran) *adj.* blue
파리 (pa-ri) *n.* fly, Paris
파마 (pa-ma) *n.* permanent (hairstyle)

파마하다 (pa-ma-ha-da) *v.* to get a permanent

파인애플 (pa-in-ae-peul) *n.* pineapple

파킹 (pa-king) *n.* parking lot

파트너 (pa-teu-neo) *n.* partner

파티 (pa-ti) *n.* party

팔 (pal) *n.* arm, eight

팔다 (pal-da) *v.* to sell

팔리다 (pal-li-da) *v.* to be sold

팔월 (pal-wol) *n.* August

팝송 (pap-song) *n.* pop song

팩스 (paek-seu) *n.* fax

팩스를 받다 (paek-seu-reul bat-da) to receive a fax

팩스를 보내다 (paek-seu-reul bo-nae-da) to send a fax

팬 (paen) *n.* pan

펜 (pen) *n.* pen

편 (pyeon) *n.* team, side, part, tendency

편도 (pyeon-do) *n.* one way

편도표 (pyeon-do-pyo) *n.* one-way ticket

편리하다 (pyeol-li-ha-da) *v.* to be convenient; 편리한 (pyeol-li-han) *adj.* convenient

편지 (pyeon-ji) *n.* letter

편하다 (pyeon-ha-da) *v.* to be comfortable; 편한 (pyeon-han) *adj.* comfortable

평균 (pyeong-gyun) *n.* average

폐쇄적이다 (pye-swae-jeog-i-da) *v.* to be closed; 폐쇄적인 (pye-swae-jeog-in) *adj.* closed

포근하다 (po-geun-ha-da) *v.* to be warm; 포근한 (po-geun-han) *adj.* warm

포기하다 (po-gi-ha-da) *v.* to give up

포도 (po-do) *n.* grape

포도주 (po-do-ju) *n.* wine

포장 (po-jang) *n.* packing, wrapping

포장센터 (po-jang-ssen-teo) *n.* retail packaging store

포장하다 (po-jang-ha-da) *n.* to pack, to wrap

포크 (po-keu) *n.* fork

표 (pyo) *n.* ticket

표정 (pyo-jeong) *n.* facial expression, look

푹 (puk) *adv.* deeply, soundly

풀 (pul) *n.* glue, grass

풀다 (pul-da) *v.* to solve a problem, to take off

풀어지다 (pul-eo-ji-da) *v.* to soften

풋볼 (put-bol) *n.* football

풍습 (pung-seup) *n.* customs

프라이팬 (peu-ra-i-paen) *n.* frying pan

프랑스 (peu-rang-seu) *n.* France

프린터 (peu-rin-teo) *n.* printer

플래시 (peul-lae-si) *n.* lantern

플룻 (peul-lut) *n.* flute

피곤하다 (pi-gon-ha-da) *v.* to be tired; 피곤한 (pi-gon-han) *adj.* tired

피다 (pi-da) *v.* to bloom

피아노 (pi-a-no) *n.* piano

피자 (pi-ja) *n.* pizza

피하다 (pi-ha-da) *v.* to avoid

필수 (pil-ssu) *adj.* required; *n.* requirement

필수적이다 (pil-ssu-jeog-i-da) *v.* to be required; 필수적인 (pil-su-jeog-in) *adj.* required

필요하다 (pil-yo-ha-da) *v.* to be necessary, to need; 필요한 (pil-yo-han) *adj.* necessary, needed

필통 (pil-tong) *n.* pencil case

ㅎ

하기야 (ha-gi-ya) *adv.* in fact, indeed

하나 (ha-na) *n.* one

하늘 (ha-neul) *n.* sky

하늘색 (ha-neul-ssaek) *n.*, *adj.* sky blue

하다 (ha-da) *v.* to do

하도 (ha-do) *adv.* too much, extremely

하루 (ha-ru) *n.* one day

하숙하다 (ha-su-ka-da) *v.* to live at a boarding house

하얀색 (ha-yan-saek) *n.*, *adj.* white

하얗다 (ha-ya-ta) *v.* to be white; 하얀 (ha-yan) *adj.* white

하차하다 (ha-cha-ha-da) *v.* to get off (a vehicle)

하키 (ha-ki) *n.* hockey

하품하다 (ha-pum-ha-da) *v.* to yawn

학교 (hak-gyo) *n.* school

학벌 (hak-beol) *n.* educational background

학생 (hak-saeng) *n.* student

한가하다 (han-ga-ha-da) *v.* to be free, to have spare time; 한가한 (han-ga-han) *adj.* free, relaxed

한국 (han-guk) *n.* Korea

한국사람 (han-guk-sa-ram) *n.* Korean person

한국어 (han-gug-eo) *n.* Korean language

한글 (han-geul) *n.* Korean alphabet

한꺼번에 (han-kkeo-beon-e) *adv.* altogether

한복 (han-bok) *n.* traditional Korean outfit

한산하다 (han-san-ha-da) *v.* to be almost empty, to be quiet; 한산한 (han-san-han) *adj.* almost empty, quiet

한식집 (han-sik-jip) *n.* Korean-style restaurant

한자 (han-jja) *n.* Chinese characters

한자어 (han-jja-eo) *n.* words derived from Chinese

한잔하다 (han-jan-ha-da) *v.* to drink alcohol

한턱내다 (han-teok-nae-da) *v.* to treat someone to a meal

할머니 (hal-meo-ni) *n.* grandmother

할머님 (hal-meo-nim) *n.* grandmother (hon.)

할아버님 (hal-a-beo-nim) *n.* grandfather (hon.)

할아버지 (hal-a-beo-ji) *n.* grandfather

할인 (hal-in) *n.* discount

할인하다 (hal-in-ha-da) *v.* to discount

함께 (ham-kke) *adv.* together

합격 (hap-gyeok) *n.* passing an exam

합격하다 (hap-gyeo-ka-da) *n.* to pass the exam

합승 (hap-seung) *n.* ride-sharing

합승하다 (hap-seung-ha-da) *n.* to share a ride

핫도그 (hat-do-geu) *n.* corn dog

항공 (hang-gong) *n.* flight, aviation

항공권 (hang-gong-kkwon) *n.* airline ticket

항공료 (hang-gong-nyo) *n.* airfare

항공사 (hang-gong-sa) *n.* airline

항공우편 (hang-gong-u-pyeon) *n.* airmail

항공편 (hang-gong-pyeon) *adv.* via airmail

항상 (hang-sang) *adv.* always

해 (hae) *n.* sun

해가 나다 (hae-ga na-da) *v.* to be sunny

해결하다 (hae-gyeol-ha-da) *v.* to solve a problem

해바라기 (hae-ba-ra-gi) *n.* sunflower

핸드폰 (haen-deu-pon) *n.* cell phone

햄버거 (haem-beo-geo) *n.* hamburger

행복 (haeng-bok) *n.* happiness

행복하다 (haeng-bo-ka-da) *v.* to be happy; 행복한 (haeng-bo-kan) *adj.* happy

행사 (haeng-sa) *n.* event

행인 (haeng-in) *n.* passerby

향수 (hyang-su) *n.* homesick, perfume

허리 (heo-ri) *n.* waist

헤드폰 (he-deu-pon) *n.* headphones

헤어지다 (he-eo-ji-da) *v.* to break up, to part, to separate

현관 (hyeon-gwan) *n.* entrance

현금 (hyeon-geum) *n.* cash

현대인 (hyeon-dae-in) *n.* modern people

현명하다 (hyeon-myeong-ha-da) *v.* to be wise; **현명한** (hyeon-myeong-han) *adj.* wise

혈압 (hyeol-ap) *n.* blood pressure

형 (hyeong) *n.* male's older brother

형님 (hyeong-nim) *n.* male's older brother (hon.)

형제 (hyeong-je) *n.* male siblings

호기심 (ho-gi-sim) *n.* curiosity

호랑이 (ho-rang-i) *n.* tiger

호박 (ho-bak) *n.* squash

호주 (ho-ju) *n.* Australia

호텔 (ho-tel) *n.* hotel

혹시 (hok-si) *adv.* by any chance

혼나다 (hon-na-da) *v.* to be frightened, to have a hard time, to be scolded

혼수 (hon-su) *n.* dowry

혼자(서) (hon-ja-(seo)) *adv.* alone, by oneself

홍차 (hong-cha) *n.* black tea

화 (hwa) *n.* anger, misfortune

화가 나다 (hwa-ga na-da) to be angry

화단 (hwa-dan) *n.* flower bed

화랑 (hwa-rang) *n.* art gallery

화려하다 (hwa-ryeo-ha-da) *v.* to be splendid, to be gorgeous; **화려한** (hwa-ryeo-han) *adj.* splendid, gorgeous

화면 (hwa-myeon) *n.* TV/computer screen

화분 (hwa-bun) *n.* flowerpot

화씨 (hwa-ssi) *adj.* Fahrenheit

화요일 (hwa-yo-il) *n.* Tuesday

화장실 (hwa-jang-sil) *n.* restroom

화장지 (hwa-jang-ji) *n.* toilet paper

화장품 (hwa-jang-pum) *n.* cosmetics

환경 (hwan-gyeong) *n.* environment

환승역 (hwang-seung-nyeok) *n.* a station to change trains
   or subways, way station

환영 (hwan-yeong) *n.* welcome

환영하다 (hwan-yeong-ha-da) *v.* to welcome

환자 (hwan-ja) *n.* patient

환하다 (hwan-ha-da) *v.* to be bright; **환한** (hwan-han) *adj.*
   bright

활달하다 (hwal-ttal-ha-da) *v.* to be outgoing; **활달한**
   (hwal-ttal-han) *adj.* outgoing

회계사 (hoe-gye-sa) *n.* accountant

회색 (hoe-saek) *n.* gray

회의 (hoe-ui) *n.* meeting

횡단보도 (hoeng-dan-bo-do) *n.* crosswalk

후 (hu) *n.* after

후손 (hu-son) *n.* descendant

후추 (hu-chu) *n.* black pepper

후회하다 (hu-hoe-ha-da) *v.* to regret

훨씬 (hwol-ssin) *adv.* by far

휴가 (hyu-ga) *n.* vacation from work

휴게실 (hyu-ge-sil) *n.* lounge

휴식 (hyu-sik) *n.* rest

휴일 (hyu-il) *n.* holiday

휴지 (hyu-ji) *n.* toilet paper, tissue paper, wastepaper

휴지통 (hyu-ji-tong) *n.* trash can

흐려지다 (heu-ryeo-ji-da) *v.* to get cloudy

흐리다 (heu-ri-da) *v.* to be cloudy; **흐린** (heu-rin) *adj.*
   cloudy

흔들다 (heun-deul-da) *v.* to shake

희다 (hui-da, hi-da) *v.* to be white; **흰** (huin) *adj.* white

흰색 (huin-saek, hin-saek) *n.*, *adj.* white

힘 (him) *n.* power, energy

힘들다 (him-deul-da) *v.* to be difficult; **힘든** (him-deun)
   adj. difficult

ENGLISH-KOREAN DICTIONARY

A

abandon *v*. 버리다 (beo-ri-da), 버려두다 (beo-ryeo-du-da)

ability *n*. 능력 (neung-nyeok), 솜씨 (som-ssi), 실력 (sil-lyeok)

abnormal *adj*. 이상이 있는 (i-sang-i in-neun), 이상이 있다 (i-sang-i it-da)

about *prep*. 약- (yak), 한- (han) .... –쯤 (jjeum), -정도 (jeong-do)

above *prep*. 위 (wi)

above zero *adj*. 영상 (yeong-sang)

abroad *adj*. 외국 (oe-guk)

absence *n*. 결석 (gyeol-sseok)

absolute *adj*. 절대적인 (jeol-ttae-jeog-in), 순수한 (sun-su-han)

absolutely *adv*. 전적으로 (jeon-jjeog-eu-ro), 완전히 (wan-jeon-hi)

academic *adj*. 학문적인 (hang-mun-jeog-in)

academic term *n*. 학기 (hak-gi)

academic year *n*. 학년 (hang-nyeon)

accept *v*. 받다 (bat-da), 받아들이다 (bad-a-deul-i-da)

acceptance *n*. 받아들임 (bad-a-deul-im), 승인 (seung-in)

accessories *n*. 액세서리 (aek-se-seo-ri), 장신구 (jang-sin-gu)

accident *n*. 사고 (sa-go)

accompany *v*. 모시다 (mo-si-da), 동반하다 (dong-ban-ha-da)

according to *prep*. -에 따르면 (e tta-reu-myeon), -에 의하면 (e ui-ha-myeon)

account *v*. 계산하다 (gye-san-ha-da)

accountant *n*. 회계사 (hoe-gye-sa)

achieve *v*. 성취하다 (seong-chwi-ha-da)

achievement *n*. 성취 (seong-chwi)

acquaintance *n*. 아는 사람 (a-neun sa-ram)

acquire *v*. 요청하다 (yo-cheong-ha-da)

active *adj*. 적극적인 (jeok-geuk-jeog-in), 적극적이다 (jeok-geuk-jeog-i-da)

activity *n*. 활동 (hwang-ttong)

actor *n.* 배우 (bae-u)

actress *n.* 여배우 (yeo-bae-u)

actually *adv.* 정말로 (jeong-mal-lo), 실제로 (sil-jje-ro)

add *v.* 더하다 (deo-ha-da)

address *n.* 주소 (ju-so)

admission *n.* 입장 (ip-jang), 입학 (i-pak), 용인 (yong-in)

admission fee *n.* 입장료 (ip-jang-nyo)

admission ticket *n.* 입장권 (ip-jang-kkwon)

admit *v.* 받아들이다 (bad-a-deul-i-da)

adult *n.* 어른 (eo-reun), 성인 (seong-in)

advantage *n.* 유익한 점 (yu-i-kan jeom)

advantageous *adj.* 유리한 (yu-ri-han), 유리하다 (yu-ri-ha-da)

advertise *v.* 광고하다 (gwang-go-ha-da)

advertisement *n.* 광고 (gwang-go)

advice *n.* 충고 (chung-go)

advise *v.* 충고하다 (chung-go-ha-da)

afraid *adj.* 무서운 (mu-seo-un), 무섭다 (mu-seop-da), 두려워하다 (du-ryeo-wo-ha-da),무서워하다 (mu-seo-wo-ha-da)

after *adv., prep.* -후에 (hu-e), -은 다음 (-eun da-eum)

afternoon *n.* 오후 (o-hu)

again *adv.* 다시 (da-si)

against *prep.* -에 대항해서 (e dae-hang-hae-seo), -에 반해서 (e ban-hae-seo)

age *n.* 나이 (na-i), 연세 (yeon-se) (*honorific*)

agree *v.* 동의하다 (dong-ui-ha-da)

agreement *n.* 동의 (dong-ui)

ahead *adv.* 미리 (mi-ri), 먼저 (meon-jeo)

aid *n.* 도움 (do-um)

air *n.* 공기 (gong-gi)

airfare *n.* 항공료 (hang-gong-nyo)

airline *n.* 항공사 (hang-gong-sa)

airline ticket *n.* 비행기표 (bi-haeng-gi-pyo), 항공권 (hang-gong-kkwon)

airmail *n.* 항공우편 (hang-gong-u-pyeon); **via airmail** *adv.* 항공편으로 (hang-gong-pyeon-eu-ro)

airplane *n.* 비행기 (bi-haeng-gi)

airport *n.* 공항 (gong-hang), 비행장 (bi-haeng-jang)

aisle *n.* 복도 (bok-do), 통로 (tong-no)

alcohol *n.* 술 (sul)

alike *adj.* 닮다 (dam-tta), 비슷하다 (bi-seu-ta-da)

alive *adj.* 살아있다 (sal-a-it-da)

all *adv.* 다 (da), 모두 (mo-du)

all right *adv.* 괜찮다 (gwaen-chan-ta)

almost *adv.* 거의 (geo-ui)

alone *adv.* 혼자서 (hon-ja-seo)

alphabet *n.* 알파벳 (al-pa-bet), 철자법 (cheol-jja-ppeop)

already *adv.* 벌써 (beol-sseo)

also *adv.* 또 (tto), -도 (do)

although *conj.* 그렇지만 (geu-reo-chi-man), -지만 (ji-man)

altogether *adv.* 모두 (mo-du), 한꺼번에 (han-kkeo-beon-e)

always *adv.* 늘 (neul), 언제나 (eon-je-na)

a.m. *n.* 오전 (o-jeon)

ambulance *n.* 앰뷸런스 (aem-byul-leon-seu)

America *n.* 미국 (mi-guk)

amount *n.* 분량 (bul-lyang), 양 (yang)

amuse *v.* 즐거워하다 (jeul-geo-wo-ha-da)

amusement *n.* 즐거움 (jeul-geo-um)

amusement park *n.* 놀이공원 (nol-i-gong-won)

analgesic *n.* 진통 (jin-tong)

ancestor *n.* 조상 (jo-sang)

ancestor-honoring rites *n.* 차례 (cha-rye)

and *conj.* 그리고 (geu-ri-go), -고 (go)

and then *conj.* 그리고 나서 (geu-ri-go na-seo)

anger *n.* 화 (hwa), 성남 (seong-nam)

angry *adj.* 화가 난 (hwa-ga nan), 화가 나다 (hwa-ga na-da)

animal *n.* 동물 (dong-mul)

animation *n.* 만화 (man-hwa)

announce *v.* 발표하다 (bal-pyo-ha-da)

announcement *n.* 발표 (bal-pyo)

annoy *v.* 귀찮게 하다 (gwi-chan-ke-ha-da), 속을 썩이다 (sog-eul sseog-i-da)

another *adj.* 다른 (da-reun)

answer *n.* 대답 (dae-da)p), 답 (dap); *v.* 대답하다 (dae-da-pa-da)

ant *n.* 개미 (gae-mi)

antenna *n.* 안테나 (an-te-na)

anxious *adj.* 걱정되는 (geok-jeong-doe-neun), 열망하는 (yeol-mang-ha-neun)

anybody *pron.* 누구든지 (nu-gu-deun-ji), 아무나 (a-mu-na)

anyplace *adv.* 어디든지 (eo-di-deun-ji), 아무 데나 (a-mu de-na)

anything *pron.* 무엇이든지 (mu-eos-i-deun-ji), 아무 거나 (a-mu geo-na)

anytime *adv.* 언제든지 (eon-je-deun-ji), 아무 때나 (a-mu ttae-na)

apartment *n.* 아파트 (a-pa-teu)

appear *v.* 나타나다 (a-ta-na-da)

appearance *n.* 외모 (oe-mo)

appetite *n.* 식성 (sik-seong), 입맛 (im-mat)

apple *n.* 사과 (sa-gwa)

application *n.* 적용 (jeog-yong), 지원서 (ji-won-seo)

apply *v.* 바르다 (ba-reu-da)

apply for *v.* 적용하다 (jeog-yong-ha-da), 지원하다 (ji-won-ha-da)

appointment *n.* 약속 (yak-sok)

appreciate *v.* 고마워하다 (go-ma-wo-ha-da)

appropriate *adj.* 적당하다 (jeok-dang-ha-da)

appropriately *adv.* 제대로 (je-dae-ro)

approximately *adv.* 약 (yak), -정도 (jeong-do)

April *n.* 사월 (sa-wol)

aptitude *n.* 적성 (jeok-seong)

architect *n.* 건축가 (geon-chuk-ga)

area *n.* 분야 (bun-ya), 지역 (ji-yeok)

argue *v.* 논쟁하다 (non-jaeng-ha-da), 싸우다 (ssa-u-da)

argument *n.* 논쟁 (non-jaeng)

arm *n.* 팔 (pal), 품 (pum)

armpit *n.* 겨드랑이 (gyeo-deu-rang-i)

army *n.* 군대 (gun-dae)

around *prep.* -쯤 (jjeum)

arrange *v.* 조정하다 (jo-jeong-ha-da), 조절하다 (jo-jeol-ha-da)

arrest *v.* 구속하다 (gu-so-ka-da), 잡아가다 (jab-a-ga-da)

arrival *n.* 도착 (do-chak)

arrive *v.* 도착하다 (do-cha-ka-da)

art *n.* 미술 (mi-sul), 예술 (ye-sul)

artery *n.* 동맥 (dong-maek)

art gallery *n.* 화랑 (hwa-rang)

artificial *adj.* 인공적인 (in-gong-jeog-in)

artist *n.* 예술가 (ye-sul-ga)

as *prep., adv.* -처럼 (cheo-reom)

as if *conj.* 마치 ... -인 것처럼 (ma-chi ... in goet cheo-reom)

ascend *v.* 올라가다 (ol-la-ga-da)

ash *n.* 재 (jae)

ashtray *n.* 재떨이 (jae-tteol-i)

Asia *n.* 아시아 (a-si-a), 동양 (dong-yang)

Asian *adj.* 동양의 (dong-yang-ui)

Asian Studies *n.* 동양학 (dong-yang-hak)

ask *v.* 물어보다 (mul-eo-bo-da), 질문하다 (jil-mun-ha-da)

ask a favor *v.* 부탁하다 (bu-ta-ka-da)

assemble *v.* 조립하다 (jo-ri-pa-da)

assembly *n.* 조립 (jo-rip)

assignment *n.* 과제 (gwa-je), 숙제 (suk-je), 할 일 (hal lil)

assist *v.* 도와주다 (do-wa-ju-da)

assistance *n.* 도와주는 사람 (do-wa-ju-neun sa-ram), 비서 (bi-seo)

association *n.* 연합 (yeon-hap), 협회 (heo-poe)

assume *v.* 가정하다 (ga-jeong-ha-da)

assumption *n.* 가정 (ga-jeong)

asthma *n.* 천식 (cheon-sik)

astonish *v.* 놀라게 하다 (nol-la-ge-ha-da)

athlete *n.* 운동선수 (un-dong-seon-su)

atmosphere *n.* 분위기 (bun-wi-gi)

attempt *n.* 시도 (si-do)

attend *v.* 다니다 (da-ni-da), 참석하다 (cham-seo-ka-da)

attorney *n.* 변호사 (byeon-ho-sa)

attract *v.* 호감을 주다 (ho-gam-eul ju-da)

attractive *adj.* 멋있는 (meos-in-neun), 매력적인 (mae-ryeok-jeog-in), 멋있다 (meos-it-da), 매력적이다 (mae-ryeok-jeog-i-da)

audible *adj.* 들리는 (deul-li-neun), 들리다 (deul-li-da)

audience *n.* 관중 (gwan-jung)

August *n.* 팔월 (pal-wol)

aunt *n.* 이모 (i-mo), 고모 (go-mo), 숙모 (sung-mo)

Australia *n.* 호주 (ho-ju)

author *n.* 저자 (jeo-ja), 작가 (jak-ga)

authority *n.* 권위 (gwon-wi), 권위자 (gwon-wi-ja)

authorized *adj.* 승인된 (seung-in-doen)

automatic *adj.* 자동 (ja-dong)

automobile *n.* 차 (cha)

autumn *n.* 가을 (ga-eul)

average *n.* 평균 (pyeong-gyun)

aviation *n.* 항공 (hang-gong)

avoid *v.* 피하다 (pi-ha-da)

awaken *v.* 깨다 (kkae-da), 일어나다 (il-eo-na-da)

awful *adj.* 나쁜 (na-ppeun)

awkward *adj.* 자연스럽지 않은 (ja-yeon-seu-reop-ji an-eun), 거북한 (geo-bu-kan), 섣부른 (seot-bu-reun)

B

baby *n.* 아기 (a-gi)

baby-sit *v.* 아이를 봐주다 (a-i-reul bwa-ju-da)

baby-sitter *n.* 아이 봐주는 사람 (a-i bwa-ju-neun sa-ram)

back *prep., adv.* 뒤 (dwi); *n.* 등 (deung)

backdoor *n.* 뒷문 (dwin-mun)

backpack *n.* 등산가방 (deung-san-ga-bang)

back row *n.* 뒷줄 (dwit-jul)

bad *adj.* 나쁜 (na-ppeun), 나쁘다 (na-ppeu-da)

bag *n.* 가방 (ga-bang)

bakery *n.* 빵집 (ppang-jjip), 제과점 (je-gwa-jeom)

balance *n.* 균형 (gyun-hyeong)

ball *n.* 공 (gong)

ballpoint pen *n.* 볼펜 (bol-pen)

banana *n.* 바나나 (ba-na-na)

bangs (hair) *n.* 앞머리 (am-meo-ri)

bank *n.* 은행 (eun-haeng)

bar *n.* 술집 (sul-jjip)

barbecued spareribs *n.* 갈비 (gal-bi)

barber *n.* 이발사 (i-bal-ssa)

barbershop *n.* 이발소 (i-bal-sso)

barely *adv.* 겨우 (gyeo-u)

barley tea *n.* 보리차 (bo-ri-cha)

baseball *n.* 야구 (ya-gu)

baseball stadium *n.* 야구장 (ya-gu-jang)

basketball *n.* 농구 (nong-gu)

basketball player *n.* 농구선수 (nong-gu-seon-su)

bath *n.* 목욕 (mog-yok)

bathroom *n.* 화장실 (hwa-jang-sil), 목욕탕 (mog-yok-tang)

beach *n.* 바닷가 (ba-dat-ga)

bean *n.* 콩 (kong)

bean sprout *n.* 콩나물 (kong-na-mul)

beautiful *adj.* 아름다운 (a-reum-da-un), 아름답다 (a-reum-dap-da)

beautiful woman *n.* 미인 (mi-in)

beauty *n.* 아름다움 (a-reum-da-um), 미인 (mi-in)

beauty shop *n.* 미장원 (mi-jang-won), 미용실 (mi-yong-sil), 머리방 (meo-ri-bang)

because *conj.* 왜냐하면... -기 때문이다 (wae-nya-ha-myeon …gi ttae-mun-i-da)

become *v.* -이/가 되다 (i/ga doe-da)

bed *n.* 침대 (chim-dae)

bedroom *n.* 침실 (chim-sil)

beef *n.* 쇠고기 (soe-go-gi), 소고기 (so-go-gi)

beer *n.* 맥주 (maek-ju)

before *prep., adv.* -전에 (jeon-e)

begin *v.* 시작하다 (si-ja-ka-da)

behind *prep., adv.* 뒤 (dwi), 뒤에 (dwi-e)

believe *v.* 믿다 (mit-da), 신뢰하다 (sil-loe-ha-da)

belly *n.* 배 (bae)

beloved *adj.* 그리운 (geu-ri-un), 그립다 (geu-rip-da)

below *prep., adv.* 밑 (mit), 밑에 (mit-e)

below zero *adj.* 영하 (yeong-ha)

belt *n.* 벨트 (bel-teu)

bench *n.* 벤치 (ben-chi)

beneath *prep., adv.* 밑 (mit)

beside *prep., adv.* 옆 (yeop), 옆에 (yeop-e)

best *n.* 최선 (choe-seon), 제일 (je-il)

best quality (of the) *adj.* 최고급 (choe-go-geup)

better *adj.* 낫다 (nat-da)

between *conj.* 사이 (sa-i), 사이에 (sa-i-e)

beverage *n.* 음료수 (eum-nyo-su)

Bible *n.* 성경책 (seong-gyeong-chaek)

bicycle *n.* 자전거 (ja-jeon-geo)

big *adj.* 큰(keun), 크다 (keu-da)

bilingual *n.* 이중언어 구사자 (i-jung-eon-eo gu-sa-ja); *adj.* 이중언어의 (i-jung-eon-eo-ui)

bill *n.* 청구서(cheong-gu-seo), 영수증 (yeong-su-jeung), 계산서 (gye-san-seo)

biology *n.* 생물학 (saeng-mul-hak)

bird *n.* 새 (sae)

birth *n.* 출생 (chul-ssaeng), 태어남 (tae-eo-nam)

birthday *n.* 생일 (saeng-il), 생신 (saeng-sin) (*honorific*)

bite *v.* 물다 (mul-da)

bitten *adj.* 물리다 (mul-li-da)

bitter *adj.* 쓰다 (sseu-da)

black *n.* 까만색 (kka-man-saek); *adj.* 까맣다 (kka-ma-ta), 까만 (kka-man)

black pepper *n.* 후추 (hu-chu)

black tea *n.* 홍차 (hong-cha)

blackboard *n.* 칠판 (chil-pan)

bland *adj.* 싱겁다 (sing-geop-da), 싱거운 (sing-geo-un)

blessing *n.* 복 (bok), 축복 (chuk-bok)

block *v.* 막다 (mak-da)

blood *n.* 피 (pi), 혈액 (hyeol-aek)

blood pressure *n.* 혈압 (hyeol-ap)

blood type *n.* 혈액형 (hyeol-ae-kyeong)

bloom *v.* 꽃이 피다 (kkoch-i pi-da)

blouse *n.* 블라우스 (beul-la-u-seu)

blow *v.* 불다 (bul-da), 바람이 불다 (ba-ram-i bul-da)

blue *n.* 파란색 (pa-ran-saek); *adj.* 파랗다 (pa-ra-ta), 파란 (pa-ran)

blue jeans *n.* 청바지 (cheong-ba-ji)

boat *n.* 배 (bae), 보트 (bo-teu)

body *n.* 몸 (mom)

body ache *n.* 몸살 (mom-sal)

boil *v.* 끓다 (kkeul-ta), 끓이다 (kkeul-i-da)

bone *n.* 뼈 (ppyeo)

book *n.* 책 (chaek)

bookcase *n.* 책장 (chaek-jang)

bookstore *n.* 책방 (chaek-bang), 서점 (seo-jeom)

border *n.* 경계 (gyeong-gye), 국경 (guk-gyeong)

bored *adj.* 심심하다 (sim-sim-ha-da), 지루하다 (ji-ru-ha-da)

boring *adj.* 심심하다 (sim-sim-ha-da), 지루하다 (ji-ru-ha-da)

born *v.* 태어나다 (tae-eo-na-da)

borrow *v.* 빌리다 (bil-li-da)

both *adv., conj.* 모두 (mo-du)

bother *v.* 귀찮게 하다 (gwi-chan-ke ha-da)

bottle *n.* 병 (byeong)

bottom *n.* 밑 (mit), 바닥 (ba-da)k)

bow *n.* 절 (jeol); *v.* 절하다 (jeol-ha-da)

bowling *n.* 볼링 (bol-ling)

box *n.* 상자 (sang-ja), 박스 (bak-seu)

boxing *n.* 권투 (gwon-tu)

boy *n.* 남자아이 (nam-ja-a-i)

boyfriend *n.* 남자친구 (nam-ja-chin-gu)

bra *n.* 브레지어 (beu-re-ji-eo), 브라자 (beu-ra-ja)

brake *n.* 브레이크 (beu-re-i-keu)

branch *n.* 가지 (ga-ji), 지사 (ji-sa)

brand *n.* 상표 (sang-pyo)

brave *adj.* 용감하다 (yong-gam-ha-da)

bread *n.* 빵 (ppang)

break *v.* 깨다 (kkae-da), 부수다 (bu-su-da)

breakfast *n.* 아침 (a-chim), 아침밥 (a-chim-ppap)

break up *v.* 헤어지다 (he-eo-ji-da)

breast *n.* 가슴 (ga-seum)

breath *n.* 숨 (sum), 호흡 (ho-heup)

breathe *v.* 숨을 쉬다 (sum-eul swi-da)

bride *n.* 신부 (sin-bu)

bridegroom *n.* 신랑 (sil-lang)

bridge *n.* 다리 (da-ri)

brief *adj.* 짧은 (jjalb-eun), 간단한 (gan-dan-han)

bright *adj.* 밝다 (balk-da)

bring *v.* 가지고 오다 (ga-ji-go o-da)

broadcast *n.* 방송하다 (bang-song-ha-da)

broadcasting *n.* 방송 (bang-song)

broadcasting station *n.* 방송국 (bang-song-guk)

brochure *n.* 안내책 (an-nae-chaek)

broken *adj.* 고장나다 (go-jang-na-da), 깨지다 (kkae-ji-da), 부러지다 (bu-reo-ji-da)

brother *n.* 오빠 (o-ppa), 형 (hyeong), 남자형제 (nam-ja-hyeong-je)

brown *n.* 밤색 (bam-saek); *adj.* 밤색의 (bam-saeg-ui); **light brown** 갈색 (gal-saek), 갈색의 (gal-saeg-ui)

brush *v.* 빗 (bit), 빗질하다 (bit-jil-ha-da)

brush hair *v.* 머리를 빗다 (meo-ri-reul bit-da)

brush teeth *v.* 이를 닦다 (i-reul dak-da)

build *v.* 집을 짓다 (jib-eul jit-da)

building *n.* 건물 (geon-mul), 빌딩 (bil-ding)

bun *n.* 둥근 빵 (dung-geun ppang)

burn *v.* 타다 (ta-da), 태우다 (tae-u-da)
bury *v.* 땅에 묻다 (ttang-e mut-da)
bus *n.* 버스 (beo-seu)
bus station *n.* 버스 터미널 (beo-seu teo-mi-neol)
bus stop *n.* 버스 정류장 (beo-seu jeong-nyu-jang), 버스
　　정거장 (beo-seu jeong-geo-jang)
business *n.* 사업 (sa-eop)
busy *adj.* 바쁜 (ba-ppeun), 바쁘다 (ba-ppeu-da)
but *conj.* 그렇지만 (geu-reo-chi-man), -지만 (gi-man)
butter *n.* 버터 (beo-tteo)
buy *v.* 사다 (sa-da), 구입하다 (gu-i-pa-da)
by *prep.* 곁에 (gyeot-e), 옆에 (yeop-e)
by all means *prep.* 꼭 (kkok)
by any chance *prep.* 혹시 (hok-si)
by any possibility *prep.* 도저히 (do-jeo-hi)
by chance *adv.* 우연히 (u-yeon-hi)
by far *adv.* 훨씬 (hwol-ssin)
by the way *conj.* 그런데 (geu-reon-de), 참 (cham)

C

cab *n.* 택시 (taek-si)
cabbage *n.* 배추 (bae-chu)
café *n.* 카페 (ka-pe), 다방 (da-bang)
cake *n.* 케이크 (ke-i-keu)
call *n.* 전화 (jeon-hwa); *v.* 전화하다 (jeon-hwa-ha-da)
calligraphy *n.* 붓글씨 (but-geul-ssi)
calm *adj.* 차분한 (cha-bun-han), 잔잔한 (jan-jan-han),
　　차분하다 (cha-bun-ha-da), 잔잔하다 (jan-jan-ha-da)
camera *n.* 사진기 (sa-jin-gi), 카메라 (ka-me-ra)
can *aux.* 할 수 있다 (hal ssu-it-da)
cancel *v.* 취소하다 (chwi-so-ha-da)
candle *n.* 초 (cho)
candy *n.* 사탕 (san-tang), 캔디 (kaen-di)
canned food *n.* 통조림 (tong-jo-rim)
cap *n.* 모자 (mo-ja)
capital *n.* 수도 (su-do)
capricious *adj.* 변덕이 심한 (byeon-deog-i sim-han),
　　변덕이 심하다 (byeon-deog-i sim-ha-da)
car *n.* 차 (cha); **used car** *n.* 중고차 (jung-go-cha)
card *n.* 카드 (ka-deu)

care *n.* 돌봄 (dol-bom); *v.* 돌보다 (dol-bo-da)

careful *adj.* 조심하다 (jo-sim-ha-da)

carrot *n.* 당근 (dang-geun)

carry *v.* 가지고 다니다 (ga-ji-go da-ni-da)

cartoon *n.* 만화 (man-hwa)

case *n.* 경우 (gyeong-u), 상자 (sang-ja)

cash *n.* 현금 (hyeon-geum), 돈 (don)

castle *n.* 성 (seong), 궁전 (gung-jeon)

casually *adv.* 아무렇지도 않게 (a-mu-reo-chi-do an-ke)

cat *n.* 고양이 (go-yang-i)

catch *v.* 잡다 (jap-da), 붙잡다 (but-jap-da)

catch a cold *v.* 감기에 걸리다 (gam-gi-e geol-li-da)

caught in the rain 비를 맞다 (bi-reul mat-da)

cause *n.* 이유 (i-yu), 원인 (won-in)

cavity *n.* 충치 (chung-chi)

cease *v.* 말다 (mal-da), 그만두다 (geu-man-du-da)

ceiling *n.* 천장 (cheon-jang)

celebration *n.* 기념 (gi-nyeom)

cello *n.* 첼로 (chel-lo)

cell phone *n.* 핸드폰 (haen-deu-pon)

Celsius *adj., n.* 섭씨 (seop-ssi)

center *n.* 센터 (ssen-teo), 중앙 (jung-ang)

central *adj.* 중앙의 (jung-ang-ui), 중부의 (jung-bu-ui)

central post office *n.* 중앙우체국 (jung-ang-u-che-guk)

chair *n.* 의자 (ui-ja)

chairman *n.* 의장 (ui-jang), -장 (jang)

chance *n.* 기회 (gi-hoe), 거스름돈 (geo-seu-reum-tton), 변화 (byeon-hwa),

change *v.* 바꾸다 (ba-kku-da)

change clothes *v.* 옷을 갈아입다 (os-eul gal-a-ip-da)

change residence *v.* 이사가다 (i-sa-ga-da)

change vehicle *v.* 갈아타다 (gal-a-ta-da)

chapter *n.* -과 (gwa)

characterize *v.* 특색을 이루다 (teuk-saeg-eul i-ru-da), -의 특성을 묘사하다 (ui teuk-seong-eul myo-sa-ha-da)

chase *v.* 쫓다 (jjot-da)

cheap *adj.* 싼 (ssan), 싸다 (ssa-da)

check *n.* 계산서 (gye-san-seo)

check out *v.* 알아보다 (al-a-bo-da), 확인하다 (hwag-in-ha-da)

cheek *n.* 뺨 (ppyam)

chef *n.* 요리사 (yo-ri-sa)

chest *n.* 가슴 (ga-seum)

chewy *adj.* 쫄깃쫄깃한 (jjol-git-jjol-ji-tan), 쫄깃쫄깃하다 (jjol-git-jjol-ji-ta-da)

chicken *n.* 닭 (dak), 닭고기 (dak-go-gi)

child *n.* 아이 (a-i); **youngest child** *n.* 막내 (mang-nae)

children *n.* 아이들 (a-i-deul)

chilly *adj.* 쌀쌀한 (ssal-ssal-han), 쌀쌀하다 (ssal-ssal-ha-da)

chin *n.* 턱 (teok)

China *n.* 중국 (jung-guk)

Chinese *n.* 중국어 (jung-gug-eo), 중국사람 (jung-guk-sa-ram); *adj.* 중국의 (jung-gug-ui)

Chinese restaurant *n.* 중국집 (jung-guk-jip), 중국식당 (jung-guk-sik-dang)

chocolate *n.* 초콜릿 (cho-kol-lit)

choice *n.* 선택 (seon-taek)

choir *n.* 합창 (hap-chang)

choke *v.* 질식시키다 (jil-ssik-si-ki-da), 숨이 막히다 (sum-i ma-ki-da)

choose *v.* 선택하다 (seon-tae-ka-da), 고르다 (go-reu-da)

church *n.* 교회 (gyo-hoe)

cigarette *n.* 담배 (dam-bae)

cinema *n.* 영화 (yeong-hwa), 영화관 (yeong-hwa-gwan)

circle *n.* 원 (won)

citron tea *n.* 유자차 (yu-ja-cha)

city *n.* 도시 (do-si)

city hall *n.* 시청 (si-cheong)

civil *adj.* 도시의 (do-si-ui)

clarinet *n.* 클라리넷 (keul-la-ri-net)

class *n.* 반 (ban), 지위 (ji-wi)

classic *n.* 고전 (go-jeon); *adj.* 고전적인 (go-jeon-jeog-in)

classical music *n.* 클래식 음악 (keul-lae-sik eum-ak)

classroom *n.* 교실 (gyo-sil)

clean *adj.* 깨끗한 (kkae-kkeu-tan), 깨끗하다 (kkae-kkeu-ta-da), 청소하다 (cheong-so-ha-da)

clear *adj.* 선명한 (seon-myeong-han), 선명하다 (seon-myeong-ha-da)

clerk *n.* 직원 (jig-won)

clock *n.* 시계 (si-gye)

close *v.* 닫다 (dat-da); *adj.* 친하다 (chin-ha-da), 가깝다 (ga-kkap-da)

closely *adv.* 자세히 (ja-se-hi)

closet *n.* 옷장 (ot-jang), 장롱 (jang-nong)

closing *n.* 폐쇄 (pye-swae), 닫음 (dat-eum)

cloth *n.* 옷감 (ot-gam)

clothes *n.* 옷 (ot)

clothing store *n.* 옷가게 (ot-ga-ge)

cloud *n.* 구름 (gu-reum)

cloudy *adj.* 흐린 (heu-rin), 흐리다 (heu-ri-da)

coast *n.* 연안 (yeon-an)

coat *n.* 코트 (ko-teu)

coffee *n.* 커피 (keo-pi)

coffee shop *n.* 카페 (ka-pe), 다방 (da-bang)

coin *n.* 동전 (dong-jeon)

coincidentally *adv.* 마침 (ma-chim)

cola *n.* 콜라 (kol-la)

cold *adj.* 추운 (chu-un), 춥다 (chup-da), 차가운 (cha-ga-un), 차갑다 (cha-gap-da); *n.* 감기 (gam-gi)

cold noodle dish *n.* 냉면 (naeng myeon)

cold water *n.* 찬물 (chan-mul), 냉수 (naeng-su)

collapse *v.* 쓰러지다 (sseu-reo-ji-da)

collect *v.* 모으다 (mo-eu-da)

colleague *n.* 동료 (dong-nyo)

college *n.* 대학 (dae-hak)

college student *n.* 대학생 (dae-hak-saeng)

color *n.* 색 (saek), 색깔 (saek-kkal)

comb *n.* 빗 (bit); *v.* 빗다 (bit-da)

come *v.* 오다 (o-da)

come in *v.* 들어오다 (deul-eo-o-da), 들어가다 (deul-eo-ga-da)

come out *v.* 나오다 (na-o-da), 나가다 (na-ga-da)

come up *v.* 올라오다 (ol-la-o-da), 올라가다 (ol-la-ga-da)

comedy *n.* 코미디 (ko-mi-di), 코메디 (ko-me-di)

comfort *v.* 편안하다 (pyeon-an-ha-da), 편하다 (pyeon-ha-da)

comfortable *adj.* 편안한 (pyeon-an-han), 편안하다 (pyeon-an-ha-da)

commit *v.* 죄를 범하다 (joe-reul beom-ha-da), 위임하다 (wi-im-ha-da), 맡기다 (mat-gi-da)

commitment *n.* 범행 (beom-haeng), 위임 (wi-im), 맡김 (mat-gim)

common *adj.* 보통의 (bo-tong-ui), 상식의 (sang-sig-ui)

commonly *adv.* 보통 (bo-tong)

community *n.* 사회 (sa-hoe), 공동사회 (gong-dong-sa-hoe)

commute *v.* 통근하다 (tong-geun-ha-da)

company *n.* 회사 (hoe-sa)

compare *v.* 비하다 (bi-ha-da), 비교하다 (bi-gyo-ha-da)

compare to *v.* -에 비해 (e bi-hae)

comparison *n.* 비교 (bi-gyo)

compartment *n.* 칸막이 (kan-mag-i), 칸막이방 (kan-mag-i-bang), 기차 침실칸 (gi-cha chim-sil-kan)

compensate *v.* 보상하다 (bo-sang-ha-da)

compete *v.* 경쟁하다 (gyeong-jaeng-ha-da)

competition *n.* 경쟁 (gyeong-jaeng)

complete *adj.* 완전한 (wan-jeon-han)

completely *adv.* 깜빡 (kkam-ppak), 완전히 (wan-jeon-hi)

computer *n.* 컴퓨터 (keom-pyu-teo)

concern *v.* 관계하다 (gwan-gye-ha-da), 관심을 갖다 (gwan-sim-eul gat-da); *n.*관계 (gwan-gye), 관심 (gwan-sim)

concerning *prep.* -에 대해서 (e dae-hae-seo)

concert *n.* 음악회 (eum-a-koe), 콘서트 (kon-seo-teu)

condition *n.* 조건 (jo-kkeon)

confirm *v.* 확실히 하다 (hawk-sil-hi-ha-da), 확인하다 (hwag-in-ha-da)

confirmation *n.* 확정 (hawk-jeong), 확인 (hwag-in)

congested *adj.* 막히다 (ma-ki-da)

congratulate *v.* 축하하다 (chu-ka-ha-da)

congratulation *n.* 축하 (chu-ka)

congregation *n.* 막힘 (ma-kim)

connection *n.* 연결 (yeon-gyeol)

conquer *v.* 정복하다 (jeong-bo-ka-da)

conscious *adj.* 의식하고 있는 (ui-si-ka-go in-neun), 지각 있는 (ji-gak in-neun)

consequence *n.* 결과 (gyeol-gwa), 중대성 (jung-dae-sseong)

conservative *adj.* 보수적인 (bo-su-jeog-in), 보수적이다 (bo-su-jeog-i-da)

consider *v.* 고려하다 (go-ryeo-ha-da)

considerate *adj.* 친절한 (chin-jeol-han), 친절하다 (chin-jeol-ha-da)

consideration *n.* 고려 (go-ryeo)

constant *adj.* 변치 않는 (byeon-chi an-neun)

construction *n.* 공사 (gong-sa); **under construction** 공사중 (gong-sa-jung)

consult *v.* 상의하다 (sang-ui-ha-da)

consult a doctor *v.* 진찰을 받다 (jin-chal-eul bat-da)

consume *v.* 소비하다 (so-bi-ha-da), 다 써버리다 (da sseo-beo-ri-da)

consumer *n.* 소비자 (so-bi-ja)

contact *n.* 연락 (yeol-lak); *v.* 연락하다 (yeol-la-ka-da), 접촉하다 (jeop-cho-ka-da)

contact lens *n.* 콘택트 렌즈 (kon-taek-teu ren-jeu); **wear contact lenses** *v.* 택트렌즈를 끼다 (kon-taek-teu-ren-jeu-reul kki-da)

contact number (telephone) *n.* 연락처 (yeol-lak-cheo)

contain *v.* 담다 (dam-tta)

container *n.* 용기 (yong-ji)

content *n.* 내용 (nae-yong)

continue *v.* 계속하다 (gye-so-ka-da), 계속되다 (gye-sok-doe-da)

contrast *n.* 대비 (dae-bi), 대비하다 (dae-bi-ha-da); **in contrast** 반면에 (ban-myeon-e)

contribute *v.* 공헌하다 (gong-heon-ha-da)

convenience store *n.* 편의점 (pyeon-ui-jeom)

convenient *adj.* 편리한 (pyeol-li-han), 편리하다 (pyeol-li-ha-da)

conversation *n.* 대화 (dae-hwa); **initiate a conversation** 이야기를 걸다 (i-ya-gi-reul geol-da)

convey *v.* 전하다 (jeon-ha-da)

conviction *n.* 신념 (sin-nyeom), 확신 (hawk-sin)

cook *n.* 요리하다 (yo-ri-ha-da), 요리사 (yo-ri-sa)

cookie *n.* 과자 (gwa-ja), 쿠키 (ku-ki)

cooking *n.* 요리 (yo-ri)

cool *adj.* 시원한 (si-won-han), 시원하다 (si-won-ha-da)

cool off *v.* 식다 (sik-da)

cooperate *v.* 협력하다 (hyeom-nyeo-ka-da)

cooperation *n.* 협력 (hyeom-nyeok)

cord *n.* 끈 (kkeun)

cordial *adj.* 간곡한 (gan-go-kan)

corn *n.* 옥수수 (ok-su-su)

correct *v.* 올바르다 (ol-ba-reu-da), 맞다 (mat-da)

cost *n.* 비용 (bi-yong)

cost money *v.* 돈이 들다 (don-i deul-da)

cost of living *n.* 생활비 (saeng-hwal-bi), 물가 (mul-kka)

cottage *n.* 시골집 (si-gol-jjip), 작은집 (jag-eun jip)

cotton *n.* 면 (myeon)

cough *n.* 기침 (gi-chim); *v.* 기침을 하다 (gi-chim-eul ha-da), 기침이 나오다 (gi-chim-i na-o-da)

counselor *n.* 카운슬러 (ka-un-seul-leo), 상담자 (sang-da-m-ja)

count *v.* 세다 (se-da)

counter *n.* 계산대; *v.* -에 달려있다 (e dal-lyeo-it-da)

D

degree (to some) *adv.* 다소 (da-so)

deposit *n.* 예금 (ye-geum); *v.* 맞기다 (mat-gi-da)

depth *n.* 깊이 (gip-i)

describe *v.* 기술하다 (gi-sul-ha-da), 묘사하다 (myo-sa-ha-da)

deserve *v.* -을 만한 가치가 있다 (eul man-han ga-chi-ga it-da)

designer *n.* 디자이너 (di-ja-i-neo)

desire *v.* 바라다 (ba-ra-da), 원하다 (won-ha-da)

desk *n.* 책상 (chaek-sang)

detail *n.* 세부사항 (se-bu-sa-hang); *adj.* 자세한 (ja-se-han)

detergent *n.* 빨래비누 (ppal-lae-ppi-nu)

develop *v.* 개발하다 (gae-bal-ha-da)

diabetes *n.* 당뇨병 (dang-nyo-ppyeong)

dial *n.* 다이얼 (da-i-eol); *v.* 다이얼을 돌리다 (da-i-eol-eul dol-li-da)

dialect *n.* 사투리 (sa-tu-ri)

diarrhea *n.* 설사 (seol-ssa)

diary *n.* 일기 (il-gi)

dictionary *n.* 사전 (sa-jeon)

die *v.* 죽다 (juk-da)

diet *n.* 다이어트 (da-i-eo-teu)

differ *v.* 다르다 (da-reu-da)

difference *n.* 차이 (cha-i), 다름 (da-reum)

different *adj.* 다른 (da-reun), 다르다 (da-reu-da)

difficult *adj.* 어려운 (eo-ryeo-un), 힘든 (him-deun), 어렵다 (eo-ryeop-da), 힘들다 (him-deul-da)

digestion *n.* 소화 (so-hwa)

digestive *adj.* 소화제 (so-hwa-je)

diligent *adj.* 근면한 (geun-myeon-han), 근면하다 (geun-myeon-ha-da)

diligently *adv.* 열심히 (yeol-ssim-hi)

dine *v.* 식사를 하다 (sik-sa-reul ha-da)

dining table *n.* 식탁 (sik-tak)

dinner *n.* 저녁 (jeo-nyeok), 저녁밥 (jeo-nyeok-bap)

direct *adj.* 직접적인 (jik-jeop-jeog-in)

direct sunshine *n.* 직사광선 (jik-sa-gwang-seon)

direction *n.* 방향 (bang-hyang), 지시 (ji-si), 용법 (yong-ppeop)

directly *adv.* 직접적으로 (jik-jeop-jeog-eu-ro)

dirt *n.* 먼지 (meon-ji), 더러운 것 (deo-reo-un geot)

dirty *adj.* 더러운 (deo-reo-un), 더럽다 (deo-reop-da)

disappear *v.* 사라지다 (sa-ra-ji-da), 없어지다 (eops-eo-ji-da)

disappoint *v.* 실망하다 (sil-mang-ha-da)

discharged *adj.* 퇴원하다 (toe-won-ha-da)

disclose *v.* 나타내다 (na-ta-nae-da), 드러내다 (deu-reo-nae-da)

discontinue *v.* 중단하다 (jung-dan-ha-da), 중지하다 (jung-ji-ha-da)

discount *n.* 할인 (hal-in); *v.* 할인하다 (hal-in-ha-da)

discover *v.* 발견하다 (bal-gyeon-ha-da)

discreet *adj.* 신중한 (sin-jung-han), 신중하다 (sin-jung-ha-da)

discuss *v.* 의논하다 (ui-non-ha-da)

disease *n.* 질병 (jil-byeong), 병 (byeong)

dish *n.* 그릇 (geu-reut), 음식 (eum-sik), 요리 (yo-ri)

dislike *v.* 미운 (mi-un), 밉다 (mip-da), 싫다 (sil-ta), 싫어하다 (sil-eo-ha-da)

dissatisfied *adj.* 불만족스러운 (bul-man-jok-seu-reo-un), 불만족스럽다 (bul-man-jok-seu-reop-da)

distance *n.* 거리 (geo-ri)

distressed *adj.* 속상한 (sok-sang-han), 속상하다 (sok-sang-ha-da)

district *n.* 지역 (ji-yeok)

divine *adj.* 신의 (sin-ui), 신성한 (sin-seong-han)

divorce *n.* 이혼 (i-hon)

do *v.* 하다 (ha-da)

doctor *n.* 의사 (ui-sa)

dog *n.* 개 (gae)

doll *n.* 인형 (in-hyeong)

domestic *adj.* 국내의 (gung-nae-ui), 가정의 (ga-jeong-ui), 길들여진 (gil-deul-yeo-jin)

domestic flight *n.* 국내선 (gung-nae-seon)

domesticate *v.* 길들이다 (gil-deul-i-da)

door *n.* 문 (mun)

doorbell *n.* 초인종 (cho-in-jong)

dormitory *n.* 기숙사 (gi-suk-sa)

dot *n.* 점 (jeom)

double *n.* 두배 (du-bae), 중복 (jung-bok)

doubt *n.* 의심 (ui-sim)

down *prep., adv.* 밑 (mit), 밑에 (mit-e)

downstairs *n.* 아래층 (a-rae-cheung)

downtown *n.* 시내 (si-nae)

dowry *n.* 혼수 (hon-su)

doze off *v.* 졸다 (jol-da)

draw *v.* 그리다 (geu-ri-da)

draw a picture *v.* 그림을 그리다 (geu-rim-eul geu-ri-da)

drawer *n.* 서랍 (seo-rap)

dream *n.* 꿈 (kkum), 희망 (hui-mang); *v.* 꿈을 꾸다 (kkum-eul kku-da)

dress *n.* 원피스 (won-pi-seu); *v.* 입히다 (i-pi-da)

dress shoe *n.* 정장구두 (jeong-jang-gu-du)

drink *n.* 마실 것 (ma-sil kkeot), 음료수 (eum-nyo-su); *v.* 마시다 (ma-si-da),

drive *v.* 운전하다 (un-jeon-ha-da)

driver *n.* 운전사 (un-jeon-sa), 운전기사 (un-jeon-gi-sa)

drop *v.* 떨어뜨리다 (tteol-eo-tteu-ri-da)

drop off *v.* 내려주다 (nae-ryeo-ju-da)

drug *n.* 약 (yak), 마약 (ma-yak)

drug-addicted *adj.* 마약 중독의 (ma-yak jung-dog-ui), 마약 중독 (ma-yak jung-dok)

drugstore *n.* 약국 (yak-guk)

dry *adj.* 마른 (ma-reun), 마르다 (ma-reu-da), 건조한 (geon-jo-han), 건조하다 (geon-jo-ha-da)

dry cleaner *n.* 세탁소 (se-tak-so)

dumb *n.* 벙어리 (beong-eo-ri); *adj.* 벙어리의 (beong-eo-ri-ui), 말을 하지 않는 (mal-eul ha-ji an-neun), 바보 같은 (ba-bo gat-eun)

during *prep.* -동안 (dong-an)

during the time *prep.* 그 동안 (geu dong-an)

dust *n.* 먼지 (meon-ji)

dye *v.* 물들이다 (mul-deul-i-da), 염색하다 (yeom-sae-ka-da)

E

each *adv.* 각각 (gak-gak)

each other *pron.* 서로서로 (seo-ro-seo-ro)

ear *n.* 귀 (gwi)

early *adj.* 이른 (i-reun); *adv.* 일찍 (il-jjik), 먼저 (meon-jeo)

earn *v.* 얻다 (eot-da), 돈을 벌다 (don-eul beol-da)

earrings *n.* 귀걸이 (gwi-geol-i)

earth *n.* 지구 (ji-gu), 땅 (ttang)

earthquake *n.* 지진 (ji-jin)

east *n.* 동쪽 (dong-jjok), 동 (dong)

east coast *n.* 동부 (dong-bu)

eastern *adj.* 동쪽의 (dong-jjog-ui)

east side *n.* 동쪽 (dong-jjok)

easy *adj.* 쉬운 (swi-un), 쉽다 (swip-da)

eat *v.* 먹다 (meok-da)

economics *n.* 경제학 (gyeong-je-hak)

economy *n.* 경제 (gyeong-je)

economy-class seat *n.* 일반석 (il-ban-seok)

editorial *adj.* 사설 (sa-seol)

educate *v.* 교육하다 (gyo-yu-ka-da), 가르치다 (ga-reu-chi-da)

education *n.* 교육 (gyo-yuk)

educational background *n.* 학벌 (hak-beol)

educator *n.* 교육자 (gyo-yuk-ja)

eel *n.* 뱀장어 (baem-jang-eo)

egg *n.* 계란 (gye-ran), 달걀 (dal-gyal)

eight *n.* 팔 (pal), 여덟 (yeo-deol)

eighty *n.* 여든 (yeo-deun)

eldest daughter *n.* 장녀 (jang-nyeo)

eldest son *n.* 장남 (jang-nam)

election *n.* 선거 (seon-geo)

elegant *adj.* 고상한 (go-sang-han), 고상하다 (go-sang-ha-da)

elementary *adj.* 기본의 (gi-bon-ui), 초보의 (cho-bo-ui)

elementary school *n.* 초등학교 (cho-deung-hak-gyo)

elementary school student *n.* 초등학생 (cho-deung-hak-saeng)

elevator *n.* 엘리베이터 (el-li-be-i-teo)

elk *n.* 큰사슴 (keun sa-seum)

e-mail *n.* 이메일 (i-me-il)

embarrassed *adj.* 당황스러운 (dang-hwang-seu-reo-un), 당황스럽다 (dang-hwang-seu-rep-da)

embarrassing *adj.* 창피한 (chang-pi-han), 창피하다 (chang-pi-ha-da)

emergency *n.* 응급상황 (eung-geup-sang-hwang)

emergency room *n.* 응급실 (eung-geup-sil)

emigrate *v.* 이민 가다 (i-min ga-da)

emotional *adj.* 감정적인 (gam-jeong-jeog-in), 감정적이다 (gam-jeong-jeog-i-da)

employ *v.* 고용하다 (go-yong-ha-da)

employee *n.* 직원 (jig-won)

employer *n.* 고용주 (go-yong-ju), 사장 (sa-jang), 주인 (ju-in)

end *n.* 끝 (kkeut), 말 (mal)

endless *adj.* 끝이 안 나는 (kkeu-chi an na-neun)

energy *n.* 에너지 (e-neo-ji), 힘 (him)

engineer *n.* 엔지니어 (en-ji-ni-eo)

England *n.* 영국 (yeong-guk)

English (language) *n.* 영어 (yeong-eo)

enjoy *v.* 즐기다 (jeul-gi-da)

enjoyable *adj.* 즐거운 (jeul-geo-un), 즐겁다 (jeul-geop-da)

enormous *adj.* 엄청난 (eom-cheong-nan), 엄청나다 (eom-cheong-na-da)

enough *adj.* 충분한 (chung-bun-han); *adv.* 충분하게 (chung-bun-ha-ge)

entering *n.* 입장 (ip-jang)

enterprise *n.* 기획 (gi-hoek), 기업 (gi-eop), 진취성 (jin-chwi-sseong)

entertain *v.* 즐겁게 하다 (jeul-geop-ge ha-da), 즐기다 (jeul-gi-da)

entertainment *n.* 오락 (o-rak), 대접 (dae-jeop), 연예 (yeon-ye)

entrance *n.* 입구 (ip-gu), 현관 (hyeon-gwan)

entrust *v.* 맡기다 (mat-gi-da)

envelope *n.* 봉투 (bong-tu)

envious *adj.* 부러운 (bu-reo-un), 부럽다 (bu-reop-da)

environment *n.* 환경 (hwan-gyeong)

equip *v.* 장비를 갖추다 (jang-bi-reul gat-chu-da)

equipment *n.* 장비 (jang-bi)

equivalence *n.* 동등 (dong-deung), 같음 (gat-eum)

escalator *n.* 에스컬레이터 (e-seu-keol-le-i-teo)

especially *adv.* 특히 (teu-ki)

essential *adj.* 필수적인 (pil-ssu-jeog-in), 필수의 (pil-ssu-ui)

estimate *v.* 평가하다 (pyeong-kka-ha-da), 평가 (pyeong-kka), 판단 (pan-dan)

ethnic group *n.* 민족 (min-jok)

Europe *n.* 유럽 (yu-reop)

European *n., adj.* 유럽의 (yu-reob-ui), 유럽인 (yu-reob-in), 유럽인의 (yu-reob-in-ui)

evening *n.* 저녁 (jeo-nyeok)

event *n.* 사건 (sa-kkeon), 행사 (haeng-sa)

eventually *adv.* 마침내 (ma-chim-nae), 결국은 (gyeol-gug-eun), 경우에 따라서는 (gyeong-u-e tta-ra-seo-neun)

every *adj.* 모든 (mo-deun), 매- (mae)

every day *n.* 매일 (mae-il), 날마다 (nal-ma-da)

every month *n.* 매달 (mae-da)l)

every week *n.* 매주 (mae-ju)

every year *n.* 매년 (mae-nyeon)

everything *pron.* 일체 (il-che), 모두 (mo-du), 모든 것 (mo-deun geot)

everywhere *adv.* 어디에나 (eo-di-e-na), 모든 곳에 (mo-deun gos-e)

evict *v.* 쫓아내다 (jjoch-a-nae-da), 퇴거시키다 (toe-geo-si-ki-da)

evidence *n.* 증거 (jeung-geo)

evident *adj.* 분명한 (bun-myeong-han)

exactly *adv.* 꼭 (kkok)

examination *n.* 시험 (si-heom), 진찰 (jin-chal), 검사 (geom-sa)

examine *v.* 시험하다 (si-heom-ha-da), 검사하다 (geom-sa-ha-da)

exception *n.* 예외 (ye-oe)

exchange *n.* 교환 (gyo-hwan); *v.* 교환하다 (gyo-hwan-ha-da)

excited *adj.* 신나다 (sin-na-da)

exciting *adj.* 신나는 (sin-na-neun), 신기한 (sin-gi-han), 신나다 (sin-na-da), 신기하다 (sin-gi-ha-da)

excuse *n.* 실례 (sil-lye); *v.* 실례하다 (sil-lye-ha-da)

exercise *n.* 운동 (un-dong), 연습 (yeon-seup); *v.* 운동하다 (un-domg-ha-da)

exercise wear *n.* 운동복 (un-dong-bok)

exist *v.* 있다 (it-da), 존재하다 (jon-jae-ha-da)

exit *n.* 출구 (chul-gu)

expense *n.* 비용 (bi-yong), 소비 (so-bi); *v.* 소비하다 (so-bi-ha-da), 돈을 쓰다 (don-eul sseu-da)

expensive *adj.* 비싼 (bi-ssan), 비싸다 (bi-ssa-da)

experience *n.* 경험 (gyeong-heom)

explain *v.* 설명하다 (seol-myeong-ha-da)

explanation *n.* 설명 (seol-myeong)

express *v.* 표현하다 (pyo-hyeon-ha-da); *adj.* 고속의 (go-sog-ui), 빠른 (ppa-reun)

express bus *n.* 고속버스 (go-sok-beo-seu)

express mail *n.* 속달우편 (sok-da)l-u-pyeon)

expressway *n.* 고속도로 (go-sok-do-ro)

extend *v.* 연장하다 (yeon-jang-ha-da)

extension *n.* 연장 (yeon-jang)

extremely *adv.* 굉장히 (goeng-jang-hi), 되게 (doe-ge)

eye *n.* 눈 (nun)

F

fabric *n.* 옷감 (ot-gam)

face *n.* 얼굴 (eol-gul)

facial expression *n.* 표정 (pyo-jeong)

fact *n.* 사실 (sa-sil)

factory *n.* 공장 (gong-jang)

fad *n.* 유행 (yu-haeng)

Fahrenheit *adj., n.* 화씨 (hwa-ssi)

failure *n.* 실패 (sil-pae), 불합격 (bul-hap-gyeok)

fair *adj.* 공평한 (gong-pyeong-han), **아름다운** (a-reum-da-un), **맑은** (malg-eun), 꽤 **많은** (kkwae man-eun)

fairly *adv.* 공평하게 (gong-pyeong-ha-ge), 꽤 (kkwae)

faith *n.* 신앙 (sin-ang), 믿음 (mid-eum)

fall *n.* 가을 (ga-eul); *v.* 떨어지다 (tteol-eo-ji-da)

familiar *adj.* 잘 알고 있는 (jal al-go in-neun), 잘 알려진 (jal al-lyeo-jin)

family *n.* 가족 (ga-jok)

family background *n.* 집안 (jib-an)

far *adj.* 먼 (meon), 멀다 (meol-da)

fare *n.* 요금 (yo-geum)

farm *n.* 농장 (nong-jang)

farmer *n.* 농부 (nong-bu)

fashion *n.* 스타일 (seu-ta-il), 유행 (yu-haeng)

fast *adj.* 빠른 (ppa-reun), 빠르다 (ppa-reu-da)

fat *n.* 지방 (ji-bang); *adj.* 뚱뚱한 (ttung-ttung-han), 뚱뚱하다 (ttung-ttung-ha-da)

father *n.* 아버지 (a-beo-ji), 아빠 (a-ppa), 신부님 (sin-bu-nim)

father-in-law *n.* 시아버지 (si-a-beo-ji), 시아버님 (si-a-beo-nim)

favor *v.* 선호하다 (seon-ho-ha-da)

feature *n.* 특징 (teuk-jing), 생김새 (saeng-gim-sae)

February *n.* 2월 (i-wol)

fee *n.* 요금 (yo-geum)

feed *v.* 먹이다 (meog-i-da)

feel *v.* 느끼다 (neu-kki-da)

feeling *n.* 느낌 (neu-kkim), 기분 (gi-bun)

female *n.* 여성 (yeo-seong), 여자 (yeo-ja); *adj.* 여성의 (yeo-seong-ui), 여자의 (yeo-ja-ui)

female student *n.* 여학생 (yeo-hak-saeng)

fetch *v.* 가져오다 (ga-jyeo-o-da), 자아내다 (ja-a-nae-da)

fever *n.* 열 (yeol), 열기 (yeol-gi)

few *adj.* 소수의 (so-su-ui), 몇몇 (myeon-myeot), 적다 (jeok-da)

field *n.* 분야 (bun-ya), 운동장 (un-dong-jang)

fifty *n.* 쉰 (swin)

fight *n.* 싸움 (ssa-um)

figure *n.* 숫자 (sut-ja), 모양 (mo-yang), 인물 (in-mul), 그림 (geu-rim)

fill *v.* 채우다 (chae-u-da), 담다 (dam-tta)

fill out *v.* 적다 (jeok-da)

filling *n.* 속 (sok)

film *n.* 필름 (pil-leum), 영화 (yeong-hwa)

final *n., adj.* 마지막 (ma-ji-mak)

finally *adv.* 결국 (gyeol-guk), 마지막으로 (ma-ji-mag-eu-ro)

financial *adj.* 경제적인 (gyeong-je-jeog-in), 금전적인 (geum-jeon-jeog-in)

find *v.* 찾다 (chat-da), 발견하다 (bal-gyeon-ha-da)

find a job *v.* 취직하다 (chwi-ji-ka-da)

find out *v.* 알아보다 (al-a-bo-da)

fine *adj.* 좋다 (jo-ta)

finger *n.* 손가락 (son-kka-rak)

finish *v.* 마치다 (ma-chi-da)

fire *n.* 불 (bul); *v.* 불이 나다 (bul-i na-da)

fire station *n.* 소방서 (so-bang-seo)

firm *n.* 단단하다 (dan-dan-ha-da), 탄탄하다 (tan-tan-ha-da)

first *n., adj., adv.* 첫 번째 (cheot beon-jjae)

first-class seat *n.* 일등석 (il-tteung-seok)

first floor *n.* 일층 (il-cheung)

fish *n.* 물고기 (mul-kko-gi), 생선 (saeng-seon)

fishing *n.* 낚시 (nak-si); go fishing 낚시 가다 (nak-si ga-da)

fit *v.* 맞다 (mat-da), 맞추다 (mat-chu-da)

five *n.* 오 (o), 다섯 (da-seot)

fix *v.* 고치다 (go-chi-da)

flag *n.* 기 (gi), 깃발 (git-bal)

flash *n.* 번쩍임 (beon-jjeog-im), *v.* 번쩍이다 (beon-jjeog-i-da)

flat *adj.* 평평한 (pyeong-pyeong-han), 평평하다 (pyeong-pyeong-ha-da)

flavor *n.* 맛 (mat)

flight *n.* 비행기 (bi-haeng-gi), 항공기 (hang-gong-gi), 항공 (hang-gong)

float *v.* 뜨다 (tteu-da)

floor *n.* 층 (cheung), 마루 (ma-ru)

florist *n.* 꽃집 (kkot-jip)

flower *n.* 꽃 (kkot)

flower pot *n.* 화분 (hwa-bun)

flower shop *n.* 꽃집 (kkot-jip)

fluid *n.* 액체 (aek-che)

flute *n.* 플루트 (peul-lu-teu)

fly *n.* 파리 (pa-ri); *v.* 날다 (nal-da)

fog *n.* 안개 (an-gae)

foggy *adj.* 안개가 낀 (an-gae-ga kkin), 안개가 끼다 (an-gae-ga kki-da)

follow *v.* 따르다 (tta-reu-da)

following *adj.* 다음의 (da-eum-ui)

fond of *adj.* 좋아하다 (jo-a-ha-da)

food *n.* 음식 (eum-sik), 먹을 것 (meog-eul kkeot)

foot *n.* 발 (bal)

football *n.* 풋볼 (put-bol), 미식축구 (mi-sik-chuk-gu)

footwear *n.* 신발 (sin-bal), 신 (sin)

for *prep.* -을 향하여 (eul hyang-ha-yeo), -을 위해 (eul wi-hae), -대신 (dae-sin), -때문에 (ttae-mun-e)

for a long time *prep.* 오랫동안 (o-raet-dong-an)

for a short time *prep.* 잠깐만 (jam-kkan-man)

for the first time *prep.* 처음으로 (cheo-eum-eu-ro)

forbid *v.* 금지하다 (geum-ji-ha-da)

force *v.* 강요하다 (gang-yo-ha-da), 강제하다 (gang-je-ha-da)

foreign *adj.* 외국의 (oe-gug-ui), 외국인의 (oe-gug-in-ui)

foreign country *n.* 외국 (oe-guk)

forest *n.* 숲 (sup)

forget *v.* 잊어버리다 (ij-eo-beo-ri-da), 잊다 (it-da)

form *v.* 형성하다 (hyeong-seong-ha-da), 만들다 (man-deul-da), 모양 (mo-yang), 폼 (pom)

formal *adj.* 형식적인 (hyeong-sik-jeog-in), 정식의 (jeong-sig-ui), 표면적인 (pyo-myeon-jeog-in)

former *adj.* 이전의 (i-jeon-ui), 전의 (jeon-ui)

fortunate *adj.* 다행이다 (da-haeng-i-da)

fortunately *adv.* 다행히 (da-haeng-hi)

forty *n.* 마흔 (ma-heun)

four *n.* 사 (sa), 넷 (net)

fowl *n.* 닭 (dak), 가금 (ga-geum), 들새 (deul-ssae)

frame *n.* 뼈대 (ppyeo-dae), 구조 (gu-jo), 체격 (che-gyeok), 틀 (teul)

free *adj.* 자유롭다 (ja-yu-rop-da), 자유로운 (ja-yu-ro-un), 공짜로 (gong-jja-ro)

free of charge *adj.* 무료 (mu-ryo)

freedom *n.* 자유 (ja-yu)

freezer *n.* 냉동실 (naeng-dong sil)

frequently *adv.* 자주 (ja-ju)

fresh *adj.* 신선한 (sin-seon-han), 신선하다 (sin-seon-ha-da), 상쾌한 (sang-kwae-han), 상쾌하다 (sang-kwae-ha-da)

freshman *n.* 일학년 (il-hang-nyeon)

Friday *n.* 금요일 (geum-yo-il)

friend *n.* 친구 (chin-gu)

friendly *adj.* 친하다 (chin-ha-da)

frightened *adj.* 놀라다 (nol-la-da)

from *prep.* -으로부터 (eu-ro-bu-teo), -에서부터 (e-seo-bu-teo)

from now on *prep.* 지금부터 (ji-geum-bu-teo), 앞으로는 (ap-eu-ro-neun)

front *n.* 앞 (ap)

fruit *n.* 과일 (gwa-il)

fruit store *n.* 과일가게 (gwa-il-kka-ge)

fry *n.* 튀김 (twi-gim); *v.* 튀기다 (twi-gi-da)

full *adj.* 가득 찬 (ga-deuk chan), 가득 차다 (ga-deuk cha-da), 바보스러운 (ba-bo-seu-reo-un), 바보스럽다 (ba-bo-seu-reop-da), 배가 부른 (bae-ga bu-reun), 배가 부르다 (bae-ga bu-reu-da)

fun *adj.* 재미있는 (jae-mi-in-neun), 재미있다 (jae-mi-it-da)

function *n.* 기능 (gi-neung)

funny *adj.* 우스운 (u-seu-un), 우습다 (u-seup-da), 웃기는 (ut-gi-neun), 재미있는 (jae-mi-in-neun)

furniture *n.* 가구 (ga-gu); **used furniture** *n.* 중고가구 (jung-go-ga-gu)

furniture store *n.* 가구점 (ga-gu-jeom)

furthermore *adv.* 더욱더 (deo-uk-deo), 더더욱 (deo-deo-uk), 더군다나 (deo-gun-da-na)

fuss (with no) *adv.* 아무렇지도 않게 (a-mu-reo-chi-do an-ke)

G

gain *v.* 얻다 (eot-da)

gain weight *v.* 몸무게가 늘다 (mom-mu-ge-ga neul-da), 살이 찌다 (sal-i jji-da)

garlic *n.* 마늘 (ma-neul)

game *n.* 게임 (ge-im), 놀이 (nol-i), 사냥감 (sa-nyang-kkam)

gang *n.* 한 떼 (han tte); *v.* 집단을 이루다 (jip-dan-eul i-ru-da)

garage *n.* 차고 (cha-go)

garden *n.* 정원 (jeong-won), 마당 (ma-dang)

gas *n.* 가스 (kka-sseu), 석유 (seog-yu), 기름 (gi-reum)

gas station *n.* 주유소 (ju-yu-so)

gate *n.* 게이트 (ge-i-teu), 문 (mun)

gather *v.* 모이다 (mo-i-da)

gaze *v.* 응시하다 (eung-si-ha-da), 응시 (eung-si)

gear *n.* 기어 (gi-eo), 전동장치 (jeon-dong-jang-chi)

generally *adv.* 대체로 (dae-che-ro), 일반적으로 (il-ban-jeog-eu-ro)

gesture *n.* 제스츄어 (je-seu-chyu-eo), 몸짓 (mom-jjit); *v.* 몸짓을 하다 (mom-jjis-eul ha-da), 제스츄어를 하다 (je-seu-chyu-eo-reul ha-da)

get *v.* 얻다 (eot-da), 받다 (bat-da), 가지다 (ga-ji-da), 되다 (doe-da)

get in/on *v.* 타다 (ta-da)

get married *v.* 결혼하다 (gyeol-hon-ha-da)

get off *v.* 내리다 (nae-ri-da)

get up *v.* 일어나다 (il-eo-na-da)

gift *n.* 선물 (seon-mul)

ginseng tea *n.* 인삼차 (in-san-cha)

girl *n.* 여자아이 (yeo-ja-a-i), 소녀 (so-nyeo)

girlfriend *n.* 여자친구 (yeo-ja-chin-gu)

give *v.* 주다 (ju-da)

give a ride *v.* 태워주다 (tae-wo-ju-da)

give regards *v.* 안부를 전하다 (an-bu-reul jeon-ha-da)

give up *v.* 포기하다 (po-gi-ha-da)

glad *adj.* 즐겁다 (jeul-geop-da), 기쁘다 (gi-ppeu-da), 반갑다 (ban-gap-da)

glass *n.* 잔 (jan)

glasses *n.* 안경 (an-gyeong)

gloss *n.* 윤기 (yun-kki)

glossy *adj.* 윤기 있다 (yun-kki it-da)

gloves *n.* 장갑 (jang-gap)

go *v.* 가다 (ga-da)

go down *v.* 내려가다 (nae-ryeo-ga-da), 내려오다 (nae-ryeo-o-da)

go grocery shopping *v.* 시장을 보다 (si-jang-eul bo-da), 장을 보다 (jang-eul bo-da)

go hiking *v.* 등산을 하다 (deung-san-eul ha-da), 등산을 가다 (deung-san-eul ga-da)

go out *v.* 나가다 (na-ga-da), 나오다 (na-o-da), 데이트하다 (de-i-teu-ha-da)

go well *v.* 어울리다 (eo-ul-li-da)

goal *n.* 목적 (mok-jeok), 득점 (deuk-jeom)

god *n.* 신 (sin)

going out *n.* 나들이 (na-deul-i), 데이트 (de-i-teu)

gold *n.* 금 (geum)

golden *adj.* 금의 (geum-ui), 금빛의 (geum-bich-ui)

goldfish *n.* 금붕어 (geum-bung-eo)

golf *n.* 골프 (gol-peu)

good *adj.* 좋은 (jo-eun), 좋다 (jo-ta); feel good 기분이 좋다 (gi-bun-i jo-ta)

good fortune *n.* 복 (bok)

good-bye *n.* 안녕히 가세요 (an-nyeong-hi ga-se-yo), 잘 가 (jal ga)

goods *n.* 물건 (mul-geon), 상품 (sang-pum)

gorgeous *adj.* 화려한 (hwa-ryeo-han), 화려하다 (hwa-ryeo-ha-da)

government *n.* 정부 (jeong-bu)

grab *v.* 잡다 (jap-da)

grade *n.* 성적 (seong-jeok), 등급 (deung-geup)

gradually *adv.* 차차 (cha-cha), 점진적으로 (jeom-jin-jeog-eu-ro)

graduate *v.* 졸업하다 (jol-eo-pa-da)

graduate school *n.* 대학원 (dae-hag-won)

graduate student *n.* 대학원생 (dae-hag-won-saeng)

grandfather *n.* 할아버지 (hal-a-beo-ji), 할아버님 (hal-a-beo-nim)

grandmother *n.* 할머니 (hal-meo-ni), 할머님 (hal-meo-nim)

grapes *n.* 포도 (po-do)

grass *n.* 풀 (pul), 잔디 (jan-di)

grateful *adj.* 고마운 (go-ma-un), 고맙다 (go-map-da)

gray *n.* 회색 (hoe-saek); *adj.* 회색의 (hoe-saeg-ui)

great *adj.* 대단한 (dae-dan-han), 대단하다 (dae-dan-ha-da)

green *n.* 초록색 (cho-rok-saek); *adj.* 초록색의 (cho-rok-saeg-ui); **light green** 연두색 (yeon-du-saek), 연두색의 (yeon-du-saeg-ui)

green onion *n.* 파 (pa)

greet *v.* 인사하다 (in-sa-ha-da)

greeting *n.* 인사 (in-sa)

grocery store *n.* 식품점 (sik-pum-jeom), 식료품 가게 (sing-nyo-pum ga-ge)

groom *n.* 신랑 (sil-lang)

ground *n.* 땅 (ttang), 바닥 (ba-dak); *adj.* 간 (gan), 빻은 (ppa-eun)

group *n.* 그룹 (geu-rup)

grow *v.* 기르다 (gi-reu-da)

grow up *v.* 자라다 (ja-ra-da)

grown-up *n.* 어른 (eo-reun), 성인 (seong-in); *adj.* 다 큰 (da-keun)

guarantee *v.* 보장하다 (bo-jang-ha-da)

guard *n.* 경계 (gyeong-gye), 경호인 (gyeong-ho-in); *v.* 경계하다 (gyeong-gye-ha-da)

guess *n.* 추측 (chu-cheuk); *v.* 추측하다 (chu-cheu-ka-da)

guest *n.* 손님 (son-nim)

guide *n.* 안내원 (an-nae-won); *v.* 안내하다 (an-nae-ha-da)

guilt *n.* 유죄 (yu-joe)

guilty *adj.* 죄책감을 느끼는 (joe-chaek-gam-eul neu-kki-neun), 죄책감을 느끼다 (joe-chaek-gam-eul neu-kki-da)

gum *n.* 잇몸 (in-mom)

H

hair *n.* 머리카락 (meo-ri-ka-rak), 머리 (meo-ri)

haircut *v.* 머리를 깎다 (meo-ri-reul kkak-da), 이발하다 (i-bal-ha-da), 머리를 자르다 (meo-ri-reul ja-reu-da)

hairdresser *n.* 미용사 (mi-yong-sa), 헤어디자이너 (he-eo-di-ja-i-neo)

hair salon *n.* 머리방 (meo-ri-bang), 미장원 (mi-jang-won), 미용실 (mi-yong-sil)

hair style *n.* 헤어스타일 (he-eo-seu-ta-il)

half *n., adj.* 반 (ban)

half-price *n., adj.* 반값 (ban-kkap)

hall *n.* 집회장 (ji-poe-jang), 현관 (hyeon-gwan), 공회당 (gong-hoe-dang)

hallway *n.* 복도 (bok-do)

ham *n.* 햄 (haem)

hamburger *n.* 햄버거 (haem-beo-geo)

hand *n.* 손 (son)

hand in *v.* 내다 (nae-da), 제출하다 (je-chul-ha-da)

handsome *adj.* 잘생긴 (jal-saeng-gin), 잘생기다 (jal-saeng-gi-da)

hang *v.* 매달리다 (mae-da-l-li-da)

hang up (the telephone) *v.* 전화를 끊다 (jeon-hwa-reul kkeun-ta)

hanger *n.* 옷걸이 (ot-geol-i)

happen *v.* (일이) 생기다 ([il-i] saeng-gi-da), (일이) 일어나다 ([il-i] il-eo-na-da)

happiness *n.* 행복 (haeng-bok)

happy *adj.* 행복한 (haeng-bo-kan), 행복하다 (haeng-bo-ka-da)

harbor *n.* 항구 (hang-gu)

hard *adj.* 어려운 (eo-ryeo-un), 어렵다 (eo-ryeop-da)

hat *n.* 모자 (mo-ja)

hate *n.* 증오 (jeung-o); *v.* 싫어하다 (sil-eo-ha-da), 증오하다 (jeung-o-ha-da)

have *v.* 가지다 (ga-ji-da), 있다 (it-da)

head *n.* 머리 (meo-ri)

headache *n.* 두통 (du-tong); **have a headache** 머리가 아프다 (meo-ri-ga a-peu-da)

headline *n.* 표제 (pyo-je)

heal *v.* 치료되다 (chi-ryo-doe-da), 치료하다 (chi-ryo-ha-da), 낫다 (nat-da)

health *n.* 건강 (geon-gang)

healthily *adv.* 건강하게 (geon-gang-ha-ge)

healthy *adj.* 건강한 (geon-gang-han), 건강하다 (geon-gang-ha-da)

hear *v.* 듣다 (deut-da)

hearing aid *n.* 보청기 (bo-cheong-gi)

heart *n.* 심장 (sim-jang), 마음 (ma-eum), 인정 (in-jeong)

heartache *n.* 속앓이 (sog-al-i); **cause heartache** 속을 썩이다 (sog-eul sseog-i-da)

heat *n.* 열 (yeol); *v.* 달구다 (dal-gu-da), 뜨겁게 하다 (tteu-geop-ge ha-da)

heater *n.* 난방장치 (nan-bang-jang-chi), 히터 (hi-teo), 스팀 (seu-tim)

heavy *adj.* 무거운 (mu-geo-un), 무겁다 (mu-geop-da)

heel *n.* 뒤꿈치 (dwi-kkum-chi); *v.* 뒤축을 대다 (dwi-chug-eul dae-da), 기울다 (gi-ul-da)

height *n.* 키 (ki), 높이 (nop-i)

hello *n.* 안녕하세요 (an-nyeong-ha-se-yo)

help *n.* 도움 (do-um); *v.* 도와주다 (do-wa-ju-da)

here *adv.* 여기 (yeo-gi)

hide *v.* 감추다 (gam-chu-da)

high *adj.* 높은 (nop-eun), 높다 (nop-da)

high-rise apartment *n.* 고층 아파트 (go-cheung a-pa-teu)

high school *n.* 고등학교 (go-deung-hak-gyo)

high school student *n.* 고등학생 (go-deung-hak-saeng)

highest *n., adj.* 최고 (choe-go)

highway *n.* 고속도로 (go-sok-do-ro)

hike *v.* 등산하다 (deung-san-ha-da)

hiking *n.* 등산 (deung-san)

hip *n.* 엉덩이 (eong-deong-i)

hire *v.* 고용하다 (go-yong-ha-da)

historical *adj.* 역사적인 (yeok-sa-jeog-in)

history *n.* 역사 (yeok-sa)

hit *v.* 치다 (chi-da)

hobby *n.* 취미생활 (chwi-mi-saeng-hwal), 취미 (chwi-mi)

hold *v.* 붙잡다 (but-jap-da), 안다 (an-tta)

hole *n.* 구멍 (gu-meong)

holiday *n.* 휴일 (hyu-il)

home *n.* 집 (jip)

homesick *n.* 향수 (hyang-su)

hometown *n.* 고향 (go-hyang)

homework *n.* 숙제 (suk-je)

honest *adj.* 정직한 (jeong-ji-kan), 정직하다 (jeong-ji-ka-da)

honeymoon *n.* 신혼여행 (sin-hon-yeo-haeng)

hope *v.* 원하다 (won-ha-da), 희망하다 (hui-mang-ha-da, hi-mang-ha-da)

horrible *adj.* 무서운 (mu-seo-un), 무섭다 (mu-seop-da)

horrified *adj.* 무서운 (mu-seo-un), 무섭다 (mu-seop-da)

horse *n.* 말 (mal)

hospital *n.* 병원 (byeong-won)

hospitalized *adj.* 입원하다 (ib-won-ha-da)

hot *adj.* 덥다 (deop-da), 뜨겁다 (tteu-geop-da)

hot temper *n.* 급한 성격 (geu-pan seong-kkyeok)

hotel *n.* 호텔 (ho-tel)

hour *n.* 시간 (si-gan)

house *n.* 집 (jip), 댁 (daek) (*honorific*)

household *n.* 살림 (sal-lim)

housewarming party *n.* 집들이 (jip-deul-i)

housewife *n.* 주부 (ju-bu)

how *adv.* 어떻게 (eo-tteo-ke)

how long *adv.* 얼마나 오래 (eol-ma-na o-rae)

how many *adv.* 얼마나 많이 (eol-ma-na man-i)

how much *adv.* 얼마나 많이 (eol-ma-na man-i)

how often *adv.* 얼마나 자주 (eol-ma-na ja-ju)

however *conj.* 그렇지만 (geu-reo-chi-man)

hug *v.* 안다 (an-tta)

huge *adj.* 엄청난 (eom-cheong-nan), 엄청나다 (eom-cheong-na-da)

human *n.* 사람 (sa-ram), 인간 (in-gan)

humid *adj.* 끈끈한 (kkeun-kkeun-han), 끈끈하다 (kkeun-kkeun-ha-da)

humidity *n.* 습기 (seup-gi)

hundred *n.* 백 (baek)

hunger *n.* 배고픔 (bae-go-peum), 기아 (gi-a)

hungry *adj.* 배고픈 (bae-go-peun), 배고프다 (bae-go-peu-da)

hunt *v.* 사냥하다 (sa-nyang-ha-da)

hurt *v.* 다치다 (da-chi-da), 다치게 하다 (da-chi-ge ha-da)

husband *n.* 남편 (nam-pyeon)

I

ice *n.* 얼음 (eol-eum)

ice cream *n.* 아이스크림 (a-i-seu-keu-rim)

icy *adj.* 미끄러운 (mi-kkeu-reo-un), 얼음이 언 (eol-eum-i eon), 쌀쌀한 (ssal-ssal-han)

idea *n.* 생각 (saeng-gak)

ideal *n.* 이상 (i-sang); *adj.* 이상적인 (i-sang-jeog-in)

if *conj.* 만약 (man-yak)

if so *prep.* 그런 경우에 (geu-reon gyeong-u-e), 그렇다면 (geu-reo-ta-myeon)

ignore *v.* 무시하다 (mu-si-ha-da)

ill *adj.* 아픈 (a-peun), 아프다 (a-peu-da)

illegal *adj.* 불법적인 (bul-ppeop-jeog-in), 불법적이다 (bul-ppeop-jeog-i-da)

illness *n.* 질병 (jil-byeong), 병 (byeong)

image *n.* 상상 (sang-sang), 이미지 (i-mi-ji)

imagine *v.* 상상하다 (sang-sang-ha-da)

immigrant *n.* 이민 (i-min)

immigrate *v.* 이민 가다 (i-min ga-da), 이민 오다 (i-min o-da)

important *adj.* 중요한 (jung-yo-han), 중요하다 (jung-yo-ha-da)

impress *v.* 감명을 주다 (gam-myeong-eul ju-da), 인상을 주다 (in-sang-eul ju-da)

impression *n.* 인상 (in-sang)

impressive *adj.* 인상적인 (in-sang-jeog-in), 인상적이다 (in-sang-jeog-i-da)

improve *v.* 늘다 (neul-da)

in *prep.* 안 (an), 속 (sok)

in a short time *prep.* 금방 (geum-bang)

in fact *adv.* 사실은 (sa-sil-eun)

in the future *prep.* 앞으로 (ap-eu-ro)

in time *prep.* 제시간 (je-si-gan)

in total *adj.* 전부 (jeon-bu)

in what way *adv.* 어떻게 (eo-tteo-ke)

inactive *adj.* 한산한 (han-san-han), 한산하다 (han-san-ha-da)

include *v.* 포함하다 (po-ham-ha-da)

inconvenient *adj.* 불편한 (bul-pyeon-han), 불편하다 (bul-pyeon-ha-da)

increase *v.* 증가하다 (jeung-ga-ha-da), 늘다 (neul-da)

indeed *adv.* 하기야 (ha-gi-ya), 사실 (sa-sil), 정말 (jeong-mal)

indigestion *n.* 소화불량 (so-hwa-bul-lyang); **have indigestion** *v.* 속이 답답하다 (sog-i dap-da-pa-da), 속이 거북하다 (sog-i geo-bu-ka-da)

individual *n.* 개인 (gae-in); *adj.* 개인의 (gae-in-ui), 개인적인 (gae-in-jeog-in)

indoors *n.* 실내 (sil-lae)

industry *n.* 산업 (san-eop)

influence *n.* 영향 (yeong-hyang); *v.* 영향을 주다 (yeong-hyang-eul ju-da)

inform *v.* 알려주다 (al-lyeo-ju-da)

information *n.* 안내 (an-nae), 정보 (jeong-bo)

inhabitant *n.* 주민 (ju-min), 거주자 (geo-ju-ja), 서식 동물 (seo-sik dong-mul)

injure v. 다치다 (da-chi-da), 상처를 입다 (sang-cheo-reul ip-da)

injury n. 부상 (bu-sang)

inn n. 여관 (yeo-gwan)

inner adj. 내면의 (nae-myeon-ui), 속안의 (sog-an-ui)

inquire v. 물어보다 (mul-eo-bo-da)

inside n., prep. 속 (sok), 안 (an)

instead of prep. 대신에 (dae-sin-e)

institute n. 기관 (gi-gwan), 연구소 (yeon-gu-so), 학원 (hag-won)

institution n. 기관 (gi-gwan), 연구소 (yeon-gu-so), 학원 (hag-won)

insurance n. 보험 (bo-heom)

insurance company n. 보험회사 (bo-heom-hoe-sa)

intellectual adj. 지적인 (ji-jjeog-in), 지적이다 (ji-jjeog-i-da)

intelligence n. 지능 (ji-neung)

intention n. 의도 (ui-do)

intentionally adv. 의도적으로 (ui-do-jeog-eu-ro), 일부러 (il-bu-reo)

interest n. 이자 (i-ja), 흥미 (heung-mi); adj. 흥미 있는 (heung-mi-in-neun), 흥미 있다 (heung-mi-it-da)

interior adj. 실내의 (sil-lae-ui)

interior design n. 실내장식 (sil-lae-jang-sik)

international adj. 국제적인 (guk-je-jeog-in)

international flight n. 국제선 (guk-je-seon)

Internet n. 인터넷 (in-teo-net)

interpreter n. 통역가 (tong-yeok-ga), 해석자 (hae-seok-ja)

intersection n. 교차로 (gyo-cha-ro)

interview n. 면접 (myeon-jeop); v. 면접하다 (myeon-jeo-pa-da)

introduce v. 소개하다 (so-gae-ha-da)

introduction n. 소개 (so-gae), 도입 (do-ip)

introverted adj. 내성적인 (nae-seong-jeog-in), 내성적이다 (nae-seong-jeog-i-da)

invitation n. 초대 (cho-dae)

invitation card n. 초대장 (cho-dae-jjang)

invite v. 초대하다 (cho-dae-ha-da)

iron n. 다리미 (da-ri-mi); v. 다리미질하다 (da-ri-mi-jil-ha-da)

item n. 사항 (sa-hang), 물건 (mul-geon)

J

jacket *n.* 재킷 (jae-kit), 자켓 (ja-ket)

January *n.* 일월 (il-wol)

Japan *n.* 일본 (il-bon)

Japanese *n.* 일본어 (il-bon-eo), 일본사람 (il-bon-ssa-ram); *adj.* 일본의 (il-bon-ui)

Japanese restaurant *n.* 일본식당 (il-bon-sik-dang), 일본음식점 (il-bon-eum-sik-jeom), 일식집 (il-ssik-jip)

jar *n.* 병 (byeong)

jealous *adj.* 부러운 (bu-reo-un), 부럽다 (bu-reop-da)

jeans *n.* 청바지 (cheong-ba-ji)

jeopardize *v.* 위태롭게 하다 (wi-tae-rop-ge-ha-da)

job *n.* 직업 (jig-eop), 직장 (jik-jang)

jog *v.* 조깅하다 (jo-ging-ha-da)

joint *n.* 관절 (gwan-jeol); *adj.* 연합의 (yeon-hab-ui)

journal *n.* 일기 (il-gi), 저널 (jeo-neol)

journalist *n.* 기자 (gi-ja)

journey *n.* 여행 (yeo-haeng), 여정 (yeo-jeong)

joy *n.* 기쁨 (gi-ppeum)

joyful *adj.* 즐거운 (jeul-geo-un), 즐겁다 (jeul-geop-da)

judge *n.* 판사 (pan-sa); *v.* 판단하다 (pan-dan-ha-da)

juice *n.* 주스 (ju-seu)

July *n.* 칠월 (chul-wol)

jump *v.* 넘다 (neom-tta), 점프하다 (jeom-peu-ha-da)

jump rope *n.* 줄넘기 (jul-leom-kki)

junction *n.* 연합 (yeon-hap), 교차점 (gyo-cha-jjeom)

June *n.* 유월 (yu-wol)

junior *n.* 삼학년 (sam-hang-nyeon)

junior high school *n.* 중학교 (jung-hak-gyo)

junior high school student *n.* 중학생 (jung-hak-saeng)

just *adv.* 그냥 (geu-nyang)

just now *adv.* 방금 (bang-geum), 금방 (geum-bang)

juvenile *n.* 청소년 (cheong-so-nyeon)

K

karaoke (room) *n.* 노래방 (no-rae-bang)

keen *adj.* 심함 (sim-ham), 심하다 (sim-ha-da)

keep *v.* 보관하다 (bo-gwan-ha-da), 지키다 (ji-ki-da)

key *n.* 열쇠 (yeol-ssoe)

kill *v.* 죽이다 (jug-i-da), 살해하다 (sal-hae-ha-da)

kind *n.* 종류 (jong-nyu); *adj.* 친절한 (chin-jeol-han), 친절하다 (chin-jeol-ha-da)

kindness *n.* 친절 (chin-jeol)

king *n.* 왕 (wang)

kitchen *n.* 부엌 (bu-eok), 주방 (ju-bang)

kite *n.* 연 (yeon)

kite-flying *n.* 연날리기 (yeon-nal-li-gi)

kitten *n.* 아기 고양이 (a-gi go-yang-i)

knit *v.* 짜다 (jja-da), 뜨개질하다 (tteu-gae-jil-ha-da)

knock *n.* 노크 (no-keu); *v.* 노크하다 (no-keu-ha-da)

know *v.* 알다 (al-da)

knowledge *n.* 지식 (ji-sik)

Korea *n.* 한국 (han-guk)

Korean *n.* 한국어 (han-gug-eo), 한국사람 (han-guk-sa-ram); *adj.* 한국의 (han-gug-ui)

Korean Airline *n.* 대한항공 (dae-han-hang-gong)

Korean restaurant *n.* 한식집 (han-sik-jip), 한국음식점 (han-gug-eum-sik-jeom), 한국식당 (han-guk-sik-dang)

L

lace *n., v.* 레이스 (re-i-seu), 끈 (kkeun), 끈으로 묶다 (kkeun-eu-ro muk-da)

lacking *adj.* 부족한 (bu-jo-kan), 부족하다 (bu-jo-ka-da)

lake *n.* 호수 (ho-su)

lamp *n.* 램프 (raem-peu)

land *n.* 땅 (ttang), 육지 (yuk-ji)

landlord *n.* 집주인 (jip-ju-in)

landscape *n.* 조경 (jo-gyeong), 풍경 (pung-gyeong)

language *n.* 말 (mal), 언어 (eon-eo)

large *adj.* 큰 (keun), 크다 (keu-da)

last *adj.* 지나간 (ji-na-gan), 지난 (ji-nan), 마지막 (ma-ji-mak)

last night *adv.* 어젯밤 (eo-jet-bam)

last time *adv.* 지난번 (ji-nan-beon), 마지막으로 (ma-ji-mag-eu-ro)

last week *adv.* 지난주 (ji-nan-ju)

last year *adv.* 작년 (jang-nyeon)

late *adj.* 늦은 (neuj-eun), 지각한 (ji-ga-kan), 늦다 (neut-da), 지각하다 (ji-ga-ka-da)

lately *adv.* 최근에 (choe-geun-e)

later *adv.* 나중에 (na-jung-e)

laugh *n.* 웃음 (us-eum); **make someone laugh** 웃기다 (ut-gi-da)

laundry *n.* 빨래 (ppal-lae); **do laundry** *v.* 빨래하다 (ppal-lae-ha-da)

law *n.* 법 (beop), 법률 (beom-nyul)

law school *n.* 법대 (beop-dae)

lawn *n.* 잔디 (jan-di)

lawyer *n.* 변호사 (byeon-ho-sa); **international lawyer** 국제변호사 (guk-je-byeon-ho-sa)

layer *n.* 층 (cheung)

lead *v.* 이끌다 (i-kkeul-da), 리드하다 (ri-deu-ha-da)

leadership *n.* 지도 (ji-do), 지도력 (ji-do-ryeok)

learn *v.* 배우다 (bae-u-da)

least *adj.* 가장 작은 (ga-jang jag-eun), 가장 적은 (ga-jang jeog-eun); **at least** 최소한 (choe-so-han)

leather *n.* 가죽 (ga-juk)

leather shoes *n.* 구두 (gu-du)

leave *v.* 남기다 (nam-gi-da), 떠나다 (tteo-na-da), 맡기다 (mat-gi-da)

left *n.* 왼쪽 (oen-jjok); **turn left** 좌회전하다 (jwa-hoe-jeon-ha-da), 왼쪽으로 돌다 (oen-jjog-eu-ro dol-da)

leg *n.* 다리 (da-ri)

legal *adj.* 법적인 (beop-jeog-in), 적법한 (jeok-beo-pan), 적법하다 (jeok-beo-pa-da)

lemon *n.* 레몬 (re-mon)

lemonade *n.* 레모네이드 (re-mo-ne-i-deu)

lend *v.* 빌려주다 (bil-lyeo-ju-da)

less *adv.* 덜 (deol)

letter *n.* 편지 (pyeon-ji)

lettuce *n.* 상추 (sang-chu)

level *n.* 수준 (su-jun), 차원 (cha-won)

library *n.* 도서관 (do-seo-gwan)

lie *n., v.* 거짓말 (jeo-jin-mal), 거짓말을 하다 (geo-jin-mal-eul ha-da)

lie down *v.* 눕다 (nup-da)

life *n.* 삶 (salm, sam), 생활 (saeng-hwal), 목숨 (mok-sum)

light *adj.* 가벼운 (ga-byeo-un), 가볍다 (ga-byeop-da), 밝은 (balg-eun), 밝다 (balk-da)

like *v.* 좋아하다 (jo-a-ha-da), 좋다 (jo-ta), 마음에 들다 (ma-eum-e deul-da); *prep.* -처럼 (cheo-reom)

likeness *n.* 선호 (seon-ho)

limit *n.* 제한 (je-han)

line *n.* 줄 (jul)

line is busy 통화중이다 (tong-hwa-jung-i-da)

link *n.* 연결 (yeon-gyeol)

lion *n.* 사자 (sa-ja)

lips *n.* 입술 (ip-sul)

liquor *n.* 술 (sul)

listen *v.* 듣다 (deut-da)

listen to music *v.* 음악을 듣다 (eum-ag-eul deut-da)

literature *n.* 문학 (mun-hak)

little *adj.* 작은 (jag-eun), 작다 (jak-da); *adv.* 약간 (yak-gan), 조금 (jo-geum)

little later *adv.* 이따가 (i-tta-ga)

live *n.* 살다 (sal-da)

live together *v.* 모여 살다 (mo-yeo-sal-da)

liver *n.* 간 (gan)

living room *n.* 응접실 (eung-jeop-sil), 거실 (geo-sil)

loan *n.* 융자 (yung-ja)

local *adj.* 지역의 (ji-yeog-ui), 지역적인 (ji-yeok-jeog-in)

location *n.* 위치 (wi-chi), 장소 (jang-so)

lock *n.* 잠금 장치 (jam-geum jang-chi), 잠기다 (jam-gi-da)

lonely *adj.* 외로운 (oe-ro-un), 외롭다 (oe-rop-da)

long *adj.* 긴 (gin), 길다 (gil-da)

long distance *n.,* **long-distance** *adj.* 장거리 (jang-geo-ri)

long-distance telephone call *n.* 장거리 전화 (jang-geo-ri jeon-hwa)

long time ago *adv.* 옛날에 (yen-nal-e)

look *n.* 외모 (oe-mo), 표정 (pyo-jeong); *v.* 보다 (bo-da), 생기다 (saeng-gi-da)

look around *v.* 구경하다 (gu-gyeong-ha-da)

look at *v.* 쳐다보다 (chyeo-da-bo-da)

look for *v.* 찾다 (chat-da)

look for a job *v.* 일자리를 구하다 (il-jja-ri-reul gu-ha-da)

look good on *v.* 어울리다 (eo-ul-li-da)

look over *v.* 살펴보다 (sal-pyeo-bo-da)

lose *v.* 잃다 (il-ta), 잃어버리다 (il-eo-beo-ri-da)

lose weight *v.* 살을 빼다 (sal-eul ppae-da)

loss *n.* 분실 (bun-sil), 손실 (son-sil), 실패 (sil-pae)

lost *adj.* 잃어버린 (il-eo-beo-rin)

lot *n.* 제비 (je-bi), 몫 (mok), 운 (un); **a lot** 많이 (man-i)

loud *adj.* 시끄러운 (si-kkeu-reo-un), 시끄럽다 (si-kkeu-reop-da)

loudspeaker *n.* 확성기 (hwak-seong-gi)

lounge *n.* 휴게실 (hyu-ge-sil)

love *n.* 사랑 (sa-rang); *v.* 사랑하다 (sa-rang-ha-da)

lovely *adj.* 사랑스러운 (sa-rang-seu-reo-un)

low *adj.* 낮은 (naj-eun), 낮다 (nat-da)

lowest *adj.* 최저 (choe-jeo)

luck *n.* 행운 (haeng-un); **luck in the midst of disaster** 불행 중 다행이다 (bul-haeng-jung da-haeng-i-da)

lucky *adj.* 다행이다 (da-haeng-i-da), 행운이다 (haeng-un-i-da)

luggage *n.* 짐 (jim)

lunch *n.* 점심 (jeom-sim)

luster *n.* 윤기 (yun-kki)

M

machine *n.* 기계 (gi-gye)

mad *adj.* 화가 난 (hwa-ga nan), 화가 나다 (hwa-ga na-da), 미친 (mi-chin), 미치다 (mi-chi-da)

magazine *n.* 잡지 (jap-ji)

magpie *n.* 까치 (kka-chi)

mail *n.* 우편물 (u-pyeon-mul), *v.* 부치다 (bu-chi-da)

mail delivery *n.* 우편배달 (u-pyeon-bae-da)l)

mailbox *n.* 우체통 (u-che-tong)

mailman *n.* 우체부 (u-che-bu)

main *adj.* 주요 (ju-yo), 주요한 (ju-yo-han)

mainly *adv.* 주로 (ju-ro)

maintain *v.* 지키다 (ji-ki-da)

major *n.* 전공 (jeon-gong); *adj.* 주요한 (ju-yo-han)

major in *v.* 전공하다 (jeon-gong-ha-da)

majority *n.* 대다수 (dae-da-su)

make *v.* 만들다 (man-deul-da)

make a noise *v.* 떠들다 (tteo-deul-da)

make a plan *v.* 계획을 세우다 (gye-hoeg-eul se-u-da)

make a telephone call *v.* 전화를 걸다 (jeon-hwa-reul geol-da), 전화하다 (jeon-hwa-ha-da)

make an effort *v.* 수고하다 (su-go-ha-da), 노력하다 (no-ryeo-ka-da)

make friends *v.* 친구를 사귀다 (chi-gu-reul sa-gwi-da)

male *n.* 남성 (nam-seong), 남자 (nam-ja)

male student *n.* 남학생 (nam-hak-saeng)

man *n.* 남자 (nam-ja), 사람 (sa-ram)

manage *v.* 다루다 (da-ru-da), 관리하다 (gwal-li-ha-da), 처리하다 (cheo-ri-ha-da)

many *adj.* 많은 (man-eun), 많다 (man-ta); *adv.* 많이 (man-i), 여러 (yeo-reo),

map *n.* 지도 (ji-do)

March *n.* 삼월 (sam-wol)

mark *v.* 표시하다 (pyo-si-ha-da)

market *n.* 상가 (sang-ga), 시장 (si-jang)

marriage *n.* 결혼 (gyeol-hon)

married couple *n.* 부부 (bu-bu)

marry *v.* 결혼하다 (gyeol-hon-ha-da)

mass *n.* 대중 (dae-jung); *adj.* 대중의 (dae-jung-ui), 다량의 (da-ryang-ui)), 한 덩어리의 (han deong-eo-ri-ui)

mass media *n.* 대중매체 (dae-jung-mae-che)

master *n.* 주인 (ju-in), 대가 (dae-ga), 선생 (seon-saeng)

master bedroom *n.* 안방 (an-ppang)

match *v.* 시합 (si-hap)

matchmaker *n.* 중매쟁이 (jung-mae-jaeng-i)

matchmaking *n.* 중매 (jung-mae)

maternal *adj.* 어머니의 (eo-meo-ni-ui)

matter *n.* 일 (il), 문제 (mun-je)

May *n.* 오월 (o-wol)

maybe *adv.* 아마 (a-ma)

me *pron.* 내 (nae), 제 (je) (*humble*)

meal *n.* 식사 (sik-sa); **before a meal** 식전에 (sik-jeon-e); **after a meal** 식후에 (si-ku-e)

mean *n.* 평균 (pyeong-gyun); *v.* 의미하다 (ui-mi-ha-da), 심술궂다 (sim-sul-gut-da)

meaning *n.* 의미 (ui-mi)

means *n.* 방법 (bang-beop), 수단 (su-dan)

meat *n.* 고기 (go-gi)

medical *adj.* 의학적인 (ui-hak-jeog-in), 의학의 (ui-hag-ui)

medical examination *n.* 진찰 (jin-chal)

medical school *n.* 의대 (ui-dae)

medicine *n.* 약 (yak), 의술 (ui-sul)

medieval *adj.* 중세기의 (jung-se-gi-ui), 중세의 (jung-se-ui)

medium *n.* 중간치 (jung-gan-chi), *adj.* 중간의 (jung-gan-ui)

meet *v.* 만나다 (man-na-da), 맞다 (mat-da)

meeting *n.* 회의 (hoe-ui)

melt *adj.* 녹다 (nok-da)

member *n.* 구성원 (gu-seong-won), 일원 (il-won)

memorable *adj.* 기억에 남는 (gi-eog-e nam-neun)

memorize *v.* 외우다 (oe-u-da)

memory *n.* 기억 (gi-eok), 기억력 (gi-eong-nyeok)

mend *v.* 수선하다 (su-seon-ha-da), 개선하다 (gae-seon-ha-da)

mention *v.* 언급하다 (eon-geu-pa-da)

menu *n.* 메뉴 (me-nyu), 차림표 (cha-rim-pyo)

merchandise *n.* 상품 (sang-pum), 물건 (mul-geon); **used merchandise** *n.* 중고품 (jung-go-pum)

mess *n.* 혼란 (hol-lan), 곤란한 상태 (gol-lan-han sang-tae), 더러운 것 (deo-reo-un geot)

message *n.* 메시지 (me-si-ji), 메세지(me-se-ji)

messy *adj.* 지저분한 (ji-jeo-bun-han), 지저분하다 (ji-jeo-bun-ha-da)

metal *n.* 금속 (geum-sok), 금속의 (geum-sog-ui)

method *n.* 방법 (bang-beop)

meticulous *adj.* 매우 신중한 (mae-u sin-jung-han), 소심한 (so-sim-han)

microphone *n.* 마이크 (ma-i-keu)

middle *n.* 중간 (jung-gan), 가운데 (ga-un-de)

middle-aged *adj.* 중년의 (jung-nyeon-ui)

Middle Ages *n.* 중세 (jung-se)

middle school *n.* 중학교 (jung-hak-gyo)

middle school student *n.* 중학생 (jung-hak-saeng)

mild *adj.* 온순한 (on-sun-han), 온화한 (on-hwa-han)

military *n.* 군대 (gun-dae), 군대의 (gun-dae-ui)

milk *n.* 우유 (u-yu)

million *n.* 백만 (baeng-man)

mindlessly *adv.* 정신없이 (jeong-sin-eops-i)

mine *pron.* 내 것 (nae goet), 내 거 (nae kkeo), 제 것 (je geot), 제 거 (je kkeo)

minor *n.* 부전공 (bu-jeon-gong); *adj.* 부수적인 (bu-su-jeog-in)

minute *n.* 분 (bun)

miss *n.* -양 (yang), *v.* 놓치다 (no-chi-da)

miss the bus *v.* 버스를 놓치다 (ppeo-sseu-reul no-chi-da)

mission *n.* 선교 (seon-gyo)

mistake *n.* 실수 (sil-ssu), 잘못 (jal-mot); **make a mistake** 잘못하다 (jal-mo-ta-da), 실수하다 (sil-ssu-ha-da)

mix *v.* 섞다 (seok-da)

mode *n.* 스타일 (seu-ta-il)

model *n.* 모델 (mo-del)

modern *adj.* 현대의 (hyeon-dae-ui), 현대적인 (hyeon-dae-jeog-in)

mom *n.* 엄마 (eom-ma)

moment *n.* 순간 (sun-gan), 잠시 (jam-si)

Monday *n.* 월요일 (wol-yo-il)

money *n.* 돈 (don), 금전 (geum-jeon)

month *n.* 달 (dal), 월 (wol); **every month** 매달 (mae-da)

moonrise *n.* 달뜨는 시각 (dal-tteu-neun si-gak)

more *adv.* 더 (deo)

more or less *adv.* 다소 (da-so)

morning *n.* 아침 (a-chim)

mosquito *n.* 모기 (mo-gi)

most *n.* 최상 (choe-sang); *adj.* 가장 (ga-jang)

mostly *adv.* 대부분 (dae-bu-bun)

mother *n.* 어머니 (eo-meo-ni), 어머님 (eo-meo-nim)

mother-in-law *n.* 시어머니 (si-eo-meo-ni), 시어머님 (si-eo-meo-nim)

motion *n.* 운동 (un-dong), 동작 (dong-jak)

mountain *n.* 산 (san)

mountain climbing *n.* 등산 (deung-san)

mountaintop *n.* 산꼭대기 (san-kkok-dae-gi)

mourn *v.* 신음하다 (sin-eum-ha-da)

mouse *n.* 쥐 (jwi)

mousse *n.* 무스 (mu-sseu)

mouth *v.* 입 (ip)

move *v.* 움직이다 (um-jig-i-da), 이사하다 (i-sa-ha-da), 옮기다 (om-gi-da)

movement *n.* 움직임 (um-jig-im)

movie *n.* 영화 (yeong-hwa)

movie theater *n.* 극장 (geuk-jang), 영화관 (yeong-hwa-gwan)

much *adj.* 많다 (man-ta), 많은 (man-eun); *adv.* 많이 (man-i); **as much as possible** 되도록 많이 (doe-do-rok man-i)

muffler *n.* 머플러 (meo-peul-leo)

mug *n.* 머그 잔 (meo-geu jan), 머그 (meo-geu)

muscle *n.* 근육 (geun-yuk)

museum *n.* 박물관 (bang-mul-gwan)

mushroom *n.* 버섯 (beo-seot)

music *n.* 음악 (eum-ak)

musical *n., adj.* 뮤지컬 (myu-ji-keol)

musical instruments *n.* 악기 (ak-gi)

musician *n.* 음악가 (eum-ak-ga)

mystery *n.* 미스터리 (mi-seu-te-ri)

mysterious *adj.* 알 수 없는 (al ssu eom-neun)

mystery novel *n.* 추리소설 (chu-ri-so-seol)

N

name *n.* 이름 (i-reum), 성함 (seong-ham)

narrow *adj.* 좁은 (job-eun), 좁다 (jop-da)

nasal *adj.* 코의 (ko-ui)

nasal congestion *n.* 코막힘 (ko-ma-kim); **have nasal congestion** 코가 막히다 (ko-ga ma-ki-da)

nation *n.* 국가 (guk-ga)

national *adj.* 국가의 (guk-ga-ui), 국립의 (gung-nib-ui)

national museum *n.* 국립 박물관 (gung-nip bang-mul-gwan)

national park *n.* 국립공원 (gung-nip-gong-won)

nationality *n.* 민족 (min-jok)

nationwide *adj.* 전국적으로 (jeon-guk-jeog-eu-ro)

natural *adj.* 자연적인 (ja-yeon-jeog-in)

naturally *adv.* 자연적으로 (ja-yeon-jeog-eu-ro)

nature *n.* 자연 (ja-yeon), 자연환경 (ja-yeon-hwan-gyeong)

nausea *n.* 체기 (che-kki), 체함 (che-ham); **have nausea** 체하다 (che-ha-da)

navy *n.* 해군 (hae-gun)

navy blue *n.* 감색 (gam-saek); *adj.* 감색의 (gam-saeg-ui)

near *adv.* 근처 (geun-cheo)

nearby *adj., adv.* 근처 (geun-cheo)

nearly *adv.* 거의 (geo-ui), -을 뻔하다 (eul ppeon-ha-da)

necessary *adj.* 필수적인 (pil-ssu-jeog-in), 필수적이다 (pil-ssu-jeog-i-da), 필요하다 (pil-yo-ha-da)

necessity *n.* 필수품 (pil-ssu-pum), 필수 (pil-ssu)

neck *n.* 목 (mok)

necklace *n.* 목걸이 (mok-geol-i)

need *n.* 필요 (pil-yo); *v.* 필요하다 (pil-yo-ha-da)

negotiate *v.* 협상하다 (hyeop-sang-ha-da)

negotiation *n.* 협상 (hyeop-sang)

neighbor *n.* 이웃 (i-ut)

neighborhood *n.* 근처 (geun-cheo), 동네 (dong-ne); *adj.* 이웃의 (i-us-ui)

nervous *adj.* 긴장한 (gin-jang-han), 긴장하다 (gin-jang-ha-da)

neutral *adj.* 중성의 (jung-seong-ui), 중간의 (jung-gan-ui)

never *adv.* 절대로 .... -않다 (jeol-ttae-ro ...an-ta)

nevertheless *conj.* 그럼에도 불구하고 (geu-reom-e-do bul-gu-ha-go)

new *adj.* 새로운 (sae-ro-un), 새 (sae)

New Year's Day *n.* 설날 (seol-lal)

newly *adv.* 새로 (sae-ro)

newlyweds *n.* 신혼 (sin-hon), 신혼부부 (sin-hon-bu-bu)

news *n.* 뉴스 (nyu-seu)

newspaper *n.* 신문 (sin-mun)

next *adj.* 다음 (da-eum), 다음의 (da-eum-ui)

next door *adj.* 옆집 (yeop-jip)

next to *adj.* 옆 (yeop), 옆의 (yeop-ui)

next year *n.* 내년 (nae-nyeon)

nice *adj.* 상냥한 (sang-nyang-han), 친절한 (chin-jeol-han), 상냥하다 (sang-nyang-ha-da), 친절하다 (chin-jeol-ha-da)

night *n.* 밤 (bam)

nine *n.* 아홉 (a-hop), 구 (gu)

ninety *n.* 아흔 (a-heun)

no *adv.* 아니오 (a-ni-o)

no fun *adj.* 재미없는 (jae-mi-eom-neun), 재미없다 (jae-mi-eop-da)

no matter how *prep.* 아무리 (a-mu-ri)

no parking *n.* 주차금지 (ju-cha-geum-ji)

nobody *pron.* 아무도 (a-mu-do)

noise *n.* 소리 (so-ri), 소음 (so-eum); **make a noise** 떠들다 (tteo-deul-da)

noisy *adj.* 시끄러운 (si-kkeu-reo-un), 시끄럽다 (si-kkeu-reop-da)

noodle *n.* 면 (myeon), 국수 (guk-su)

normal *adj.* 정상의 (jeong-sang-ui), 정상이다 (jeong-sang-i-da)

north *n.* 북 (buk), 북쪽 (buk-jjok)

North Korea *n.* 북한 (bu-kan)

northern *adj.* 북쪽의 (buk-jjog-ui)

nose *n.* 코 (ko)

not *adv.* 안 (an), -지 않다 (ji an-ta)

not at all *adv.* 도저히 (do-jeo-hi), 통 (tong)

not enough *adj.* 모자라다 (mo-ja-ra-da), 부족하다 (bu-jo-ka-da)

not exist *v.* 없다 (eop-da)

not have *v.* 없다 (eop-da)

not know *v.* 모르다 (mo-reu-da)

not know what to do *v.* 어쩔 줄 모르다 (eo-jjeol jjul mo-reu-da)

not particularly *adv.* 별로 (byeol-lo)

not really *adv.* 별로 (byeol-lo)

not recognize *v.* 몰라보다 (mol-la-bo-da)

note *n.* 메모 (me-mo); *v.* 메모하다 (me-mo-ha-da)

notebook *n.* 공책 (gong-chaek), 노트 (no-teu)

nothing *pron.* 아무 것도 (a-mu-geot-do)

notice *n.* 주의 (ju-ui), 통지 (tong-ji), 예고 (ye-go)

novel *n.* 소설 (so-seol); *adj.* 신기하다 (sin-gi-ha-da)

novelty *n.* 신기함 (sin-gi-ham), 새로운 것 (sae-ro-un-geot)

November *n.* 십일월 (sib-il-wol)

now *adv.* 지금 (ji-geum), 이제 (i-je)

nuclear *adj.* 핵의 (haeg-ui), 원자핵의 (won-ja-haeg-ui)

number *n.* 숫자 (sut-ja), 번호 (beon-ho)

nurse *n.* 간호사 (gan-ho-sa), 간호원 (gan-ho-won)

nutrition *n.* 영양 (yeong-yang), 영양소 (yeong-yang-so)

nutritious *adj.* 영양의 (yeong-yang-ui), 영양분이 있는 (yeong-yang-bun-i in-neun)

O

o'clock *n.* -시 (si)

obligation *n.* 의무 (ui-mu), 책임 (chaeg-im)

obstacle *n.* 장애 (jang-ae), 장애물 (jang-ae-mul)

obtain *v.* 얻다 (eot-da), 획득하다 (hoek-deu-ka-da)

obvious *adj.* 명백한 (myeong-bae-kan)

occupation *n.* 직업 (jig-eop)

occur *v.* (일이) 일어나다 ([il-i] il-eo-na-da), (일이) 발생하다 ([il-i] bal-ssaeng-ha-da)

ocean *n.* 바다 (ba-da), 대양 (dae-yang)

October *n.* 시월 (si-wol)

odd *adj.* 홀수의 (hol-ssu-ui), 짝이 안 맞는 (jjag-i an man-neun), 기묘한 (gi-myo-han)

offer *v.* 제안하다 (je-an-ha-da)

office *n.* 사무실 (sa-mu-sil)

officer *n.* 장교 (jang-gyo), 공무원 (gong-mu-won)

official *adj.* 공식적인 (gong-sik-jeog-in)

often *adv.* 자주 (ja-ju)

old *adj.* 늙은 (neulg-eun), 늙다 (neulk-da), 낡은 (nalg-eun), 낡다 (nalk-da)

once *adv.* 한번 (han-beon)

once in a while *adv.* 가끔 (ga-kkeum)

oncoming *adj.* 접근하는 (jeop-geun-ha-neun), 다가오는 (da-ga-o-neun)

one *n.* 일 (il), 하나 (ha-na)

one time *adv.* 한번 (han-beon)

one-way *n.* 일방통행 (il-bang-tong-haeng); *adj.* 일방통행의 (il-bang-tong-haeng-ui)

one-way ticket *n.* 편도표 (pyeon-do-pyo)

onion *n.* 양파 (yang-pa)

only *adv.* 단지 (dan-ji), -만 (man)

open *v.* 열다 (yeol-da)

opening *n.* 개장 (gae-jang)

opera *n.* 오페라 (o-pe-ra)

operation *n.* 수술 (su-sul)

opponent *n.* 상대편 (sang-dae-pyeon)

opportunity *n.* 기회 (gi-hoe)

opposed *adj.* 반대의 (ban-dae-ui), 대립된 (dae-rip-doen)

opposite *n.* 반대 (ban-dae)

optician *n.* 검안의 (geom-an-ui), 안경점 (an-gyeong-jeom)

or *conj.* -거나 (geo-na), -이나 (i-na)

orange *n.* 주황색 (ju-hwang-saek), 오렌지색 (o-ren-ji-saek); *adj.* 주황색의 (ju-hwang-saeg-ui), 오렌지색의 (o-ren-ji-saeg-ui)

orchestra *n.* 오케스트라 (o-ke-seu-teu-ra), 관현악단 (gwan-hyeon-ak-dan)

order *n.* 명령 (myeong-nyeong), 주문 (ju-mun), 차례 (cha-rye); *v.* 주문하다 (ju-mun-ha-da), 음식을 시키다 (eum-sig-eul si-ki-da)

organ *n.* 오르간 (o-reu-gan), 기관 (gi-gwan)

organic *adj.* 유기체의 (yu-gi-che-ui), 유기적 (yu-gi-jeok)

organic food *n.* 자연식품 (ja-yeon-sik-pum)

organization *n.* 조직 (jo-jik), 조직체 (jo-jik-che), 단체 (dan-che)

organize *v.* 조직하다 (jo-ji-ka-da), 구성하다 (gu-seong-ha-da)

originally *adv.* 원래 (wol-lae)

other *adv.* 다른 (da-reun)

out *n.* 밖 (bak); *adv.* 밖에 (bakk-e)

out of order *adj.* 고장난 (go-jang-nan), 고장나다 (go-jang-na-da)

outdoors *n.* 실외 (sil-oe), 야외 (ya-oe)

outer *adj.* 밖의 (bakk-ui), 외부의 (oe-bu-ui)

outgoing *adj.* 활달한 (hwal-ttal-han), 활달하다 (hwal-ttal-ha-da)

outside *n., adv.* 밖 (bak)

over *prep., adv.* 넘다 (neom-tta), 끝나다 (kkeun-na-da)

overeat *v.* 과식하다 (gwa-si-ka-da)

overlap *v.* 겹치다 (gyeop-chi-da)

overpass *n.* 육교 (yuk-gyo)

own *v.* 가지다 (ga-ji-da), 소유하다 (so-yu-ha-da)

P

pack *v.* 포장하다 (po-jang-ha-da)

package *n.* 소포 (so-po)

packing *n.* 포장 (po-jang)

pain *n.* 고통 (go-tong), 아픔 (a-peum)

painful *adj.* 고통스러운 (go-tong-seu-reo-un), 아픈 (a-peun)

painkiller *n.* 진통제 (jin-tong-je)

paint *n.* 페인트 (pe-in-teu); *v.* 그리다 (geu-ri-da), 칠을
하다 (chil-eul ha-da)

painter *n.* 미술가 (mi-sul-ga), 화가 (hwa-ga)

painting *n.* 그림 (geu-rim)

pair *n.* 짝 (jjak)

pan *n.* 팬 (paen); **frying pan** 프라이팬 (peu-ra-i-paen)

pants *n.* 바지 (ba-ji)

paper *n.* 종이 (jong-i), 서류 (seo-ryu)

paper cup *n.* 종이컵 (jong-i-keop)

paper plate *n.* 종이접시 (jong-i-jeop-si)

parcel *n.* 소포 (so-po)

parents *n.* 부모 (bu-mo)

park *n.* 공원 (gong-won); *v.* 주차하다 (ju-cha-ha-da),
차를 세우다 (cha-reul se-u-da)

parking lot *n.* 주차장 (ju-cha-jang)

parliament *n.* 국회 (gu-koe), 의회 (ui-hoe)

part *n.* 부분 (bu-bun); *v.* 헤어지다 (he-eo-ji-da)

part-time job *n.* 아르바이트 (a-reu-ba-i-teu)

participate *v.* 참석하다 (cham-seo-ka-da)

particular *adj.* 특정한 (teuk-jeong-han)

particularly *adv.* 특히 (teu-ki)

partly *adv.* 부분적으로 (bu-bun-jeog-eu-ro)

partner *n.* 파트너 (pa-teu-neo), 협동자 (hyeop-dong-ja),
배우자 (bae-u-ja)

party *n.* 파티 (pa-ti)

pass *v.* 지나가다 (ji-na-ga-da), 합격하다 (hap-gyeo-ka-
da), 통과하다 (tong-gwa-ha-da), 전하다 (jeon-ha-da)

pass away *v.* 돌아가시다 (dol-a-ga-si-da)

pass by *v.* 지나가다 (ji-na-ga-da), 지내다 (ji-nae-da)

passerby *n.* 지나가는 사람 (ji-na-ga-neun sa-ram), 행인
(haeng-in)

passive *adj.* 소극적인 (so-geuk-jeog-in), 소극적이다 (so-
geuk-jeog-i-da)

passport *n.* 여권 (yeo-kkwon)

pastime *n.* 오락 (o-rak), 소일거리 (so-il-kkeo-ri)

pastor *n.* 목사님 (mok-sa-nim)

paternal *adj.* 아버지의 (a-beo-ji-ui)

path *n.* 길 (gil), 작은 길 (jag-eun gil), 통로 (tong-no)

patience *n.* 인내심 (in-nae-sim)

patient *adj.* 인내심이 많은 (in-nae-sim-i man-eun), 인내심이 많다 (in-nae-sim-i man-ta), 환자 (hwan-ja)

pattern *n.* 무늬 (mu-nui), mu-ni), 패턴 (pae-tteon)

pay *v.* 돈을 내다 (don-eul nae-da), 돈을 지불하다 (don-eul ji-bul-ha-da)

pay by credit card *v.* 카드로 내다 (ka-deu-ro nae-da)

payment *n.* 지불 (ji-bul), 월급 (wol-geup)

pea *n.* 콩 (kong)

peace *n.* 평화 (pyeong-hwa)

peacefully *adv.* 평화롭게 (pyeong-hwa-rop-ge)

pear *n.* 배 (bae)

pen *n.* 펜 (pen), 볼펜 (bol-pen)

pencil *n.* 연필 (yeon-pil)

people *n.* 사람들 (sa-ram-deul), 민족 (min-jok)

pepper *n.* 고추 (go-chu)

percentage *n.* 퍼센트 (peo-sen-teu)

perhaps *adv.* 아마 (a-ma)

period *n.* 기간 (gi-gan), 생리기간 (saeng-ni-gi-gan)

permanent (hairstyle) *n.* 파마 (pa-ma); **get a permanent** *v.* 파마하다 (pa-ma-ha-da)

permanent with large/small rollers *n.* 굵은/가는 파마 (gulg-eun/ga-neun pa-ma)

person *n.* 사람 (sa-ram)

personal *adj.* 개인적인 (gae-in-jeog-in)

personality *n.* 성격 (seong-kkyeok)

personally *adv.* 개인적으로 (gae-in-jeog-eu-ro)

pharmacy *n.* 약국 (yak-guk), 약방 (yak-bang)

photo *n.* 사진 (sa-jin)

photocopy *n.* 복사 (bok-sa); *v.* 복사하다 (bok-sa-ha-da)

photograph *n.* 사진 (sa-jin)

physical *adj.* 육체의 (yuk-che-ui), 물질의 (mul-jjil-ui), 자연의 (ja-yeon-ui), 물리학의 (mul-li-hag-ui)

physical checkup *n.* 신체검사 (sin-che-geom-sa)

physical therapist *n.* 물리치료사 (mul-li-chi-ryo-sa)

piano *n.* 피아노 (pi-a-no); **play piano** 피아노를 치다 (pi-a-no-reul chi-da)

pick out *v.* 뽑다 (ppop-da)

pick up a package *v.* 소포를 찾다 (so-po-reul chat-da)

pick up *v.* 따다 (tta-da), 집다 (jip-da)

picnic *n.* 소풍 (so-pung)

picture *n.* 그림 (geu-rim), 사진 (sa-jin); **take a picture** 사진을 찍다 (sa-jin-eul jjik-da)

picture frame *n.* 사진틀 (sa-jin-teul)

piece *n.* 조각 (jo-gak), 쪽 (jjok)

pile up *v.* 쌓아놓다 (ssa-a-no-ta), 쌓이다 (ssa-i-da)

pineapple *n.* 파인애플 (pa-in-ae-peul)

ping-pong *n.* 탁구 (tak-gu)

pink *n.* 분홍색 (bun-hong-saek); *adj.* 분홍색의 (bun-hong-saeg-ui)

place *n.* 장소 (jang-so)

plain *adj.* 평범한 (pyeong-beom-han), 밋밋한 (min-mi-tan)

plan *n.* 계획 (gye-hoek); *v.* 계획하다 (gye-hoe-ka-da); **make plans** 계획을 짜다 (gye-hoeg-eul jja-da)

plane *n.* 평면 (pyeong-myeon), 비행기 (bi-haeng-gi), 평평한 (pyeong-pyeong-han)

planet *n.* 혹성 (hok-seong), 유성 (yu-seong)

plant *n.* 식물 (sing-mul)

plastic *n.* 플라스틱 (peul-la-seu-tik), 비닐 (bi-nil)

platform *n.* 플랫폼 (peul-laet-pom), 교단 (gyo-dan)

play *v.* 놀다 (nol-da)

play basketball *v.* 농구하다 (nong-gu-ha-da)

play tennis *v.* 테니스를 치다 (te-ni-seu-reul chi-da)

player *n.* 운동선수 (un-dong-seon-su)

playground *n.* 운동장 (un-dong-jang)

plaza *n.* 광장 (gwang-jang)

pleasant *adj.* 즐거운 (jeul-geo-un), 기쁜 (gi-ppeun), 즐겁다 (jeul-geop-da), 기쁘다 (gi-ppeu-da)

please *v.* -아/어 주세요 (a/eo ju-se-yo), 기쁘게 하다 (gi-ppeu-ge ha-da)

plot *n.* 플롯 (peul-lot), 줄거리 (jul-geo-ri)

pluck *v.* 따다 (tta-da)

p.m. *n.* 오후 (o-hu)

poem *n.* 시 (si)

poet *n.* 시인 (si-in)

point *n.* 점 (jeom); *v.* 지적하다 (ji-jeo-ka-da)

poison *n.* 독 (dok), 독성 (dok-seong)

poisonous *adj.* 독성의 (dok-seong-ui), 독성이 있는 (dok-seong-i in-neun)

police *n.* 경찰 (gyeong-chal)

police station *n.* 경찰서 (gyeong-chal-sseo)

political science *n.* 정치학 (jeong-chi-hak)

politician *n.* 정치인 (jeong-chi-in)

politics *n.* 정치 (jeong-chi)

poor *adj.* 가난한 (ga-nan-han), 가난하다 (ga-nan-ha-da), 불쌍한 (bul-ssang-han), 불쌍하다 (bul-ssang-ha-da)

popular *adj.* 대중 (dae-jung), 대중적인 (dae-jung-jeog-in)

popularity *n.* 인기 (in-kki)

population *n.* 인구 (in-gu)

pork *n.* 돼지고기 (dwae-ji-go-gi)

port *n.* 항구 (hang-gu), 항구도시 (hang-gu-do-si)

position *n.* 위치 (wi-chi)

positive *adj.* 적극적인 (jeok-geuk-jeog-in), 적극적이다 (jeok-geuk-jeog-i-da)

possess *v.* 가지다 (ga-ji-da), 소유하다 (so-yu-ha-da)

possibility *n.* 가능성 (ga-neung-sseong)

possible *adj.* 가능한 (ga-neung-han), 가능하다 (ga-neung-ha-da)

post office *n.* 우체국 (u-che-guk)

post office clerk *n.* 우체국 직원 (u-che-guk jig-won)

postage *n.* 우편요금 (u-pyeon-nyo-geum)

postcard *n.* 우편엽서 (u-pyeon-nyeop-seo)

potato *n.* 감자 (gam-ja)

power *n.* 힘 (him)

powerful *adj.* 힘이 있는 (him-i in-neun), 힘이 있다 (him-i it-da)

practical *adj.* 실제적인 (sil-jje-jeog-in), 실제적이다 (sil-jje-jeog-i-da), 실리적인 (sil-li-jeog-in), 실리적이다 (sil-li-jeog-i-da)

practice *n.* 연습 (yeon-seup); *v.* 연습하다 (yeon-seu-pa-da)

pray *v.* 기도하다 (gi-do-ha-da)

prayer *n.* 기도 (gi-do)

precise *adj.* 간략한 (gal-lya-kan), 간략하다 (gal-lya-ka-da)

prefer *v.* 우대하다 (u-dae-ha-da), 선호하다 (seon-ho-ha-da)

prepare *v.* 준비하다 (jun-bi-ha-da)

prepare food *v.* 음식을 차리다 (eum-sig-eul cha-ri-da)

prescription *n.* 처방전 (cheo-bang-jeon)

present *n.* 선물 (seon-mul)

president *n.* 사장 (sa-jang), 대통령 (dae-tong-nyeong);
    vice president 부사장 (bu-sa-jang), 부통령 (bu-tong-
    nyeong)

press *n.* 신문사 (sin-mun-sa); *v.* 누르다 (nu-reu-da),

pressure *n.* 압력 (am-nyeok), 스트레스 (seu-teu-re-sseu)

pretty *adj.* 예쁜 (ye-ppeun), 예쁘다 (ye-ppeu-da)

prevent *v.* 예방하다 (ye-bang-ha-da)

price *n.* 가격 (ga-gyeok)

prices *n.* 물가 (mul-kka)

priest *n.* 성직자 (seong-jik-ja)

print *n.* 프린트 (peu-rin-teu); *v.* 프린트하다 (peu-rin-teu-
    ha-da)

prison *n.* 감옥 (gam-ok)

prisoner *n.* 죄수 (joe-su)

privilege *n.* 특권 (teuk-gwon); *v.* 특권을 주다 (teuk-
    gwon-eul ju-da)

prize *n.* 상 (sang), 상품 (sang-pum)

probable *adj.* 있음직한 (iss-eum-ji-kan), 있음직한 일
    (iss-eum-ji-kan il)

probably *adv.* 아마 (a-ma)

problem *n.* 문제 (mun-je)

produce *v.* 생산하다 (saeng-san-ha-da), 만들어내다
    (man-deul-eo-nae-da)

product *n.* 생산품 (saeng-san-pum)

production *n.* 생산 (saeng-san)

profession *n.* 전문직 (jeon-mun-jik), 전문 (jeon-mun),
    직업 (jig-eop)

professor *n.* 교수님 (gyo-su-nim)

profit *n.* 이익 (i-ik), 이윤 (i-yun)

program *n.* 프로그램 (peu-ro-geu-raem)

promise *n.* 약속 (yak-sok); *v.* 약속하다 (yak-so-ka-da)

pronounce *v.* 발음하다 (bal-eum-ha-da)

pronunciation *n.* 발음 (bal-eum)

proof *n.* 증거 (jeung-geo), 증명 (jeung-myeong)

proper *adj.* 적당한 (jeok-dang-han), 적당하다 (jeok-
    dang-ha-da)

properly *adv.* 제대로 (je-dae-ro)

prosecute *v.* 해내다 (hae-nae-da), 기소하다 (gi-so-ha-da)

prosecutor *n.* 검사 (geom-sa)

protect *v.* 보호하다 (bo-ho-ha-da)

protection *n.* 보호 (bo-ho)

prudent *adj.* 신중한 (sin-jung-han), 신중하다 (sin-jung-ha-da)

pub *n.* 술집 (sul-jjip)

public *adj.* 공공의 (gong-gong-ui), 대중의 (dae-jung-ui), 공중의 (gong-jung-ui)

public bath *n.* 대중 목욕탕 (dae-jung mog-yok-tang)

public restroom *n.* 공중화장실 (gong-jung-hwa-jang-sil)

public transportation *n.* 대중교통 (dae-jung-gyo-tong)

publish *v.* 발행하다 (bal-haeng-ha-da), 발간하다 (bal-gan-ha-da)

pumpkin *n.* 호박 (ho-bak)

pupil *n.* 제자 (je-ja), 학생 (hak-saeng)

puppet *n.* 인형 (in-hyeong)

puppy *n.* 강아지 (gang-a-ji)

purchase *v.* 사다 (sa-da), 구입하다 (gu-i-pa-da)

pure *adj.* 순수한 (sun-su-han), 순수하다 (sun-su-ha-da)

purple *n.* 보라색 (bo-ra-saek); *adj.* 보라색의 (bo-ra-saeg-ui)

purpose *n.* 목적 (mok-jeok)

push *v.* 밀다 (mal-da), 강요하다 (gang-yo-ha-da)

put *v.* 갖다 놓다 (gat-da-no-ta), 두다 (du-da), 얹다 (eon-tta), 넣다 (neo-ta)

put a stamp on *v.* 우표를 붙이다 (u-pyo-reul bu-chi-da)

put down *v.* 놓다 (no-ta)

put into *v.* 담다 (dam-tta)

put on *v.* 옷을 입다 (os-eul ip-da), 신발을 신다 (sin-bal-eul sin-tta), 안경을 끼다 (an-gyeong-eul kki-da), 모자를 쓰다 (mo-ja-reul sseu-da), 시계를 차다 (si-gye-reul cha-da)

Q

quality *n.* 질 (jil)

quantity *n.* 양 (yang)

queen *n.* 여왕 (yeo-wang), 왕비 (wang-bi)

question *n.* 질문 (jil-mun)

quick *adj.* 빠른 (ppa-reun), 빠르다 (ppa-reu-da)

quickly *adv.* 빨리 (ppal-li)

quiet *adj.* 조용한 (jo-yong-han), 한산한 (han-san-han), 조용하다 (jo-yong-ha-da), 한산하다 (han-san-ha-da)

quietly *adv.* 조용하게 (jo-yong-ha-ge)

quit *v.* 그만두다 (geu-man-du-da), 끊다 (kkeun-ta)
quite *adv.* 완전히 (wan-jeon-hi), 아주 (a-ju)

R

radio *n.* 라디오 (ra-di-o)
radish *n.* 무 (mu)
rail *n.* 레일 (re-il)
railroad *n.* 기찻길 (gi-chat-gil)
rain *n.* 비 (bi); *v.* 비가 오다 (bi-ga o-da)
raincoat *n.* 비옷 (bi-ot)
raise *v.* 기르다 (gi-reu-da), 올리다 (ol-li-da)
ramen *n.* 라면 (ra-myeon)
rare *adj.* 드문 (deu-mun), 드물다 (deu-mul-da)
rather *adv.* 오히려 (o-hi-ryeo), 차라리 (cha-ra-ri)
raw *adj.* 날- (nal), 날것의 (nal-geos-ui), 익지 않은 (ik-ji an-eun)
react *v.* 반응하다 (ban-eung-ha-da)
reaction *n.* 반응 (ban-eung)
read *v.* 읽다 (ilk-da), 독서하다 (dok-seo-ha-da)
reading *n.* 독서 (dok-seo)
ready *adj.* 준비된 (jun-bi-doen), 준비되다 (jun-bi-doe-da)
real *adj.* 진짜 (jin-jja), 진짜의 (jin-jja-ui)
reality *n.* 현실 (hyeon-sil), 진실 (jin-sil), 사실 (sa-sil)
realize *v.* 느끼다 (neu-kki-da), 깨닫다 (kkae-da-t-da)
really *adv.* 정말 (jeong-mal), 참 (cham)
reason *n.* 이유 (i-yu)
reasonable *adj.* 이해할 수 있는 (i-hae-hal ssu in-neun), 납득할 수 있는 (nap-deu-kal ssu in-neun)
reasoning *n.* 추리 (chu-ri)
receipt *n.* 영수증 (yeong-su-jeung)
receive *v.* 받다 (bat-da)
recent *adj.* 최근 (choe-geun), 최근의 (choe-geun-ui)
recently *adv.* 최근에 (choe-geun-e)
recipe *n.* 처방 (cheo-bang), 조리법 (jo-ri-ppeop), 만드는 법 (man-deu-neun beop)
recognition *n.* 인식 (in-sik), 알아봄 (al-a-bom)
recognize *v.* 알아보다 (al-a-bo-da), 인식하다 (in-si-ka-da)
recommend *v.* 추천하다 (chu-cheon-ha-da)

recommendation *n.* 추천 (chu-cheon), 추천서 (chu-cheon-seo)

record *n.* 레코드 (re-ko-deu); *v.* 기록하다 (gi-ro-ka-da), 녹음하다 (nog-eum-ha-da), 녹화하다 (no-kwa-ha-da)

record store *n.* 음악사 (eum-ak-sa), 레코드 가게 (re-ko-deu ga-ge)

recover *v.* 낫다 (nat-da), 회복하다 (hoe-bo-ka-da)

recreation *n.* 오락 (o-rak), 레크레이션 (re-keu-re-i-syeon)

recruit *v.* 모집하다 (mo-ji-pa-da)

red *n.* 빨간색 (ppal-gan-saek); *adj.* 빨간 (ppal-gan), 빨갛다 (ppal-ga-ta)

reduce *v.* 줄이다 (jul-i-da)

refill *v.* 다시 채우다 (da-si chae-u-da), 다시 채움 (da-si chae-um)

refreshing *adj.* 상쾌한 (sang-kwae-han), 상쾌하다 (sang-kwae-ha-da)

refrigerator *n.* 냉장고 (naeng-jang-go)

refuse *v.* 거절하다 (geo-jeol-ha-da)

regarding *prep.* -에 대한 (e dae-han), -에 대해서 (e dae-hae-seo)

region *n.* 지방 (ji-bang), 지역 (ji-yeok)

register *n.* 카운터 (ka-un-teo); *v.* 등록하다 (deung-no-ka-da)

registered mail *n.* 등기우편 (deung-gi-u-pyeon)

regret *v.* 후회하다 (hu-hoe-ha-da)

regular *adj.* 규칙적인 (gyu-chik-jeog-in), 규칙적이다 (gyu-chik-jeog-i-da)

regular price *n.* 정가 (jeong-kka)

regulation *n.* 규칙 (gyu-chik)

relation *n.* 관계 (gwan-gye)

relationship *n.* 관계 (gwan-gye), 사이 (sa-i)

relative *n.* 친척 (chin-cheok)

relatively *adv.* 비교적 (bi-gyo-jeok)

relics *n.* 유적 (yu-jeok), 유물 (yu-mul)

relieve *v.* 경감하다 (gyeong-gam-ha-da), 안도하게 하다 (an-do-ha-ge ha-da), 구원하다 (gu-won-ha-da), 해임하다 (hae-im-ha-da)

relieve stress *v.* 스트레스를 풀다 (seu-teu-re-seu-reul pul-da)

religion *n.* 종교 (jong-gyo)

religious *adj.* 종교적인 (jong-gyo-jeog-in)

remain *v.* 남다 (nam-tta)

remain in one's memory *v.* 기억에 남다 (gi-eog-e nam-tta)

remember *v.* 기억하다 (gi-eo-ka-da), 기억나다 (gi-eong-na-da)

remind *v.* 생각나게 하다 (saeng-gang-na-ge ha-da), 기억나게 하다 (gi-eong-na-ge ha-da)

reminder *n.* 생각나게 하는 것 (saeng-gang-na-ge ha-neun geot), 생각나게 하는 사람 (saeng-gang-na-ge ha-neun sa-ram), 독촉장 (dok-chok-jang)

renew *v.* 갱신하다 (gaeng-sin-ha-da), 새롭게 하다 (sae-rop-ge ha-da)

rent *v.* 빌려주다 (bil-lyeo-ju-da), 빌리다 (bil-li-da)

rental car *n.* 렌트카 (ren-teu-ka)

repair *v.* 고치다 (go-chi-da)

repeat *v.* 반복하다 (ban-bo-ka-da)

replace *v.* 제자리에 놓다 (je-ja-ri-e no-ta), 대신하다 (dae-sin-ha-da), 되돌리다 (doe-dol-li-da)

replacement *n.* 제자리에 둠 (je-ja-ri-e dum), 교체 (gyo-che), 바꾸어 놓음 (ba-kku-eo no-eum)

reply *v.* 응답하다 (eung-da-pa-da)

reporter *n.* 기자 (gi-ja)

represent *v.* 대표하다 (dae-pyo-ha-da)

representative *n.* 대표자 (dae-pyo-ja); *adj.* 대표적인 (dae-pyo-jeog-in)

reputation *n.* 평판 (pyeong-pan), 명성 (myeong-seong)

request *n.* 요청 (yo-cheong); *v.* 요청하다 (yo-cheong-ha-da)

required *adj.* 필수의 (pil-ssu-ui)

requirement *n.* 필수 (pil-ssu)

rescue *v.* 구하다 (gu-ha-da), 구조하다 (gu-jo-ha-da)

research *n.* 연구 (yeon-gu); *v.* 연구하다 (yeon-gu-ha-da)

resemble *adj.* 닮은 (dalm-eun), 닮다 (dam-tta)

reservation *n.* 예약 (ye-yak); **make a reservation** 예약하다 (ye-ya-ka-da)

reserve *v.* 예약하다 (ye-ya-ka-da)

residence *n.* 주거지 (ju-geo-ji)

responsible *adj.* 책임이 있는 (chaeg-im-i in-neun), 책임이 있다 (chaeg-im-i it-da), 책임감이 강한 (chaeg-im-gam-i gang-han), 책임감이 강하다 (chaeg-im-gam-i gang-ha-da)

rest *n.* 휴식 (hyu-sik), 나머지 (na-meo-ji); **take a rest** 쉬다 (swi-da), 휴식을 취하다 (hyu-sig-eul chwi-ha-da)

restaurant *n.* 식당 (sik-dang), 음식점 (eum-sik-jeom)

restroom *n.* 화장실 (hwa-jang-sil)

result *n.* 결과 (gyeol-gwa)

return *v.* 돌아오다 (dol-a-o-da), 돌려주다 (dol-lyeo-ju-da)

reward *n.* 보상 (bo-sang)

rewarding *adj.* 득이 되는 (deug-i doe-neun), 가치가 있는 (ga-chi-ga in-neun)

rice *n.* 쌀 (ssal), 밥 (bap)

rice cake *n.* 떡 (tteok)

rice-cake soup *n.* 떡국 (tteok-guk)

rich *n.* 부자 (bu-ja), 부유한 (bu-yu-han)

ride *v.* 차를 타다 (cha-reul-ta-da)

ride together *v.* 합승하다 (hap-seung-ha-da), 동승하다 (dong-seung-ha-da)

right *n., adj.* 오른쪽 (o-reun-jjok), 옳은 (ol-eun), 옳다 (ol-ta); **turn right** 우회전하다 (u-hoe-jeon-ha-da), 오른쪽으로 돌다 (o-reun-jjog-eu-ro dol-da)

ring *n.* 반지 (ban-ji), 고리 (go-ri)

rinse *v.* 헹구다 (heng-gu-da)

rinse one's mouth *v.* 양치질하다 (yang-chi-jil-ha-da)

rip *v.* 쪼개다 (jjo-gae-da), 찢다 (jjit-da)

rise *v.* 일어서다 (il-eo-seo-da), 기상하다 (gi-sang-ha-da), 떠오르다 (tteo-o-reu-da), 치솟다 (chi-sot-da), 나타나다 (na-ta-na-da)

risk *n.* 위험 (wi-heom)

road *n.* 길 (gil), 도로 (do-ro), 차도 (cha-do), 거리 (geo-ri)

road construction *n.* 도로공사 (do-ro-gong-sa)

road map *n.* 도로지도 (do-ro-ji-do)

rob *v.* 훔치다 (hum-chi-da), 강도질하다 (gang-do-jil-ha-da)

robber *n.* 강도 (gang-do)

robbery *n.* 강도사건 (gang-do-sa-kkeon)

rock *n.* 돌 (dol), 바위 (ba-wi)

role *n.* 역할 (yeo-kal), 배역 (bae-yeok)

roller blade *n.* 롤러스케이트 (rol-leo seu-ke-i-teu); *v.* 롤러스케이트를 타다 (rol-leo seu-ke-i-teu-reul ta-da)

roof *n.* 지붕 (ji-bung)

room *n.* 방 (bang)

roughly *adv.* 대충 (dae-chung), 거칠게 (geo-chil-ge),
　　마구 (ma-gu)
round *adj.* 둥근 (dung-geun), 둥글다 (dung-geul-da)
round trip *n.* 왕복 (wang-bok)
route *n.* 도로 (do-ro), 통로 (tong-no), 루트 (ru-teu)
row *n.* 줄 (jul)
rule *n.* 룰 (rul), 규칙 (gyu-chik), 지배하다 (ji-bae-ha-da)
rumor *n.* 소문 (so-mun)
run *v.* 뛰다 (ttwi-da), 달리다 (dal-li-da)
runny nose *n.* 콧물 (kkon-mul); **have a runny nose**
　　콧물이 나오다 (kkon-mul-i na-o-da)
rush *adj.* 급한 (geu-pan), 서두르는 (seo-du-reu-neun),
　　급하다 (geu-pa-da), 서두르다 (seo-du-reu-da)
rush hour *n.* 러시아워 (reo-si-a-wo)
ruthless *adj.* 무정한 (mu-jeong-han), 잔인한 (jan-in-han)

S

sacrifice *v.* 희생하다 (hui-saeng-ha-da, hi-saeng-ha-da)
sad *adj.* 슬픈 (seul-peun), 섭섭한 (seop-seo-pan), 슬프다
　　(seul-peu-da), 섭섭하다 (seop-seo-pa-da)
safe *adj.* 안전한 (an-jeon-han), 안전하다 (an-jeon-ha-da)
safely *adv.* 안전하게 (an-jeon-ha-ge)
safety *n.* 안전 (an-jeon)
salary *n.* 월급 (wol-geup)
salesperson *n.* 세일즈맨 (sse-il-jeu-maen), 점원 (jeom-
　　won)
salt *n.* 소금 (so-geum)
salty *adj.* 짠 (jjan), 짜다 (jja-da)
same *adj.* 같은 (gat-eun), 같다 (gat-da)
sample *n.* 샘플 (ssaem-peul)
sandals *n.* 샌들 (ssaen-deul)
sandwich *n.* 샌드위치 (ssaen-deu-wi-chi)
sanitary *adj.* 위생의 (wi-saeng-ui)
sanitary pad *n.* 생리대 (saeng-ni-dae)
satisfy *v.* 만족한 (man-jo-kan), 만족하다 (man-jo-ka-da)
Saturday *n.* 토요일 (to-yo-il)
sauna *n.* 사우나 (ssa-u-na)
save *v.* 절약하다 (jeol-ya-ka-da), 아끼다 (a-kki-da),
　　남겨두다 (nam-gyeo-du-da), 살리다 (sal-li-da)
say *v.* 말하다 (mal-ha-da)

scallion *n.* 파 (pa)

scared *adj.* 겁이 나는 (geob-i na-neun), 겁이 나다 (geob-i na-da)

scarf *n.* 스카프 (seu-ka-peu), 머플러 (meo-peul-leo)

schedule *n.* 스케줄 (seu-ke-jul)

scheduled time *n.* 제시간 (je-si-gan)

scholarship *n.* 장학금 (jang-hak-geum)

school *n.* 학교 (hak-gyo)

science *n.* 과학 (gwa-hak)

scientific *adj.* 과학적인 (gwa-hak-jeog-in)

scientist *n.* 과학자 (gwa-hak-ja)

scissors *n.* 가위 (ga-wi)

scold *v.* 혼내다 (hon-nae-da)

sculpture *n.* 조각 (jo-gak), 조각품 (jo-gak-pum)

sea *n.* 바다 (ba-da)

search *v.* 찾다 (chat-da)

season *n.* 계절 (gye-jeol); *v.* 양념하다 (yang-nyeom-ha-da)

seat *n.* 자리 (ja-ri), 좌석 (jwa-seok)

seaweed *n.* 미역 (mi-yeok); **seaweed soup** 미역국 (mi-yeok-guk)

second *n.* 초 (cho), 두 번째 (du-beon-jjae)

second floor *n.* 이층 (i-cheung)

second daughter *n.* 차녀 (cha-nyeo)

second son *n.* 차남 (cha-nam)

secret *n.* 비밀 (bi-mil)

secretary *n.* 비서 (bi-seo)

secretly *adv.* 몰래 (mol-lae)

security *n.* 안전 (an-jeon)

see *v.* 보다 (bo-da)

seek *v.* 찾다 (chat-da)

seem *v.* -으로 보이다 (eu-ro bo-i-da), -하는 것 같다 (ha-neun geot gat-da)

select *v.* 뽑다 (ppop-da)

selection *n.* 선택 (seon-taek)

self *n.* 자신의 (ja-sin-ui)

self-service *n.* 셀프서비스 (ssel-peu-sseo-bi-seu)

selfish *adj.* 이기적인 (i-gi-jeog-in), 이기적이다 (i-gi-jeog-i-da)

sell *v.* 팔다 (pal-da)

semester *n.* 학기 (hak-gi)

send *v.* 보내다 (bo-nae-da)

send a letter *v.* 편지를 부치다 (pyeon-ji-reul bu-chi-da)

send an E-mail *v.* 이메일을 보내다 (i-me-il-eul bo-nae-da)

sender *n.* 보내는 사람 (bo-nae-neun sa-ram)

senior citizen *n.* 사학년 (sa-hang-nyeon)

sense *n.* 센스 (ssen-seu)

sensible *adj.* 민감한 (min-gam-han), 느낌이 오는 (neu-kkim-i o-neun)

sentence *n.* 문장 (mun-jang), 선고하다 (seon-go-ha-da)

separate *adj.* 분리된 (bul-li-doen), 분리되다 (bul-li-doe-da), 나누어진 (na-nu-eo-jin), 나누어지다 (na-nu-eo-ji-da), 헤어진 (he-eo-jin), 헤어지다 (he-eo-ji-da)

separately *adv.* 따로 (tta-ro)

September *n.* 구월 (gu-wol)

serious *adj.* 심각한 (sim-ga-kan), 심각하다 (sim-ga-ka-da)

seriously *adv.* 심하게 (sim-ha-ge)

serve *v.* 섬기다 (seom-gi-da), 근무하다 (geun-mu-ha-da)

service *n.* 서비스 (sseo-bi-sseu)

sesame oil *n.* 참기름 (cham-gi-reum)

sesame seed *n.* 참깨 (cham-kkae)

seven *n.* 칠 (chil), 일곱 (il-gop)

seventy *n.* 일흔 (il-heun)

several *adj.* 여러 (yeo-reo)

severe *adj.* 심한 (sim-han), 심하다 (sim-ha-da)

sew *v.* 꿰매다 (kkwe-mae-da), 바느질하다 (ba-neu-jil-ha-da)

sewer *n.* 재봉사 (jae-bong-sa), 재봉틀 (jae-bong-teul), 하수구 (ha-su-gu)

sex *n.* 성 (seong), 성별 (seong-byeol)

sexual *adj.* 성적인 (seng-jjeog-in)

sexually *adv.* 성적으로 (seong-jjeog-eu-ro)

shake *v.* 흔들다 (heun-deul-da)

shallow *adj.* 얕은 (yat-eun), 얕다 (yat-da)

shame *n.* 부끄러움 (bu-kkeu-reo-um)

shameful *adj.* 부끄러운 (bu-kkeu-reo-un), 창피한 (chang-pi-han), 부끄럽다 (bu-kkeu-reop-da), 창피하다 (chang-pi-ha-da)

shampoo *n.* 샴푸 (syam-pu); *v.* 머리를 감다 (meo-ri-reul gam-tta), 샴푸하다 (syam-pu-ha-da)

shape *n.* 모양 (mo-yang)

share *n.* 배당 (bae-dang), 주식 (ju-sik); *v.* 분배하다 (bun-bae-ha-da), 공유하다 (gong-yu-ha-da)

share a ride *v.* 합승하다 (hap-seung-ha-da)

shave *n.* 면도 (myeon-do); *v.* 면도하다 (myeon-do-ha-da)

shine *n.* 햇별 (haet-byeot), 햇빛 (haet-bit), 윤기 (yun-kki)

ship *n.* 배 (bae)

shirt *n.* 셔츠 (syeo-cheu)

shoe *n.* 신발 (sin-bal), 신 (sin); **leather shoes** 구두 (gu-du)

shoe store *n.* 신발가게 (sin-bal-kka-ge)

shoot *v.* 쏘다 (sso-da)

shop *n.* 가게 (ga-ge), 상점 (sang-jeom); *v.* 쇼핑하다 (syo-ping-ha-da)

shopping center *n.* 쇼핑센터 (syo-ping-ssen-teo)

shopping district *n.* 상가 (sang-ga), 상가지역 (sang-ga-ji-yeok)

short *adj.* 짧은 (jjalb-eun), 짧다 (jjal-tta), 키가 작은 (ki-ga jag-eun), 키가 작다 (ki-ga jak-da)

short pants *n.* 반바지 (ban-ba-ji)

short-sleeved shirt *n.* 반소매셔츠 (ban-so-mae syeo-cheu), 반소매남방 (ban-so-mae nam-bang)

shortly *adv.* 짧게 (jjal-kke)

shorts *n.* 반바지 (ban-ba-ji)

shot *v.* 발포 (bal-po), 탄환 (tan-hwan); **get a shot** 주사를 맞다 (ju-sa-reul mat-da)

shoulder *n.* 어깨 (eo-kkae)

shout *v.* 소리 지르다 (so-ri ji-reu-da)

show *v.* 보여주다 (bo-yeo-ju-da)

shower *n.* 소나기 (so-na-gi); *v.* 샤워하다 (sya-wo-ha-da)

sibling *n.* 형제 (hyeong-je)

sick *adj.* 아픈 (a-peun), 아프다 (a-peu-da)

sickness *n.* 질병 (jil-byeong)

side *n.* 옆 (yeop), 편 (pyeon)

side dish *n.* 반찬 (ban-chan)

sideline *n.* 부업 (bu-eop)

sidewalk *n.* 인도 (in-do), 보도 (bo-do)

sight *n.* 시각 (si-gak), 조망 (jo-mang), 바라봄 (ba-ra-bom)

sightsee *v.* 구경하다 (gu-gyeong-ha-da)

sightseeing *n.* 구경 (gu-gyeong)

sign *n.* 사인 (ssa-in); *v.* 사인하다 (ssa-in-ha-da); traffic sign 교통신호 (gyo-tong-sin-ho)

sign language *n.* 수화 (su-hwa)

significance *n.* 의의 (ui-ui), 중요성 (jung-yo-sseong)

signify *v.* 의미하다 (ui-mi-ha-da), 중대하다 (jung-dae-ha-da)

silence *n.* 고요 (go-yo), 조용함 (jo-yong-ham), 침묵 (chim-muk)

silent *adj.* 조용한 (jo-yong-han), 고요한 (go-yo-han)

silk *n.* 실크 (ssil-keu)

similar *adj.* 비슷한 (bi-seu-tan), 비슷하다 (bi-seu-ta-da)

similarity *n.* 유사점 (yu-sa-jjeom)

simple *adj.* 간단한 (gan-dan-han), 간단하다 (gan-dan-ha-da), 단순한 (dan-sun-han), 단순하다 (dan-sun-ha-da)

simultaneously *adv.* 동시에 (dong-si-e), 일제히 (il-jje-hi)

since *prep., conj., adv.* -이래 (i-rae), -(이)기 때문에 ([i]-gi ttae-mun-e)

sincere *adj.* 성실한 (seong-sil-han), 성실하다 seong-sil-ha-da)

sing *v.* 노래하다 (no-rae-ha-da); **sing a song** 노래 부르다 (no-rae bu-reu-da)

singer *n.* 가수 (ga-su)

single *n.* 독신 (dok-sin), 혼자 (hon-ja)

single bed *n.* 1인용 침대 (il-in-nyong chim-dae)

single-family house *n.* 단독주택 (dan-dok-ju-taek)

single out *v.* 뽑다 (ppop-da)

single room *n.* 독방 (dok-bang)

sink *v.* 가라앉다 (ga-ra-an-tta)

sister *n.* 자매 (ja-mae), 언니 (eon-ni), 누나 (nu-na), 여동생 (yeo-dong-saeng)

sister-in-law *n.* 형수 (hyeong-su), 동서 (dong-seo), 시누이 (si-nu-i), 올케 (ol-ke), 처제 (cheo-je), 처형 (cheo-hyeong)

sit *v.* 앉다 (an-tta)

site *n.* 위치 (wi-chi), 장소 (jang-so); *v.* 위치를 잡다 (wi-chi-reul jap-da)

six *n.* 육 (yuk), 여섯 (yeo-seot)

sixty *n.* 예순 (ye-sun)

size *n.* 사이즈 (ssa-i-jeu)

skate *n.* 스케이트 (seu-ke-i-teu); *v.* 스케이트를 타다 (seu-ke-i-teu-reul ta-da)

ski *n.* 스키 (seu-ki); *v.* 스키를 타다 (seu-ki-reul ta-da)

ski resort *n.* 스키장 (seu-ki-jang)

skill *n.* 솜씨 (som-ssi), 실력 (sil-lyeok)

skinny *adj.* 마른 (ma-reun), 말랐다 (mal-lat-da)

skip *v.* 건너뛰다 (geon-neo-ttwi-da)

skip a meal *v.* 끼니를 거르다 (kki-ni-reul geo-reu-da)

skirt *n.* 스커트 (seu-keo-teu), 치마 (chi-ma)

sky *n.* 하늘 (ha-neul)

sky-blue *n.* 하늘색 (ha-neul-saek); *adj.* 하늘색의 (ha-neul-saeg-ui)

sleep *n.* 잠 (jam); *v.* 자다 (ja-da), 주무시다 (ju-mu-si-da) (*honorific*)

sleeping car *n.* 기차 침대차 (gi-cha chim-dae-cha)

sleeping pills *n.* 수면제 (su-myeon-je)

sleepy *adj.* 졸린 (jol-lin), 졸리다 (jol-li-da)

slice *v.* 썰다 (sseol-da)

slice thin *v.* 얇게 썰다 (yal-kke sseol-da)

slim *adj.* 날씬한 (nal-ssin-han), 날씬하다 (nal-ssin-ha-da)

slippery *adj.* 미끄러운 (mi-kkeu-reo-un), 미끄럽다 (mi-kkeu-reop-da)

slow *adj.* 느린 (neu-rin), 느리다 (neu-ri-da)

slowly *adv.* 천천히 (cheon-cheon-hi)

small *adj.* 작은 (jag-eun), 작다 (jak-da)

smell *n.* 냄새 (naem-sae); *v.* 냄새가 나다 (naem-sae-ga na-da), 냄새를 맡다 (name-sae-reul mat-da)

smoke *n.* 연기 (yeon-gi); *v.* 담배를 피우다 (dam-bae-reul pi-u-da); **no smoking** 금연 (geum-yeon)

sneakers *n.* 운동화 (un-dong-hwa)

snow *n.* 눈 (nun); *v.* 눈이 오다 (nun-i o-da)

so *conj.* 그래서 (geu-rae-seo)

so-so 그저 그래요 (geu-jeo geu-rae-yo)

soap *n.* 비누 (bi-nu)

sob *n.* 흐느낌 (heu-neu-kkim); *v.* 흐느껴 울다 (heu-neu-kkyeo ul-da)

sober *adj.* 술 취하지 않은 (sul chwi-ha-ji an-eun), 냉정한 (naeng-jeong-han), 맑은 정신의 (malg-eun jeong-sin-ui)

soccer *n.* 축구 (chuk-gu); **play soccer** 축구 하다 (chuk-gu-ha-da)

sociable *adj.* 사교적인 (sa-gyo-jeog-in), 사교적이다 (sa-gyo-jeog-i-da)

social *adj.* 사회의 (sa-hoe-ui), 사교적인 (sa-gyo-jeog-in)

society *n.* 사회 (sa-hoe)

sock *n.* 양말 (yang-mal)

soda *n.* 콜라 (kol-la), 사이다 (sa-i-da)

sofa *n.* 소파 (sso-pa)

soft *adj.* 부드러운 (bu-deu-reo-un), 부드럽다 (bu-deu-reop-da); **turn soft** 풀어지다 (pul-eo-ji-da)

soldier *n.* 군인 (gun-in)

solution *n.* 해결책 (hae-gyeol-chaek), 용액 (yong-aek)

solve *v.* (문제를) 풀다 ([mun-je-reul] pul-da), 해결하다 (hae-gyeol-ha-da)

some *adj.* 몇몇 (myeon-myeot), 약간의 (yak-gan-ui)

somebody *pron.* 누군가 (nu-gun-ga)

someone *pron.* 누구 (nu-gu)

something *pron.* 뭔가 (mwon-ga)

sometime *adv.* 언젠가 (eon-jen-ga)

sometime ago *adv.* 얼마 전에 (eol-ma jeon-e)

sometimes *adv.* 가끔 (ga-kkeum), 가끔씩 (ga-kkeum-ssik)

son *n.* 아들 (a-deul)

son-in-law *n.* 사위 (sa-wi)

song *n.* 노래 (no-rae)

soon *adv.* 곧 (got)

sophomore *n.* 이학년 (i-hang-nyeon)

sore *adj.* 아픈 (a-peun), 슬픈 (seul-peun), 쓰라린 (sseu-ra-rin)

sore throat *n.* 후두염 (hu-du-yeom), 목 아픔 (mog-a-peum)

sorry *adj.* 미안하다 (mi-an-ha-da), 안되다 (an-doe-da), 섭섭하다 (seop-seo-pa-da)

sort *n.* 종류 (jong-nyu), 성질 (seong-jil); **a sort of** 일종의 (il-jjong-ui)

sort out *v.* 골라버리다 (gol-la beo-ri-da), 골라내다 (gol-la-nae-da), 가려내다 (ga-ryeo-nae-da)

sound *n.* 소리 (so-ri); *v.* 소리가 나다 (so-ri-ga na-da), 들리다 (deul-li-da)

soundly *adv.* 푹 (puk)

soup *n.* 수프 (su-peu), 국 (guk)

sour *adj.* 신 (sin), 시다 (si-da)

south *n.* 남 (nam), 남쪽 (nam-jjok)

South America *n.* 남미 (nam-mi)

South Asia *n.* 동남아 (dong-nam-a)

South Korea *n.* 남한 (nam-han)

southern *adj.* 남쪽의 (nam-jjog-ui)

soy sauce *n.* 간장 (gan-jang)

soybean *n.* 콩 (kong)

space *n.* 자리 (ja-ri)

spacious *adj.* 넓은 (neolb-eun), 넓다 (neol-tta)

speak *v.* 말하다 (mal-ha-da)

special *adj.* 특별한 (teuk-byeol-han), 특별하다 (teuk-byeol-ha-da)

special event *n.* 특별한 일 (teuk-byeol-han il)

specialty *n.* 전문 (jeon-mun)

species *n.* 종류 (jong-nyu), 종 (jong)

specify *v.* 명시하다 (myeong-si-ha-da)

speech *n.* 연설 (yeon-seol)

speech style *n.* 말씨 (mal-ssi)

speed *n.* 속도 (sok-do); *v.* 속도를 내다 (sok-do-reul nae-da)

speed limit *n.* 속도제한 (sok-do-je-han)

spend *v.* 소비하다 (so-bi-ha-da)

spend money *v.* 돈을 쓰다 (don-eul sseu-da)

spend time *v.* 시간을 보내다 (si-gan-eul bo-nae-da)

spicy *adj.* 매운 (mae-un), 맵다 (map-da)

spinach *n.* 시금치 (si-geum-chi)

spine *n.* 척추 (cheok-chu), 등뼈 (deung-ppyeo)

splendid *adj.* 화려한 (hwa-ryeo-han), 화려하다 (hwa-ryeo-ha-da)

sports *n.* 스포츠 (seu-po-cheu)

sports game *n.* 경기 (gyeong-gi), 시합 (si-hap)

sports shoes *n.* 운동화 (un-dong-hwa)

spot *n.* 점 (jeom), 얼룩 (eol-luk)

spread *v.* 깔다 (kkal-da), 펴서 바르다 (pyeo-seo ba-reu-da)

spring *n.* 봄 (bom)

squash *n.* 호박 (ho-bak)

stage *n.* 무대 (mu-dae); *v.* 연출하다 (yeon-chul-ha-da)

stamp *n.* 우표 (u-pyo)

stand *v.* 서다 (seo-da), 참다 (cham-tta)

star *n.* 별 (byeol)

start *v.* 시작하다 (si-ja-ka-da)

state *n.* 상태 (sang-tae), 국가 (guk-ga); *adj.* 국가의 (guk-ga-ui); *v.* 진술하다 (jin-sul-ha-da), 지정하다 (ji-jeong-ha-da)

statement *n.* 성명 (seong-myeong), 진술 (jin-sul)

station *n.* (기차)역 ([gi-cha]-yeok), (고속버스)터미널 ([go-sok-beo-seu]-teo-mi-neol)

stationery *n.* 학용품 (hag-yong-pum)

stationery store *n.* 문방구 (mun-bang-gu), 문구점 (mun-gu-jeom)

statistics *n.* 통계 (tong-gye)

stay *v.* 머무르다 (meo-mu-reu-da), 있다 (it-da)

stay up all night *v.* 밤을 새우다 (bam-eul sae-u-da)

steal *v.* 훔치다 (hum-chi-da)

steam *n.* 스팀 (seu-tim)

steel *n.* 강철 (gang-cheol)

steer *v.* 휘젓다 (hwi-jeot-da)

steering wheel *n.* 자동차 핸들 (ja-dong-cha haen-deul)

step *n.* 걸음 (geol-eum); *v.* 걷다 (geot-da)

stick *v.* 붙이다 (bu-chi-da)

sticker *n.* 스티커 (seu-ti-keo)

stiff *adj.* 경사진 (gyeong-sa-jin), 경사지다 (gyeong-sa-ji-da)

still *adv.* 아직도 (a-jik-do); stay still 가만히 있다 (ga-man-hi it-da)

sting *v.* 쏘다 (sso-da)

stir *v.* 젓다 (jeot-da)

stir-fry *n.* 볶다 (bok-da)

stomach *n.* 위 (wi), 위장 (wi-jang), 배 (bae)

stomachache *n.* 위통 (wi-tong), 복통(bok-tong); **have a stomachache** 배가 아프다 (bae-ga a-peu-da)

stone *n.* 돌 (dol), 돌멩이 (dol-meng-i)

stop *v.* 서다 (seo-da), 멈추다 (meom-chu-da), 세우다 (se-u-da), 그만두다 (geu-man-du-da)

store *n.* 가게 (ga-ge), 상점 (sang-jeom)

store clerk *n.* 상점 점원 (sang-jeom jeom-won)

store sign *n.* 간판 (gan-pan)

story *n.* 이야기 (i-ya-gi)

straight *adv.* 똑바로 (ttok-ba-ro)

strange *adj.* 이상한 (i-sang-han), 이상하다 (i-sang-ha-da)

strawberry *n.* 딸기 (ttal-gi)

street *n.* 길 (gil), 거리 (geo-ri), 찻길 (chat-gil)

strength *n.* 힘 (him), 세기 (se-gi)

stress *n.* 스트레스 (seu-teu-re-seu); **feel stress** 스트레스를 받다 (seu-teu-re-seu-reul bat-da); **have no stress** 스트레스가 없다 (seu-teu-re-seu-ga eop-da)

stress accumulates 스트레스가 쌓이다 (seu-teu-re-seu-ga ssa-i-da)

stress is relieved 스트레스가 풀리다 (seu-teu-re-seu-ga pul-li-da)

string *n.* 줄 (jul)

stripe *n.* 줄무늬 (jul-mu-nui, jul-mu-ni)

strong *adj.* 힘이 센 (hin-i sen), 강한 (gang-han), 힘이 세다 (him-i se-da), 강하다 (gang-ha-da)

struggle *v.* 버둥거리다 (beo-dung-geo-ri-da), 노력하다 (no-ryeo-ka-da)

student *n.* 학생 (hak-saeng)

study *n.* 서재 (seo-jae); *v.* 공부하다 (gong-bu-ha-da)

stuffy *adj.* 속이 답답한 (sog-i dap-da-pan), 속이 답답하다 (sog-i dap-da-pa-da)

style *n.* 스타일 (seu-ta-il)

stylish *adj.* 멋있는 (meos-in-neun), 멋있다 (meos-it-da)

subject *n.* 주제 (ju-je), 전공 (jeon-gong), 과목 (gwa-mok)

substantially *adv.* 꽤 (kkwae)

suburbs *n.* 교외 (gyo-oe), 근교 (geun-gyo)

subway *n.* 지하철 (ji-ha-cheol)

subway station *n.* 지하철역 (ji-ha-cheol-lyeok), 전철역 (jeon-cheol-lyeok)

such *adv.* 그러한 (geu-reo-han), 그와 같은 (geu-wa gat-eun)

suddenly *adv.* 갑자기 (gap-ja-gi)

suffer *v.* 피로워하다 (goe-ro-wo-ha-da)

suffering *n.* 피로움 (goe-ro-um), 고통 (go-tong)

sufficient *adj.* 충분한 (chung-bun-han), 충분하다 (chung-bun-ha-da)

sugar *n.* 설탕 (seol-tang)

suggest *v.* 제안하다 (je-an-ha-da)

suggestion *n.* 제안 (je-an)

suit *n.* 소송 (so-song), 옷 한 벌 (ot han-beol); *v.* 적합하다 (jeo-ka-pa-da), 적합하게 하다 (jeo-ka-pa-ge ha-da)

suitable *adj.* 적당한 (jeok-dang-han), 어울리는 (eo-ul-li-neun)

suite *n.* 한 벌 (han beol), 한 세트 (han sse-teu); **wedding suite** 결혼 예복 (gyeol-hon ye-bok)

summer *n.* 여름 (yeo-reum)

sun *n.* 해 (hae), 태양 (tae-yang)

Sunday *n.* 일요일 (il-yo-il)

sunrise *n.* 해뜨는 시각 (hae-tteu-neun si-gak)

sunset *n.* 해지는 시각 (hae-ji-neun si-gak)

sunset glow *n.* 저녁노을 (jeo-nyeok no-eul)

supermarket *n.* 슈퍼마켓 (syu-peo-ma-ket), 슈퍼 (syu-peo)

supper *n.* 저녁 (jeo-nyeok), 저녁밥 (jeo-nyeok-bap)

support *n.* 지지 (ji-ji), *v.* 지지하다 (ji-ji-ha-da), 뒷바라지하다 (dwit-ba-ra-ji-ha-da)

sure *adj.* 확실하다 (hwak-sil-ha-da), 확신하다 (hwak-sin-ha-da)

surface *n.* 표면 (pyo-myeon), 겉 (geot)

surgery *n.* 수술 (su-sul); *v.* 수술하다 (su-sul ha-da); **have surgery** 수술 받다 (su-sul bat-da)

surprise *adj.* 놀란 (nol-lan), 놀라다 (nol-la-da)

surprise party *n.* 깜짝 파티 (kkam-jjak pa-ti)

survive *v.* 생존하다 (saeng-jon-ha-da)

swarm *v.* 몰리다 (mol-li-da)

swear *v.* 맹세하다 (maeng-se-ha-da), 욕하다 (yo-ka-da)

sweat *n.* 땀 (ttam); *v.* 땀을 흘리다 (ttam-eul heul-li-da)

sweet *adj.* 단 (dan); 달다 (dal-da)

sweet rice drink *n.* 식혜 (si-kye)

sweetener *n.* 감미료 (gam-mi-ryo)

swim *v.* 수영하다 (su-yeong-ha-da)

swimming pool *n.* 수영장 (su-yeong-jang)

swimsuit *n.* 수영복 (su-yeong-bok)

switch *v.* 바꾸다 (ba-kku-da)

swollen *adj.* 부은 (bu-eun), 붓다 (but-da)

sympathy *n.* 인정 (in-jeong), 동정 (dong-jeong)

symphony *n.* 심포니 (ssim-po-ni)

symptom *n.* 증상 (jeung-sang)

T

table *n.* 테이블 (te-i-beul)

table tennis *n.* 탁구 (tak-gu)

tablespoon *n.* 큰술 (keun-sul)

take *v.* 택하다 (tae-ka-da), 모시다 (mo-si-da)

take a shower *v.* 샤워하다 (sya-wo-ha-da)

take a test *v.* 시험을 보다 (si-heom-eul bo-da)

take an X-ray *v.* 엑스레이를 찍다 (ek-seu-re-i-reul jjik-da)

take away *v.* 뺏다 (ppaet-da)

take care of *v.* 챙기다 (chaeng-gi-da), 돌보다 (dol-bo-da), 손질하다 (son-jil-ha-da), 몸조리하다 (mom-jo-ri-ha-da)

take medicine *v.* 약을 먹다 (yag-eul meok-da)

take off *v.* 옷을 벗다 (os-eul beot-da), 신발을 벗다 (sin-bal-eul beot-da), 장갑을 빼다 (jang-gab-eul ppae-da), 시계를 풀다 (si-gye-reul pul-da)

take the trouble to *v.* 수고하다 (su-go-ha-da)

take time *v.* 시간이 걸리다 (si-gan-i geol-li-da)

talent *n.* 재능 (jae-neung)

talk *v.* 말하다 (mal-ha-da), 이야기하다 (i-ya-gi-ha-da)

tall *adj.* 키가 큰 (ki-ga keun), 키가 크다 (ki-ga keu-da)

tame *adj.* 길든 (gil-deun), 길들이다 (gil-deul-i-da)

tampon *n.* 지혈마개 (ji-hyeol-ma-gae), 탬폰 (taem-pon)

tape *n.* 테이프 (te-i-peu)

task *n.* 일 (il), 임무 (im-mu)

taste *n.* 맛 (mat)

tasteful *adj.* 맛이 있는 (mas-i in-neun)

tasteless *adj.* 맛이 없는 (mas-i eom-neun), 맛이 없다 (mas-i eop-da)

tasty *adj.* 맛이 있는 (mas-i in-neun), 맛이 있다 (mas-i it-da)

tax *n.* 세금 (se-geum)

taxi *n.* 택시 (taek-si)

taxi fare *n.* 택시비 (taek-si-bi)

taxi stand *n.* 택시 타는 곳 (taek-si-ta-neun got)

tea *n.* 차 (cha)

teach *v.* 가르치다 (ga-reu-chi-da)

teacher *n.* 선생님 (seon-saeng-nim)

team *n.* 팀 (tim)

teaspoon *n.* 작은술 (jag-eun-sul), 티스푼 (ti-seu-pun)

teenager *n.* 십대 (sip-dae)

telephone *n.* 전화 (jeon-hwa), 전화기 (jeon-hwa-gi)

telephone bill *n.* 전화비 (jeon-hwa-bi)

telephone book *n.* 전화번호부 (jeon-hwa-beon-ho-bu)

telephone booth *n.* 공중전화 박스 (gong-jung-jeon-hwa bak-seu)

telephone card *n.* 전화카드 (jeon-hwa-ka-deu)

telephone company *n.* 전화국 (jeon-hwa-guk)

telephone number *n.* 전화번호 (jeon-hwa-beon-ho)

television *n.* 텔레비전 (tel-le-bi-jeon)

television screen *n.* 화면 (hwa-myeon)

temperature *n.* 온도 (on-do), 기온 (gi-on)

temporarily *adv.* 당분간 (dang-bun-gan)

ten *n.* 십 (sip), 열 (yeol)

ten thousand *n.* 만 (man)

tend *v.* -을 향하다 (eul hyang-ha-da), -는 경향이 있다 (neun gyeong-hyang-i it-da), -을 돌보다 (eul dol-bo-da)

tendency *n.* 경향 (gyeong-hyang)

tender *adj.* 연한 (yeon-han), 연하다 (yeon-ha-da)

tennis *n.* 테니스 (te-ni-seu)

tent *n.* 텐트 (ten-teu)

test *n.* 시험 (si-heom)

textbook *n.* 교과서 (gyo-gwa-seo), 교재 (gyo-jae)

thank *v.* 감사하다 (gam-sa-ha-da), 고맙다 (go-map-da)

thankful *adj.* 감사한 (gam-sa-han), 고마운 (go-ma-un)

thaw *v.* 녹이다 (nog-i-da)

theater *n.* 극장 (geuk-jang), 영화관 (yeong-hwa-gwan)

theme *n.* 주제 (ju-je)

then *adv.* 그러면 (geu-reo-myeon), 그리고 나서 (geu-ri-go na-seo)

there *adv.* 거기 (geo-gi)

therefore *adv.* 그래서 (geu-rae-seo), 그러므로 (geu-reo-meu-ro)

thesis *n.* 논문 (non-mun)

thick *adj.* 두꺼운 (du-kkeo-un), 두껍다 (du-kkeop-da)

thief *n.* 도둑 (do-duk)

thin *adj.* 얇은 (yalb-eun), 얇다 (yal-tta)

thing *n.* 물건 (mul-geon)

think *v.* 생각하다 (saeng-ga-ka-da)

thirsty *adj.* 목이 마른 (mog-i ma-reun), 목이 마르다 (mog-i ma-reu-da)

thirty *n.* 서른 (seo-reun)

thought *n.* 생각 (saeng-gak)

thousand *n.* 천 (cheon)

threat *n.* 협박 (hyeop-bak)

three *n.* 삼 (sam), 셋 (set)

through *prep.* -을 통과하여 (eul tong-gwa-ha-yeo), -을 통해서 (eul tong-hae-seo)

throw *v.* 던지다 (deon-ji-da)

thunderstorm *n.* 천둥 (cheon-dung)

Thursday *n.* 목요일 (mog-yo-il)

ticket *n.* 표 (pyo), 티켓 (ti-ket); **admission ticket** 입장권 (ip-jang-kkwon)

ticket booth *n.* 매표소 (mae-pyo-so)

ticket holder *n.* 입장객 (ip-jang-gaek)

tie *n.* 넥타이 (nek-ta-i)

tiger *n.* 호랑이 (ho-rang-i)

time *n.* 시간 (si-gan), 때 (ttae); **after a long time** 오랜만에 (o-raen-man-e)

tire *n.* 타이어 (ta-i-eo)

tired *adj.* 피곤한 (pi-gon-han), 피곤하다 (pi-gon-ha-da)

tissue paper *n.* 휴지 (hyu-ji), 크리넥스 (keu-ri-nek-seu)

title *n.* 제목 (je-mok)

to *prep.* -에게 (e-ge), -한테 (han-te), -께 (kke)

today *n.* 오늘 (o-neul)

together *adv.* 다같이 (da ga-chi); **get together** 모이다 (mo-i-da)

toilet *n.* 화장실 (hwa-jang-sil)

toilet paper *n.* 휴지 (hyu-ji), 화장지 (hwa-jang-ji)

tomato *n.* 토마토 (to-ma-to), 도마도 (do-ma-do)

tomorrow *n.* 내일 (nae-il)

tone *n.* 음질 (eum-jil), 어조 (eo-jo), 색조 (saek-jo), 기품 (gi-pum); *v.* 가락을 붙이다 (ga-rag-ul bu-chi-da), 가락을 떠다 (ga-rag-eul tti-da)

too *adv.* 또 (tto)

too much *adv.* 너무 (neo-mu)

tools *n.* 기구 (gi-gu), 연장 (yeon-jang)

tooth *n.* 이 (i), 이빨 (i-ppal)

toothache *n.* 치통 (chi-tong); **have a toothache** 이가 아프다 (i-ga a-peu-da)

toothbrush *n.* 칫솔 (chit-sol)

toothpaste *n.* 치약 (chi-yak)

top *n.* 위 (ui)

touch *v.* 치다 (chi-da), 건드리다 (geon-deu-ri-da)

tour *n.* 여행 (yeo-haeng), 관광 (gwan-gwang)

tourist *n.* 관광객 (gwan-gwang-gaek)

town *n.* 도시 (do-si), 마을 (ma-eul)

toy *n.* 장난감 (jang-nan-kkam)

trace *v.* 추적하다 (chu-jeo-ka-da), 선을 긋다 (seon-eul geut-da), 발자국 (bal-jja-guk)

track *n.* 지나간 자국 (ji-na-gan ja-guk); *v.* 뒤를 쫓다 (dwi-reul jjot-da)

trade *n.* 무역 (mu-yeok); *v.* 교환하다 (gyo-hwan-ha-da)

tradition *n.* 전통 (jeon-tong)

traditional *adj.* 전통적인 (jeon-tong-jeog-in)

traditional national holiday *n.* 명절 (myeong-jeol)

traffic *n.* 교통 (gyo-tong); *adj.* 교통의 (gyo-tong-ui)

traffic light *n.* 신호등 (sin-ho-deung)

traffic sign *n.* 교통 표지판 (gyo-tong-pyo-ji-pan)

traffic ticket *n.* 교통위반 딱지 (gyo-tong-wi-ban ttak-ji); **get a traffic ticket** 딱지를 떼다 (ttak-ji-reul tte-da)

train *n.* 기차 (gi-cha)

train station *n.* 기차역 (gi-cha-yeok)

train ticket *n.* 기차표 (gi-cha-pyo)

training *n.* 훈련 (hul-lyeon)

transfer *v.* 갈아타다 (gal-a-ta-da)

translate *v.* 번역하다 (beon-yeo-ka-da)

translation *n.* 번역 (beon-yeok)

transportation *n.* 교통 (gyo-tong), 교통편 (gyo-tong-pyeon)

trash *n.* 쓰레기 (sseu-re-gi)

trash can *n.* 휴지통 (hyu-ji-tong), 쓰레기통 (sseu-re-gi-tong)

travel *n.* 여행 (yeo-haeng); *v.* 여행하다 (yeo-haeng-ha-da)

travel agency *n.* 여행사 (yeo-haeng-sa)

travel agent *n.* 여행사 직원 (yeo-haeng-sa jig-won)

traveler *n.* 여행객 (yeo-haeng-gaek)

traveler's check *n.* 여행자수표 (yeo-haeng-ja su-pyo)

treasure *n.* 보물 (bo-mul)

treat *v.* 모시다 (mo-si-da)

treat a meal *v.* 한턱 내다 (ha-teok nae-da), 대접하다 (dae-jeo-pa-da), 접대하다 (jeop-dae-ha-da)

treat a patient *v.* 치료하다 (chi-ryo-ha-da)

tree *n.* 나무 (na-mu)

tree branch *n.* 나뭇가지 (na-mut-ga-ji)

trend *n.* 방향 (bang-hyang), 경향 (gyeong-hyang); *v.* -는 경향을 띠다 (neun gyeong-hyang-eul tti-da)

trendy *adj.* 유행하는 (yu-haeng-ha-neun)

trial *n.* 시도 (si-do), 공판 (gong-pan), 시련 (si-ryeon)

trim *v.* 다듬다 (da-deum-tta); **trim one's bangs** 앞머리를 다듬다 (am-meo-ri-reul da-deum-tta)

trip *n.* 여행 (yeo-haeng)

trip over a rock *v.* 돌에 걸리다 (dol-e geol-li-da)

trouble *n.* 문제 (mun-je), 큰일 (keun-il)

truck *n.* 트럭 (teu-reok)

true *adj.* 진짜 (jin-jja), 정말 (jeong-mal)

trust *v.* 믿다 (mit-da)

truth *n.* 진실 (jin-sil), 사실 (sa-sil); **to tell the truth** *v.*
사실은 (sa-sil-eun)

try *v.* 해보다 (hae-bo-da)

T-shirt *n.* 티셔츠 (ti-syeo-cheu)

Tuesday *n.* 화요일 (hwa-yo-il)

tuition *n.* 학비 (hak-bi), 과외비 (gwa-oe-bi)

turn *v.* 돌다 (dol-da), 차례 (cha-rye)

turn in *v.* 내다 (nae-da), 제출하다 (je-chul-ha-da)

turn into *v.* -이/가 되다 (i/ga doe-da)

turn off *v.* 끄다 (kkeu-da)

turn on *v.* 켜다 (kyeo-da)

tutor *n.* 가정교사 (ga-jeong-gyo-sa)

twenty *n.* 스물 (seu-mul)

twin beds *n.* 1인용 침대 한 쌍 (il-in-nyong chim-dae
han-ssang)

twins *n.* 쌍둥이 (ssang-dung-i)

two *n.* 이 (i), 둘 (dul)

type *n.* 종류 (jong-nyu)

U

ugly *adj.* 못생긴 (mot-saeng-gin), 못생기다 (mot-saeng-
gi-da)

umbrella *n.* 우산 (u-san)

unable *adj.* 못하다 (mo-ta-da)

unauthorized *adj.* 승인되지 않은 (seung-in-doe-ji
an-eun)

uncle *n.* 삼촌 (san-chon), 큰아버지 (keun a-beo-ji),
작은아버지 (jag-eun a-beo-ji)

uncomfortable *adj.* 거북하다 (geo-bu-ka-da), 불편하다
(bul-pyeon-ha-da)

uncomplicated *adj.* 복잡하지 않은 (bok-ja-pa-ji an-eun),
까다롭지 않은 (kka-da-rop-ji an-eun)

unconscious *adj.* 의식이 없는 (ui-sig-i eom-neun)

unconsciousness *n.* 무의식 (mu-ui-sik), 인사불성 (in-sa-
bul-sseong)

under *prep., adv.* 밑 (mit), 아래 (a-rae), 밑에 (mit-e);
   under construction 공사 중 (gong-sa jung)

under-floor heating *n.* 온돌 (on-dol)

underground *n.* 지하 (ji-ha)

underpass *n.* 지하도 (ji-ha-do)

understand *v.* 이해하다 (i-hae-ha-da), 알다 (al-da)

underwear *n.* 속옷 (sog-ot)

unexpected *adj.* 기대하지 않은 (gi-dae-ha-ji an-eun)

unexpectedly *adv.* 오히려 (o-hi-ryeo)

unhappiness *n.* 불행 (bul-haeng)

uninteresting *adj.* 재미없는 (jae-mi-eom-neun),
   재미없다 (jae-mi-eop-da)

union *n.* 조합 (jo-hap)

unit *n.* 단위 (dan-wi)

unite *v.* 결합하다 (gyeol-ha-pa-da), 하나가 되다 (ha-na-
   ga doe-da)

university *n.* 대학교 (dae-hak-gyo)

unkind *adj.* 불친절한 (bul-chin-jeol-han), 불친절하다
   (bul-chin-jeol-ha-da)

unkindness *n.* 불친절 (bul-chin-jeol)

unknown *adj.* 알려지지 않은 (al-lyeo-ji-ji an-eun)

unlock *v.* 자물쇠를 열다 (ja-mul-soe-reul yeol-da),
   자물쇠가 풀리다 (ja-mul-soe-ga pul-li-da)

until *prep., conj.* -까지 (kka-ji)

up *n.* 위 (wi), 위에 (wi-e)

urgent *adj.* 급하다 (geu-pa-da)

usage *n.* 사용법 (sa-yong-ppeop), 용법 (yong-ppeop)

use *v.* 사용하다 (sa-yong-ha-da), 쓰다 (sseu-da)

used *adj.* 중고 (jung-go)

used to *adj.* 익숙해지다 (ik-su-kae-ji-da)

useful *adj.* 유용한 (yu-yong-han), 유용하다 (yu-yong-
   ha-da)

useless *adj.* 쓸모 없는 (sseul-mo-eom-neun), 쓸모 없다
   (sseul-mo-eop-da)

usual *adj.* 보통 (bo-tong)

usually *adv.* 보통 (bo-tong), 주로 (ju-ro)

utilize *v.* 이용하다 (i-yong-ha-da)

V

vacancy *n.* 공허 (gong-heo), 공석 (gong-seok), 방심
   (bang-sim)

vacant *adj.* 비어있는 (bi-eo-in-neun), 공허한 (gong-heo-han), 한가한 (han-ga-han)

vacation *n.* 방학 (bang-hak), 휴가 (hyu-ga)

vacuum *v.* 청소하다 (cheong-so-ha-da)

vacuum cleaner *n.* 청소기 (cheong-so-gi)

valid *adj.* 확실한 근거가 있는 (hwak-sil-han geun-geo-ga in-neun), 타당한 (ta-dang-han)

valuable *adj.* 가치 있는 (ga-chi in-neun), 가치 있다 (ga-chi-it-da)

value *n.* 가치 (ga-chi)

vary *n.* 다양한 (da-yang-han), 다양하다 (da-yang-ha-da)

vegetable store *n.* 채소가게 (chae-so-ga-ge), 야채가게 (ya-chae-ga-ge)

vegetables *n.* 야채 (ya-chae)

vegetarian *n.* 채식주의자 (chae-sik-ju-ui-ja)

vehicle *n.* 자동차 (ja-dong-cha)

vending machine *n.* 자동 판매기 (ja-dong-pan-mae-gi), 자동 발매기 (ja-dong-bal-mae-gi)

very *adv.* 굉장히 (goeng-jang-hi), 아주 (a-ju), 되게 (doe-ge)

via *prep.* -을 통과해서 (eul tong-gwa-hae-seo), -을 통해서 (eul tong-hae-seo)

victim *n.* 희생자 (hui-saeng-ja), (hi-saeng-ja)

victory *n.* 승리 (seung-ni)

view *n.* 전망 (jeon-mang)

village *n.* 마을 (ma-eul)

vinegar *n.* 식초 (sik-cho)

violet *n.* 보라색 (bo-ra-saek); *adj.* 보라색의 (bo-ra-saeg-ui)

violin *n.* 바이올린 (ba-i-ol-lin)

visa *n.* 비자 (bi-ja)

visible *adj.* 볼 수 있는 (bol-ssu in-neun), 보이는 (bo-i-neun)

vision *n.* 시력 (si-ryeok)

visit *v.* 방문하다 (bang-mun-ha-da)

visit a sick person *v.* 문병 가다 (mun-byeong-ga-da)

visitor *n.* 방문객 (bang-mun-gaek), 입장객 (ip-jang-gaek)

vitamin *n.* 비타민 (bi-ta-min)

vocabulary *n.* 단어 (dan-eo)

voice *n.* 목소리 (mok-so-ri)

volleyball *n.* 배구 (bae-gu)

volume *n.* 볼륨 (bol-lyum), 권 (gwon)
vomit *v.* 토하다 (to-ha-da), 구토하다 (gu-to-ha-da)
vote *v.* 선거하다 (seon-geo-ha-da), 투표하다 (tu-pyo-ha-da)
vouch *v.* 보증하다 (bo-jeung-ha-da)

W

wage *n.* 임금 (im-geum)
wagon *n.* 수레 (su-re)
waist *n.* 허리 (heo-ri)
wait *v.* 기다리다 (gi-da-ri-da)
waiter *n.* 종업원 (jong-eob-won)
waitress *n.* 여종업원 (yeo-jong-eob-won)
wake up *v.* 일어나다 (il-eo-na-da), 깨다 (kkae-da)
walk *v.* 걷다 (geot-da), 걸어가다 (geol-eo-ga-da)
wall *n.* 벽 (byeok), 장벽 (jang-byeok)
wallet *n.* 지갑 (ji-gap)
want *v.* 원하다 (won-ha-da), 원함 (won-ham)
wardrobe *n.* 옷장 (ot-jang), 장롱 (jang-nong)
warm *adj.* 따뜻한 (tta-teu-tan), 따뜻하다 (tta-teu-ta-da)
warn *v.* 경고하다 (gyeong-go-ha-da)
warnings *n.* 주의점 (ju-ui-jjeom)
wash *v.* 씻다 (ssit-da)
wash dishes *v.* 설거지하다 (seol-geo-ji-ha-da)
wash one's face *v.* 세수하다 (se-su-ha-da)
wash hair *v.* 머리를 감다 (meo-ri-reul gam-tta)
wash hands *v.* 손을 씻다 (son-eul ssit-da)
wash laundry *v.* 빨래하다 (ppal-lae-ha-da)
washer *n.* 세탁기 (se-tak-gi)
wasp *n.* 까다로운 사람 (kka-da-ro-un sa-ram)
wastepaper *n.* 휴지 (hyu-ji)
watch *v.* 보다 (bo-da), 시계 (si-gye)
watch out *v.* 조심하다 (jo-sim-ha-da)
watch TV *v.* 텔레비전을 보다 (tel-le-bi-jeon-eul bo-da)
watchmaker *n.* 시계방 (si-gye-bbang)
water *n.* 물 (mul)
watermelon *n.* 수박 (su-bak)
wave *v.* 손을 흔들다 (son-eul heun-deul-da), 파도 (pa-do)
way *n.* 길 (gil), 방법 (bang-beop)
weapon *n.* 무기 (mu-gi)

wear *v.* 옷을 입다 (os-eul ip-da), 신발을 신다 (sin-bal-eul sin-tta), 시계를 차다 (si-gye-reul cha-da), 장갑을 끼다 (jang-gab-eul kki-da), 모자를 쓰다 (mo-ja-reul sseu-da)

weather *n.* 날씨 (nal-ssi)

weather forecast *n.* 일기예보 (il-gi-ye-bo)

wedding *n.* 결혼식 (gyeol-hon-sik)

wedding gown *n.* 웨딩드레스 (we-ding-deu-re-sseu)

wedding hall *n.* 결혼식장 (gyeol-hon-sik-jang)

Wednesday *n.* 수요일 (su-yo-il)

week *n.* 주 (ju), 주일 (ju-il)

weekday *n.* 평일 (pyeong-il), 주중 (ju-jung)

weekend *n.* 주말 (ju-mal)

welcome *n., v.* 환영 (hwan-yeong), 환영하다 (hwan-yeong-ha-da)

well *adv.* 잘 (jal), 글쎄요 (geul-sse-yo); **go well** 잘 되다 (jal doe-da)

west *n.* 서 (seo), 서쪽 (seo-jjok)

west coast *n.* 서부 (seo-bu)

west side *n.* 서쪽 (seo-jjok)

western *adj.* 서쪽의 (seo-jjog-ui)

wet *adj.* 젖은 (jeoj-eun), 젖다 (jeot-da)

whale *n.* 고래 (go-rae)

what *pron.* 뭐 (mwo), 무슨 (mu-seun)

what day *adv.* 며칠 (myeo-chil)

what kind *adv.* 어떤 (eo-tteon)

what matter *adv.* 웬일 (wen-nil)

whatever *pron.* 아무 거나 (a-mu geo-na)

wheel *n.* 수레바퀴 (su-re-ba-kwi), 자동차 핸들 (ja-dong-cha haen-deul)

when *adv.* 언제 (eon-je)

whenever *conj.* 아무 때나 (a-mu ttae-na)

where *adv.* 어디 (eo-di)

wherever *conj.* 아무 데나 (a-mu de-na)

which *pron.* 어떤 (eo-tteon), 어느 (eo-neu)

while *conj.* -동안 (dong-an), -으면서 (eu-myeon-seo); **a little while ago** 아까 (a-kka); **after a while** 잠시 후 (jam-si hu)

whine *v.* 흐느껴 울다 (heu-neu-kkyeo ul-da), 투덜대다 (tu-deol-dae-da), 징징거리다 (jing-jing-geo-ri-da)

white *n., adj.* 하얀 (ha-yan), 하얗다 (ha-ya-ta), 하얀색 (ha-yan-saek)

who *pron.* 누구 (nu-gu)

whoever *pron.* 아무나 (a-mu-na)

whole *adj.* 모든 (mo-deun), 전체의 (jeon-che-ui)

whose *pron.* 누구의 (nu-gu-ui)

why *adv.* 왜 (wae)

wide *adj.* 넓은 (neolb-eun), 넓다 (neol-tta)

widow *n.* 과부 (gwa-bu)

widower *n.* 홀아비 (hol-a-bi)

width *n.* 넓이 (neolb-i)

wife *n.* 아내 (a-nae), 집사람 (jip-sa-ram), 부인 (bu-in) (*honorific*), 사모님 (sa-mo-nim) (*honorific*)

will *aux.* -을 것이다 (eul kkeos-i-da)

win *v.* 이기다 (i-gi-da), 상을 타다 (sang-eul ta-da)

wind *n.* 바람 (ba-ram); *v.* 바람이 불다 (ba-ram-i bul-da)

window *n.* 창문 (chang-mun); **window seat** 창측 좌석 (chang-cheuk jwa-seok)

windy *adj.* 바람이 부는 (ba-ram-i bu-neun)

wine *n.* 포도주 (po-do-ju)

winter *n.* 겨울 (gyeo-ul)

wire *n.* 철사 (cheol-ssa), 전선 (jeon-seon); *v.* 전보를 치다 (jeon-bo-reul chi-da)

wise *adj.* 현명한 (hyeon-myeong-han), 현명하다 (hyeon-myeong-ha-da)

wish *v.* 바라다 (ba-ra-da), 희망하다 (hui-mang-ha-da, hi-mang-ha-da)

with *prep.* -와 같이 (wa ga-chi)

withdraw *v.* 도로 찾다 (do-ro chat-da), 출금하다 (chul-geum-ha-da)

without *prep.* -없이 (eops-i)

without any reason *adv.* 그냥 ((geu-nyang)

without fail *adv.* 반드시 (ban-deu-si)

woman *n.* 여자 (yeo-ja), 여성 (yeo-seong)

wonder *v.* 궁금하다 (gung-geum-ha-da)

wonderful *adj.* 훌륭한 (hul-lyung-han), 훌륭하다 (hul-lyung-ha-da)

wood *n.* 나무 (na-mu)

wooden *adj.* 나무로 만든 (na-mu-ro man-deun)

woods *n.* 숲 (sup)

wool *n.* 모 (mo), 모직 (mo-jik)

word *n.* 단어 (dan-eo), 말 (mal), 말씀 (mal-sseum) (*honorific*)

work *n.* 일 (il); *v.* 일하다 (il-ha-da)

workaholic *n.* 일벌레 (il-beol-lae)

workplace *n.* 직장 (jik-jang)

world *n.* 세상 (se-sang)

worry *v.* 걱정하다 (geok-jeong-ha-da), 고민하다 (go-min-ha-da)

worse *adj.* 더 나쁜 (deo na-ppeun)

worst *adj.* 최악의 (choe-ag-ui)

wrap *v.* 싸다 (ssa-da), 포장하다 (po-jang-ha-da)

wrapping paper *n.* 포장지 (po-jang-ji)

wreck *n.* 난파 (nan-pa); *v.* 난파하다 (nan-pa-ha-da), 난파시키다 (nan-pa-si-ki-da)

wrestling *n.* 레슬링 (re-seul-ling)

write *v.* 쓰다 (sseu-da)

write down *v.* 적다 (jeok-da)

writer *n.* 작가 (jak-ga)

wrong *adj.* 틀리다 (teul-li-da), 잘못되다 (jal-mot-doe-da)

X

X-ray *n.* 엑스레이 (ek-seu-re-i)

Y

yacht *n.* 요트 (yo-teu)

yard *n.* 마당 (ma-dang), 정원 (jeong-won)

year *n.* 해 (hae), 년 (nyeon); **this year** *adv.* 올해 (ol-hae), 금년 (geum-nyeon)

yell *v.* 소리지르다 (so-ri ji-reu-da)

yellow *n.* 노란색 (no-ran-saek); *adj.* 노란 (no-ran), 노랗다 (no-ra-ta)

yes *adv.* 네 (ne), 예 (ye)

yesterday *n.* 어제 (eo-je)

yet *adv.* 아직 (a-jik)

young *adj.* 어린 (eo-rin), 어리다 (eo-ri-da), 젊은 (jeolm-eun), 젊다 (jeom-tta)

Z

zest *n.* 풍미 (pung-mi), 맛 (mat), 풍취 (pung-chwi)
zip code *n.* 우편번호 (u-pyeon-beon-ho)
zipper *n.* 지퍼 (ji-peo)
zone *n.* 지역 (ji-yeok)
zoo *n.* 동물원 (dong-mul-won)
zucchini *n.* 호박 (ho-bak)

A BRIEF KOREAN GRAMMAR

1. Pronouns

Personal Pronouns

Singular	Plain	Honorific	Humble
1st person (I, me, myself)	나 / 내 na / nae	---	저 / 제 jeo / je
2nd person (you)	너 neo	---	---
3rd person (he, she, it, etc.)	이/그/저사람 i/geu/jeo-sa-ram	이/그/저분 i/geu/jeo-bun	---
	이/그/저것 i/geu/jeo-geot	---	---

The use of personal pronouns is not common in Korean, except for the first person pronoun. With the second and third person, usually either the name or title is used.

Plural	Plain	Honorific	Humble
1st person (we)	우리(들) u-ri-(deul)	---	저희(들) jeo-hui-(deul)
2nd person (you all)	너희(들) neo-hui-(deul)	---	---
3rd person (they)	이/그/저사람들 i/geu/jeo-sa-ram-deul	이/그/저분들 i/geu/jeo-bun-deul	---
	이/그/저것들 i/geu/jeo-geot-deul	---	---

Possessive Pronouns

Singular	Plain	Honorific	Humble
1st person (my)	내 nae	---	제 je
2nd person (your)	네 ne	---	---
3rd person (his/hers/its)	이/그/저 사람들(의) i/geul jeo-sa-ram-deul-(ui)	이/그/저분(의) i/geul jeo-bun-deul-(ui)	---

Plural	Plain	Honorific	Humble
1st person (our)	우리(들)(의) u-ri-(deul)-(ui)	---	저희(들)(의) jeo-hui-(deul)-(ui)
2nd person (your)	너희(들)(의) neo-hui-(deul)-(ui)	---	---
3rd person (their)	이/그/저 사람들(의) i/geuljeo-sa-ram-deul-(ui)	이/그/저분들(의) i/geuljeo-bun-deul-(ui)	---
	이/그/저것들(의) i/geuljeo-geot-deul-(ui)	---	---

Plural nouns in English use a plural suffix, e.g. the "s" in "fields". In Korean, the plural suffix –다 (-ta, -da) is optional and rarely used.

2. Demonstratives

For the topic markers, subject markers and object markers, please see particles below.

이 (i)
this (*near speaker*)

이것/이거 i-geot/i-geo	이건 (*topic*) i-geon	이게 (*subj.*) i-ge	이걸 (*obj.*) i-geol
여기 (place) yeo-gi	이쪽 (direction) i-jjok	이사람 (person) i-sa-ram	이분 (person, hon.) i-bun

그 (geu)
that (*near listener*)

그것/그거 (topic)	그건 (topic)	그게 (*subj.*)	그걸 (*obj.*)
geu-geot/ *geu-geo*	*geu-geon*	*geu-ge*	*geu-geol*

거기	그쪽	그사람	그분
(place)	(direction)	(person)	(person, hon.)
geo-gi	*geu-jjok*	*geu-sa-ram*	*geu-bun*

저 (jeo)
that over there (*away from both speaker and listener*)

저것/저거	저건 (topic)	저게 (*subj.*)	저걸 (*obj.*)
jeo-geot/ *jeo-geo*	*jeo-geon*	*jeo-ge*	*jeo-geol*

저기	저쪽	저사람	저분
(place)	(direction)	(person)	(person, hon.)
jeo-gi	*jeo-jjok*	*jeo-sa-ram*	*jeo-bun*

3. Particles

Particles are words that indicate the context in which one is to understand the noun, phrase, or sentence to which they are attached. They are usually short, often no more than a syllable, and some have functions similar to such English prepositions as *in, to, at,* and *with.* Others are used as markers for the subject and object nouns in a sentence. Remember that particles always come after the sentence elements they modify. Occasionally, different particles are used depending on whether the word to which they are attached ends with a consonant or a vowel.

Subject

-이 (-i) (*used after a consonant*)	**학생이** (hak-saeng-*i*) *student* (+ subject marker [*subj.*])
-가 (-ga) (*used after a vowel*)	**의사가** (ui-sa-*ga*) *doctor* (+ *subj.*)

-께서 (-kke-seo) *(honorific)*

아버지께서
(a-beo-ji-kke-seo)
father (+ *subj.*)

Object

-을 (-eul)
(used after a consonant)

책상을
(chaek-sang-eul)
desk (+ object marker
  [*obj.*])

-를 (-reul)
(used after a vowel)

의자를
(ui-ja-reul)
chair (+ *obj.*)

Topic

-은 (-eun)
(used after a consonant)

한국말은
(han-gung-mal-eun)
Korean language (+
  topic marker [*top.*])

-는 (-nuen)
(used after a vowel)

한국어는
(han-gug-eo-neun)
Korean language (+*top.*)

Dative (Indirect Object)

-에게 (-e-ge)

친구에게
(chin-gu-e-ge)
to my friend

-한테 (-han-te)
(colloquial)

친구한테
(chin-gu-han-te)
to my friend

-께 (-kke)
(honorific)

아버지께
(a-beo-ji-kke)
to my father

Source

-에게서 (-e-ge-seo)

친구에게서
(chin-gu-e-ge-seo)
from my friend

-한테서 (-han-te-seo)
(*colloquial*)

친구한테서
(chin-gu-han-te-seo)
from my friend

Location

-에 (-e)
(*current*)

학교에 있어요.
(hak-gyo-e iss-eo-yo.)
I am in school.

(*destination*)

학교에 가요.
(hak-gyo-e ga-yo.)
I go to school.

-에서 (-e-seo)
(*place of action*)

학교에서 공부해요.
(hak-gyo-e-seo gong-bu-
hae-yo.)
I study at school.

(*starting point of action*)

학교에서 왔어요.
(hak-gyo-e-seo wass-
eo-yo.)
I came from the school.

-(으)로 ([-eu]-ro)
(*direction of action*)

서울로 가요.
(seo-ul-lo ga-yo.)
I go to Seoul.

-에서 . . . –까지
(from . . . to . . .)
(-e-seo ... -kka-ji)

미국에서 한국까지
(mi-gug-e-seo han-guk-
kka-ji)
from America to Korea

Time

-에 (-e)
(at, on . . .)

아침에
(a-chim-e)
in the morning

-부터 . . . -까지
(from . . . until. . .)
(-bu-teo ... -kka-ji)

아침부터 저녁까지
(a-chim-bu-teo jeo-
nyeok-kka-ji)
*from morning until
evening*

Purpose

-(으)러 (in order to)
([-eu]-reo)

친구 만나러
(chin-gu man-na-reo)
*in order to meet my
friend*

-(으)려고 (in order to)
([-eu]-ryeo-go)

서울에 가려고
(seo-ul-e ga-ryeo-go)
in order to go to Seoul

Miscellaneous

-(으)로 (by means of)
([-eu]-ro)

비행기로
(bi-haeng-gi-ro)
(transportation)

볼펜으로
(bol-pen-eu-ro)
(instrument)

-도 (also)
(-do)

나도 가고 싶어요.
(na-do ga-go sip-eo-yo.)
I also want to go.

-만 (only, just)
(-man)

콜라만 주세요.
(col-la-man ju-se-yo)
*Please give me a Coke
only.*

-(이)나 ([-i]-na)
(or something, just)

오늘 집에서 잠<u>이나</u>
잘래요.
(o-neul jib-e-seo jam-<u>i-na</u> jal-lae-yo.)
I'll just stay home and sleep today.

(as many as; already)

오늘 커피를 세잔<u>이나</u>
마셨어요.
(o-neul keo-pi-reul se jan-<u>i-na</u> ma-syeoss-eo-yo.)
I already drank three cups of coffee today.

-밖에 (nothing but, only)
(-bakk-e)

다섯 사람<u>밖에</u> 안
왔어요.
(da-seot sa-ram-<u>bakk-e</u> an wass-eo-yo.)
Only five people came.

(-밖에 always accompanies a negative verb. [Verbs are discussed below in Numbers 6, 7, and 8.])

-에 (-e) (per, for)

한 상자<u>에</u> 2000
원이<u>에</u>요.
(han sang-ja-<u>e</u> i-cheon-won-i-<u>e</u>-yo.)
It's 2000 won [Korean currency] per box.

4. Question Words

누가
(nu-ga)
who (*subject*)

<u>누가</u> 간호원이세요?
(<u>nu-ga</u> gan-ho-won-i-se-yo?)
Who's the nurse?

누구
(nu-gu)
who

<u>누구</u>를 찾으세요?
(<u>nu-gu</u>-reul chaj-eu-se-yo?)
Who are you looking for?

무슨
(mu-seun)
what kind of; what

<u>무슨</u> 일을 하세요?
(<u>mu-seun</u> il-eul ha-se-yo?)
What kind of work do you do?
What do you do for a living?

무엇   <u>무엇</u>을 좋아하세요?
(mu-eot)   (<u>mu-eos</u>-eul jo-a-ha-se-yo?)
what   *What do you like?*

뭐   <u>뭐</u>가 제일 어려우세요?
(mwo)   (<u>mwo</u>-ga je-il eo-ryeo-u-se-yo?)
what (colloquial)   *What is the most difficult thing for*
                                      you?

어느   <u>어느</u> 나라 사람이세요?
(eo-neu)   (<u>eo-neu</u> na-ra sa-ram-i-se-yo?)
which   *Which country are you from?*

어디   <u>어디</u> 사세요?
(eo-di)   (<u>eo-di</u> sa-se-yo?)
where   *Where do you live?*

어떻게   부산에 <u>어떻게</u> 가요?
(eo-tteo-ke)   (bu-san-e <u>eo-tteo-ke</u> ga-yo?)
how   *How can I get to Pusan?*

어떤   <u>어떤</u> 사람을 좋아하세요?
(eo-tteon)   (<u>eo-tteon</u> sa-ram-eul jo-a-ha-se
what kind of   yo?)
                                What kind of people do you like?

언제   <u>언제</u> 한국에 가세요?
(eon-je)   (<u>eon-je</u> han-gug-e ga-se-yo?)
when   *When are you leaving for Korea?*

얼마나   한국에 <u>얼마나</u> 계실 거예요?
(eol-ma-na)   (han-gug-e <u>eol-ma-na</u> gye-sil geo
how long/many/much   ye-yo?)
                                How long are you staying in
                                Korea?

왜   <u>왜</u> 한국에 가세요?
(wae)   (<u>wae</u> han-gug-e ga-se-yo?)
why   *Why are you going to Korea?*

5. Indefinite Pronouns

누가   <u>누가</u> 왔어요.
(nu-ga)   (<u>nu-ga</u> wass-eo-yo.)
someone/anyone   *There is someone.*

누구
(nu-gu)
someone/anyone

누구를 데리고 올 거예요.
(nu-gu-reul de-ri-go ol geo-ye-yo.)
I am bringing someone.

무슨
(mu-seun)
some kind of

무슨 냄새가 나요.
(mu-seun naem-sae-ga na-yo.)
I smell something.

뭐
(mwo)
something/anything

뭐 좀 샀어요.
(mwo jom sass-eo-yo.)
I bought something.

무엇
(mu-eot)
something/anything

(original form of 뭐 *mwo*)

어느
(eo-neu)
one

어느 날 갑자기 귀가 잘 안 들렸어요.
(eo-neu-nal gap-ja-gi gwi-ga jal an deul-lyeoss-eo-yo.)
One day I couldn't hear all of a sudden.

어디
(eo-di)
somewhere/anywhere

어디 좀 가고 싶어요.
(eo-di jom ga-go sip-eo-yo.)
I want to go somewhere.

어떻게
(eo-tteo-ke)
somehow

어떻게 좀 해 보세요.
(eo-tteo-ke jom hae bo-se-yo)
Please do something.

어떤
(eo-tteon)

some

어떤 사람이 집에 왔어요.
(eo-tteon sa-ram-i jib-e wass-eo-yo.)
Somebody came to our house.

언제
(eon-je)
sometime/anytime

언제 한번 만날까요?
(eon-je han-beon man-nal-kka-yo?)
Should we meet sometime?

누구든지
(nu-gu-deun-ji)
whoever/whomever

누구든지 안젤라를 좋아해요.
(nu-gu-deun-ji an-jel-la-reul jo-a hae-yo.)
Whomever you ask, they all like Angela.

뭐든지
(mwo-deun-ji)
whatever; anything

저는 <u>뭐든지</u> 다 잘 먹어요.
(jeo-neun <u>mwo-deun-ji</u> da jal
  meog-eo-yo.)
*Whatever the food is, I will eat
  very well.*

어느 것이든지
(eo-neu geos-i- deun-ji)
whichever

한국음식은 <u>어느 것이든지</u> 다
좋아해요.
(han-gug-eum-sig-eun <u>eo-neu
  geos-i-deun-ji</u> da jo-a-hae-yo.)
*I like all Korean food, whichever
  dish it may be.*

어디든지
(eo-di-deun-ji)
wherever

주말에는 <u>어디든지</u> 여행을 가고
싶어요.
(ju-mal-e-neun <u>eo-di-deun-ji</u> yeo-
  haeng-eul ga-go sip-eo-yo.)
*Wherever the destination may be, I
  want to travel on weekends.*

어떻게든지
(eo-tteo-ke-deun-ji)
whatsoever,
  no matter what

<u>어떻게든지</u> 외국에 한번 가고
싶어요.
(<u>eo-tteo-ke-deun-ji</u> oe-gug-e han
  beon ga-go sip-eo-yo.)
*No matter what I want to go
  abroad once.*

어떤 것이든지
(eo-tteon
  geos-i-deun-ji)
whichever/whatever

저는 영화는 <u>어떤 것이든지</u> 다
봐요.
(jeo-neun yeong-hwa-neun <u>eo-
  tteon geos-i-deun-ji</u> da bwa-yo.)
*I like all movies, whatever kind
  you might think of.*

언제든지
(eon-je-deun-ji)
whenever

<u>언제든지</u> 우리 집에 놀러
오세요.
(<u>eon-je-deun-ji</u> u-ri-jib-e nol-leo
  o-se-yo.)
*Come to my house whenever you
  like.*

6. Word Formation

Noun Formation

To form nouns from a verb, add **-기** (-gi) or **-는 것** (-neun-geot) after the verb stem.

Verb	Noun
걷다 (geot-da) *walk*	**걷기 / 걷는 것** (geot-gi)/ (geon-neun geot) *walking*
노래하다 (no-rae-ha-da) *sing*	**노래하기 / 노래하는 것** (no-rae-ha-gi) / (no-rae-ha-neun geot) *singing*
쇼핑가다 (syo-ping-ga-da) *shop*	**쇼핑가기 / 쇼핑가는 것** (syo-ping-ga-gi) / (syo-ping-ga-neun geot) *shopping*
자다 (ja-da) *sleep*	**자기 / 자는 것** (ja-gi) / (ja-neun geot) *sleeping*

Verb Formation

To form verbs from a noun, add **-하다** (-ha-da) to the noun.

Noun	Verb
일 (il) *work*	**일하다** (il-ha-da) *to work*
공부 (gong-bu) *study*	**공부하다** (gong-bu-ha-da) *to study*
생각 (saeng-gak) *thinking*	**생각하다** (saeng-ga-ka-da) *to think*
수영 (su-yeong) *swimming*	**수영하다** (su-yeong-ha-da) *to swim*

Noun Modifier Formation

A construction consisting of [clause + ~는 / (으)ㄴ] before a noun is called a relative clause. It is a type of noun-modifying construction. Relative clauses in Korean have the following characteristics: (a) the modifying clause precedes the modified noun; (b) there are no relative pronouns such as *which, who,* and *that* as in English.

	Verb: 읽다 / 가다 (ilk-da/ ga-da) [to read, to go]	Adjective: 좋다 / 싸다 (jo-ta/ ssa-da) [to be good, to be cheap]	있다/없다 (it-da/ eop-da) [to exist, not to exist]	이다 (i-da) [to be]
Past / **Retrospective** **(Imperfect)**	-던 읽던 / 가던 (ilk-deon/ ga-deon)	-던 좋던 / 싸던 (jo-teon/ ssa-deon)	-던 있던 / 없던 (it-deon/ eop-deon)	-던 이던 (i-deon)
Past / **Completed**	-(으)ㄴ 읽은 / 간 (ilgeun/gan)			
Present / **Ongoing**	-는 읽는 / 가는 (ilk-neun/ ga-neun)	-(으)ㄴ 좋은 / 싼 (jo-eun /ssan)	-는 있는 / 없는 (in-neun/ eom-neun)	-ㄴ 인 (in)
Future / **Unrealized**	-(으)ㄹ 읽을 / 갈 (ilg-eul/gal)	-(으)ㄹ 좋을 / 쌀 (joeul/ssal)	-(으)ㄹ 있을/ 없을 (iss-eul/ eops-eul)	-ㄹ 일 (il)

Adverb Formation

To form an adverb from an adjective, add **-게** (-ge) after the adjective stem.

Adjective   *Adverb*

재미있다   **재미있게**
(jae-mi-it-da)   (jae-mi-it-ge)
interesting   *interestingly*

늦다   **늦게**
(neut-da)   (neut-ge)
late   *late*

바쁘다   **바쁘게**
(ba-ppeu-da)   (ba-ppeu-ge)
busy   busily

시끄럽다   **시끄럽게**
(si-kkeu-reop-da)   (si-kkeu-reop-ge)
loud   *loudly*

7. Tenses

Korean verbs have three tenses: present, past, and future. The rules for conjugating them in the tenses appear below. Please note that verbs are conjugated by tense only and not by person.

Present:

verb stem + **-아/어요**
(-a/eo-yo)

지금 한국에 가요.
(ji-geum han-gug-e ga-yo.)
I am leaving for Korea now.

Past:

verb stem + **-았/었어요**
(-ass/eoss-eo-yo)

작년에 한국에 갔어요.
(jang-nyeon-e han-gug-e gass-eo-yo.)
I went to Korea last year.

Future (probability in the future):

verb stem + -(으)ㄹ 거예요

(-[eu]l kkeo-ye-yo)

내년에 한국에 갈 거예요.

(nae-nyeon-e han-gug-e gal kkeo-ye-yo.)

I will go to Korea next year.

8. Negation of Verbs

Short-form Negation

안-	안 먹어요.
(an-)	(an meog-eo-yo.)
don't	*I don't eat.*

공부 안 해요.

(gong-bu an hae-yo.)

I don't study.

못-	못 먹어요.
(mot-)	(mot meog-eo-yo.)
can't	*I can't eat.*

공부 못해요.

(Gong-bu mo-tae-yo.)

I can't study.

Long-form Negation

-지 않다	먹지 않아요.
(-ji anta)	(meok-ji an-a-yo.)
	I don't eat.

-지 못하다	먹지 못해요.
(ji mo-ta-da)	(meok-ji mo-tae-yo.)
	I can't eat.

-지 말다 (request only)	먹지 마세요.
(-ji mal-da)	(meok-ji ma-se-yo)
	Please don't eat it.

Special Negation Words

있다 (it-da) versus 없다 (eop-ta)

> **있어요**
> (iss-eo-yo)
> *there is . . .*

> **없어요**
> (eops-eo-yo)
> *there is not . . .*

이다 (i-da) versus 아니다 (a-ni-da)

> **이에요.**
> (i-e-yo)
> *it is. . .*
> **아니에요.**
> (a-ni-e-yo)
> *it is not . . .*

알다 (al-da) versus 모르다 (mo-reu-da)

> **알아요**
> (al-a-yo . . .)
> *I know . . .*

> **몰라요**
> (mol-la-yo . . .)
> *I don't know . . .*

좋다 (jo-ta) versus 싫다 (sil-ta)

> **좋아요**
> (jo-a-yo . . .)
> *I like . . .*

> **싫어요**
> (sil-eo-yo . . .)
> *I don't like . . .*

좋아하다 (jo-a-ha-da) vs. 싫어하다 (sil-eo-ha-da)

좋아해요
(jo-a-hae-yo . . .)
s/he likes . . .

싫어해요
(sil-eo-hae-yo . . .)
s/he doesn't like . . .

9. Honorific Expressions

Korean is a language whose honorific patterns are highly systematic. Honorific forms appear in hierarchical address/reference terms and titles, some commonly used nouns and verbs, the pronoun system, particles, and verb suffixes. Sentences in Korean can hardly be composed without knowledge of one's social relationship with the listener or reference to age, social status, and kinship. Honorific forms are used when a social or familial superior, a distant peer, or a stranger must be referred to or spoken to with respect.

Nouns

	Plain	*Honorific*	*Humble*
age	나이 (na-)	연세 (yeon-se)	
name	이름 (i-reum)	성함 (seong-ham)	
birthday	생일 (saeng-il)	생신 (saeng-sin)	
word	말 (mal)	말씀 (mal-sseum)	말씀 (mal-ssum)
house	집 (jip)	댁 (daek)	
meal	밥 (bap)	진지 (jin-ji)	
counter	사람/명 (sa-ram/ myeong)	분 (bun)	

Pronouns

	Plain	Honorific	Humble
he/she	이/그/저 사람 (i/geu/jeo-sa-ram)	이/그/저분 (i/geu/jeo-bun)	
I	나는/내가 (na-neun/nae-ga)		저는/제가 (jeo-neun /je-ga)
my	내 (nae)		제 (je)
we	우리 (u-ri)		저희 (jeo-hui)

Verbs

	Plain	Honorific	Humble
see/meet	보다/만나다 (bo-da/man-na-da)	보시다/만나시다 bo-si-da/man-na-si-da	뵙다 bwoep-da
be/exist/stay	있다 (it-da)	계시다 (gye-si-da)	
die	죽다 (juk-da)	돌아가시다 (dol-a-ga-si-da)	
be well/fine	잘 있다 (jal it-da)	안녕하시다 (an-nyeong-ha-si-da)	
sleep	자다 (ja-da)	주무시다 (ju-mu-si-da)	
eat	먹다 (meok-da)	드시다/잡수시다 deu-si-da/jap-su-si-da	
give	주다 (ju-da)	주시다 (ju-si-da)	드리다 (deu-ri-da)
speak	말하다 (mal-ha-da)	말씀하시다 (mal-sseum-ha-si-da)	말씀드리다 (mal-sseum-deu-ri-da)

	Plain	*Honorific*	*Humble*
ask	물어보다 (mul-eo-bo- -da)	물어보시다 (mul-eo-bo- si-da)	여쭈어보다 (yeo-jju-eo- da)

Particles

subject	-이/가 (-I)/(-ga)	-께서 (-kke-seo)
topic	-은/는 (-eun)/(neun)	-께서는 (-kke-seo-neun)
goal	-한테/에게 (-han-te) /(e-ge)	-께 (-kke)

10. Irregular Verbs

In Korean, there are verbs that change their final sound before a suffix that begins with a certain sound. These verbs are commonly called irregular. There are nine types, as shown below.

ㄷ-Irregular Verbs
ㄷ-irregular verbs are those whose stem-final ㄷ becomes ㄹ when before a vowel, as in 듣는다 (deut-neun-da) vs. 들어요 (deul-eo-yo) [to listen], 걷는다 (geot-neun-da) vs. 걸어요 (geol-eo-yo) [to walk], 묻는다 (mut-neun-da) vs. 물어요(mul-eo-yo) [to ask].

ㅂ-Irregular Verbs
ㅂ- irregular verbs are those whose final ㅂ sound becomes 우 before a vowel, as in 가깝다 (ga-kkap-da) vs. 가까워요 (ga-kka-wo-yo) [to be close], 어렵다 (eo-reop-da) vs. 어려워요 (eo-ryeo-wo-yo) [to be difficult], 쉽다 (swip-da) vs. 쉬워요 (swi-wo-yo) [to be easy], 춥다 (chup-da) vs. 추워요 (chu-wo-yo) [to be cold], 덥다 (deop-da) vs. 더워요 (deo-wo-yo) [to be hot], 무겁다 (mu-geop-da) vs. 무거워요 (mu-geo-wo-yo) [to be heavy].

ㅅ-Irregular Verbs

ㅅ-irregular verbs are those whose final ㅅ is deleted before a vowel, as in 짓는다 (jit-neun-da) vs. 지어요 (ji-eo-yo) [to build], 붓는다 (but-neun-da) vs. 부어요 (bu-eo-yo) [to pour], 젓는다 (jeot-neun-da) vs. 저어요 (jeo-eo-yo) [to stir], 잇는다 (it-neun-da) vs. 이어요 (i-eo-yo) [to connect].

으-Irregular Verbs

으-irregular verbs are those whose final 으 is deleted before another vowel. All 으- final verbs follow this pattern, as in 쓰다 (sseu-da) vs. 써요 (sseo-yo) [to write], 바쁘다 (ba-ppeu-da) vs. 바빠요 (ba-ppa-yo) [to be busy], 크다 (keu-da) vs. 커요 (keo-yo) [to be big], 예쁘다 (ye-ppeu-da) vs. 예뻐요 (ye-ppeo-yo) [to be pretty], 나쁘다 (na-ppeu-da) vs. 나빠요 (na-ppa-yo) [to be bad], 아프다 (a-peu-da) vs. 아파요 (a-pa-yo) [to be sick].

ㄹ-Irregular Verbs

ㄹ-irregular verbs are those whose stem-final ㄹ is deleted before the consonants ㄴ, ㅂ, or ㅅ, as in 알아요 (al-a-yo) vs. 아세요 (a-se-yo) [to know], 놀아요 (nol-a-yo) vs. 놉니다 (nop-ni-da) [to play], 돌아요 (dol-a-yo) vs. 도니까 (do-ni-kka) [to turn]. All ㄹ- final verbs follow this pattern.

르-Irregular Verbs

르-irregular verbs are those whose final -르 becomes -ㄹㄹ before a suffix beginning with –eo or –a, as in 부르다 (bu-reu-da) vs. 불러요 (bul-leo-yo) [to call], 모르다 (mo-reu-da) vs. 몰라요 (mol-la-yo) [to not know], 빠르다 (ppa-reu-da) vs. 빨라요 (ppal-la-yo) [to be fast].

러-Irregular Verbs

러-irregular verbs are those that have the ㄹ inserted before a suffix beginning with –eo or –a, as in 푸르다 (pu-reu-da) [to be blue] vs. 푸르러서 (pu-reu-reo-seo) [since it is blue]. 이르다 (i-reu-da) and 누르다 (nu-reu-da) also follow this pattern.

여-Irregular Verbs

여-irregular verbs are those that undergo vowel change
(from ㅏ to ㅐ) before a suffix beginning with –eo or –a, as
in 하다 (ha-da) [to do] vs. 해서 (hae-seo) [because
someone does something]. All verbs ending with
–하다 follow this pattern, such as 좋아하다 (jo-a-ha-da),
싫어하다 (sil-eo-ha-da), 여행하다 (yeo-haeng-ha-da), and
수영하다 (su-yeong-ha-da).

ㅎin Irregular Verbs

ㅎirregular verbs are those whose final -ㅎ is deleted
before a nasal consonant (ㄴ, ㄹ, or ㅁ) and a vowel. They
may undergo further phonological change with the
subsequent vowel, as in 빨갛다 (ppal-ga-ta) [to be red] vs.
빨간 ppal-gan [red], 하얗다 (ha-ya-ta) [to be white] vs.
하야니까 (ha-ya-ni-kka) [because it is white], 파랗다 (pa-
ra-ta) vs. 파라면 (pa-ra-myeon) [if it is blue]. 노랗다 (no-
ra-ta), 까맣다 (kka-ma-ta), 이렇다 (i-reo-ta), 그렇다 (geu-
reo-ta), 저렇다 (jeo-reo-ta), and 어떻다 (eo-tteo-ta) follow
this pattern.

11. Passive Verbs

Active	*Passive*	*Example*
보다 (bo-da) *to see*	보이다 (bo-i-da) *to be seen*	저기 신호등이 보여요. (jeo-gi sin-ho-deung-i bo-yeo-yo.) *I see the traffic light over there.*
쓰다 (sseu-da) *to use*	쓰이다 (sseu-i-da) *to be used*	이 약이 감기에 잘 쓰여요. (i-yag-i gam-gi-e jal sseu-yeo-yo.) *This medicine is often used for colds.*
닫다 (dat-da) *to close*	닫히다 (da-chi-da) *to be closed*	바람에 문이 닫혔어요. (ba-ram-e mun-i da- chyeoss-eo-yo.) *The door was closed by the wind.*

Active	**Passive**	**Example**
막다	막히다	차가 많아서 길이 막혀요.
(mak-da)	(ma-ki-da)	(cha-ga man-a-seo gil-i ma-kyeo-yo.)
to block	*to be blocked*	*The street is blocked due to many cars.*
잡다	잡히다	도둑이 경찰한테 잡혔어요.
(jap-da)	(ja-pi-da)	(do-dug-i gyeong-chal-han-te ja-pyess-eo-yo.)
to catch	*to be caught*	*The thief was caught by the policeman.*
물다	물리다	우체부가 개한테 물렸어요.
(mul-da)	(mul-li-da)	(u-che-bu-ga gae-han-te mul-lyeoss-eo-yo.)
to bite	*to be bitten*	*The mailman was bitten by a dog.*
열다	열리다	가게문이 열렸어요.
(yeol-da)	(yeol-li-da)	(ga-ge-mun-i yeol lyeoss-eo-yo.)
to open	*to be open*	*The store door is open.*
듣다	들리다	음악 소리가 들려요.
(deut-da)	(deul-li-da)	(eum-ak so-ri-ga deul lyeo-yo.)
to hear	*to be heard*	*Music is heard by me.*
팔다	팔리다	요즘 집이 잘 팔려요.
(pal-da)	(pal-li-da)	(yo-jeum jib-i jal pal-lyeo-yo.)
to sell	*to be sold*	*Houses are sold quickly these days.*
뺏다	뺏기다	개한테 사과를 뺏겼어요.
(ppaet-da)	(ppaet-gi-da)	(gae-han-te sa-gwa-reul ppaet-gyeoss-eo-yo.)
to take away	*to be taken away*	*My apple was taken away by the dog.*

Active	Passive	Example
안다 (an-tta) *to hold*	안기다 (an-gi-da) *to be held*	아이가 엄마한테 안겼어요. (a-i-ga eom-ma-ha-te an-gyeoss-eo-yo.) *The baby was being held* *by the mother.*
쫓다 (jjot-da) *to chase*	쫓기다 (jjot-gi-da) *to be chased*	쥐가 고양이한테 쫓겨요. (jwi-ga go-yang-i han-te jjot-gyeo-yo.) *A mouse is being chased* *by a cat.*

12. Causative Verbs

Plain	Causative	Example
먹다 (meok-da) *to eat*	먹이다 (meog-i-da) *to feed someone*	엄마가 아기한테 우유를 먹여요. (eom-ma-ga a-gi-han-te u-yu-reul meog- yeo-yo.) *The mother is feeding* *the baby.*
죽다 (juk-da) *to die*	죽이다 (jug-i-da) *to kill someone*	제가 파리를 죽였어요. (je-ga pa-ri-reul jug- yeoss-eo-yo.) *I killed the fly.*
끓다 (kkeul-ta) *to boil*	끓이다 (kkeul-i-da) *to boil something*	라면을 먹으려고 물을 끓여요. (ra-myeon-eul meog-eu- ryeo-go mul-eul kkeul-yeo-yo.) *I'm boiling water to* *cook ramen.*

Plain	Causative	Example
입다 (ip-da) *to wear*	입히다 (i-pi-da) *to dress someone*	엄마가 아기한테 옷을 입혀요. (eom-ma-ga a-gi-han-te os-eul i-pyeo-yo.) *The mother is dressing the baby.*
눕다 (nup-da) *to lie down*	눕히다 (nu-pi-da) *to lay someone down*	엄마가 아기를 침대에 눕혀요. (eom-ma-ga a-gi-reul chim-dae-e nu-pyeo-yo.) *The mother is laying the baby down on the bed.*
앉다 (an-tta) *to sit*	앉히다 (an-chi-da) *to seat someone*	엄마가 아기를 의자에 앉혀요. (eom-ma-ga a-gi-reul ui-ja-e an-chyeo-yo.) *The mother is seating the baby on the chair.*
울다 (ul-da) *to cry*	울리다 (ul-li-da) *to make someone cry*	형이 동생을 울려요. (hyeong-i dong-saeng-eul ul-lyeo-yo.) *The older brother makes his younger sibling cry.*
얼다 (eol-da) *to freeze*	얼리다 (eol-li-da) *to freeze something*	물을 얼려서 얼음을 만들어요. (mul-eul eol-lyeo-seo eol-eum-eul man-deul-eo-yo.) *You can freeze water to make ice.*
벗다 (beot-da) *to take off*	벗기다 (beot-gi-da) *to undress someone*	엄마가 아기 옷을 벗겨요. (eom-ma-ga a-gi os-eul beot-geo-yo.) *The mother is undressing the baby.*

Plain	*Causative*	*Example*
웃다 (ut-da) *to laugh*	웃기다 (ut-gi-da) *to make some- one laugh*	형이 동생을 웃겨요. (hyeong-i dong-saeng- eul ut-gyeo-yo.) *The older brother makes his younger sibling laugh.*
신다 (sin-tta) *to wear*	신기다 (sin-gi-da) *to put shoes on someone*	엄마가 아기한테 신발을 신겨요. (eom-ma-ga a-gi-han-te sin-bal-eul sin- gyeo-yo.) *The mother is putting shoes on the baby.*
자다 (ja-da) *to sleep*	재우다 (jae-u-da) *to put some- one to sleep*	엄마가 아기를 침대에 재워요. (eom-ma-ga a-gi-reul chim-dae-e jae-wo-yo.) *The mother is putting the baby to sleep on the bed.*
타다 (ta-da) *to burn*	태우다 (tae-u-da) *to burn something*	실수로 생선을 태웠어요. (sil-su-ro saeng-seon-eul tae-woss-eo-yo.) *I burned the fish by mistake.*
깨다 (kkae-da) *to wake*	깨우다 (kkae-u-da) *to wake some- one up*	엄마가 아침에 아이를 깨워요. (eom-ma-ga a-chim-e a- i-reul kkae-wo-yo.) *The mother wakes up the baby in the morning.*

13. Connectives

Noun Connectives

때문에
(ttae-mun-e)
because of

차 사고 때문에 길이 막혔어요.
(cha sa-go ttae-mun-e gil-i ma-
kyeoss-eo-yo.)
*There's traffic because of the
accident.*

-만에
(-man-e)
in

대학교 때 친구를 5년만에
우연히 만났어.
(dae-hak-gyo ttae chin-gu-reul o
nyeon-man-e u-yeon-hi man-
nass-eo.)
*I ran into my college friend, whom
I had not seen in five years.*

-만큼
(-man-keum)
as much as

동생이 형만큼 키가 커요.
(dong-saeng-i hyeong-man-keum
ki-ga keo-yo.)
*The younger sibling is as tall as
the older brother.*

-말고
(-mal-go)
not [...]; instead

육개장 말고 불고기 드세요.
(yuk-gae-jang mal-go bul-go-gi
deu-se-yo.)
*Eat bulgogi instead of yuk-gae-
jang.*

과 *(used after
a consonant)*
(-gwa)
with, and

책상과 의자를 샀어요.

(chaek-sang-gwa ui-ja-reul sass-
eo-yo.)
I bought a desk and a chair.

-와 *(used after a vowel)*
(-wa)
with, and

의자와 책상을 샀어요.
(ui-ja-wa chaek-sang-eul sass-
eo-yo.)
I bought a chair and a desk.

-이나 *(used after
a consonant)*
(-i-na)
or

신문이나 책을 읽어요.

(sin-mun-i-na chaeg-eul ilg-
eo-yo.)
I read a newspaper or a book.

-나 *(used after a vowel)* 커피나 차를 마셔요.
(-na)   (keo-pi-na cha-reul ma-syeo-yo.)
or   *I drink a coffee or a tea.*

-이랑 *(used after*   책상이랑 의자를 샀어요.
a consonant)
(-i-rang)   (chaek-sang-i-rang ui-ja-reul sass-
with, and (colloquial)   eo-yo.)
                             I bought a desk and a chair.

-랑 *(used after a vowel)* 친구랑 음악을 들어요.
(-na)   (chin-gu-rang eum-ag-eul deul-
with, and (colloquial)   eo-yo.)
                             I listen to music with my friend.

-하고   책상하고 의자를 샀어요.
(-ha-go)   (chaek-sang-ha-go ui-ja-reul sass-
with, and (colloquial)   eo-yo.)
                             I bought a desk and a chair.

Clausal Connectives

-거나   주말에 영화를 보거나 쇼핑을
(-geo-na)   해요.
or   (ju-mal-e yeong-hwa-reul bo-geo-
                             na syo-ping-eul hae-yo.)
                             I usually watch a movie or go
                             shopping on weekends.

-게   사진 좀 찍게 사진기 좀 빌려
(-ge)   주세요.
in order that; to   (sa-jin jom jjik-ge sa-jin-gi jom
                             bil-lyeo ju-se-yo.)
                             Can I borrow your camera to take
                             some pictures?

-고   아파트가 조용하고 깨끗해요.
(-go)   (a-pa-teu-ga jo-yong-ha-go kkae-
and   kkeu-tae-yo.)
                             The apartment is quiet and clean.

-고 나서

(-go na-seo)

after

점심 먹고 나서 공원에 갔어요.

(jeom-sim meok-go na-seo gong-won-e gass-eo-yo.)

We went to a park after we ate lunch.

-기 때문에

(-gi ttae-mun-e)

because

날씨가 나쁘기 때문에 밖에 안 나갔어요.

(nal-ssi-ga na-ppeu-gi ttae-mun-e bakk-e an na-gass-eo-yo.)

We didn't go outside because the weather was bad.

-기 위해서

(-gi wi-hae-seo)

in order to

한국어를 배우기 위해서 한국에 왔어요.

(ha-gug-eo-reul bae-u-gi wi-hae-seo han-gug-e wass-eo-yo.)

I came to Korea to learn Korean.

-기 전에

(-gi jeon-e)

before

점심 먹기 전에 공원에 갔어요.

(jeom-sim meok-gi jeon-e gong-won-e gass-eo-yo.)

I went to the park before lunch.

-느라고

(-neu-ra-go)

as a result of . . . ing; because of

인터넷 하느라고 텔레비전을 못 봤어요.

(in-teo-net ha-neu-ra-go tel-le-bi-jeon-eul mot bwass-eo-yo.)

Because of the Internet, I did not watch TV.

-는 길에

(-neun gil-e)

on one's way

우체국에 가는 길에 시장에도 갔어요.

(u-che-gug-e ga-neun gil-e si-jang-e-do gass-eo-yo.)

On my way to the post office, I stopped by the market.

-는 동안

(-neun dong-an)

during; while

빨래를 하는 동안 신문을 읽어요.

(ppal-lae-reul ha-neun dong-an sin-mun-eul ilg-eo-yo.)

While I do laundry I read the newspaper.

-는 바람에
(-neun ba-ram-e)
as a result of; because

넘어지는 바람에 다쳤어요.
(neom-e-ji-neun ba-ram-e da-cheoss-eo-yo.)
Because I fell, I hurt myself.

-는데(에)
(-neun-de-[e])
in/for . . . -ing

김치찌개 끓이는데 뭐가 필요해요?
(gim-chi-jji-gae kkeul-i-neun-de mwo-ga pil-yo-hae-yo?)
What do you need in order to make kimchi-jii-gae [Korean dish]?

-다가
(-da-ga)
while doing something

뛰다가 넘어졌어요.
(ttwi-da-ga neom-eo-jeoss-eo-yo.)
I fell while I was running.

-아/어 가지고
(-a/eo ga-ji-go)
1) because

냉장고가 작아 가지고 너무 불편해요.
(naeng-jang-go-ga jag-a ga-ji-go neo-mu bul-pyeon-hae-yo.)
Because the refrigerator is so small, it is inconvenient.

-아/어 가지고
(-a/eo ga-ji-go)
2) by doing

한국어 배워 가지고 한국에서 일할 거예요.
(han-gug-eo-reul bae-wo ga-ji-go han-gug-e-seo il-hal kkeo-yeo-yo.)
By learning Korean, I will be able to work in Korea.

-아/어서
(-a/-eo-seo)
since

아파트가 멀어서 버스 타고 와요.
(a-pa-teu-ga meol-eo-seo beo-seu ta-go wa-yo.)
I take the bus since the apartment is far away.

-았/-었다가
(-at/-eot-da-ga)
speaker's past experience

지하철 탔다가 사람이 많아서 혼났어요.
(ji-ha-cheol-eul tat-da-ga sa-ram-i man-a-seo hon-nass-eo-yo.)
I had a hard time because there were so many people in the subway.

-았/-었더니
-at/-eot-deo-ni
speaker's past experience

버스를 탔더니 사람이 너무 많았어요.
(beo-seu-reul tat-deo-ni sa-ram-i neo-mu man-ass-eo-yo.)
There were many people in the bus when I rode it.

-(으)니까
([-eu]-ni-kka)
1) because; since

지금 시간 없으니까 택시 타세요.
(ji-geum si-gan-i eops-eu-ni-kka taek-si ta-se-to.)
Take a taxi because there isn't enough time.

-(으)니까
([-eu]-ni-kka)
2) logical sequence

전화 하니까 친구가 집에 없었어요.
(jeon-hwa ha-ni-kka chin-gu-ga jib-e eops-eoss-eo-yo.)
I called my friend but he/she was not home.

-(으)러
([-eu]-reo)
in order to

옷을 사러 백화점에 가요.
(os-eul sa-reo ba-kwa-jeom-e ga-yo.)
I am going to the mall in order to buy clothes.

-(으)려고
([-eu]-ryeo-go)
intending to

여행 가려고 준비했어요.
(yeo-haeng ga-ryeo-go jun-bi-haess-eo-yo.)
I prepared to take a trip.

-(으)려다가
([-eu]-ryeo-da-ga)
about to do, but

뭔가 말하려다가 그만됐어요.
(mwon-ga mal-ha-ryeo-da-ga geu-man-dwoss-eo-yo.)
I was going to say something but I stopped.

-(으)려면
([-eu]-ryeo-myeon)
if one intends to

편지 부치려면 우체국에 가세요.
(pyeon-ji bu-chi-ryeo-myeon u-che-gug-e ga-se-yo.)
If you want to mail your letter go to the post office.

-(으)면
([-eu]-myeon)
if

돈이 많으면 뭐 할 거예요?
(don-i man-eu-myeon mwo hal
    kkeo-ye-yo?)
*If you had a lot of money, what
    would you do?*

-(으)면 ... -(으)ㄹ수록
([-eu]-myeon . . . eul-su-rok)
the more . . . the more. . .

이 영화는 보면 볼수록 더
재미있어요.
(i yeong-hwa-neun bo-myeon
    bol-su-rok deo jae-mi-
    iss-eo-yo.)
*The more you see of this
    movie, the more you will
    like it.*

-(으)면서
([-eu]-myeon-seo)
1) while

아침 먹으면서 신문을 읽어요.
(a-chim meog-eu-myeon-seo sin-
    mun-eul ilg-eo-yo.)
*While I eat breakfast I read the
    newspaper.*

-(으)면서
([-eu]-myeon-seo)
2) even though

돈도 없으면서 비싼 차를 타고
다녀요.
(don-do eops-eu-myeon-seo bi-
    ssan cha-reul ta-go da-nyeo-yo.)
*He/she is driving an expensive car
    even though he/she does not
    have money.*

-은 후/다음에
(-eun hu/da-eum-e)
after

점심 먹은 후에 공원에 갔어요.
(jeom-sim meog-eun hu-e gong-
    won-e gass-eo-yo.)
*I went to the park after I had
    lunch.*

-은/는/을지
(-eun)/(-neun)/(eul-jji)
indirect questions

이 신발이 동생한테 잘 맞을지
잘 모르겠어요.
(sin-bal-i dong-saeng-han-te jal
    maj-eul-jji jal mo-reu-gess-
    eo-yo.)
*I am not sure if these shoes will fit
    my younger brother/sister.*

-은/-는데
(-eun)/(-neun-de)
but

아파트가 조용한데 안
   깨끗해요.
(a-pa-teu-ga jo-yong-han-de an
   kkae-kkeu-tae-yo.)
*The apartment is quiet but not
   clean.*

-은/-는데도
(-eun)/(-neun-de-do)
despite; although

음식을 많이 먹었는데도 아직도
   배가 고파요.
(eum-sig-eul man-i meog-eon-
   neun-de-do a-jik-do bae-ga
   go-pa-yo.)
*Although I ate a lot I am still
   hungry.*

-을 때
(-eul ttae)
when

시간 있을 때 텔레비전을 봐요.
(sin-gan iss-eul ttae tel-le-bi-jeon-
   eul bwa-yo.)
Watch TV when you have time.

-을까봐
(-eul-kka-bwa)
*for fear that;
   worry that*

한국 날씨가 너무 추울까봐
   걱정이에요.
(han-guk nal-ssi-ga neo-mu chu-
   ul-kka-bwa geok-geong-i-e-yo.)
*I am afraid the weather in Korea
   is too cold.*

-을 만큼
(-eul man-keum)
*to the extent/
   as much as*

음식은 먹을 만큼만 가지고
   오세요.
(eum-sig-eun meog-eul man-
   keum-man ga-ji-go o-se-yo.)
*Please bring only as much food as
   you can finish.*

-을 테니까
(-eul-te-ni-kka)
*because one will . . .,
   so*

내일 갈 테니까 맛있는 음식
   많이 준비하세요.
(nae-il gal te-ni-kka mas-in-neun
   eum-sik man-i jun-bi-ha-se-yo.)
*I will be there tomorrow, so please
   prepare enough food.*

-이/가 아니라
(-i/-ga a-ni-ra)
it is not . . . but . . .

화가 난 게 아니라 아픈 거예요.
(hwa-ga nan ge a-ni-ra a-peun
   geo-yeo-yo.)
I am not angry but sick.

-이라면
(-i-ra-myeon)
if it is . . .

내가 만일 부자라면 좋은 차를 사겠다.
(nae-ga man-il bu-ja-ra-myeon jo-eun cha-reul sa-get-da.)
If I were rich I would buy a good car.

-이라서
(-i-ra-seo)
because; since

오늘은 일요일이라서 학교에 안 가요.
(o-neul-eun il-yo-il-i-ra-seo hak-gyo-e an ga-yo.)
I am not going to school today since it is Sunday.

-자마자
(-ja-ma-ja)
as soon as

아침에 일어나자마자 화장실에 가요.
(a-chim-e il-eo-na-ja-ma-ja hwa-jang-sil-e ga-yo.)
I go to the bathroom as soon as I get up in the morning.

-지만
(-ji-man)
but

아파트가 조용하지만 안 깨끗해요.
(a-pa-teu-ga jo-yong-ha-ji-man an kkae-kkeu-tae-yo.)
The apartment is quiet but not clean.

아무 . . . –(이)나
(a-mu . . . [-i]-na)
any

저는 아무 음식이나 다 잘 먹어요.
(jeo-neun a-mu eum-sig-i-na da jal meog-eo-yo.)
I can eat any kind of food.

아무리 . . . -아/어도
(a-mu-ri . . . -a/-eo-do)
no matter how

아무리 기다려도 택시가 안 와요.
(a-mu-ri gi-da-ryeo-do taek-si-ga an wa-yo.)
No matter how long I wait for the taxi, it's not coming.

얼마나 . . . -은/는지
(eol-ma-na . . .
   –eun)/(-neun-ji)
so . . . that . . .

서울에 사람이 얼마나 많은지
깜짝 놀랐어요.
(seo-ul-e sa-ram-i eol-ma-na man-
   eun-ji kkam-jjak nol-lass-eo-yo.)
*I was so surprised that there are
   so many people in Seoul.*

하나도 안/못 . . .
(ha-na-do an/mot . . .)
not at all

바빠서 영화도 하나도 못 봐요.
(ba-ppa-seo yeong-hwa-do ha-na-
   do mot bwa-yo.)
*I cannot watch movies at all
   because I am so busy.*

Sentence Connectives

그리고
(geu-ri-go)
and

아파트가 조용해요. 그리고
깨끗해요.
(a-pa-teu-ga jo-yong-hae-yo geu-
   ri-go kkae-kkeu-tae-yo.)
The apartment is quiet and clean.

그래서
(geu-rae-seo)
so

아파트가 멀어요. 그래서 버스
타고 와요.
(a-pa-teu-ga meol-eo-yo geu-rae-
   seo beo-seu ta-go wa-yo.)
*The apartment is far away so I
   took the bus.*

그런데
(geu-reon-de)
but (spoken form)

아파트가 조용해요. 그런데 안
깨끗해요.
(a-pa-teu-ga jo-yong-hae-yo geu-
   reon-de an kkae-kkeu-tae-yo.)
*The apartment is quiet but not
   clean.*

그렇지만
(geu-reo-chi-man)
but (written form)

아파트가 조용해요. 그렇지만
안 깨끗해요.
(a-pa-teu-ga jo-yong-hae-yo geu-
   reo-chi-man an kkae-kkeu-
   tae-yo.)
*The apartment is quiet. However,
   it is not clean.*

14. Sentence Endings & Helping Verbs

-거든요
(-geo-deun-yo)
you see, because . . .

지난 주에 비자를 받았거든요.
(ji-nan ju-e bi-ja-reul bad-at-geo-
    deun-yo.)
You see, I got my visa last week.

-게 되다
(-ge doe-da)
a change of events

한국을 좋아하게 됐어요.
(han-gug-eul jo-a-ha-ge dwaess-
    eo-yo.)
I came to like Korea.

-게 하다
(-ge ha-da)
*make someone/
    something*

아이들이 방에 못 들어오게 해
    주세요.
(a-i-deul-i bang-e mot deul-eo-o-
    ge hae ju-se-yo.)
*Please make the children stay out
    of the room.*

-게요
(-ge-yo)
intend to

지금 청소하게요.
(ji-geum cheong-so-ha-ge-yo.)
I am going to clean now.

-겠습니다
(-get-seum-ni-da)
announcement

오늘의 날씨를 말씀
    드리겠습니다.
(o-neul-ui nal-ssi-reul mal-sseum
    deu-ri-get-seum-ni-da).
I will tell you today's weather.

-고 싶다/싶어하다
(-go sip-da/
    sip-eo-ha-da)
want to

갈비를 먹고 싶어요. (-고 싶다
    [first person only])
(gal-bi-reul meok-go sip-eo-yo.)
I want to eat galbi [Korean dish].

-고 있다/-계시다
(-go it-da)/(-gye-si-da)
progressive

지금 밥 먹고 있어요. (-고
    계시다 [honorific])
(ji-geum bap meok-go iss-eo-yo.)
S/he is eating right now.

-군요
(-gun-yo)
exclamation

아직 집에 계셨군요!
(a-jik jib-e gye-syeot-gun-yo!)
You are still home!

-기 시작하다
(-gi si-ja-ka-da)
begin to

한국어를 배우기 시작했어요.
(han-gug-eo-reul bae-u-gi si-ga-
kaess-eo-yo.)
I began to learn Korean.

-기 싫다
(-gi sil-ta)
I don't want to

버스 타기 싫어요.
(beo-seu ta-gi sil-eo-yo.)
I don't want to ride the bus.

-기가 불편하다
-gi-ga bul-pyeon-
ha-da
it is inconvenient to

버스 타기가 불편해요.
(beo-seu ta-gi-ga bul-pyeon-hae-
yo.)
It is inconvenient to ride the bus.

-기가 쉽다
(-gi-ga swip-da)
it is easy to

버스 타기가 쉬워요.
(beo-seu ta-gi-ga swi-wo-yo.)
It is easy to ride the bus.

-기가 어렵다
(-gi-ga eo-ryeop-da)
it is difficult to

버스 타기가 어려워요.
(beo-seu ta-gi-ga eo-ryeo-wo-yo.)
It is difficult to ride the bus.

-기가 편하다
(-gi-ga pyeon-ha-da)
it is convenient to

버스 타기가 편해요.
(beo-seu ta-gi-ga pyeon-hae-yo)
It is convenient to ride the bus.

-기는 하다
(-gi-neun ha-da)
*as for. . . -ing,
I did. But . . .*

많이 자기는 했는데 아직도
졸려요.
(man-i ja-gi-neun han-neun-de a-
jik-do jol-lyeo-yo.)
I slept a lot, but I am still sleepy.

-기는요?
(-gi-neun-yo?)
no way

한국말을 잘하기는요? 잘
못해요.
(han-gung-mal-eul jal-ha-gi-neun-
yo? jal mo-tae-yo.)
*No way do I speak Korean well! I
can't speak well.*

-기도 하다
(-gi-do ha-da)
they also did

시간 있으면 가끔 볼링 치기도
해요.
(si-gan iss-eo-myeon ga-kkeum
bol-ling chi-gi-do hae-yo.)
*I sometimes go bowling when I
have time, as they also did.*

-기로 하다
(-gi-ro ha-da)
decide/plan to

여름에 한국에 가기로 했어요.
(yeo-reum-e han-gug-e ga-gi-ro
    haess-eo-yo.)
*We/I plan to go Korea this
    summer.*

-내요
(-nyae-yo)
*indirect speech
  (question)*

동물원에 가내요.
(dong-mul-won-e ga-nyae-yo.)
*Someone asked if I am going to
    the zoo.*

-네요
(-ne-yo)
*surprise/admira-
  tion/sympathy*

미국에서 오래 살았네요.
(mi-gug-e-seo o-rae sal-an-ne-yo.)
*My goodness, you lived in
    America for a long time.*

-는 길이다
(-neun gil-i-da)
be on one's way

지금 우체국에 가는 길이에요.
(ji-geum u-che-gug-e ga-neun gil-
    i-e-yo.)
I am on my way to the post office.

-는 중이다
(-neun jung-i-da)
in the process of

지금 청소하는 중이에요.
(ji-geum cheong-so-ha-neun jung-
    i-e-yo.)
I am in the middle of cleaning up.

-다/-라면서요?
(-da)/(-ra-myeon-
  seo-yo?)
confirming information

한국에 간다면서요?
(han-gug-e gan-da-myeon-seo-
    yo?)
I heard you are going to Korea.

-대요/(-이)래요
(-dae-yo)/([-i]-rae-yo)
*indirect speech
  (statement)*

동물원에 간대요.
(dong-mul-won-e gan-dae-yo.)
I heard s/he is going to the zoo.

-더라고(요)
(-deo-ra-go-yo)
speaker's experience

마이클 조던이 정말 농구를 잘
  하더라고.
(ma-i-keul jo-deon-i jeong-mal
    nong-gu-reul jal ha-deo-ra-
    go.)
*Michael Jordan plays basketball
    very well, in my experience.*

-던데요
(-deon-de-yo)
speaker's experience

호텔 식당 음식이 아주
맛있던데요.
(ho-tel sik-dang eum-sig-i a-ju
mas-it-deon-de-yo.)
*The food at the hotel restaurant
was delicious, in my
experience.*

-래요
(-rae-yo)
*indirect speech
(request)*

동물원에 가래요.
(dong-mul-won-e ga-rae-yo.)
Somebody told me to go to the zoo.

-만 . . . -으면 되다
(-man . . . -eu-
myeon doe-da)
all one needs is . . .

이젠 비행기표만 사면 돼요.
(i-jen bi-haeng-gi-pyo-man sa-
myeon dwae-yo.)
*All I need to buy is an airplane
ticket.*

-아/어 버리다
(-a)/(-eo beo-ri-da)
to get done/finish

남은 스파게티를 동생이 다
먹어 버렸어요.
(nam-eun seu-pa-ge-ti-reul dong-
saeng-i meog-eo-beo-ryeoss-
eo-yo.)
*My younger brother/sister finished
the leftover spaghetti.*

-아/어 보다
(-a)/(-eo bo-da)
try doing

김치 먹어 봤어요?
(gim-chi meog-eo bwass-eo-yo?)
*Have you tried kimchi [Korean
dish]?*

-아/어 보이다
-a/-eo bo-i-da
*someone/
something looks*

케이크가 맛있어 보여요.
(ke-i-keu-ga mas-iss-eo bo-yeo-
-yo.)
The cake looks delicious.

-아/어 본 적이 없다
(-a)/(-eo bon jeog-i
eop-da)
*there has been
no occasion of*

스키 타 본 적이 없어요.
(seu-ki ta bon jeog-i eops-eo-yo.)

I have never skied before.

-아/어 본 적이 있다
(a)/(-eo bon jeog-i
it-da)
*there has been
an occasion of*

스키 타 본 적이 있어요.
(seu-ki ta bon jeog-i iss-eo-yo.)

I have skied before.

-아/어 있다
(-a)/(-eo it-da)
be . . . -ing (state)

한 상자에 사과가 10개 들어
있어요.
(han sang-ja-e sa-gwa-ga yeol-
kkae deul-eo iss-eo-yo.)
There are ten apples in a box.

-아/어 주다/드리다
(-a)/(-eo ju-da)/
(deu-ri-da)
benefactive

다시 설명해 주세요. (-아/어
드리다[*humble*])
(da-si seol-myeong-hae ju-se-yo.)
Please explain to me again.

-아/어도 되다
(-a)/(-eo-do doe-da)
permission

이 케이크 먹어도 돼요?
(i ke-i-keu meog-eo-do dwae-yo.)
May I eat this cake?

-아/어야 되다/하다
(-a)/(-eo-ya
doe-da)/(ha-da)
necessity

매일 운동해야 돼요.
(mae-il un-dong-hae-ya dwae-yo.)

One needs to exercise every day.

-아/어야지요
(-a)/(-eo-ya-ji-yo)
surely have to/ should

피곤한데 일찍 자야지요.
(pi-gon-han-de il-jjik ja-ya-ji-yo.)
*You must be tired. You should go
to sleep early.*

**-아/어야할지
모르겠다**
(-a)/(-eo-ya-hal-jji
mo-reu-get-da)
*don't know-
[Qword] to*

뭘 사야할지 모르겠어요.

(mwol sa-ya-hal-jji mo-reu-
gess-eo-yo.)
I don't know what to buy.

-아/어지다
(-a)/(-eo-ji-da)
become, get to be

날씨가 추워졌어요.
(nal-ssi-ga chu-wo-jeoss-eo-yo.)
The weather became cold.

-아/어 하다
(-a)/(-eo-ha-da)
*feeling of the
third person*

어머니가 케이크를 아주
좋아하세요.
(eo-meo-ni-ga ke-i-keu-reul a-ju
jo-a-ha-se-yo.)
My mother really likes cake.

-았/었으면 하다
(-ass)/(-eoss-eu-
myeon ha-da)
wish

앞으로 한국에서 살았으면
해요.
(a-peu-ro han-gug-e-seo sal-ass-
eu-myeon hae-yo.)
*I wish to live in Korea in the
future.*

-(으)면 좋겠다
([-eu]-myeon
jo-ket-da)
speaker's wish; want

피곤해서 잤으면 좋겠어요.
(pi-gon-hae-seo jass-eu-myeon jo-
kess-eo-yo.)
I am tired. I want to sleep.

-(으)려고 하다
([-eu]-ryeo-go ha-da)
intend to

너무 피곤해서 자려고 해요.
(neo-mu pi-gon-hae-seo ja-ryeo-
go hae-yo.)
I am so tired, I am going to sleep.

-(으)면 안 되다
([-eu]-myeon
an doe-da)
prohibition

아니오, 먹으면 안 돼요.
(a-ni-o meog-eu-myeon an dwae-
yo.)
No, please don't eat.

-은/는 거예요
(-eun)/(-neun geo-
ye-yo)
the fact is

잇몸 때문에 이가 아픈 거예요.
(in-mom ttae-mun-e i-ga a-peun
geo-ye-yo.)
*My teeth hurt a lot because of the
chewing gum.*

-은/는 줄 알다
(-eun)/(-neun jul al-da)
I thought. . . .

미국사람인줄 알았어요.
(mi-guk-sa-ram-in-jul al-ass-
eo-yo.)
I thought you were American.

-은/는 척하다
(-eun)/(-neun
cheo-ka-da)
to pretend to

친구가 내 말을 못 들은
척했어요.
(chin-gu-ga nae mal-eul mot deul-
eun cheo-kaess-eo-yo.)
My friend pretended not to listen.

-은/는 편이다

(-eun)/(-neun
pyeon-i-da)
relatively

우리 부모님은 건강하신
편이에요.
(u-ri bu-mo-nim-eun geon-gang-
ha-sin pyeon-i-e-yo.)
My parents are relatively healthy.

-은/는/을 것 같다

(-eun)/(-neun)/
(-eul geot gat-da)
it seems/looks like

어제 비가 온 것 같아요.
(eo-je bi-ga on-geot gat-a-yo.)

It looks like it rained yesterday.

지금 비가 오는 것 같아요.
(ji-geum bi-ga o-neun-geot gat-a-
yo.)
It looks like it's raining now.

내일 비가 올 것 같아요.
(nae-il bi-ga ol-kkeot gat-a-yo.)
*It looks like it's going to rain
tomorrow.*

-은/는/을 모양이다

(-eun)/(-neun)/
(-eul mo-yang-i-da)
it appears

기분이 좋은 모양이에요.
(gi-bun-i jo-eun mo-yang-i-e-yo.)

You appear to be in a good mood.

**-은/는/을 줄 모르다
몰랐어요.**

(-eun)/(-neun)/
(-eul jul mo-reu-da)
don't know

한국음식이 이렇게 맛있는 줄

(han-gug-eum-sig-i i-reo-ke mas-
in-neun jul mol-lass-eo-yo.)
*I didn't know that Korean food
was so delicious.*

-은/는/을 줄 알다

(-eun)/(-neun)/
(-eul jul al-da)
know; thought

음식이 아직 많은 줄 알았어요.
(eum-sig-i a-jik man-eun-jul al-
ass-eo-yo.)
*I thought there was plenty of food
left.*

-은/는데요

(-eun)/(-neun-de-yo)
*presenting background
information*

마이클씨 지금 집에 없는데요.
(ma-i-keul-ssi ji-geum jib-e eom
neun-de-yo.)
Michael is not home right now.

-은/는지 ... 되다
(-eun)/(-neun-ji ... doe-da)
It has been [time] since

한국에 온지 일년 됐어요.
(han-gug-e on-ji il-lyeon dwaess-eo-yo.)
It has been one year since I came to Korea.

-은/는지 모르다
(-eun)/(-neun-ji mo-reu-da)
don't know that . . .

우체국이 어디 있는지 몰라요.
(u-che-gug-i eo-di in-neun-ji mol-la-yo.)
I don't know where the post office is.

-은/는지 알다
(-eun)/(-neun-ji al-da)
know that . . .

우체국이 어디 있는지 아세요?
(u-che-gug-i eo-di in-neun-ji a-se-yo?)
Do you know where the post office is?

-은가/는가/나보다
(-eun-ga)/(-neun-ga)/(na-bo-da)
it seems that . . . / I guess

오늘 기분이 좋은가봐요.
(o-neul gi-bun-i jo-eun-ga-bwa-yo.)
I guess you are in a good mood today.

-은/는요?
(-eun/-neun-yo)
what about. . . ?

저는 집이 좀 멀어요.
마이클씨는요?
(jeo-neun jib-i jom meol-eo-yo. ma-i-keul-ssi-neun-yo.)
My house is pretty far away. What about yours, Michael?

-(으)ㄹ 뻔하다
(-eul ppeon-ha-da)
almost, nearly

지갑을 잃어버릴 뻔했어요.
(ji-gab-eul il-eo-beo-ril ppeon-haess-eo-yo.)
I almost lost my wallet.

-(으)ㄹ 수 있다/없다
(-eul ssu it-da)/(-eop-da)
potential

내일 갈 수 없어요.
(nae-il gal-ssu eops-eo-yo.)

I cannot go tomorrow.

-(으)ㄹ 줄 모르다
(-eul jjul mo-reu-da)
not know how to

테니스 칠 줄 몰라요.
(te-ni-seu chil jjul mol-la-yo.)
I don't know how to play tennis.

-(으)ㄹ 줄 알다
(-eul jjul al-da)
know how to

테니스 칠 줄 알아요.
(te-ni-seu chil jjul al-a-yo.)
I know how to play tennis.

-(으)ㄹ 걸 그랬다
(-eul kkeol geu-raet-da)
*regret for a past
  action*

우산을 가지고 나올 걸
  그랬어요.
(u-san-eul ga-ji-go na-ol kkeol
  geu-raess-eo-yo.)
*I should have brought my
  umbrella.*

-(으)ㄹ게요
(-eul-kke-yo)
willingness

이따가 다시 올게요.
(i-tta-ga da-si ol-kke-yo)
I will come back later.

-(으)ㄹ까 생각하다
(-eul-kka saeng-ga-ka-da)
think about

선물로 뭘 살까 생각하고
  있어요.
(seon-mul-lo mwol sal-kka saeng-
  ga-ka-go iss-eo-yo.)
*I am thinking about what to buy
  for a gift.*

-(으)ㄹ까 하다
(-eul-kka ha-da)
thinking of –ing

주말에 영화 보러 갈까 해요.
(ju-mal-e yeong-hwa bo-reo gal-
  kka hae-yo.)
*I am thinking of going to the
  movies this weekend.*

-(으)ㄹ까요?
(-eul-kka-yo)
1) Shall I/we. . . ?

한국어로 말할까요?
(han-gug-eo-ro mal-hal-kka-yo?)
Should I speak in Korean?

-(으)ㄹ까요?
(-eul-kka-yo?)
2) Do you think ....?

내일 날씨가 좋을까요?
(nae-il nal-ssi-ga jo-eul-kka-yo?)
*Do you think tomorrow's weather
  will be nice?*

-(으)ㄹ래요.
(-eul-lae-yo.)
intention

영화 보러 갈래요.
(yeong-hwa bo-reo gal-lae-yo.)
I will go to see a movie.

-잖아요
(-jan-a-yo)
you know

밖에 비가 오잖아요.
(bakk-e bi-ga o-jan-a-yo.)
It's raining outside.

-재요
(-jae-yo)
*indirect speech
(suggestion)*

동물원에 가재요.
(dong-mul-won-e ga-jae-yo.)
He/she asked me to go to the zoo.

-지요
(-ji-yo)
suggestion

길이 많이 막히는데 지하철
타고 가지요.
(gil-i man-i ma-ki-neun-de ji-ha-
cheol ta-go ga-ji-yo.)
*We should take the subway since
there is heavy traffic.*

-지요?/-죠?
(-ji-yo?)/(-jyo?)
seeking agreement

오늘 날씨가 참 좋지요?
(o-neul nal-ssi-ga cham
jo-chi-yo?)
Isn't today's weather really nice?

**(마치) -은/-는/
-을 것 같다**
([ma-chi] -eun/-neun/
-eul geot gat-da)
as if

두 사람이 마치 형제인 것 같이
닮았어요.
(du sa-ram-i ma-chi hyeong-je-in
geot ga-chi dalm-ass-eo-yo.)
*The two people look alike as if
they were brothers.*

**(차라리) . . .
이/가 더 낫다**
([cha-ra-ri] . . .
i/ga deo nat-da]
had better

차라리 혼자 사는 게 더
낫겠어요.
(cha-ra-ri hon-ja sa-neun ge deo
nat-gess-eo-yo.)
It is better to live alone.

15. Indirect Quotation
Standard Form (Colloquial Form)

Statement:

-는/-ㄴ다고 해요 (-는/-ㄴ대요)
(-neun/-n-da-go hae-yo [-neun/-n-dae-yo])

> 밥을 먹는다고 해요. / 밥을 먹는대요.
> (bab-eul meong-neun-da-go hae-yo.) / (bab-eul meong-neun-dae-yo.)
> *Someone said (he/she) is eating.*

-라고 해요 (-래요)
(-ra-go hae-yo [-rae-yo])

> 의사라고 해요. / 의사래요.
> (ui-sa-ra-go hae-yo.) / (ui-sa-rae-yo.)
> *Someone said (he/she) is a doctor.*

Question:

-냐고 해요 (-내요)
(-nya-go-hae-yo [nyae-yo])

> 밥을 먹냐고 해요. / 밥을 먹내요.
> (bab-eul meong-nya-go hae-yo.) / (bab-eul meong-nyae-yo.)
> *Someone asked if (he/she) is eating.*

Proposal:

-자고 해요 (-재요)
(-ja-go hae-yo [-jae-yo])

> 밥을 먹자고 해요. / 밥을 먹재요.
> (bab-eul meok-ja-go hae-yo.) / (bab-eul meok-jae-yo.)
> *Someone said let's eat.*

Request:

-(으)라고 해요 /-(으)래요
([eu]-ra-go hae-yo)/([eu]-rae-yo)

밥을 먹으라고 해요. / 밥을 먹으래요.

(bab-eul meog-eu-ra-go hae-yo.) / (bab-eul meog-eu-rae-yo.)

Someone told me to eat.

16. Word Order

Korean is a predicate-final language. All sentences end with the predicate, i.e. the verb or adjective. All other elements in the sentence, such as the subject or object, appear before the predicate. Korean particles, the equivalent of English prepositions (e.g. *from, in, with,* or *to*), always appear after the noun or pronoun to which they're related. The elements before the predicate can be placed in any order as long as the sentence ends with the predicate, a tendency that has led to Korean being called a "free word order" language.

Consider this English sentence:

Michael eats breakfast at a restaurant in the morning.

Let's break it down into its component parts:

Michael <subject>
    eats <predicate>
        breakfast <object>
            at a restaurant <location> (*at* is the preposition/particle)
                in the morning <time> (*in* is the preposition/particle)

Now let's convert this to a Korean structural pattern:

Michael (+ subject marker) <subject>
    the morning + in <time + time particle>
        a restaurant + at <location + location particle>
            breakfast (+ object marker) <object>
                eats <predicate>

So, in Korean, this would be:

마이클이   **아침에**   **식당에서**   **밥을**   **먹는다.**
(ma-i-keul-i) (a-chim-e) (sik-dang-e-seo) (bab-eul) (meong-neun-da)
Michael   *the morning-in* *a restaurant-at* *breakfast* *eats.*

Other possibilities include:

식당에서   **아침에**   **마이클이**   **밥을**   **먹는다.**
(sik-dang-e-seo) (a-chim-e) (ma-i-keul-i) (bab-eul) (meong-neun-da)
a restaurant-at *the morning-in* *Michael* *breakfast* *eats.*

아침에   **마이클이**   **식당에서**   **밥을**   **먹는다.**
(a-chim-e) (ma-i-keul-i) (sik-dang-e-seo) (bab-eul) (meong-neun-da)
the morning-in *Michael* *a restaurant-at* *breakfast* *eats.*

As can be seen, the sentence elements can be arranged in any order as long as the sentence ends with the predicate.

17. Speech Levels

Korean has four speech levels indicating the speaker's personal relationship with the listener. These speech levels are denoted by sentence-final suffixes attached to the predicates. These suffixes are illustrated below.

	Statement	Question	Request	Suggestion
deferential	-습/ㅂ니다 (-seum/-m-ni-da)	-습/ㅂ니까? (-seum/m-ni-kka)	-(으)십시오 ([-eu]-sip-si-o)	N/A
polite	-아/어요 (-a/eo-yo)	-아/어요? (-a/eo-yo)	-아/어요 (-a/eo-yo)	-아/어요 (-a/eo-yo)
intimate	-아/어 (-a/eo)	-아/어? (-a/eo)	-아/어 (-a/eo)	-아/어 (-a/eo)
plain	-은/는/ㄴ다 (-eun/neun/n-da)	-니? (-ni)	-아/어라 (-a/eo-ra)	-자 (-ja)

For example, 먹습니다 (meok-seum-ni-da), 먹어요 (meog-eo-yo), 먹어 (meog-eo), and 먹는다 (meong-neun-da) all means "(someone) eats," expressed in different speech levels.

The most common level used when speaking to an adult is the polite one. While the deferential level is used (mostly by male speakers) in formal situations such as news reports or public lectures, the polite level is widely used by both males and females in daily conversation.

The intimate level and the plain level would be used by an older person to a younger one, by a child to his or her siblings, or between close friends whose friendship began in childhood or adolescence.

PHRASEBOOK CONTENTS

Lesson 1. Greetings
인사 (in-sa)

1. Cultural Notes

In Korea, bowing is the most common way to show
courtesy when you greet someone. Usually, the younger
person initiates bowing and the older person responds. In
general, it is courteous to bend your head and waist about
15 degrees when you greet someone. Adult males often
bow and shake hands simultaneously using one or both
hands. Sometimes you will be asked whether you have
eaten. It is just a way to greet someone in Korea.

2. Model Phrases

Hello / Good morning / Good afternoon / Good evening.
안녕하세요?
(an-nyeong-ha-se-yo)

Goodbye (to one who is leaving).
안녕히 가세요.
(an-nyeong-hi ga-se-yo)

Good-bye (if you are the one leaving).
안녕히 계세요.
(an-nyeong-hi gye-se-yo)

Nice to meet you. (*lit.* It's a first time to see you.)
처음 뵙겠습니다.
(cheo-eum boep-get-seum-ni-da)

Nice to meet you.
만나 뵙게 돼서 반갑습니다.
(man-na boep-ge dwae-seo ban-gap-seum-ni-da)

See you later.
다음에 또 뵙겠습니다.
(da-eum-e tto boep-get-seum-ni-da)

Welcome. (*lit.* Please come hurry.)
어서 오세요.
(eo-seo o-se-yo)

Thank you.
감사합니다.
(gam-sa-ham-ni-da)

Thank you for your help.
도와주셔서 감사합니다.
(do-wa-ju-syeo-seo gam-sa-ham-ni-da)

> You are welcome. (*lit.* Not at all.)
> **천만에요.**
> (cheon-man-e-yo)

> You are welcome. (*lit.* Don't mention it.)
> **무슨 말씀을요.**
> (mu-seun mal-sseum-eul-yo)

I am sorry.
죄송합니다.
(joe-song-ham-ni-da)

Excuse me.
실례합니다.
(sil-lye-ham-ni-da)

3. Everyday Conversation

How are you these days?
요즘 어떻게 지내세요?
(yo-jeum eo-tteo-ke ji-nae-se-yo)

> (Thanks to you), I am fine.
> **(덕분에) 잘 지내요.**
> ([deok-bun-e] jal ji-nae-yo)

> I am a little busy.
> **좀 바빠요.**
> (jom ba-ppa-yo)

> So-so.
> **그저 그래요.**
> (geu-jeo geu-rae-yo)

Not so good.
별로예요.
(byeol-lo-ye-yo)

Not so good. / I am not doing too well.
별로 잘 못 지내요.
(byeol-lo jal mot ji-nae-yo)

Lesson 2. Asking about Someone & Telling about Yourself
소개하기 (so-gae-ha-gi)

1. Cultural Notes

In Korean, the family name comes first and the given name follows. When getting to know someone, address him or her using their full name, followed by –씨 (ssi), which means Mr. or Ms. After getting acquainted, it is acceptable to address a person by his or her first name, again followed by –씨 (ssi). In business situations, it is most common to address another by last name and title.

When first meeting someone, Koreans often ask personal questions, such as about one's marriage status or age. These are cultural conventions, as Koreans have to know that information to determine the sentence endings to be used when speaking to one.

In Korean culture, modesty is an important virtue. When one is complemented for doing something well or is envied one's occupation, one should respond "no" rather than "thank you".

2. Model Phrases

What is your name?
성함이 어떻게 되세요?
(seong-ham-i eo-tteo-ke doe-se-yo)

> My name is Michael.
> **마이클이에요.**
> (ma-i-keul-i-e-yo)

How old are you?
연세가 어떻게 되세요?
(yeon-se-ga eo-tteo-ke doe-se-yo)

> I am thirty-two years old.
> **서른 둘이에요.**
> (seo-reun dul-i-e-yo)

Where are you from? (*lit.* Where is your hometown?)
고향이 어디세요?
(go-hyang-i eo-di-se-yo)

Where are you from? / Where do you live? (*lit.* Where is
   your house?)
집이 어디세요?
(jib-i eo-di-se-yo)

> I am from San Diego.
> **샌디에고예요.**
> (saen-di-e-go-ye-yo)

Where are you from? (*lit.* Which country are you from?)
어디에서 오셨어요?
(eo-di-e-seo o-syeoss-eo-yo)

> I am from America.
> **미국에서 왔어요.**
> (mi-gug-e-seo wass-eo-yo)

When is your birthday?
생일이 언제세요?
(saeng-il-i eon-je-se-yo)

> My birthday is June 30th. (*lit.* It is June 30th.)
> **6월 30일이에요.**
> (yu-wol sam-sib-il-i-e-yo)

What do you do for living?
무슨 일을 하세요?
(mu-seun il-eul ha-se-yo)

What is your occupation?
어떤 직장에 다니세요?
(eo-tteon jik-jang-e da-ni-se-yo)

> I am a doctor.
> **의사예요.**
> (ui-sa-ye-yo)

> I am working in a hospital.
> **병원에 다녀요.**
> (byeong-won-e da-nyeo-yo)

What is your major?
뭘 전공하세요?
(mwol jeon-gong-ha-se-yo)

What is your major? (*lit.* What do you study?)
뭘 공부하세요?
(mwol gong-bu-ha-se-yo)

> My major is Linguistics. (*lit.* I am studying
>   Linguistics.)
> **언어학을 공부해요.**
> (eon-eo-hag-eul gong-bu-hae-yo)

Are you married?
결혼하셨어요?
(gyeol-hon-ha-syeoss-eo-yo)

> Yes, I am.
> **네, 했어요.**
> (ne, haess-eo-yo)

> No, I am not.
> **아니오, (아직) 안 했어요.**
> (a-ni-o, [a-jik] an haess-eo-yo)

How many people are in your family?
가족이 몇 분이세요?
(ga-jog-i myeot bun-i-se-yo)

How many people are in your family?
가족이 어떻게 되세요?
(ga-jog-i eo-tteo-ke doe-se-yo)

> There are three: Father, Mother, and myself.
> **아버지, 어머니, 저 모두 셋이에요.**
> (a-beo-ji, eo-meo-ni, jeo mo-du ses-i-e-yo)

** Making an excuse **

Since I am an American, I don't speak Korean fluently.
저는 미국사람이라서 한국어를 잘 못해요.
(jeo-neun mi-guk-sa-ram-i-ra-seo han-gug-eo-reul jal mo-
    tae-yo)

Because I am not a Korean, I don't know much about
    Korea.
저는 한국사람이 아니라서 한국에 대해서 잘 몰라요.
(jeo-neun han-guk-sa-ram-i a-ni-ra-seo han-gug-e dae-hae-
    seo jal mol-la-yo)

3. Vocabulary

Jobs

businessman	사업가 (sa-eop-ga)
civil servant	공무원 (gong-mu-won)
computer graphic designer	컴퓨터 그래픽 디자이너 (ceom-pyu-teo geu-rae-pik di-ja-i-neo)
doctor	의사 (ui-sa)
driver	운전사 (un-jeon-sa)
journalist	기자 (gi-ja)
lawyer	변호사 (byeon-ho-sa)
nurse	간호원 (gan-ho-won)
office employee	회사원 (hoe-sa-won)
pastor	목사 (mok-sa)
pharmacist	약사 (yak-sa)
professor	교수 (gyo-su)
secretary	비서 (bi-seo)
singer	가수 (ga-su)
soldier	군인 (gun-in)
sportsman	운동선수 (un-dong-seon-su)
student	학생 (hak-saeng)
teacher	선생 (seon-saeng)
writer	작가 (jak-ga)

Academic majors

anthropology	인류학 (il-lyu-hak)
architecture	건축학 (geon-chuk-hak)
Asian studies	동양학 (dong-yang-hak)
biology	생물학 (saeng-mul-hak)
business management	경영학 (gyeong-yeong-hak)
chemistry	화학 (hwa-hak)
economics	경제학 (gyeong-je-hak)
education	교육학 (gyo-yuk-hak)
engineering	공학 (gong-hak)
fine arts	미술 (mi-sul)
history	역사학 (yeok-sa-hak)
law	법학 (beo-pak)
linguistics	언어학 (eon-eo-hak)
literature	문학 (mun-hak)

mathematics	수학 (su-hak)
medicine	의학 (ui-hak)
music	음악 (eum-ak)
physics	물리학 (mul-li-hak)
political science	정치학 (jeong-chi-hak)
psychology	심리학 (sim-ni-hak)
sociology	사회학 (sa-hoe-hak)

Family terms

aunt (maternal)	이모 (i-mo)
aunt (paternal)	고모 (go-mo)
older brother	형 (hyeong) [male speaker]
	오빠 (o-ppa) [female speaker]
younger brother	남동생 (nam-dong-saeng)
children	아이들 (a-i-deul)
cousin	사촌 (sa-chon)
daughter	딸 (ttal)
daughter-in-law	며느리 (myeo-neu-ri)
father	아버지 (a-beo-ji)
father-in-law	장인어른 (jang-in-eo-reun) [male speaker]
	시아버님 (si-a-beo-nim) [female speaker]
grandchildren	손주 (son-ju)
grandson	손자 (son-ja)
granddaughter	손녀 (son-nyeo)
grandfather	할아버지 (hal-a-beo-ji)
grandmother	할머니 (hal-meo-ni)
husband	남편 (nam-pyeon)
mother	어머니 (eo-meo-ni)
mother-in-law	장모님 (jang-mo-nim) [male speaker]
	시어머님 (si-eo-meo-nim) [female speaker]
nephew	(남자) 조카 ([nam-ja] jo-ka)
niece	(여자) 조카 ([yeo-ja] jo-ka)
older sister	누나 (nu-na) [male speaker]
	언니 (eon-ni) [female speaker]
younger sister	여동생 (yeo-dong-saeng)
son	아들 (a-deul)
son-in-law	사위 (sa-wi)

uncle (maternal)	외삼촌 (oe-sam-chon)
uncle (paternal)	삼촌 (sam-chon)
wife (one's own)	아내 (a-nae), 집사람 (jip-sa-ram), 처 (cheo)
wife (another's)	부인 (bu-in)

Country & Nationality

America / American	미국 (mi-guk) / 미국사람 (mi-guk-sa-ram)
Australia / Australian	호주 (ho-ju) / 호주사람 (ho-ju-sa-ram)
Canada / Canadian	캐나다 (kae-na-da) / 캐나다사람 (kae-na-da-sa-ram)
China / Chinese	중국 (jung-guk) / 중국사람 (jung-guk-sa-ram)
England / English	영국 (yeong-guk) / 영국사람 (yeong-guk-sa-ram)
Europe / European	유럽 (yu-reop) / 유럽사람 (yu-reop-sa-ram)
France / French	프랑스 (peu-rang-seu) / 프랑스사람 (peu-rang-seu-sa-ram)
Germany / German	독일 (dok-il) / 독일사람 (dok-il-sa-ram)
Japan / Japanese	일본 (il-bon) / 일본사람 (il-bon-sa-ram)
Korea / Korean	한국 (han-guk) / 한국사람 (han-guk-sa-ram)
Spain / Spanish	스페인 (seu-pe-in) / 스페인사람 (seu-pe-in-sa-ram)

Lesson 3. Colors & Shapes
색깔과 모양
(saek-kkal-gwa mo-yang)

1. Cultural Notes

In Korean, the words for colors take the form of nouns, predicates, or modifiers. The word "color" in Korean is 색 (saek) or 색깔 (saek-kkal). Traditionally, Korean has not distinguished between blue and green, and referred to both as 파란색 (pa-ran-saek), which means "blue". When contemporary Koreans want to indicate green, they say 초록색 (cho-rok-saek), which means "grass green". Examples demonstrating usage appear below the vocabulary list.

2. Model Phrases

What color is this?
이게 무슨 색이에요?
(i-ge mu-seun saeg-i-e-yo)

> It's blue.
> **파란색이에요.**
> (pa-ran-saeg-i-e-yo)

What color do you like?
무슨 색을 좋아하세요?
(mu-seun saeg-eul jo-a-ha-se-yo)

> I like blue.
> **파란색을 좋아해요.**
> (pa-ran-saeg-eul jo-a-hae-yo)

What color is the sky?
하늘 색깔이 어때요?
(ha-neul saek-kkal-i eo-ttae-yo)

> It's blue.
> **파래요.**
> (pa-rae-yo)

What color of clothes did s/he wear?
무슨 색깔 옷을 입었어요?
(mu-seun saek-kkal os-eul ib-eoss-eo-yo)

She/he wore blue clothes.
파란색 옷을 입었어요.
(pa-ran-saek os-eul ib-eoss-eo-yo)

3. Vocabulary

Name of colors

Color	Noun	Noun-Modifier	Predicate (Verb)
red	**빨간색** (ppal-gan-saek)	**빨간** (ppal-gan)	**빨개요** (ppal-gae- yo)
black	**까만색** (kka-man-saek)	**까만** (kka-man)	**까매요** (kka-mae-yo)
white	**하얀색** (ha-yan-saek)	**하얀** (ha-yan)	**하얘요** (ha-yae-yo)
blue	**파란색** (pa-ran-saek)	**파란** (pa-ran)	**파래요** (pa-rae-yo)
yellow	**노란색** (no-ran-saek)	**노란** (no-ran)	**노래요** (no-ra-yo)
green	**초록색** (cho-rok-saek)	**초록색** (cho-rok-saek)	**초록색이에요** (cho-rok-saeg-i-e-yo)
gray	**회색** (hoe-saek)	**회색** (hoe-saek)	**회색이에요** (hoe-saeg-i-e-yo)
pink	**분홍색** (bun-hong-saek)	**분홍색** (bun-hong-saek)	**분홍색이에요** (bun-hong-saeg-i-e-yo)
purple	**보라색** (bo-ra-saek)	**보라색** (bo-ra-saek)	**보라색이에요** (bo-ra-saeg-i-e-yo)
orange	**주황색** (ju-hwang-saek)	**주황색** (ju-hwang-saek)	**주황색이에요** (ju-hwang-saeg-i-e-yo)
light green	**연두색** (yeon-du-saek)	**연두색** (yeon-du-saek)	**연두색이에요** (yeon-du-saeg-i-e-yo)

Examples of usage:

Noun:	The color red.	**빨간색** (ppal-gan-saek)
Noun-Modifier:	A red apple.	**빨간 사과** (ppal-gan sa-gwa)
Predicate (Verb):	The apple is red.	**사과가 빨개요.** (sa-gwa-ga ppal- gae-yo)

Light, Darkness, and Patterns

light **연(한)** (yeon[-han])

연한 노란색 (yeon-han no-ran-saek)
연노란색 (yeon-no-ran-saek)
연노랑색 (yeon-no-rang-saek)

dark **진(한)** (jin [-han])

진한 노란색 (jin-han no-ran-saek)
진노란색 (jin-no-ran-saek)
진노랑색 (jin-no-rang-saek)

checkered	**체크무늬** (che-keu-mu-nui, che-keu-mu-ni)
striped	**줄무늬** (jul-mu-nui, jul-mu-ni)
flower pattern	**꽃무늬** (kkon-mu-nui, kkon-mu-ni)

Names of shapes

oval	**타원형** (ta-won-hyeong)
rectangle	**직사각형** (jik-sa-ga-kyeong)
circle	**원형** (won-hyeong)
	동그라미 (dong-geu-ra-mi)
square	**정사각형** (jeong-sa-ga-kyeong)
triangle	**정삼각형** (jeong-sam-ga-kyeong)
cube	**정육면체** (jeong-yung-myeon-che)

Lesson 4. Telling Time
시간 si-gan

1. Cultural Notes

The particle –에 (-e) accompanies most time expressions, which include the words for hour, day, month, and year. The exceptions: 그제 (geu-je) [the day before yesterday], 어제 (eo-je) [yesterday], 오늘 (o-neul) [today], 내일 (nae-il) [tomorrow], 모래 (mo-rae) [the day after tomorrow], 올해 (ol-hae) [this year], 매일 (mae-il) [every day], 매주 (mae-ju) [every week], 매월 (mae-wol) [every month], and 매년 (mae-nyeon) [every year]. Also, when writing dates in Korean, remember to write in the order of year, month, and date.

2. Model Phrases

What time is it now?
지금 몇 시예요?
(ji-geum myeot si-ye-yo)

> It's 2:45.
> **두시 사십오분이에요.**
> (du-si sa-sib-o-bun-i-e-yo)

> It's fifteen minutes to three.
> **세시 십오분 전이에요.**
> (se-si sib-o-bun jeon-i-e-yo)

What date is today?
오늘이 며칠이에요?
(o-neul-i myeo-chil-i-e-yo)

> It's April 2ⁿᵈ.
> **사월 이일이에요.**
> (sa-wol i-il-i-e-yo)

What day is tomorrow?
내일이 무슨 요일이에요?
(nae-il-i mu-seun yo-il-i-e-yo)

It's Tuesday.
화요일이에요.
(hwa-yo-il-i-e-yo)

What time do you go to work?
몇 시에 직장에 가세요?
(myeot si-e jik-jang-e ga-se-yo)

I leave at 8:00.
여덟시에 가요.
(yeo-deol-ssi-e ga-yo)

What are you going to do this weekend?
이번 주말에 뭐 하실 거예요?
(i-beon ju-mal-e mwo ha-sil kkeo-ye-yo)

I am going to visit the zoo.
동물원에 갈 거예요.
(dong-mul-won-e gal kkeo-ye-yo)

When does it rain a lot in Korea?
한국은 언제 비가 많이 와요?
(han-gug-eun eon-je bi-ga man-i wa-yo)

It rains the most in June.
유월에 비가 제일 많이 와요.
(yu-wol-e bi-ga je-il man-i wa-yo)

3. Vocabulary

Time & Minutes

A.M.   **오전** (o-jeon)
P.M.   **오후** (o-hu)

1 o'clock	**한시** (han-si)
2 o'clock	**두시** (du-si)
3 o'clock	**세시** (se-si)
4 o'clock	**네시** (ne-si)
5 o'clock	**다섯시** (da-seot-si)
6 o'clock	**여섯시** (yeo-seot-si)
7 o'clock	**일곱시** (il-gop-si)
8 o'clock	**여덟시** (yeo-deol-ssi)
9 o'clock	**아홉시** (a-hop-si)

10 o'clock	열시 (yeol-ssi)
11 o'clock	열한시 (yeol-han-si)
12 o'clock	열두시 (yeol-ttu-si)
5 minutes	오분 (o-bun)
10 minutes	십분 (sip-bun)
15 minutes	십오분 (sib-o-bun)
20 minutes	이십분 (i-sip-bun)
25 minutes	이십오분 (i-sib-o-bun)
30 minutes	삼십분 (sam-sip-bun)
	반 ban
35 minutes	삼십오분 (sam-sib-o-bun)
40 minutes	사십분 (sa-sip-bun)
	이십분 전 i-sip-bun jeon
45 minutes	사십오분 (sa-sib-o-bun)
	십오분 전 (sib-o-bun jeon)
50 minutes	오십분 (o-sip-bun)
	십분 전 (sip-bun jeon)
55 minutes	오십오분 (o-sib-o-bun)
	오분 전 o-bun jeon

Months

January	일월 (il-wol)	July	칠월 (chil-wol)
February	이월 (i-wol)	August	팔월 (pal-wol)
March	삼월 (sam-wol)	September	구월 (gu-wol)
April	사월 (sa-wol)	October	시월 (si-wol)
May	오월 (o-wol)	November	십일월 (sib-il-wol)
June	유월 (yu-wol)	December	십이월 (sib-i-wol)

Days of the Month

1st	일일 (il-il)	7th	칠일 (chil-il)
2nd	이일 (i-il)	8th	팔일 (pal-il)
3rd	삼일 (sam-il)	9th	구일 (gu-il)
4th	사일 (sa-il)	10th	십일 (sib-il)
5th	오일 (o-il)	20th	이십일 (i-sib-il)
6th	육일 (yug-il)	30th	삼십일 (sam-sib-il)

Days of the Week

Monday	월요일 (wol-yo-il)	Friday	금요일 (geum-yo-il)
Tuesday	화요일 (hwa-yo-il)	Saturday	토요일 (to-yo-il)
Wednesday	수요일 (su-yo-il)	Sunday	일요일 (il-yo-il)
Thursday	목요일 (mog-yo-il)		

Other Expressions

the day before yesterday	그제 (geu-je), 그저께 (geu-jeo-kke)
yesterday	어제 (eo-je)
today	오늘 (o-neul)
tomorrow	내일 (nae-il)
the day after tomorrow	모레 (mo-re)
last week	지난주 (ji-nan-ju)
this week	이번주 (i-beon-jju)
next week	다음주 (da-eum-jju)
last month	지난달 (ji-nan-dal)
this month	이번달 (i-beon-ttal)
next month	다음달 (da-eum-ttal)
last year	작년 (jang-nyeon)
this year	올해 (ol-hae), 금년 (geum-nyeon)
next year	내년 (nae-nyeon)
every day	매일 (mae-il)
every week	매주 (mae-ju)
every month	매월 (mae-wol)
every year	매년 (mae-nyeon)
weekdays	주중 (ju-jung)
weekend	주말 (ju-mal)
end of a month	월말 (wol-mal)
end of a year	연말 (yeon-mal)

Lesson 5. Shopping
쇼핑하기 (syo-ping-ha-gi)

1. Cultural Notes

In Korea, it is common to negotiate prices except in department stores and supermarkets, where all items have price tags. Although growing numbers of merchants accept credit cards, cash is preferred. All prices are tax-inclusive. Stores are usually open between 9 a.m. and 10 p.m., although some are open 24 hours or until midnight. It is advisable to carry sufficient cash at all times, as ATM machines are rare outside of banks. Since many stores are reluctant to let customers try on clothes before purchasing, it is important to know one's clothing size when shopping. Stores generally do not give full refunds for purchases, although exchanges for other products are possible.

2. Model Phrases

Asking for assistance

Welcome. May I help you? (lit. What are you looking for?)
어서 오세요. 뭘 찾으세요?
(eo-seo o-se-yo mwol chaj-eu-se-yo)

I want to see a digital camera.
디지털 카메라를 좀 보려고 하는데요.
(di-ji-teol ka-me-ra-reul jom bo-ryeo-go ha-neun-de-yo)

I want to see a digital camera. (lit. I am looking for a digital camera.)
디지털 카메라를 찾는데요.
(di-ji-teol ka-me-ra-reul chan-neun-de-yo)

You are? We have many digital cameras in here.
그러세요? 카메라는 이쪽에 많이 있어요.
(geu-reo-se-yo ka-me-ra-neun i-jjog-e man-i iss-eo-yo)

How about this one? This design is very popular these days.
이건 어떠세요? 요즘 이 디자인이 유행이에요.
(i-geon eo-tteo-se-yo yo-jeum i di-ja-in-i yu-haeng-i-e-yo)

I don't like this one.
이 디자인은 별로 마음에 안 드는데요.
(i di-ja-in-eun byeol-lo ma-eum-e an deu-neun-de-yo)

Can you show me another one?
다른 걸로 좀 보여주세요.
(da-reun geol-lo jom bo-yeo-ju-se-yo)

I am not looking for anything special.
특별히 찾는 건 없는데요.
(teuk-byeol-hi chan-neun geon eom-neun-de-yo)

Can I just look around?
그냥 구경 좀 해도 돼요?
(geu-nyang gu-geong jom hae-do dwae-yo)

> Sure, please feel free to look around.
> 그럼요. 천천히 구경하세요.
> (geu-reom-yo cheon-cheon-hi gu-gyeong-ha-se-yo)

> Please feel free to look around.
> 천천히 골라 보세요.
> (cheon-cheon-hi gol-la bo-se-yo)

What time do you open?
몇 시에 가게문을 여세요
(myeot si-e ga-ge-mun-eul yeo-se-yo)

What time do you close?
몇 시에 가게문을 닫으세요?
(myeot si-e ga-ge-mun-eul dad-eu-se-yo)

> We open/close at 9:00.
> 9시에 열어요 / 닫아요.
> (a-hop-si-e yeol-eo-yo / dad-a-yo)

It's too expensive. Can you offer a discount?
너무 비싼데요. 좀 깎아 주세요.
(neo-mu bi-ssan-de-yo jom kkakk-a ju-se-yo)

> I am sorry, but I can't.
> 죄송하지만 그렇게는 안되겠는데요.
> (joe-song-ha-ji-man geu-reo-ke-neun an-doe-gen-neun-
> de-yo)

It doesn't cost too much. If you go to other stores, the price is much higher.
이거 안 비싼 거예요. 다른 집에 가시면 더 비싸요.
(i-geo an bi-ssan geo-yeo-yo da-reun jib-e ga-si-myeon deo bi-ssa-yo)

We don't carry that item.
그런 건 저희 집에서 안 파는데요.
(geu-reon geon jeo-hi jib-e-seo an pa-neun-de-yo)

Please go to Yongsan Electric Complex [to purchase that item].
용산전자상가에 한번 가 보세요.
(yong-san-jeon-ja-sang-ga-e han-beon ga bo-se-yo)

I am very sorry, but all digital cameras are sold out.
죄송하지만 디지털 카메라는 지금 다 팔렸는데요.
joe-song-ha-ji-man di-ji-teol ka-me-ra-neun ji-geum da pal-lyeon-neun-de-yo

Would you visit us again next week?
다음 주에 다시 한번 와 주시겠어요?
(da-eum jju-e da-si han-beon wa ju-si-gess-eo-yo)

Paying

How much are these all together?
이거 전부 얼마지요?
(i-geo jeon-bu eol-ma-ji-yo)

It is very expensive / inexpensive.
정말 비싸네요 / 싸네요.
(jeong-mal bi-ssa-ne-yo / ssa-ne-yo)

Where do I pay?
어디에서 계산을 합니까?
(eo-di-e-seo gye-san-eul ham-ni-kka)

Where do I pay? (*lit.* Where is the place to pay?)
계산하는 곳이 어디 있습니까?
(gye-san-ha-neun gos-i eo-di iss-eum-ni-kka)

Do you take a credit card or traveler's check?
신용카드 / 크레딧 카드나 여행자 수표도 받으세요?
(sin-yong-ka-deu / keu-re-dit-ka-deu-na yeo-haeng-ja su-pyo-do bad-eu-se-yo)

How long is the warranty?
애프터서비스 기간이 얼마나 되지요?
(ae-peu-teo-sseo-bi-seu gi-gan-i eol-ma-na doe-ji-yo)

Is the warranty certificate included inside?
품질 보증서가 안에 들어 있나요?
(pum-jil bo-jeung-seo-ga an-e deul-eo in-na-yo)

May I have a receipt?
영수증 좀 주시겠어요?
(yeong-su-jeung jom ju-si-gess-eo-yo)

Delivery

May I have this wrapped?
이거 포장 좀 해 주시겠어요?
(i-geo po-jang jom hae ju-si-gess-eo-yo)

May I have this delivered?
배달도 해 주세요?
(bae-dal-do hae ju-se-yo)

> Sure. Please give me your address and phone number.
> **그럼요. 주소하고 전화번호 좀 주시겠어요?**
> (geu-reom-nyo ju-so-ha-go jeon-hwa-beon-ho jom ju-si-gess-eo-yo)

How long does it take [for delivery]?
얼마나 걸리는데요?
(eol-ma-na geol-li-neun-de-yo)

> One day is enough.
> **하루면 됩니다.**
> (ha-ru-myeon doem-ni-da)

> It will take about two days.
> **이틀 정도 걸리겠는데요.**
> (i-teul jeong-do geol-li-gen-neun-de-yo)

Shopping for Clothes or Shoes

May I try this on?
이거 좀 입어봐도 될까요?
(i-geo jom ib-eo-bwa-do doel-kka-yo)

> Sure. Please do.
> 그럼요. 입어보세요.
> (geu-reom-nyo ib-eo-bo-se-yo)

Where is the fitting room?
어디에서 입어보죠?
(eo-di-e-so ib-eo-bo-jyo)

> The fitting rooms are on that side.
> 저쪽에 탈의실이 있어요.
> (jeo-jjog-e tal-ui-sil-i iss-eo-yo)

It's too tight.
좀 작은데요.
(jom jag-eun-de-yo)

It's too loose.
좀 큰데요.
(jom keun-de-yo)

May I try a smaller size? (*lit.* Please give me a larger/smaller one)
좀 더 작은 걸로 줘 보세요.
(jom deo jag-eun geol-lo jwo bo-se-yo)

May I try a larger size? (*lit.* Please give me a larger/smaller one)
좀 더 큰 걸로 줘 보세요.
(jom deo keun geol-lo jwo bo-se-yo)

It's too narrow. (for shoes only)
볼이 좀 좁은데요.
(bol-i jom job-eun-de-yo)

It's too wide. (for shoes only)
볼이 좀 넓은데요.
(bol-i jom neolb-eun-de-yo)

Don't you have a wider one? (for shoes only)
볼이 좀 더 넓은 거 없으세요?
(bol-i jom deo neolb-eun geo eops-eu-se-yo)

Don't you have a narrower one? (for shoes only)
볼이 좀 더 좁은 거 없으세요?
(bol-i jom deo job-eun geo eops-eu-se-yo)

It fits well.
잘 맞네요.
(jal man-ne-yo)

It does not fit.
잘 안 맞네요.
(jal an man-ne-yo)

I would like to get this. / I will take this.
이걸로 주세요.
(i-geol-lo ju-se-yo)

Do you have this in different color?
이거하고 똑같은 디자인으로 다른 색깔은 없으세요?
(i-geo-ha-go ttok-gat-eun di-ja-in-eu-ro da-reun saek-kkal-eun eops-eu-se-yo)

Would you show me a long sleeve shirt that would match these pants?
이 바지하고 어울릴만한 긴팔 셔츠 좀 보여주시겠어요?
(i ba-ji-ha-go eo-ul-lil man-han gin-pal syeo-cheu ha-na bo-yeo-ju-si-gess-eo-yo)

Can I wash it in water?
이거 물빨래해도 되나요?
(i-geo mul-ppal-lae-hae-do doe-na-yo)

Can I wash it in a washing machine? [Water washing is inferred.]
이거 막 빨아도 되나요?
(i-geo mak ppal-a-do doe-na-yo)

> Sure, you can use your washing machine for it.
> **그럼요. 그냥 세탁기에 넣고 돌리셔도 돼요.**
> (geu-reom-nyo geu-nyang se-tak-gi-e neo-ko dol-li-syeo-do dwae-yo)

No, this is not for machine wash, so please dry clean it.
아니오, 이건 물빨래하면 안 되니까 꼭 드라이
하셔야 돼요.
(a-ni-o i-geon mul-ppal-lae-ha-myeon an doe-ni-kka
kkok deu-ra-i ha-syeo-ya dwae-yo)

3. Vocabulary

Kind of Stores

bakery	빵집 (ppang-jjip), 제과점 (je-gwa-jeom)
bank	은행 (eun-haeng)
bookstore	서점 (seo-jeom), 책방 (chaek-bang)
café	다방 (da-bang)
clothing store	옷가게 (ot-ga-ge)
coffee shop	카페 (ka-pe)
convenience store	편의점 (pyeon-ui-jeom), 가게 (ga-ge)
department store	백화점 (bae-kwa-jeom)
drugstore	약국 (yak-guk), 약방 (yak-bang)
florist/flower shop	꽃집 (kkot-jip), 화원(hwa-won)
jewelry dealer	금방(geum-ppang), 보석상 (bo-seok-sang)
photo shop	사진관 (sa-jin-gwan)
post office	우체국 (u-che-guk)
shoe store	신발가게 (sin-bal-kka-ge), 구두가게 (gu-du-kka-ge)
supermarket	슈퍼마켓 (syu-peo-ma-ket)
teahouse	찻집 (chat-jip)
toy store	장난감 가게 (jang-nan-kkam ga-ge)
wholesale store	마트 (ma-teu)

Clothing

blouse	블라우스 (beul-la-u-seu)
bow tie	나비 넥타이 (na-bi nek-ta-i)
bra	브라자 (beu-ra-ja)
casual	캐주얼 (kae-ju-eol)
casual style	캐주얼 스타일 (kae-ju-eol seu-ta-il)
coat	코트 (co-teu)

dress (one-piece)	원피스	(won-pi-seu)
(two-piece)	투피스	(tu-pi-seu)
(three-piece)	쓰리피스	(sseu-ri-pi-seu)
dress shirts	와이셔츠	(wa-i-syeo-cheu)
short sleeve	짧은 소매	(jjalb-eun so-mae)
long sleeve	긴 소매	(gin so-mae)
formal style	정장 스타일	(jeong-jang seu-ta-il)
glove	장갑	(jang-gap)
hat	모자	(mo-ja)
jacket	자켓	(ja-ket)
mitten	벙어리 장갑	(beong-eo-ri jang-gap)
muffler/scarf	목도리	(mok-do-ri)
necktie	넥타이	(nek-ta-i)
pants	바지	(ba-ji)
long pants	긴바지	(gin-ba-ji)
short pants	반바지	(ban-ba-ji)
jeans	청바지	(cheong-ba-ji)
cotton pants	면바지	(myeon-ba-ji)
wool pants	양복바지	(yang-bok-ba-ji)
pantyhose	스타킹	(seu-ta-king)
scarf	스카프	(seu-ka-peu)
shirt	셔츠	(syeo-cheu)
skirt	치마	(chi-ma)
short skirt	짧은 치마	(jjalb-eun chi-ma)
mini-skirt	미니 스커트	(mi-ni-seu-keo-teu)
long skirt	긴치마	(gin-chi-ma)
socks	양말	(yang-mal)
suit	정장	(jeong-jang)
sweater	스웨터	(seu-we-teo)
tennis/golf shirt	남방	(nam-bang)
underwear	속옷	(sog-ot)
briefs/panties	팬티	(paen-ti)
undershirt	런닝셔츠	(reon-ning syeo-cheu)
vest	조끼	(jo-kki)
hi-support underwear	거들	(geo-deul)

Putting On and Taking Off Clothes

Korean has different verbs for "to put on" or "to wear" and "to take off," depending on how the item is worn. For example, 입다 (ip-da) is for apparel other than headgear, footwear, or gloves. 신다 (sin-tta) is for footwear only and 끼다 (kki-da) is for things that fit tightly.

Item	Putting On Verb	Taking Off Verb
clothes / 옷 (ot)	입다 (ip-da)	벗다 (beot-da)
shoes / 신발 (sin-bal)	신다 (sin-tta)	벗다 (beot-da)
socks / 양말 (yang-mal)	신다 (sin-tta)	벗다 (beot-da)
hat / 모자 (mo-ja)	쓰다 (sseu-da)	벗다 (beot-da)
glasses / 안경 (an-gyeong)	끼다 (kki-da)	벗다 (beot-da) 빼다 (ppae-da)
gloves, mittens / 장갑 (jang-gap)	끼다 (kki-da)	벗다 (beot-da) 빼다 (ppae-da)
ring / 반지 (ban-ji)	끼다 (kki-da)	빼다 (ppae-da)
hairpin / 머리핀 (meo-ri-pin)	꼽다 (kkop-da)	빼다 (ppae-da)
muffler / 목도리 (mok-do-ri)	매다 (mae-da)	풀다 (pul-da)
scarf / 스카프 (seu-ka-peu)	두르다 (du-reu-da)	끄르다 (kkeu-reu-da)
necktie / 넥타이 (nek-ta-i)	매다 (mae-da)	풀다 (pul-da) 끄르다 (kkeu-reu-da)
belt / 벨트 (bel-teu)	차다 (cha-da) 하다 (ha-da)	풀다 (pul-da) 끄르다 (kkeu-reu-da)

Sizes

Women's Dresses

USA	4	6	8	10	12
Korea	44	55	66	77	88

Shirts and blouses

USA	X-large	large	medium	small
Korea	특대 (teuk-dae)	대 (dae)	중 (jung) 중간 (jung-gan)	소 (so) 작은 (jag-eun)

Men's Suits

USA	36	38	40	42	44
Korea	90	95	100	105	110

Shoes

USA	5	5.5	6	6.5	7	7.5	8	8.5	9	9.5	10
Korea	225	230	235	240	245	250	255	260	265	270	275

* Size differs by brand.
* Dress pants: Korea uses inches for the dress pants.

Lesson 6. Barber Shops & Beauty Salons
이발소와 미장원
(i-bal-sso-wa mi-jang-won)

1. Cultural Notes

Appointments are not required for barbershops or beauty
salons. Waits are short for walk-in customers, and free tea
and soft drinks are often provided. Tips are not expected.
Hair salons offer more stylish haircuts, and younger men
prefer them to barbershops, which generally serve an older
clientele.

2. Model Phrases

I would like to get a haircut. How long do I have to wait?
머리를 좀 자르고 싶은데 얼마나 기다리면 돼요?
(meo-ri-reul jom ja-reu-go sip-eun-de eol-ma-na gi-da-ri-
   myeon dwae-yo)

> About 20 minutes.
> **한 20분이면 될 것 같은데요.**
> (han i-sip-bun-i-myeon doel geot gat-eun-de-yo)

> Please sit here to wait.
> **이쪽에 앉아서 잠깐만 기다리세요.**
> (i-jjog-e anj-a-seo jam-kkan-man gi-da-ri-se-yo)

> Would you like to read some magazines while waiting?
> **기다리시는 동안 잡지 좀 보시겠어요?**
> (gi-da-ri-si-neun dong-an jap-ji jom bo-si-gess-eo-yo)

I would like to get a perm. How long will it take?
파마를 좀 하려고 하는데 시간이 얼마나 걸려요?
(pa-ma-reul jom ha-ryeo-go ha-neun-de si-gan-i eol-ma-na
   geol-leo-yo)

> It will take about three hours for a straight perm.
> **스트레이트 파마는 한 세시간 걸려요.**
> (Seu-teu-re-i-teu pa-ma-neun han se-si-gan
>   geol-lyeo-yo)

It will take about two hours for a regular perm.
보통 파마는 한 두시간 정도면 돼요.
(bo-tong pa-ma-neun han du-si-gan jeong-do-myeon
    dwae-yo)

How would you like your hair done?
머리 어떻게 해 드릴까요?
(meo-ri eo-tteo-ke hae deu-ril-kka-yo)

I would like to have a fashionable style.
요즘 유행하는 스타일로 해 주세요.
(yo-jeum yu-haeng-ha-neun seu-ta-il-lo hae ju-se-yo)

Please cut it short in the back and on the sides
뒷머리랑 옆머리는 좀 짧게 깎아 주세요.
(dwin-meo-ri-rang yeom-meo-ri-neun jom jjal-kke kkakk-a
    ju-se-yo)

Please cut just a little in the front.
앞머리는 조금만 깎아 주세요.
(am-meo-ri-neun jo-geum-man kkakk-a ju-se-yo)

Please don't change this style, just trim it a little shorter.
머리 모양은 바꾸지 말고 그냥 좀 짧게 다듬어 주세요.
(meo-ri mo-yang-eun ba-kku-ji mal-go geu-nyang jom jjal
    kke da-deum-eo ju-se-yo)

Do you want a shave? (for men only)
면도도 해 드릴까요?
(myeon-do-do hae deu-ril-kka-yo)

Yes, please.   No, thanks.
네, 좀 해 주세요.   아니오, 괜찮아요.
(ne jom hae ju-se-yo)   (a-ni-o gwaen-chan-a-yo)

How do I take care of this hairstyle?
이 머리 어떻게 손질해야 되죠?
(i meo-ri eo-tteo-ke son-jil-hae-ya doe-jyo)

Please dry it completely with a towel and put on some
    mousse.
수건으로 잘 말리고 무스를 살짝 발라 주세요.
(su-geon-eu-ro jal mal-li-go mu-sseu-reul sal-jjak bal-la
    ju-se-yo)

Please come here to have your hair shampooed.
이쪽으로 오셔서 머리 감으세요.
(i-jjog-eu-ro o-syeo-seo meo-ri gam-eu-se-yo)

The water is too hot.
물이 너무 뜨겁네요.
(mul-i neo-mu tteu-geom-ne-yo.)

The water is too cold.
물이 너무 차갑네요.
(mul-i neo-mu cha-gam-ne-yo.)

Please make it cooler.
좀 더 시원하게 해 주세요.
(jom deo si-won-ha-ge/tta-tteu-ta-ge hae ju-se-yo)

Please make it warmer.
좀 더 따뜻하게 해 주세요.
(jom deo si-won-ha-ge/tta-tteu-ta-ge hae ju-se-yo)

3. Vocabulary

Style

hair in back	뒷머리	(dwin-meo-ri)
hair in front	앞머리	(am-meo-ri)
hair on sides	옆머리	(yeom-meo-ri)
short hair	짧은 머리	(jjalb-eun meo-ri)
	머리가 짧다	(meo-ri-ga jjal-tta)
long hair	긴 머리	(gin meo-ri)
	머리가 길다	(meo-ri-ga gil-da)
thin hair	가는 머리	(ga-neun meo-ri)
	머리가 가늘다	(meo-ri-ga ga-neul-da)
thick hair	굵은 머리	(gulg-eun meo-ri)
	머리가 굵다	(meo-ri-ga gulk-da)
curly hair	곱슬머리	(gop-seul meo-ri)
	머리가 곱슬곱슬하다	(meo-ri-ga gop-seul-gop-seul-ha-da)

coarse hair	뻣뻣한 머리 (ppeot-ppeo-tan meo-ri)
	머리가 뻣뻣하다 (meo-ri-ga ppeot-ppeo-ta-da)
soft hair	부드러운 머리 (bu-deu-reo-un meo-ri)
	머리가 부드럽다 (meo-ri-ga bu-deu-reop-da)
straight hair	직모 (jing-mo)
bald	대머리 (dae-meo-ri)
oily	지성 (ji-seong)
normal	중성 (jung-seong)
dry	건성 (geon-seong)
permanent wave hair	파마머리 (pa-ma meo-ri)
shoulder-length hair	단발머리 (dan-bal meo-ri)
crew cut	스포츠 형 (seu-po-cheu-hyeong)
straight permanent	스트레이트 파마 (seu-teu-re-i-teu pa-ma)
perm with large curls	굵은 파마 (gulg-eun pa-ma)
woman's hairdresser	미용사 (mi-yong-sa)
	헤어 디자이너 (he-eo di-ja-i-neo)
man's hairdresser	이발사 (i-bal-ssa)
to brush one's hair	머리를 빗다 (meo-ri-reul bit-da)
to dye	염색하다 (yeom-sae-ka-da)
to get hair blown-dry	드라이하다 (deu-ra-i-ha-da)
to get a haircut (men)	머리를 깎다 (meo-ri-reul kkak-da)
to get a haircut (women)	머리를 자르다 (meo-ri-reul ja-reu-da)
to get a permanent	파마하다 (pa-ma-ha-da)
to get hair towel-dried	머리를 말리다 (meo-ri-reul mal-li-da)
to apply hair mousse	무스를 바르다 (mu-sseu-reul ba-reu-da)
to apply hair gel	젤리를 바르다 (jel-li-reul ba-reu-da)
to apply hair spray	스프레이를 하다 (seu-peu-re-i-reul ha-da)
to rinse out / wash out	머리를 헹구다 (meo-ri-reul heng-gu-da)
	린스하다 (rin-seu-ha-da)

to shampoo	머리를 감다 (meo-ri-reul gam-tta)
	샴푸하다 (syam-pu-ha-da)
to trim hair	머리를 다듬다 (meo-ri-reul da-deum-tta)

Lesson 7. Hospitals & Drugstores
병원과 약국
(byeong-won-gwa yak-guk)

1. Cultural Notes

Appointments are not required for hospital visits. One may have to wait awhile in a general hospital, but in others, patients are seen within 30 minutes. The telephone number for emergencies is 119.

2. Model Phrases

Things You May Hear from a Doctor

What brings you here? (*lit.* Why did you come here?)
어떻게 오셨어요?
(eo-tteo-ke o-syeoss-eo-yo)

Where and how does it hurt?
어디가 어떻게 아프세요?
(eo-di-ga eo-tteo-ke a-peu-se-yo)

Take off your clothes and put on this gown.
옷을 벗고 가운으로 갈아입으세요.
(os-eul beot-go kka-un-eu-ro gal-a-ib-eu-se-yo)

Please sit down.
여기 앉으세요.
(yeo-gi anj-eu-se-yo)

Please lie down.
여기 누우세요.
(yeo-gi nu-u-se-yo)

Please stand up now.
이제 일어나세요.
(i-je il-eo-na-se-yo)

Take a deep breath.
숨을 크게 쉬어 보세요.
(sum-eul keu-ge swi-eo bo-se-yo)

Hold your breath.
숨을 잠깐만 멈춰 보세요.
(sum-eul jam-kkan-man meom-chwo bo-se-yo)

Say "Ah!"
'아' 해 보세요.
(a hae bo-se-yo)

We will do some tests.
검사를 좀 해야 되겠는데요.
(geom-sa-reul jom hae-ya doe-gen-neun-de-yo)

How long has it been since your last period?
마지막으로 생리하신 게 언제지요?
(ma-ji-mag-eu-ro saeng-ni-ha-sin ge eon-je-ji-yo)

You have a cavity.
충치가 생겼군요.
(chung-chi-ga saeng-gyeot-gun-yo)

We have to pull that tooth.
이를 뽑아야겠네요.
(i-reul ppob-a-ya-gen-ne-yo)

We have to treat it.
치료를 좀 해야겠습니다.
(chi-ryo-reul jom hae-ya-gess-eum-ni-da)

Please rinse your mouth.
양치질 하십시오.
(yang-chi-jil ha-sip-si-o)
입을 헹구세요.
(ib-eul heng-gu-se-yo)

You need to wear glasses.
안경을 좀 끼셔야겠는데요.
(an-gyeong-eul jom kki-syeo-ya-gen-neun-de-yo)

You need an eye exam.
시력검사를 좀 받으셔야겠네요.
(si-ryeok-geom-sa-reul jom bad-eu-syeo-ya-gen-ne-yo)

Does it hurt a lot?
많이 아프세요?
(man-i a-peu-se-yo)

This will hurt a bit.

좀 아프실 겁니다.

(jom a-peu-sil kkeom-ni-da)

It is serious.

증상이 좀 심한데요.

(jeung-sang-i jom sim-han-de-yo)

It is not that serious.

증상이 별로 심하지 않군요.

(jeung-sang-i byeol-lo sim-han-ji an-kun-yo)

You are three months pregnant.

임신 3개월입니다.

(im-sin sam-gae-wol-im-ni-da)

Take two pills after every meal, three times a day.

이 약을 하루에 3번씩 식후에 2알씩 드세요.

(i yag-eul ha-ru-e se-beon-ssik si-ku-e du-al-ssik deu-se-yo)

Take one cup, on an empty stomach, in the morning and
afternoon.

이 약을 아침저녁 공복에 한컵씩 드세요.

(i yag-eul a-chim-jeo-nyeok gong-bog-e han-keop-ssik du-
se-yo)

Things You May Say to a Doctor

I am dizzy and have no energy.

어지럽고 기운이 없어요.

(eo-ji-reop-go gi-un-i eops-eo-yo)

I have had diarrhea and have been throwing up all night.

밤새도록 설사하고 토했어요.

(bam-sae-do-rok seol-ssa-ha-go to-haess-eo-yo)

I cannot breathe easily.

숨을 잘 못 쉬겠어요.

(sum-eul jal mot swi-gess-eo-yo)

I lost consciousness for a while.

잠깐 동안 정신을 잃었어요.

(jam-kkan-ttong-an jeong-sin-eul il-eoss-eo-yo)

I feel like throwing up.
토할 것 같아요.
(to-hal kkeot gat-a-yo)

I think I have a cavity.
이가 썩은 것 같아요.
(i-ga sseog-eun geot gat-a-yo)

My gums are swollen frequently, and I bleed when I brush
my teeth.
잇몸이 자주 붓고 양치질할 때 잇몸에서 피가 나요.
(in-mom-i ja-ju but-go yang-chi-jil-hal ttae in-mom-e-seo
pi-ga-na-yo)

Can I have my frames repaired here?
여기에서 안경테를 좀 고칠 수 있을까요?
(yeo-gi-e-seo an-gyeong-te-reul jom go-chil ssu iss-eul-
kka-yo)

I would like to have a pair of glasses.
안경을 좀 맞추려고 하는데요.
(an-gyeong-eul jom mat-chu-ryeo-go ha-neun-de-yo)

I would like to have a pair of contact lenses.
콘텍트 렌즈를 좀 맞추려고 하는데요.
(kon-tek-teu-ren-jeu-reul jom mat-chu-ryeo-go ha-neun-
de-yo)

Please call an ambulance.
앰뷸런스를 좀 불러 주시겠어요?
(aem-byul-leon-seu-reul jom bul-leo ju-si-gess-eo-yo)

How is his/her condition?
상태가 어떤가요?
(sang-tae-ga eo-tteon-ga-yo)

Does the doctor speak English?
의사선생님이 영어를 할 줄 아시나요?
(ui-sa-seon-saeng-nim-i yeong-eo-reul hal jjul a-si-na-yo)

I prefer a female doctor.
의사선생님이 여자분이었으면 좋겠는데요.
(ui-sa-seon-saeng-nim-i yeo-ja-bun-i-eoss-eu-myeon
jo-ken-neun-de-yo)

I prefer a male doctor.

의사선생님이 남자분이었으면 좋겠는데요.

(ui-sa-seon-saeng-nim-i nam-ja-bun-i-eoss-eu-myeon
   jo-ken-neun-de-yo)

3. Vocabulary

Hospitals & Calling for Medical Help

hospital, clinic	병원	(byeong-won)
dentistry	치과	(chi-kkwa)
dermatology	피부과	(pi-bu-kkwa)
external department	외과	(oe-kkwa)
internal department	내과	(nae-kkwa)
obstetrics & gynecology	산부인과	(san-bu-in-kkwa)
ophthalmology (eye)	안과	(an-kkwa)
optician	안경원	(an-gyeong-won)
	안경가게	(an-gyeong-kka-ge)
Oriental herb clinic	한의원	(han-ui-won)
orthopedics	정형외과	(jeong-hyeong-oe-kkwa)
otorhinology (NET)	이비인후과	(i-bi-in-hu-kkwa)
pediatrics	소아과	(so-a-kkwa)
plastic surgery	성형외과	(seong-hyeong-oe-kkwa)
urology	비뇨기과	(bi-nyo-gi-kkwa)
doctor	의사	(ui-sa)
herb doctor	한의사	(han-ui-sa)
nurse	간호사	(gan-ho-sa)
pharmacist	약사	(yak-sa)
emergency room	응급실	(eung-geup-sil)
operating room	수술실	(su-sul-sil)
ward	입원실	(ib-won-sil)
reception desk	접수처	(jeop-su-cheo)
information desk	접수처	(jeop-su-cheo)
medicine window	투약처	(tu-yak-cheo)
pharmacy	투약처	(tu-yak-cheo)
ambulance	구급차	(gu-geup-cha)
blood type	혈액형	(hyeol-ae-kyeong)
health insurance card	의료보험카드	(ui-ryo-bo-heom-ka-deu)
prescription	처방전	(cheo-bang-jeon)

wheelchair	휠체어 (hwil-che-eo)
pills	먹는 약 (meong-neun nyak)
ointment	바르는 약 (ba-reu-neun nyak)
	연고 (yeon-go)
eye drop	안약 (an-yak)
herb medicine	한약 (han-yak)
liquid medicine	물약 (mul-lyak)
powdered medicine	가루약 (ga-ru-yak)
tablet/pill	알약 (al-lyak)
bandage	반창고 (ban-chang-go)
	대일밴드 (dae-il-baen-deu)
iodine	소독약 (so-dong-nyak)
antibiotics	항생제 (hang-saeng-je)
pain killer	진통제 (jin-tong-je)
sunblock lotion	선블락 (sseon-beul-lak)
after a meal	식후(에) (si-ku-[e])
before a meal	식전(에) (sik-jeon-[e])
on an empty stomach	공복에 (gong-bog-e)
astigmatic	난시 (nan-si)
farsighted	원시 (won-si)
nearsighted	근시 (geun-si)

Medical Services

to apply an ointment	연고를 바르다 (yeon-go-reul ba-reu-da)
to apply lotion to an eye	안약을 넣다 (an-yag-eul neo-ta)
to get a general examination (testing)	종합검사를 하다/받다 (jong-hap-geom-sa-reul ha-da/bat-da)
to get acupuncture	침을 맞다 (chim-eul mat-da)
to get an injection	주사를 맞다 (ju-sa-reul mat-da)
to go to a hospital regularly	통원치료를 하다/받다 (tong-won-chi-ryo-reul ha-da/bat-da)
to have a blood test	혈액검사를 하다/받다 (heol-aek-geom-sa-reul ha-da/bat-da)

to have a urine test	소변검사를 하다/받다 (so-byeon-geom-sa-reul ha-da/bat-da)
to be examined (in an herbal clinic)	진맥을 하다/받다 (jin-maeg-eul ha-da/bat-da)
to be examined (in a hospital)	진찰을 하다/받다 (jin-chal-eul ha-da/bat-da)
to hospitalize	입원하다 (ib-won-ha-da)
to operate	수술을 하다/받다 (su-sul-eul ha-da)
to release	퇴원하다 (toe-won-ha-da)
to take medicine	약을 먹다 (yag-eul meok-da)
to take an X-ray	엑스레이를 찍다 (ek-seu-re-i-reul jjik-da)

Body Parts

bone	뼈 (ppyeo)
duodenum	십이지장 (sib-i-ji-jang)
esophagus	식도 (sik-do)
flesh	살 (sal)
genitalia	생식기 (saeng-sik-gi)
heart	심장 (sim-jang)
joint	관절 (gwan-jeol)
kidney	신장 (sin-jang)
large intestine	대장 (dae-jang)
liver	간장 (gan-jang)
lungs	폐 (pye, pe)
muscle	근육 (geun-yuk)
nervous system	신경 (sin-gyeong)
skin	피부 (pi-bu)
small intestine	소장 (so-jang)
spine	척추 (cheok-chu)
stomach	위 (wi)
throat	기관지 (gi-gwan-ji)
vein	혈관 (hyeol-gwan), 핏줄 (pit-jul)
ankle	발목 (bal-mok)

anus	항문	(hang-mun)
arm	팔	(pal)
back	등	(deung)
butt, hip	엉덩이	(eong-deong-i)
calf	종아리	(jong-a-ri)
chest/breast	가슴	(ga-seum)
chin	턱	(teok)
ear	귀	(gwi)
elbow	팔목	(pal-mok)
eye	눈	(nun)
face	얼굴	(eol-gul)
finger	손가락	(son-kka-rak)
fingernail	손톱	(son-top)
foot	발	(bal)
gum	잇몸	(in-mom)
hand	손	(son)
head	머리	(meo-ri)
knee	무릎	(mu-reup)
leg	다리	(da-ri)
mouth	입	(ip)
neck	목	(mok)
nose	코	(ko)
shoulder	어깨	(eo-kkae)
thigh	허벅지	(heo-beok-ji)
toe	발가락	(bal-kka-rak)
toenail	발톱	(bal-top)
tooth	이	(i)
waist	허리	(heo-ri)
wrist	손목	(son-mok)

Illnesses and Symptoms

to be dizzy	어지럽다	(eo-ji-reop-da)
to be lacking in energy	기운이 없다	(gi-un-i eop-da)
to be pregnant	임신하다	(im-sin-ha-da)
to be swollen	붓다	(but-da)
to be tired	피곤하다	(pi-gon-ha-da)
to bleed	피가 나다	(pi-ga na-da)
to cough	기침을 하다	(gi-chim-eul ha-da)
to get hurt	상처가 나다	(sang-cheo-ga na-da)
to get injured	다치다	(da-chi-da)

to have indigestion	소화가 안 되다
	(so-hwa-ga an-doe-da)
to have arthritis	관절염에 걸리다
	(gwan-jeol-lyeom-e geol-li-da),
	관절염이다
	(gwan-jeol-lyeom-i-da)
to have been unconscious	정신을 잃다 (jeong-sin-eul il-ta)

to have been vomiting	토하다 (to-ha-da)
to have chest congestion	가슴이 답답하다
	(ga-seum-i dap-da-pa-da)
to have a cold	감기에 걸리다
	(gam-gi-e geol-li-da)
to have cramps	생리통이 있다
	(saeng-ni-tong-i it-da)
to have diabetes	당뇨가 있다 (dang-nyo-ga it-da)
to have diarrhea	설사를 하다 (seol-ssa-reul ha-da)
to have difficulty breathing	숨쉬기가 힘들다
	(sum-swi-gi-ga him-deul-da),
	호흡이 곤란하다
	(ho-heub-i gol-lan-ha-da)
to have a fever	열이 나다 (yeol-i na-da)
to have a fracture or a broken bone	뼈가 부러지다
	(ppyeo-ga bu-reo-ji-da)

to have a gastric ulcer	위염이 있다 (wi-yeom-i it-da)
to have a headache	머리가 아프다
	(meo-ri-ga a-peu-da),
	두통이 있다 (du-tong-i it-da)
to have a heart attack	심장마비가 오다
	(sim-jang-ma-bi-ga o-da)
to have high blood pressure	고혈압이다 (go-hyeol-ab-i-da)
	혈압이 높다 (hyeol-ab-i nop-da)

to have an infection	염증이 생기다
	(yeom-jjeung-i saeng-gi-da)
to have low blood pressure	저혈압이다 (jeo-hyeol-ab-i-da)
	혈압이 낮다 (hyeol-ab-i nat-da)

| to have a miscarriage | 유산하다 (yu-san-ha-da) |

to have muscle pain	근육통이 생기다 (geun-yuk-tong-i saeng-gi-da), 근육통이 있다 (geun-yuk-tong-i it-da)
to have nasal congestion	코가 막히다 (ko-ga ma-ki-da)
to have pain	통증이 있다 (tong-jjeung-i it-da)
to have a runny nose	콧물이 나다 (kon-mul-i na-da)
to have a sore throat	목감기에 걸리다 (mok-gam-gi-e geol-li-da), 목이 붓다 (mog-i but-da)
to have a sprained ankle	발목을 삐다 (bal-mog-eul ppi-da)
to have stomach pain	배가 아프다 (bae-ga a-peu-da) 복통이 있다 (bok-tong-i it-da)
to have sunstroke	일사병에 걸리다 (il-ssa-ppeong-e geol-li-da)
to have throbbing pain in an eye	눈이 따갑다 (nun-i tta-gap-da)
to have a toothache	이가 아프다 (i-ga a-peu-da) 치통이 있다 (chi-tong-i it-da)
to practice contraception	피임하다 (pi-im-ha-da)

Lesson 8. Food & Restaurants
음식과 음식점
(eum-sik-gwa eum-sik-jeom)

1. Cultural Notes

In a Korean restaurant, you do not need to wait to be shown to a table. You may sit at any open table you desire. Many restaurants have their menu posted on the wall. Tipping is not expected. Side dishes and a bowl of rice are included in the order, and extra side dishes and rice can be served with a nominal charge. When one is ready to place an order, wave or call the waiter or waitress. You will receive one bill unless you request otherwise. If you sit in a private room in a restaurant, you are required to take off your shoes. The above explanations, however, are not applicable to a hotel restaurant. A hotel restaurant follows American customs.

2. Model Conversations

Welcome. Please have a seat here.
어서 오세요. 이쪽으로 앉으세요.
(eo-seo o-se-yo i-jjog-eu-ro anj-eu-se-yo)

May we sit by the window?
저쪽 창가에 앉아도 돼요?
(jeo-jjok chang-ga-e anj-a-do dwae-yo)

Sure. You can take any seat that you like.
그럼요. 아무 데나 좋으신 데 앉으세요.
(geu-reom-yo a-mu de-na jo-eu-sin de anj-eu-se-yo)

We are ready to order. (*lit*. Please take our order.)
여기 주문 좀 받으세요.
(yeo-gi ju-mun jom bad-eu-se-yo)

What would you like to order?
뭐 드시겠어요?
(mwo deu-si-gess-eo-yo)
뭐 주문하시겠어요?
(mwo ju-mun-ha-si-gess-eo-yo)

One kimchi stew and one squid stir-fry, please.
김치찌개 하나하고 오징어 볶음 하나만 주세요.
(gim-chi-jji-gae ha-na-ha-go o-jing-eo bokk-eum ha-na-
    man ju-se-yo)

We are in hurry, so can you please speed up the order?
시간이 없으니까 좀 빨리 해 주세요.
(si-gan-i eops-eu-ni-kka jom ppal-li hae ju-se-yo)

OK, no problem. Please wait a moment.
네, 그러세요. 잠깐만 기다리세요.
(ne geu-reo-se-yo jam-kkan-man gi-da-ri-se-yo)

Who ordered a squid stir-fry?
어느 분이 오징어 볶음이세요?
(eo-neu bun-i o-jing-eo bokk-eum-i-se-yo)

Me. Please put it on this side.
저요. 이쪽으로 놓아주세요.
(jeo-yo i-jjog-eu-ro no-a-ju-se-yo)

Would you bring us some more water and side dishes?
여기 물하고 반찬 좀 더 주시겠어요?
(yeo-gi mul-ha-go ban-chan jom deo ju-si-gess-eo-yo)

This tastes a little bland, so would you please pass me salt?
**음식이 약간 싱거운 것 같은데 소금 좀 갖다
    주시겠어요?**
(eum-sig-i yak-gan sing-geo-un geot gat-eun-de so-geum
    jom gat-da ju-si-gess-eo-yo)

OK, one moment. I will bring it soon.
잠깐만 기다리세요. 금방 갖다 드릴게요.
(jam-kkan-man gi-da-ri-se-yo geum-bang gat-da deu-
    ril-kke-yo)

How much is it in total?
여기 모두 얼마예요?
(yeo-gi mo-du eol-ma-ye-yo)

It's 35,000-won in total.
전부 3만 5천원이에요.
(jeon-bu sam-man o-cheon-won-i-e-yo)

Here it is.
여기요.
(yeo-gi-yo)
여기 있어요.
(yeo-gi-iss-eo-yo)

Here is the change–5000 won. Thank you. Please come again.
여기 거스름돈 5천이요. 고맙습니다. 다음에 또 오세요.
(yeo-gi geo-seu-reum-tton o-cheon-won-i-yo go-map-seum-ni-da da-eum-e tto o-se-yo)

3. Vocabulary

Meals

breakfast   **아침** (a-chim)

    to have breakfast   **아침을 먹다**
(a-chim-eul meok-da)
아침식사를 하다
(a-chim-sik-sa-reul ha-da)

lunch   **점심** (jeom-sim)

    to have lunch   **점심을 먹다**
(jeom-sim-eul meok-da)
점심식사를 하다
(jeom-sim-sik-sa-reul ha-da)

dinner   **저녁** (jeo-nyeok)

    to have dinner   **저녁을 먹다**
(jeo-nyeog-eul meok-da)
저녁식사를 하다
(jeo-nyeok-sik-sa-reul ha-da)

snack   **간식** (gan-sik)

    to have a snack   **간식을 먹다**
(gan-sig-eul meok-da)
간식을 하다
(gan-sig-eul ha-da)

Restaurants

Chinese food	중식 (jung-sik)
Chinese restaurant	중식당 (jung-sik-dang)
Japanese food	일식 (il-ssik)
Japanese restaurant	일식당 (il-ssik-dang)
Korean food	한식 (han-sik)
Korean restaurant	한식당 (han-sik-dang)
Western-style food	양식 (yang-sik)
Western-style restaurant	양식당 (yang-sik-dang)
customer	손님 (son-nim)
waiter, waitress	종업원 (jong-eob-won)
check, bill	계산서 (gye-san-seo)
change	거스름돈 (geo-seu-reum-tton)
food	음식 (eum-sik)
beverage	음료수 (eum-nyo-su)
menu	메뉴 (me-nyu)
seat	자리 (ja-ri)
to order	주문하다 (ju-mun-ha-da)
	시키다 (si-ki-da)

Tastes

to be blended	싱겁다 (sing-geop-da)
to be salty	짜다 (jja-da)
to be sour	시다 (si-da)
to be spicy/hot	맵다 (maep-da)
to be sweet	달다 (dal-da)
to be tart	쓰다 (tteu-da)
undercooked	덜 익다 (deol ik-da)
overcooked	너무 익다 (neo-mu ik-da)
burnt	타다 (ta-da)
to be full	배가 부르다 (bae-ga bu-reu-da)
to be hungry	배가 고프다 (bae-ga go-peu-da)
to be thirsty	목이 마르다 (mog-i ma-reu-da)
to drink alcohol	술을 마시다 (sul-eul ma-si-da)
to get drunk	술에 취하다 (sul-e chwi-ha-da)
to be delicious	맛이 있다 (mas-i it-da)
to taste bad	맛이 없다 (mas-i eop-da)

Basics for Korean-style dishes

cooked rice	밥 (bap)
white rice	쌀밥 (ssal-bap)
barley rice	보리밥 (bo-ri-bap)
mixed-grain rice	잡곡밥 (jap-gok-bap)
fried rice	볶음밥 (bokk-eum-bap)
mixed-vegetable rice	비빔밥 (bi-bim-ppap)
soup	국 (guk)
seaweed soup	미역국 (mi-yeok-guk)
dried-cod soup	북어국 (bug-eo-kkuk)
bean sprout soup	콩나물국 (kong-na-mul-kkuk)
kimchi	김치 (gim-chi)
cabbage kimchi	배추김치 (bae-chu-gim-chi)
radish kimchi	총각김치 (chong-gak-gim-chi)
diced-radish kimchi	깍두기 (kkak-du-gi)
kimchi soup	물김치 (mul-gim-chi)
side dishes	반찬 (ban-chan)

Ways of Cooking & Sample Dishes

broiled	구이 (gu-i)
broiled fish	생선구이 (saeng-seon-gu-i)
BBQ beef	불고기 (bul-go-gi)
BBQ short-ribs	갈비구이 (gal-bi-gu-i)
seasoned seaweed	김구이 (gim-gu-i)
broth	탕 (tang)
fish broth	매운탕 (mae-un-tang)
short-ribs broth	갈비탕 (gal-bi-tang)
deep-fried	튀김 (twi-gim)
fried vegetable s	야채튀김 (ya-chae-twi-gim)
fried fish	생선튀김 (saeng-seon-twi-gim)
(hard-) boiled	조림 (jo-rim)
boiled fish	생선조림 (saeng-seon-jo-rim)
boiled tofu	두부조림 (du-bu-jo-rim)
pan-broiled	볶음 (bokk-eum)
broiled squid	오징어 볶음 (o-jing-eo bokk-eum)
broiled octopus	낙지볶음 (nak-ji-bokk-eum)
pan-fried	부침 (bu-chim)
seafood pancake	해물파전 (hae-mul-pa-jeon)

bean pancake	빈대떡	(bin-dae-tteok)
seasoned	무침	(mu-chim)
seasoned sprout	콩나물 무침	(kong-na-mul mu-chim)
seasoned spinach	시금치 무침	(si-geum-chi mu-chim)
steamed	찜	(jjim)
steamed short-ribs	갈비찜	(gal-bi-jjim)
steamed angler fish	아구찜	(a-gu-jjim)
stew	찌개	(jji-gae)
kimchi stew	김치찌개	(gim-chi-jji-gae)
bean-paste stew	된장찌개	(doen-jang-jji-gae)
seasoned-beef stew	육개장	(yuk-gae-jang)
noodles	국수	(guk-su)
cold-noodle soup	물냉면	(mul-laeng-myeon)
hot-paste noodles	비빔냉면	(bi-bim-naeng-myeon)
mixed-vegetable noodle	잡채	(jap-chae)

Western-style dishes

steak	비프스테이크	(bi-peu-seu-te-i-keu)
hamburger	함박스테이크	(ham-bak-seu-te-i-keu)
corn dog	핫도그	(hat-do-geu)
fish fillet	생선가스	(saeng-seon-kka-seu)
pork cutlet	돈가스	(don-kka-seu),
	포크커틀릿	(po-keu-keo-teul-lit)
salad	샐러드	(ssael-leo-deu),
	사라다	(sa-ra-da)
sandwich	샌드위치	(saen-deu-wi-chi)
soup	수프	(su-peu)
pizza	피자	(pi-ja)
spaghetti	스파게티	(seu-pa-ge-ti)
french fries	프렌치 프라이	(peu-ren-chi-peu-ra-i)

Meats

meat	고기	(go-gi)
beef	소고기	(so-go-gi)
chicken	닭고기	(dak-go-gi)
duck	오리고기	(o-ri-go-gi)
fish	생선	(saeng-seon)

goat	염소고기 (yeom-so-go-gi)
pork	돼지고기 (dwae-ji-go-gi)
crab cake	게맛살 (ge-mat-sal)
fish cake	어묵 (eo-muk), 오뎅 (o-deng)
egg	계란 (gye-ran)
ham	햄 (haem)
sausage	소세지 (sso-se-ji)
dumpling	만두 (man-du)

Fish

fish	생선 (saeng-seon)
clam	조개 (jo-gae)
cod	명태 (myeong-tae)
frozen cod	동태 (dong-tae)
dried cod	북어 (bug-eo)
croaker	조기 (jo-gi)
dried croaker	굴비 (gul-bi)
eel	뱀장어 (baem-jang-eo)
hair-tail	갈치 (gal-chi)
halibut	넙치 (neop-chi)
herring	청어 (cheong-eo)
mackerel	고등어 (go-deung-eo)
mackerel-pike	꽁치 (kkong-chi)
mud fish	미꾸라지 (mi-kku-ra-ji)
mussel	홍합 (hong-hap)
oyster	굴 (gul)
perch	농어 (nong-eo)
plaice	가자미 (ga-ja-mi)
salmon	연어 (yeon-eo)
small octopus	낙지 (nak-ji)
squid	오징어 (o-jing-eo)
tuna	참치 (cham-chi)

Vegetables

vegetables	야채 (ya-chae), 채소 (chae-so)
bean sprout	콩나물 kong-na-nul
bell pepper	피망 pi-mang
broccoli	브로컬리 beu-ro-keol-li
cabbage	양배추 (yang-bae-chu)

Asian cabbage	배추 (bae-chu)
carrot	당근 (dang-geun)
corn	옥수수 (ok-su-su)
cucumber	오이 (o-i)
garlic	마늘 (ma-neul)
ginger	생강 (saeng-gang)
green onion	파 (pa)
lettuce	양상추 (yang-sang-chu)
Asian lettuce	상추 (sang-chu)
mushroom	버섯 (beo-seot)
onion	양파 (yang-pa)
parsley	파슬리 (pa-seul-li)
pea	완두콩 (wan-du-kong)
pepper	고추 (go-chu)
potato	감자 (gam-ja)
radish	무 (mu)
rice	쌀 (ssal)
spinach	시금치 (si-geum-chi)
sweet potato	고구마 (go-gu-ma)
tomato	토마토 (to-ma-to)

Seasonings

seasonings	양념 (yang-nyeom)
pepper	후추 (hu-chu)
red-pepper paste	고추장 (go-chu-jang)
red-pepper powder	고춧가루 (go-chut-ga-ru)
salt	소금 (so-geum)
sesame oil	참기름 (cham-gi-reum)
sesame seed	깨소금 (kkae-so-geum)
soybean paste	된장 (doen-jang)
soy sauce	간장 (gan-jang)
sugar	설탕 (seol-tang)
vinegar	식초 (sik-cho)

Fruit

fruit	과일 (gwa-il)
apple	사과 (sa-gwa)
Asian melon	참외 (cham-oe)
banana	바나나 (ba-na-na)

cherry	앵두 (aeng-du)
grapes	포도 (po-do)
grapefruit	자몽 (ja-mong)
melon	메론 (me-ron)
orange	오렌지 (o-ren-ji)
peach	복숭아 (bok-sung-a)
pear	배 (bae)
persimmons	감 (gam)
pineapple	파인애쁠 (pa-in-ae-peul)
plum	자두 (ja-du)
raspberry	산딸기 (san-ttal-gi)
strawberry	딸기 (ttal-gi)
tangerines	귤 (gyul)
watermelon	수박 (su-bak)

Nuts

nut	콩 (kong)
chestnut	밤 (bam)
ginkgo nut	은행 (eun-haeng)
peanut	땅콩 (ttang-kong)
pine nut	잣 (jat)
walnut	호두 (ho-du)

Drinks

drink	마실 것(ma-sil-kkeot), 음료수 (eum-nyo-su)
water	물 (mul)
coffee	커피 (keo-pi)
cola	콜라 (kol-la)
7-Up™	사이다 (sa-i-da)
juice	주스 (ju-seu)
apple juice	사과주스 (sa-gwa-ju-seu)
grape juice	포도주스 (po-do-ju-seu)
orange juice	오렌지 주스 (o-ren-ji-ju-seu)
persimmons juice	수정과 (su-jeong-gwa)
strawberry juice	딸기주스 (ttal-gi-ju-seu)
sweet rice juice	식혜 (si-ke)

tea	홍차	(hong-cha)
barley tea	보리차	(bo-ri-cha)
corn tea	옥수수차	(ok-su-su-cha)
citron tea	유자차	(yu-ja-cha)
ginger tea	생강차	(saeng-gang-cha)
ginseng tea	인삼차	(in-sam-cha)
green tea	녹차	(nok-cha)
beer	맥주	(maek-ju)
soju	소주	(so-ju)
Western liquor	양주	(yang-ju)
wine	포도주	(po-do-ju)
red wine	적포도주	(jeok-po-do-ju)
white wine	백포도주	(baek-po-do-ju)

Lesson 9. Weather
날씨 (nal-ssi)

1. Cultural Notes

Korea is located in the East Asian monsoon belt and has four distinct seasons. Due to its location, Korea has monsoon season in the summer. Typhoons, the Pacific Ocean equivalent of hurricanes, are unwelcome annual visitors. About 70% of rainfall comes between June and August. The hottest month is August and the coldest month is January. Average temperature of August is above 25°C (about 77°F) and January is below -4°C (approx. 30°F).

2. Model Phrases

Did you listen to a weather forecast?
일기예보 들으셨어요?
(il-gi-ye-bo deul-eu-syeoss-eo-yo)

What did the forecast say about the weather for tomorrow?
내일은 날씨가 어떻대요?
(nae-il-eun nal-ssi-ga eo-tteo-tae-yo)

> It said it will rain in the morning but will be sunny in the afternoon.
> **내일 오전에는 비가 오고 오후부터 맑아질 거래요.**
> (nae-il o-jeon-e-neun bi-ga o-go o-hu-bu-teo malg-a-jil kkeo-rae-yo)

On which channel can I see the weather forecast?
어디에서 일기예보를 하지요?
(eo-di-e-seo il-gi-ye-bo-reul ha-ji-yo)

> It's on channel 7, towards the end of 9 o'clock news.
> **7번 채널에서 9시 뉴스가 거의 끝날 때쯤 해요.**
> (chil-beon chae-neol-e-seo a-hop-si nyu-seu-ga geo-ui kkeun-nal ttae-jjeum hae-yo)

It was warm yesterday, but a little cold today.
어제는 날씨가 따뜻했는데 오늘은 좀 춥네요.
(eo-je-neun nal-ssi-ga tta-tteu-taen-neun-de o-neul-eun jom chum-ne-yo)

Now it's winter, so the weather is getting cold.
이제 겨울이 됐으니까 날씨가 점점 추워지지요.
(i-je gyeo-ul-i dwaess-eu-ni-kka nal-ssi-ga jeom-jeom
chu-wo-ji-ji-yo)

How is the weather in Korea in general?
한국은 보통 날씨가 어때요?
(han-gug-eun bo-tong nal-ssi-ga eo-ttae-yo)

It is very nice in spring and fall.
봄 가을에는 날씨가 아주 좋아요.
(bom ga-eul-e-neun nal-ssi-ga a-ju jo-a-yo)

It rains a lot and is very hot in summer.
여름에는 비가 많이 오고 아주 더워요.
yeo-reum-e-neun bi-ga man-i o-go a-ju deo-wo-yo

It is cold and windy in winter.
겨울에는 춥고 바람이 많이 불어요.
(gyeo-ul-e-neun chup-go ba-ram-i man-i bul-eo-yo)

3. Vocabulary

the ice freezes	얼음이 얼다	(eol-eum-i eol-da)
the lightning strikes	번개가 치다	(beon-gae-ga chi-da)
the wind blows	바람이 불다	(ba-ram-i bul-da)
to be cloudy	구름이 끼다	(gu-reum-i kki-da)
to be foggy	안개가 끼다	(an-gae-ga kki-da)
to be sunny	날씨가 좋다	(nal-ssi-ga jo-ta)
to frost	서리가 내리다	(seo-ri-ga nae-ri-da)
to hail	우박이 내리다	(u-bag-i nae-ri-da)
to have a drought	가뭄이 들다	(ga-mum-i deul-da)
to have a flood	홍수가 나다	(hong-su-ga na-da)
to have a rainy season	장마가 들다	(jang-ma-ga deul-da)
to rain	비가 오다	(bi-ga o-da)
to snow	눈이 오다	(nun-i o-da)
to thunder	천둥이 치다	(cheon-dung-i chi-da)
to be chilly	쌀쌀하다	(ssal-ssal-ha-da)
to be cold	춥다	(chup-da)
to be cool	시원하다	(si-won-ha-da)
to be hot	덥다	(deop-da)

to be hot and muggy	무덥다 (mu-deop-da)
to be warm	따뜻하다 (tta-tteu-ta-da)
to become clean	맑아지다 (malg-a-ji-da)
to get cloudy	흐려지다 (heu-ryeo-ji-da),
	구름이 끼다 (gu-reum-i kki-da)
to get cold	추워지다 (chu-wo-ji-da)
to get hot	더워지다 (deo-wo-ji-da)
the temperature is high	기온이 높다 (gi-on-i nop-da)
the temperature is low	기온이 낮다 (gi-on-i nat-da)

There is a big temperature difference between night and
day.
일교차가 심하다.
(il-gyo-cha-ga sim-ha-da)

There is a small temperature difference between night and
day.
일교차가 적다.
(il-gyo-cha-ga jeok-da)

The atmospheric pressure is high.
기압이 높다.
(gi-ab-i nop-da)
고기압이다.
(go-gi-ab-i-da)

The atmospheric pressure is low.
기압이 낮다.
(gi-ab-i nat-da)
저기압이다
(jeo-gi-ab-i-da)

above zero	영상 (yeong-sang)
below zero	영하 (yeong-ha)
Celsius	섭씨 (seop-ssi)
Fahrenheit	화씨 (hwa-ssi)
weather forecast	일기예보 (il-gi-ye-bo)

Seasons

spring	봄 (bom)
summer	여름 (yeo-reum)
fall	가을 (ga-eul)
winter	겨울 (gyeo-wul)

Lesson 10.   Leisure Activities
여가활동
(yeo-ga-hwal-ttong)

1. Cultural Notes

There is a lot to see and do in Seoul. There are numerous movie theaters, sports events, shopping malls, museums, palaces, markets, and restaurants. There are also several theme parks, bowling alleys, ice skating arenas, several good parks, and a zoo. There are also indoor skiing and golf ranges, saunas, hot pools, many traditional performances, and occasional concerts.

2. Model Phrases

Where do I have to go to watch a baseball game?
야구경기를 보려면 어디로 가야 되나요?
(ya-gu-gyeong-gi-reul bo-ryeo-myeon eo-di-ro ga-ya doe-na-yo)

You can go to the Jamsil stadium.
잠실운동장에 가시면 돼요.
(jam-sil-un-dong-jang-e ga-si-myeon dwae-yo)

What time does the national museum open?
국립박물관은 몇 시에 문을 열지요?
(gung-nip-bang-mul-gwan-eun myeot si-e mun-eul yeol-ji-yo)

It will open around 10:00 A.M.
한 10시쯤 열 거예요.
(han yeol-ssi-jjeum yeol kkeo-ye-yo)

Is there a discount for students or seniors?
학생이나 경로 우대자는 값을 할인해 주나요?
(hak-saeng-i-na gyeong-no u-dae-ja-neun gaps-eul hal-in-hae ju-na-yo)

Sure. Please show your ID in the ticket booth.
그럼요. 표 파는 곳에서 신분증을 보여 주세요.
(geu-reom-nyo pyo pa-neun gos-e-seo sin-bun-jjeung-eul bo-yeo ju-se-yo)

How much is a ticket?
표가 한 장에 얼마지요?
(pyo-ga han jang-e eol-ma-ji-yo)

> It's 10,000 won.
> **만원이에요.**
> (man-won-i-e-yo)

Then give me three, please.
그럼 세 장만 주세요.
(geu-reom se jang-man ju-se-yo)

What time does the movie start?
몇 시에 영화가 시작해요?
(myeot si-e yeong-hwa-ga si-ja-kae-yo)

> We only have tickets for the 4:30 p.m. showing.
> **지금 4시 30분 표만 남아 있어요.**
> (ji-geum ne-si sam-sip-bun pyo-man nam-a iss-eo-yo)

How long is the movie?
이 영화 다 보는데 몇 시간이나 걸려요?
(i yeong-hwa da bo-neun-de myeot si-gan-i-na
geol-lyeo-yo)

> About 2 hours, I guess.
> **한 두시간 정도 걸릴 거에요.**
> (han du-si-gan jeong-do geol-lil kkeo-ye-yo)

Are the seats numbered or can I take any seat?
**자리가 지정돼 있나요, 아니면 아무 데나 앉아도
되나요?**
(ja-ri-ga ji-jeong-dwae in-na-yo a-ni-myeon a-mu de-na
anj-a-do doe-na-yo)

> Seat numbers are designated in your ticket.
> **표에 보시면 좌석 번호가 써 있어요.**
> (pyo-e bo-si-myeon jwa-seok beon-ho-ga sseo
> iss-eo-yo)

> Please go inside and ask a guide.
> **들어가셔서 안내원한테 물어보세요.**
> (deul-eo-ga-syeo-seo an-nae-won-han-te mul-eo-
> bo-se-yo)

Is the movie subtitled?
이 영화에 영어 자막이 나오나요?
(i yeong-hwa-e yeong-eo ja-mag-i na-o-na-yo)

Of course.
그럼요.
(geu-reom-nyo)

3. Vocabulary

Sports

to play baseball	**야구를 하다** (ya-gu-reul ha-da)
to play basketball	**농구를 하다** (nong-gu-reul ha-da)
to play football	**미식축구를 하다** (mi-sik-chuk-gu-reul ha-da)
to play soccer	**축구를 하다** (chuk-gu-reul ha-da)
to play volleyball	**배구를 하다** (bae-gu-reul ha-da)
(to go) watch a baseball game	**야구 구경을 가다/하다** (ya-gu gu-gyeong-eul ga-da/ha-da)
(to go) watch a basketball game	**농구 구경을 가다/하다** (nong-gu gu-gyeong-eul ga-da/ha-da)
(to go) watch a football game	**미식축구 구경을 가다/하다** (mi-sik-chuk-gu gu-gyeong-eul ga-da/ha-da)
(to go) watch a soccer game	**축구 구경을 가다/하다** (chuk-gu gu-gyeong-eul ga-da/ha-da)
(to go) watch a volleyball game	**배구 구경을 가다/하다** (bae-gu gu-gyeong-eul ga-da/ha-da)
to ride a bicycle	**자전거를 타다** (ja-jeon-geo-reul ta-da)
to roller blade	**롤러 스케이트를 타다** (rol-leo seu-ke-i-teu-reul ta-da)

to skate	스케이트를 타다
	(seu-ke-i-teu-reul ta-da)
to ski	스키를 타다
	(seu-ki-reul ta-da)
to play golf	골프를 치다
	(gol-peu-reul chi-da)
to play ping-pong	탁구를 치다
	(tak-gu-reul chi-da)
to play tennis	테니스를 치다
	(te-ni-seu-reul chi-da)
to go mountain climbing	등산을 하다/가다
	(deung-san-eul ha-da/ga-da)
to go for a walk	산책을 하다
	(san-chaeg-eul ha-da)
to box	권투를 하다
	(gwon-tu-reul ha-da)
to wrestle	레슬링을 하다
	(re-seul-ling-eul ha-da)
to jog	조깅을 하다
	(jo-ging-eul ha-da)
to swim	수영을 하다
	(su-yeong-eul ha-da)
to travel	여행을 하다/가다
	(yeo-haeng-eul ha-da/ga-da)

Musical Instruments

to play . . .	플롯을 (peul-lus-eul)
the cello	첼로 (chel-lo)
the clarinet	클라리넷 (keul-la-ri-net)
the drums	드럼 (deu-reom)
the flute	불다 (bul-da)
the guitar	기타 (gi-ta)
the piano	피아노를 치다
	(pi-a-no-reul chi-da)
the trumpet	트럼펫 (teu-reom-pet)
the viola	비올라 (vi-ol-la)
the violin	바이올린을 켜다
	(va-i-ol-in-eul kyeo-da)

Other Pastimes

to play computer games	컴퓨터 게임을 하다 (keom-pyu-teo ge-im-eul ha-da)
to play video games	비디오 게임을 하다 (vi-di-o ge-im-eul ha-da)
to go to a concert	음악회에 가다 (eum-a-koe-e ga-da)
to go to a karaoke room	노래방에 가다 (no-rae-bang-e ga-da)
to go to a museum	박물관에 가다 (bang-mul-gwan-e ga-da)
to go to an art gallery	미술관에 가다 (mi-sul-gwan-e ga-da)
to go to watch a movie	영화 구경을 가다/하다 (yeong-hwa gu-gyeong-eul ga-da/ha-da)
to go to watch a play	연극 구경을 가다/하다 (yeon-geuk gu-gyeong-eul ga-da/ha-da)
to watch TV	텔레비전을 보다 (tel-le-bi-jeon-eul bo-da)
to watch a videotape	비디오를 보다 (vi-di-o-reul bo-da)
to play a card game	트럼프를 치다 (teu-reom-peu-reul chi-da) 카드놀이를 하다 (ka-deu nol-i-reul ha-da)
to play an Asian card game	화투를 치다 (hwa-tu-reul chi-da)
to dance	춤을 추다 (chum-eul chu-da)
to draw a picture	그림을 그리다 (geu-rim-eul geu-ri-da)
to go fishing	낚시를하다 (nak-si-reul ha-da)
to listen to music	음악을 듣다 (eum-ag-eul deut-da)
to read a book	책을 읽다 (chaeg-eul ilk-da)
to sing a song	노래를 부르다 (no-rae-reul bu-reu-da)
to sleep	잠을 자다 (jam-eul ja-da)
to take a picture	사진을 찍다 (sa-jin-eul jjik-da)

Lesson 11.   Banks
은행 (eun-haeng)

1. Cultural Notes

Banks in Korea are usually open from 9:00 a.m. to 4:30 p.m. during the weekdays and closed on weekends. All banks provide currency exchange services. Customers pay utility bills at the bank and any number of services, including balance transfers, can be done at an ATM.

Korea is a cash-oriented society. Many small shops do not accept credit cards, and personal checks do not exist. Only banks can issue checks. For opening accounts and other transactions, a personal seal (도장 do-jang) is required in lieu of a signature. It is common for a Korean to possess several personal seals, including one registered with the local government.

2. Model Phrases

Exchanging currency

I would like to exchange some money.
환전을 좀 하고 싶은데요.
(hwan-heon-eul jom ha-go sip-eun-de-yo)

> Please go to window number 7.
> **그럼 7번 창구로 가십시오.**
> (geu-reom chil-beon chang-gu-ro ga-sip-si-o)

> Do you see the sign "Exchange Window" over there?
> **저쪽에 환전창구라고 써 있지요?**
> (jeo-jjog-e hwan-jeon-chang-gu-ra-go sseo-it-ji-yo)

I see it. Thank you.
네, 고맙습니다.
(ne go-map-seum-ni-da)

I would like to exchange some money.
돈을 좀 바꾸려고 하는데요.
(don-eul jom ba-kku-ryeo-go ha-neun-de-yo)

What is the exchange rate today?
오늘 환율이 어떻게 되나요?
(o-neul hwan-nyul-i eo-tteo-ke doe-na-yo)

It's 1300원 per dollar.
달러당 1300원이에요.
(dal-leo-dang cheon-sam-baeg-won-i-e-yo)

How much do you want to exchange?
얼마나 바꾸시게요?
(eol-ma-na ba-kku-si-ge-yo)

$500.00, please.
500불만 바꿔 주세요.
(o-baek-bul-man ba-kkwo ju-se-yo)

Would you please fill out this application form?
그럼 여기 신청서 좀 써 주시겠어요?
(geu-reom yeo-gi sin-cheong-seo jom sseo
　　ju-si-gess-eo-yo)

And please show me your passport or ID card.
그리고 여권이나 신분증 좀 보여주세요.
(geu-ri-go yeo-kkwon-i-na sin-bun-jjeung jom
　　bo-yeo-ju-se-yo)

Here it is.
여기 있어요.
(yeo-gi iss-eo-yo)

Do you want cash or check?
돈은 현금으로 드릴까요, 아니면 수표로 드릴까요?
(don-eun hyeon-geum-eu-ro deu-ril-kka-yo a-ni-myeon
　　su-pyo-ro deu-ril-kka-yo)

May I have my check and please give me my change in
　　cash.
전부 수표로 주시고 잔돈만 현금으로 주세요.
(jeon-bu su-pyo-ro ju-si-go jan-don-man hyeon-geum-eu-ro
　　ju-se-yo)

Here you are. A fee of 5000 won has been deducted.
여기 있습니다. 수수료 5,000원 공제하고 드렸습니다.
(yeo-gi it-seum-ni-da su-su-ryo o-cheon-won
　　gong-je-ha-go deu-ryeot-seum-ni-da)

Good-bye.
안녕히 가십시오.
(an-nyeong-hi ga-sip-si-o)

Opening a Bank Account

I would like to open a bank account for myself.
통장을 만들려고 하는데요.
(tong-jang-eul man-deul-lyeo-go ha-neun-de-yo)

> You do? May I see your ID, please?
> 그러세요? 그럼 신분증 좀 주시겠습니까?
> (geu-reo-se-yo geu-reom sin-bun-jjeung jom ju-si-get-
> seum-ni-kka)

Is my passport acceptable?
여권이면 되죠?
(yeo-kkwon-i-myeon doe-jyo)

> Sure. How much do you want to deposit?
> 그럼요. 얼마 예금하시겠습니까?
> (geu-reom-nyo eol-ma ye-geum-ha-si-get-seum-ni-kka)

300,000 won, please.
30만원이요.
(sam-sim-man-won-i-yo)

> Would you please write your name, address and pin
>   number here?
> 이 신청서에 손님 성함하고 주소하고 비밀번호 좀
>   써 주십시오.
> (i sin-cheong-seo-e son-nim seong-ham-ha-go ju-so-ha-
>   go bi-mil-beon-ho jom sseo ju-sip-si-o)

Is this OK?
이렇게 쓰면 되나요?
(i-reo-ke sseu-myeon doe-na-yo)

> Yes. Do you have your signature seal with you?
> 네, 됐습니다. 그런데 혹시 도장 있으세요?
> (ne dwaet-seum-ni-da geu-reon-de hok-si do-jang iss-
>   eu-se-yo)

No, I don't
아니오, 없는데요.
(a-ni-o eom-neun-de-yo)

> Then you can just sign here instead.
> **그럼 그냥 사인만 하셔도 돼요.**
> (geu-reom geu-nyang ssa-in-man ha-syeo-do dwae-yo)

> You need an ATM card too, right?
> **현금카드도 필요하시죠?**
> (hyeon-geum ka-deu-do pil-yo-ha-si-jyo)

Yes, please.
네, 해 주세요.
(ne hae ju-se-yo)

> Wait a moment, please...
> **잠깐만 기다리세요....**
> (jam-kkan-man gi-da-ri-se-yo)

> I have your bank book and ATM card ready for you.
> **여기 손님 통장하고 현금카드 있습니다.**
> (yeo-gi son-nim tong-jang-ha-go hyeon-geum-ka-deu
>   it-seum-ni-da)

3. Vocabulary

Korean Currency

$1.00 = apprx. 1100원 (won)

Coins:

1원	**일원**	(il-won)
10원	**십원**	(sib-won)
50원	**오십원**	(o-sib-won)
100원	**백원**	(baeg-won)
500원	**오백원**	(o-baeg-won)

Bills:

1000원	**천원**	(cheon-won)
5000원	**오천원**	(o-cheon-won)
10,000원	**만원**	(man-won)

Checks (official checks are similar to traveler's checks, which are issued at a bank):

cheque	수표 (su-pyo)
personal cheque	자기앞수표 (ja-gi-ap su-pyo)
exchange rate	환율 (hwan-nyul)
fee, charge	수수료 (su-su-ryo)
the exchange rate goes down	환율이 내리다 (hwan-nyul-i nae-ri-da)
the exchange rate goes up	환율이 오르다 (hwan-nyul-i o-reu-da)
to exchange money	환전을 하다 (hwan-jeon-eul-ha-da)
to withdraw	돈을 찾다 (don-eul chat-da)
to deposit	저금하다 (jeo-geum-ha-da), 예금하다 (ye-geum-ha-da)
bank account application	은행거래신청서 (eun-haeng-geo-rae-sin-cheong-seo)
deposit slip	입금표 (ip-geum-pyo)
withdrawal slip	출금표 (chul-geum-pyo)
pin number	비밀번호 (bi-mil-beon-ho)
deposit and withdrawal record	통장 (tong-jang)
signature seal	도장 (do-jang)
ATM card	현금카드 (hyeon-geum-ka-deu)
ATM machine	현금지급기 (hyeon-geum-ji-geup-gi)

Lesson 12.   Post Office
우체국 (u-che-guk)

1. Cultural Notes

Post offices are usually open on weekdays from 9:00 a.m. to 5:00 p.m. and Saturdays from 9:00 a.m. to 1:00 p.m. They offer a great deal more than the U.S. postal service. One can do one's banking, mail order local specialties, make train reservations, and buy express bus tickets. In the majority of offices, one can buy stamps from vending machines. When sending mail, please remember to write the address macro-to-micro style, beginning with the country and ending with the person's name.

2. Model Phrases

Sending Mail

How long does it take to send this to Los Angeles?
이거 LA까지 얼마나 걸려요?
(i-geo el-e-i-kka-ji eol-ma-na geol-lyeo-yo)

> How would you like to send it?
> **어떻게 보내실 건데요?**
> (eo-tteo-ke bo-nae-sil kkeon-de-yo)
> **뭘로 보내실 건데요?**
> (mwol-lo bo-nae-sil kkeon-de-yo)

The fastest way, please.
제일 빨리 가는 것으로 해 주세요.
(je-il ppal-li ga-neun geos-eu-ro hae ju-se-yo)

> The express mail takes only three days, but the price is quite high. Is it urgent?
> **속달우편은 3일이면 되는데 좀 비싸요. 급하세요?**
> (sok-dal-u-pyeon-eun san-il-i-myeon doe-neun-de jom bi-ssa-yo geu-pa-se-yo)

Not really. What would be a good option for this?
별로요. 그럼 어떤 게 좋을까요?
(byeol-lo-yo geu-reom eo-tteon ge jo-eul-kka-yo)

First-class mail takes about one week.
항공편으로 보내시면 한 일주일 정도 걸려요.
(hang-gong-pyeon-eu-ro bo-nae-si-myeon han il-jju-il
jeong-do geol-lyeo-yo)

I will take that, then.
그럼 그걸로 할게요.
(geu-reom geu-geol-lo hal-kke-yo)

Do you want to register this?
등기우편으로 해 드릴까요?
(deung-gi-u-pyeon-eu-ro hae deu-ril-kka-yo)

No, thanks.
아니오, 괜찮아요.
(a-ni-o gwaen-chan-a-yo)

Would you please write the name and address of the
recipient on this form?
여기에 받으실 분 주소하고 성함 좀 써 주시겠어요?
(yeo-gi-e bad-eu-sil bun ju-so-ha-go seong-ham jom
sseo ju-si-gess-eo-yo)

Is this OK?
이렇게 쓰면 되나요?
(i-reo-ke sseu-myeon doe-na-yo)

Sure. You are all set.
네, 됐습니다.
(ne dwaet-seum-ni-da)

Mail-ordering Local Specialties

I would like to mail order some local specialties.
특산품을 우편주문하고 싶은데요.
(teuk-san-pum-eul u-pyeon-ju-mun-ha-go sip-eun-de-yo)

You do? We have some samples over there. Please look
around.
**그러세요? 저쪽에 견본품들이 있어요. 한번 골라
보세요.**
(geu-reo-se-yo jeo-jjog-e gyeon-bon-pum-deul-i iss-eo-
yo han-beon gol-la bo-se-yo)

I would like to take those Ginsengs.

이 인삼으로 할게요.

(i in-sam-eu-ro hal-kke-yo)

How long does it take for them to be delivered, if I order now?

그런데 지금 주문하면 배달하는데 며칠이나 걸리나요?

(geu-reon-de ji-geum ju-mun-ha-myeon bae-dal-ha-neun-de myeo-chil-i-na geol-li-na-yo)

It will take about a week.

한 일주일 정도면 돼요.

(han il-jju-il jeong-do-myeon dwae-yo)

Reserving Train and Bus Tickets

I would like to reserve two express bus tickets to Kyung-Ju.

경주행 고속버스표 2장만 예매하고 싶은데요.

(gyeong-ju-haeng go-sok-beo-seu-pyo du-jang-man ye-mae-ha-go sip-eun-de-yo)

When would you like to leave?

언제 가실 건데요?

(eon-je ga-sil kkeon-de-yo)

This Friday, around 8:00 a.m.

이번 주 토요일 아침 8시쯤이요.

(i-beon jju to-yo-il a-chim yeo-deol-ssi-jjeum-i-yo)

8:00 a.m. tickets are not available. Is 8:30 a.m. OK for you?

8시 표는 지금 없는데 8시 30분도 괜찮으세요?

(yeo-deol-ssi pyo-neun ji-geum eom-neun-de yeo-deol-ssi sam-sip-bun-do gwaen-chan-eu-se-yo)

I guess I have no choice. I will take them.

할 수 없죠. 그걸로 주세요.

(hal ssu eop-jyo geu-geol-lo ju-se-yo

3. Vocabulary

to buy a stamp	우표를 사다
	(u-pyo-reul sa-da)
to mail-order a local specialty	특산품을 우편주문
	하다
	(teuk-san-pum-eul
	u-pyeon-ju-mun-ha-da)
to make a reservation for a train ticket	기차표를 예매하다
	(gi-cha-pyo-reul ye-mae-ha-da)
to put on a stamp	우표를 붙이다
	(u-pyo-reul bu-chi-da)
to receive a letter	편지받다
	(pyeon-ji bat-da)
to receive a package	소포를 받다
	(so-po-reul bat-da)
to send a letter	편지부치다
	(pyeon-ji bu-chi-da)
to send a package	소포를부치다
	(so-po-reul bu-chi-da)
to write a letter	편지를 쓰다
	(pyeon-ji-reul sseu-da)
to write a reply	답장을 쓰다
	(dap-jang-eul sseu-da)
to write an address	주소를 쓰다
	(ju-so-reul sseu-da)
recipient	받는 사람
	(ban-neun sa-ram)
	수취인 (su-chwi-in)
sender	보내는 사람
	(bo-nae-neun sa-ram)
	수신인 (su-sin-in)
address	주소 (ju-so)
name (full name)	성함 (seong-ham)
	성명 (seong-myeong)
	이름 (i-reum)
central post office	중앙우체국
	(jung-ang-u-che-guk)
mailbox	우체통 (u-che-tong)
post office employee	우체국 직원
	(u-che-guk jig-won)

postage	우편요금 (u-pyeon-nyo-geum)
postman	우체부 (u-che-bu)
zip code	우편번호 (u-pyeon-beon-ho)
air mail, first class mail	항공 우편 (hang-gong u-pyeon)
express mail	빠른 우편 (ppa-reun u-pyeon), 속달우편 (sok-dal-u-pyeon)
registered mail	등기 우편 (deung-gi u-pyeon)
regular mail, ground mail	보통 우편 (bo-tong u-pyeon), 일반우편 (il-ban u-pyeon)
box	상자 (sang-ja)
envelope	편지봉투 (pyeon-ji-bong-tu)
letter	편지 (pyeon-ji)
stationery	편지지 (pyeon-ji-ji)
package	소포 (so-po)
postcard	엽서 (yeop-seo)
sample product	견본품 (gyeon-bon-pum)
local specialty	특산품 (teuk-san-pum)

Lesson 13. Transportation
교통 (gyo-tong)

1. Cultural Notes

When traveling in Korea, using public transportation has many advantages. Street signs are inadequate in most places and Seoul has heavy traffic almost all day long. Using the subway is the best way to be on time for an appointment. Subway tickets can be purchased through either vending machines or ticket windows. Using the city bus is tricky if you do not know the routes well. Taxi fare in Korea is considerably less than in the U.S. You may call for a taxi to come pick you up, but most people hail them from the street.

Though officially discouraged, ride sharing in taxis is very common during peak hours. Taxi drivers stop several times to serve more than one party, and each party pays the fare individually. Tipping is not required.

Using the train or an express bus is the most common way to travel within local areas. When traffic conditions are normal, it takes about five hours to travel from Seoul to Pusan. Generally, only one way tickets are issued. If you need a return ticket, you may buy that upon arriving at your destination.

When driving, beware of jaywalkers. You will often see jaywalkers in most cities. At gas stations, you will not find self-service. Tipping is not required at the gas station. The posted price for gas is per liter.

Transportation methods

airplane	비행기 (bi-haeng-gi)	
boat, ship	배 (bae),	
	여객선 (yeo-gaek-seon)	
bus	버스 (beo-seu),	
	시내버스 (si-nae-ppeo-seu),	
	시외버스 (si-oe-ppeo-seu)	
express bus	고속버스 (go-sok-ppeo-seu)	
rental car	렌트카 (ren-teu-ka)	
subway	지하철 (ji-ha-cheol)	

taxi   택시 (taek-si),
          일반택시 (il-ban-taek-si),
          모범택시 (mo-beom-taek-si)
train   기차 (gi-cha)

2. Model Phrases

(1) At the Airport
비행기 타기 (bi-haeng-gi ta-gi)

Where do I check in?
실례지만 수속하는 곳이 어디지요?
(sil-lye-ji-man su-so-ka-neun gos-i eo-di-ji-yo)

> Please go straight and you can find it on your left.
> **똑바로 가시다 보면 왼쪽에 있습니다.**
> (ttok-ba-ro ga-si-da bo-myeon oen-jjog-e
>   it-seum-ni-da)

> May I have your passport and ticket, please?
> **여권하고 비행기표 좀 주시겠습니까?**
> (yeo-kkwon-ha-go bi-haeng-gi-pyo jom ju-si-get-seum-
>   ni-kka)

Here they are.
여기요.
(yeo-gi-yo)

> Where do you want to go?
> **어디까지 가십니까?**
> (eo-di-kka-ji ga-sim-ni-kka)

To Japan.
일본이요.
(il-bon-i-yo)

> Are you going there alone?
> **혼자 가십니까?**
> (hon-ja ga-sim-ni-kka)

Yes, alone.
네, 혼자예요.
(ne hon-ja-ye-yo)

How many bags would you like to check in?
짐은 몇 개나 부치실 겁니까?
(jim-eun myeot gae-na bu-chi-sil kkeom-ni-kka)

Two. And can I bring these on board?
두 개요. 그리고 이건 가지고 타도 되죠?
(du-gae-yo geu-ri-go i-geon ga-ji-go ta-do doe-jyo)

Yes, you can bring up to two.
네. 두 개까지 괜찮습니다.
(ne du-gae-kka-ji gwaen-chan-seum-ni-da)

What kind of seat do you prefer?
좌석은 어느 쪽으로 드릴까요?
(jwa-seog-eun eo-neu jjog-eu-ro deu-ril-kka-yo)

A window seat, please.
창측으로 주세요.
(chang-cheug-eu-ro ju-se-yo)

Do you need anything else?
혹시 더 필요한 게 있으십니까?
(hok-si deo pil-yo-han ge iss-eu-sim-ni-kka)

Can I have my mileage registered in this card?
이 카드에 마일리지 좀 넣어 주시겠어요?
(i ka-deu-e ma-il-li-ji jom neo-eo ju-si-gess-eo-yo)

Yes, please let me have it.
네, 이리 주십시오.
(ne i-ri ju-sip-si-o)

Here are your passport and boarding pass.
여기 손님 여권하고 보딩패스 있습니다.
(yeo-gi son-nim yeo-kkwon-ha-go bo-ding-pae-sseu
  it-seum-ni-da)

The gate number is 38 and your seat number is 27A.
게이트는 38번이고 좌석번호는 27A입니다.
(ge-i-teu-neun sam-sip-pal-beon-i-go jwa-seok-beon-
  ho-neun i-sip-chil-e-i-im-ni-da)

Have a nice trip.
즐거운 여행 되십시오.
(jeul-geo-un yeo-haeng doe-sip-si-o)

Vocabulary

airport fee	공항이용료 (gong-hang-i-yong-nyo)
airline ticket	비행기표 (bi-haeng-gi-pyo)
airplane	비행기 (bi-haeng-gi)
airport	비행장 (bi-haeng-jang)
	공항 (gong-hang)
arrival	도착하는 곳 (do-cha-ka-neun got)
baggage claim	수하물 찾는 곳 (su-ha-nul chan-neun got)
boarding pass	보딩패스 (bo-ding-pae-sseu)
check-in counter	수속 (su-sok)
customs	세관 (se-gwan)
departure	출발하는 곳 (chul-bal-ha-neun got)
departure check	출국심사 (chul-guk-sim-sa)
entry check	입국심사 (ip-guk-sim-sa)
ground transportation	차 타는 곳 (cha ta-neun got)
passport	여권 (yeo-kkwon)
VISA (credit card)	비자 (bi-ja)
domestic airlines	국내선 (gung-nae-seon)
international airlines	국제선 (guk-je-seon)
citizen	내국인 (nae-gug-in)
foreigner	외국인 (oe-gug-in)

(2) Traveling by train or express bus
기차나 고속버스 타기
(gi-cha-na go-sok-ppeo-sseu ta-gi)

Two tickets to Pusan please.
부산행 두 장만 주세요.
(bu-san-haeng du-jang-man ju-se-yo)

Two. It's 20,000 won.
두 장이요. 20,000원입니다.
(du-jang-i-yo i-man-won-im-ni-da)

What time does the train leave?
이거 몇 시 표지요?
(i-geo myeot si pyo-ji-yo)
몇 시에 출발하지요?
(myeot si-e chul-bal-ha-ji-yo)

At 12:30.
12시 30분인데요.
(yeol-ttu-si sam-sip-bun-in-de-yo)

Then, what time will it arrive in Pusan?
그럼 몇 시에 부산에 도착하나요?
(geu-reom myeot si-e bu-san-e do-cha-ka-na-yo)

It takes about 5 hours.
보통 5시간 정도 걸려요.
(bo-tong da-seot-si-gan jeong-do geol-lyeo-yo)

Where is the riding spot?
기차 타는 데가 어디죠?
(gi-cha ta-neun de-ga eo-di-jyo)

Do you see the sign "Busanhaeng" at platform
number 7?
저기 7번 플랫폼에 '부산행'이라고 써 있지요?
(jeo-gi chil-beon peul-laet-pom-e bu-san-haeng-i-ra-go
sseo it-ji-yo)

Please wait over there.
그쪽에 가서 기다리세요.
(geu-jjog-e ga-seo gi-da-ri-se-yo)

Do I have to change trains or does the train go directly to
the stop?
중간에 기차를 갈아타야 되나요, 아니면 바로 가나요?
(jung-gan-e gi-cha-reul gal-a-ta-ya doe-na-yo a-ni-myeon
ba-ro ga-na-yo)

It goes directly there, so you don't need to change.
직행이니까 갈아타지 않으셔도 돼요.
(ji-kaeng-i-ni-kka gal-a-ta-ji an-eu-syeo-do dwae-yo)

Excuse me. Is this seat taken? May I sit here?
실례지만 여기 자리 있습니까? 좀 앉아도 될까요?
(sil-lye-ji-man yeo-gi ja-ri it-seum-ni-kka jom anj-a-do
doel-kka-yo)

No, it's not taken. Please have a seat.
아무도 없어요. 앉으세요.
(a-mu-do eops-eo-yo anj-eu-se-yo)

I am sorry, but this seat is taken.
죄송하지만 누가 있는데요.
(joe-song-ha-ji-man nu-ga in-neun-de-yo)

Excuse me. Do you know where the lost-and-found office is?
실례지만 혹시 분실물 신고소가 어디 있는지 아세요?
(sil-lye-ji-man hok-si bun-sil-mul sin-go-so-ga eo-di in-neun-ji a-se-yo)

I'm not sure.
잘 모르겠는데요.
(jal mo-reu-gen-neun-de-yo)

Go straight, and you can see the office on your right side.
쭉 가시다가 보면 오른쪽에 있어요.
(jjuk ga-si-da bo-myeon o-reun-jjog-e iss-eo-yo)

Due to a passing train going to Seoul, departure is delayed.
상행선 기차 통과 관계로 잠시 출발이 지연되고 있습니다.
(sang-haeng-seon gi-cha tong-gwa gwan-gye-ro jam-si chul-bal-i ji-yeon-doe-go it-seum-ni-da)

Please stay seated for a moment.
자리에 앉아서 잠시 기다려 주시기 바랍니다.
(ja-ri-e anj-a-seo jam-si gi-da-ryeo ju-si-gi ba-ram-ni-da)

We will now begin to check tickets.
지금부터 가지고 계신 좌석표 검사를 실시하겠습니다.
(ji-geum-bu-teo ga-ji-go gye-sin jwa-seok-pyo geom-sa-reul sil-ssi-ha-get-seum-ni-da)

Please be prepared.
준비해 주시기 바랍니다.
(jun-bi-hae ju-si-gi ba-ram-ni-da)

Vocabulary

A first-class train ticket offers the fastest and best way to travel by rail in Korea. It stops at the least number of stations and it has the most amenities, including a dining room. The other three classes of train—second, third, and pigeon—go slower and have more stops, with second-class travel stopping the least and pigeon-class stopping the most.

First-class (*lit.* New Community)　**새마을호**
(sae-ma-eul-ho)

- Fastest and best way to travel by train.
- Stops at least number of stations.
- Has the most amenities, including a dining room.

Second-class (*lit.* Asian Hibiscus)　**무궁화호**
(mu-gung-hwa-ho)

Third-class (*lit.* Unification)　**통일호**
(tong-il-ho)

- Stops at almost every station.

Fourth-class (*lit.* pigeon)　**비둘기호**
(bi-dul-gi-ho)

- Slowest and stops every station.

in-bound train to Seoul　**상행선**
(sang-haeng-seon)

out-bound train from Seoul　**하행선**
(ha-haeng-seon)

seating ticket　**좌석표**
(jwa-seok-pyo)

(3) Taking a Taxi
택시 타기 (taek-si-ta-gi)

Where shall I take you?
어디로 모실까요? /
(eo-di-ro mo-sil-kka-yo)
어디까지 가십니까?
(eo-di-kka-ji ga-sim-ni-kka)

Dongdaemoon market, please.
동대문 시장까지 좀 부탁합니다.
(dong-dae-mun si-jang-kka-ji jom bu-ta-kam-ni-da)

OK. Is it OK if you ride with other passengers?
**알겠습니다. 그런데 죄송하지만 합승 좀 해도
되겠습니까?**
(al-get-seum-ni-da geu-reon-de joe-song-ha-ji-man
hap-seung jom hae-do doe-get-seum-ni-kka)

Go ahead. By the way, the traffic is so heavy.
네, 그러세요. 그런데 길이 많이 막히네요.
(ne geu-reo-se-yo geu-reon-de gil-i man-i ma-ki-ne-yo)

It is as usual in downtown Seoul.
서울 시내는 언제나 이래요.
(seo-ul si-nae-neun eon-je-na i-rae-yo)

Gee... I am late for my appointment...
큰일 났네요. 약속시간에 늦었는데...
(keun-il nan-ne-yo yak-sok-si-gan-e neuj-eon-neun-de)

We are almost there. Where do you want me to stop?
거의 다 왔는데 어디 세워 드릴까요?
(geo-ui da wan-neun-de eo-di se-wo deu-ril-kka-yo)

Under the overpass there, please.
저기 육교 밑에 세워 주세요.
(jeo-gi yuk-gyo mit-e se-wo ju-se-yo)

The fare is 9,600 won.
요금은 9,600원 나왔습니다.
(yo-geum-eun gu-cheon-yuk-baeg-won na-wat-seum-
ni-da)

Here is a 10,000 won bill. Keep the change please.
여기 10,000원짜리요. 잔돈은 그냥 가지세요.
(yeo-gi man-won-jja-ri-yo jan-don-eun geu-nyang
ga-ji-se-yo)

Thank you. Good-bye.
고맙습니다. 안녕히 가세요.
(go-map-seum-ni-da an-nyeong-hi ga-se-yo)

(4) Taking the Subway
지하철 타기 (ji-ha-cheol ta-gi)

Buying a Ticket

Two tickets for zone 1, please.
1구간 두장이요.
(il-gu-gan du-jang-i-yo)

One ticket to Dongdaemoon Stadium please.
동대문 운동장 한 장만 주세요.
(dong-dae-mun un-dong-jang han-jang-man ju-se-yo)

The incoming train is going to Sadang.
지금 사당, 사당행 열차가 도착하고 있습니다.
(ji-geum sa-sang sa-dang-haeng yeol-cha-ga do-cha-ka-go it-seum-ni-da)

For your safety, please step back behind the safety line.
승객 여러분의 안전을 위해 안전선 밖으로 한걸음 물러서 주시기 바랍니다.
(seung-gaek yeo-reo-bun-ui an-jeon-eul wi-hae an-jeon-seon bakk-eu-ro han-geol-eum mul-leo-seo ju-si-gi ba-ram-ni-da)

This train is to Sadang.
이번 열차는 사당, 사당행 열차입니다.
(i-beon yeol-cha-neun sa-dang sa-dang-haeng yeol-cha-im-ni-da)

This stop is Samsonkyo station.
이번 정차할 역은 삼선교, 삼선교역입니다.
(i-beon jeong-cha-hal yeog-eun san-seon-gyo san-seon-gyo yeog-im-ni-da)

Please use the exit to your left.
내리실 문은 왼쪽입니다.
(nae-ri-sil mun-eun oen-jjog-im-ni-da)

Next stop is Haehwa station.
다음은 혜화역에서 정차하겠습니다.
(da-eum-eun hye-hwa-yeog-e-seo jeong-cha-ha-get-seum-ni-da)

If your destination is Chungmuro or Uljiro, please get
off at this station and transfer to line number 3.
**충무로나 을지로 방면으로 가시는 손님들께서는
이번 역에서 하차하셔서 3호선 열차로
갈아타시기 바랍니다.**
(chung-mu-ro-na eul-jji-ro bang-myeon-eu-ro ga-si-
neun son-nim-deul-kke-seo-neun i-beon yeog-e-
seo ha-cha-ha-syeo-seo sam-ho-seon yeol-cha-ro
gal-a-ta-si-gi ba-ram-ni-da)

Vocabulary

closed line	미개통구간	(mi-gae-tong-gu-gan)
exit	나가는 곳	(na-ga-neun got)
left	왼쪽	(oen-jjok)
right	오른쪽	(o-reun-jjok)
subway map	수도권 전철 노선도	
	(su-do-kkwon jeon-cheol no-seon-do)	
transfer platform	갈아타는 곳	(gal-a-ta-neun got)
waystation	환승역	(hwan-seung-nyeok)

(5) Car Rental
차 빌리기 (cha bil-li-gi)

I would like to rent a car. How much is it per day?
차를 좀 빌리고 싶은데요. 하루에 얼마지요?
(cha-reul jom bil-li-go sip-eun-de-yo ha-ru-e eol-ma-ji-yo)

Do you want a compact car or a sedan?
소형차로 하실 건가요, 중형차로 하실 건가요?
(so-hyeong-cha-ro ha-sil kkeon-ga-yo jung-hyeong-
cha-ro ha-sil kkeon-ga-yo)

A compact car, please.
소형차요.
(so-hyeong-cha-yo)

How many days do you want the rental?
며칠이나 쓰실 건데요?
(myeo-chil-i-na sseu-sil kkeon-de-yo)

Four days, please.
한 4일만 해 주세요.
(han sa-il-man hae ju-se-yo)

It's 50,000 won per day, including insurance.
그럼 보험료 포함해서 하루에 50,000원이에요.
(geu-reom bo-heom-nyo po-ham-hae-seo ha-ru-e o-
man-won-i-e-yo)

May I have your ID and driver's license, please?
신분증하고 운전면허증 좀 주시겠어요?
(sin-bun-jjeung-ha-go un-jeon-myeon-heo-jjeung jom
ju-si-gess-eo-yo)

Here it is.
여기요.
(yeo-gi-yo)

Your total is 200,000 won with tax. Please sign here.
세금 포함해서 모두 20만원입니다. 여기 사인 좀 해
주세요.
(se-geum po-ham-hae-seo mo-du i-sim-man-won-im-
ni-da yeo-gi ssa-in jom hae ju-se-yo)

OK, now all set?
그러죠. 그럼 이제 다 됐나요?
(geu-reo-jyo geu-reom i-je da dwaen-na-yo)

Yes, here are your credit card and ID.
네, 다 됐습니다. 여기 카드하고 신분증 있습니다.
(ne da dwaet-seum-ni-da yeo-gi ka-deu-ha-go sin-bun-
jjeung it-seum-ni-da)

Vocabulary

car insurance	자동차 보험료
	(ja-dong-cha bo-heom-nyo)
driver's license	운전면허증
	(un-jeon-myeon-heo-jjeung)
international driver's license	국제면허증
	(guk-je-myeon-heo-jjeung)
personal ID	신분증 (sin-bun-jjeung)

(6) Gas Station
기름 넣기 (gi-reum neo-ki)

Welcome. How high do you want to fill it?
어서 오세요. 얼마나 넣어 드릴까요?
(eo-seo-o-se-yo eol-ma-na neo-eo deu-ril-kka-yo)

Fill it up, please.
꽉 채워 주세요.
(kkwak chae-wo ju-se-yo)

Please fill up to 50,000 won only.
50,000원 어치만 넣어 주세요.
(o-man-won-eo-chi-man neo-eo ju-se-yo)

(7) Direction
길 물어보기 (gil mul-eo-bo-gi)

I am lost. Could you tell me where I am?
길을 잃어버린 것 같은데 실례지만 여기가 어디죠?
(gil-eul il-eo-beo-rin geot gat-eun-de sil-lye-ji-man yeo-gi-ga eo-di-jyo)

You are in front of Banghak middle school. Where are you going?
방학 중학교 앞인데요. 어디로 가시게요?
(bang-hak jung-hak-gyo ap-in-de-yo eo-di-ro ga-si-ge-yo)

How can I get to Dream Land?
드림랜드로 가려면 어떻게 가야 되나요?
(deu-rim-raen-deu-ro ga-ryeo-myeon eo-tteo-ke ga-ya doe-na-yo)

Go straight to this street, and turn left in the first traffic signal.
그럼 이 길로 똑바로 가시다가 첫 번째 신호등에서 좌회전하세요.
(geu-reom i gil-lo ttok-ba-ro ga-si-da-ga cheot-beon-jjae sin-ho-deung-e-seo jwa-hoe-jeon-ha-se-yo)

You made a wrong turn. You have to turn back.
길을 잘 못 드셨는데요. 다시 돌아가셔야 돼요.
(gil-eul jal mot deu-syeon-neun-de-yo da-si dol-a-ga-syeo-ya dwae-yo)

Vocabulary

traffic signal	신호등 (sin-ho-deung)
crosswalk	횡단보도 (hoeng-dan-bo-do)
overpass	육교 (yuk-gyo)
underpass	지하도 (ji-ha-do)
intersection	교차로 (gyo-cha-ro)
four-way intersection	사거리 (sa-geo-ri)
three-way intersection	삼거리 (sam-geo-ri)
to go straight	직진하다 (jik-jin-ha-da)
	똑바로 가다 (ttok-ba-ro ga-da)
to go back	되돌아 가다 (doe-dol-a ga-da)
to turn left	좌회전하다 (jwa-hoe-jeon-ha-da)
	왼쪽으로 가다 (oen-jjog-eu-ro ga-da)
to turn right	우회전하다 (u-hoe-jeon-ha-da)
	오른쪽으로 가다 (o-reun-jjog-eu-ro ga-da)
to jaywalk	무단횡단을 하다 (mu-dan hoeng-dan-eul ha-da)

Lesson 14. Communications & Media
통신수단과 대중매체
(tong-sin-su-dan-gwa dae-jung-mae-che)

1. Phone and Fax

(1) Cultural Notes

Phone cards are the most common means of paying for a public phone and are available at most convenience stores. Some public phones accept credit cards, but only a few take coins. If you wish to make an international call, you must enter the prefix 001, 002, 007, or 008, followed by the appropriate country prefix. You then enter the actual phone number. When you want to make a long-distance call, the number must be preceded the area code (see below). You then follow the same instructions as for regular phones. You can look up a number in the telephone book or dial 114 for directory service. Telephone books can be found under the telephone in the telephone booth.

In case of emergency, 112 (Police Dept.) or 119 (Fire Dept.) can be dialed toll-free from any phone. These numbers connect you to an operator at the emergency service centers. When you speak to the operator, you need to state your name, your location, what the problem is, and ask for appropriate assistance.

In Korea, it is not easy to send or receive a fax unless one has a fax machine in one's house. Usually you can use fax service at a stationery store or a copy service store near a university. However, the fee is very high.

Country Prefixes

Australia	61
Canada	1
China	86
France	33
Germany	49
Japan	81
Korea	82
Taiwan	886
UK	44
USA	1

Long-Distance Area Codes

강원	(gang-won)	33
경기	(gyeong-gi)	31
경남	(gyeong-nam)	55
경북	(gyeong-buk)	54
광주	(gwang-ju)	62
대구	(dae-gu)	53
대전	(dae-jeon)	42
부산	(bu-san)	51
서울	(seo-ul)	2
울산	(ul-ssan)	52
인천	(in-cheon)	32
전남	(jeon-nam)	61
전북	(jeon-buk)	63
제주	(je-ju)	64
충남	(chung-nam)	41
충북	(chung-buk)	43

(2) Model Phrases

Excuse me. May I use the phone?
죄송하지만 전화 좀 써도 될까요?
(joe-song-ha-ji-man jeon-hwa jom sseo-do doel-kka-yo)

> Sure. Please.
> **그럼요. 쓰세요.**
> (geu-reom-nyo sseu-se-yo)

Hello, is this the residence of Mr. Kangjin Lee?
여보세요, 거기 이강진씨 댁이지요?
(yeo-bo-se-yo geo-gi i-gang-jin-ssi daeg-i-ji-yo)

> Yes, it is.
> **네, 그런데요.**
> (ne geu-reon-de-yo)

> No, you have the wrong number.
> **아니오, 전화 잘 못 거신 것 같은데요.**
> (a-ni-o jeon-hwa jal mot geo-sin geot gat-eun-de-yo)

May I talk to Mr. Lee?
실례지만 이강진씨 좀 바꿔 주시겠습니까?
(sil-lye-ji-man i-gang-jin-ssi jom ba-kkwo ju-si-get-seum-
ni-kka)

Is Mr. Lee at home now?
죄송하지만 이강진씨 지금 댁에 계십니까?
(joe-song-ha-ji-man i-gang-jin-ssi ji-geum daeg-e gye-sim-
ni-kka)

> This is he.
> **전데요.**
> (jeon-de-yo)

> Wait a moment, please.
> **네, 잠깐만 기다리세요.**
> (ne jam-kkan-man gi-da-ri-se-yo)

> He is not in now.
> **지금 집에 없는데요.**
> (ji-geum jib-e eom-neun-de-yo)

Really? Then when will he be back home?
그러세요? 그럼 언제쯤 집에 돌아오시나요?
(geu-reo-se-yo geu-reom eon-je-jjeum jib-e
dol-a-o-si-na-yo)

> Maybe around 8:00 tonight.
> **아마 저녁 8시쯤 돌아올 거예요.**
> (a-ma jeo-nyeok yeo-deol-ssi-jjeum dol-a-ol
> kkeo-ye-yo)

> I don't know. I am not sure.
> **글쎄요. 저도 잘 모르겠는데요.**
> (geul-sse-yo jeo-do jal mo-reu-gen-neun-de-yo)

> Would you like to leave a message?
> **뭐 전하실 말씀 있으시면 메모 해 드릴까요?**
> (mwo jeon-ha-sil mal-sseum iss-eu-si-myeon me-mo
> hae deu-ril-kka-yo)

Yes, may I leave a message, then?
네, 그럼 죄송하지만 메모 좀 남겨 주시겠어요?
(ne geu-reom joe-song-ha-ji-man me-mo jom nam-gyeo ju-
si-gess-eo-yo)

No, that's OK.
아니오, 괜찮습니다.
(a-ni-yo gwaen-chan-seum-ni-da)

Then I will call him again around 8:00.
그럼 제가 8시쯤에 다시 전화하겠습니다.
(geu-reom je-ga yeo-deol-ssi-jjeum-e da-si jeon-hwa-ha-
     get-seum-ni-da)

This is Marcia Hartsock.
저는 마샤 핫삭이라고 하는데요.
(jeo-neun ma-sya-hat-sag-i-ra-go ha-neun-de-yo)

Would you please tell him that I called?
전화 왔었다고 좀 전해 주시겠어요?
(jeon-hwa wass-eot-da-go jom jeon-hae-ju-si-gess-eo-yo)

It's ringing, but no one is answering the phone.
신호는 가는데 전화를 안 받는데요.
(sin-ho-neun ga-neun-de jeon-hwa-reul an
     ban-neun-de-yo)

The answering machine is on.
자동 응답기가 받는데요.
(ja-dong eung-dap-gi-ga ban-neun-de-yo)

Please leave a message on the answering machine.
자동 응답기에 메모를 남겨 주세요.
(ja-dong eung-dap-gi-e me-mo-reul nam-gyeo ju-se-yo)

The line is still busy.
전화가 계속 통화중이에요.
(jeon-hwa-ga gye-sok tong-hwa-jung-i-e-yo)

Maybe the phone is out of order.
전화가 고장난 것 같아요.
(jeon-hwa-ga go-jang-nan geot gat-a-yo)

The line has been disconnected.
전화가 끊어졌어요.
(jeon-hwa-ga kkeun-eo-jeoss-eo-yo)

I am sorry. I must have dialed the wrong number.
죄송합니다. 전화를 잘 못 건 것 같아요.
(joe-song-ham-ni-da jeon-hwa-reul jal mot geon geot
    gat-a-yo)

It seems like no one is home.
집에 아무도 없나봐요.
(jib-e a-mu-do eom-na-bwa-yo)

Can I send a fax to this number?
혹시 이 번호로 팩스를 보내도 될까요?
(hok-si i beon-ho-ro paek-seu-reul bo-nae-do doel-kka-yo)

Do you have a fax machine?
혹시 집에 팩스가 있으세요?
(hok-si jib-e paek-seu-ga iss-eu-se-yo)

What is the area code?
지역번호가 어떻게 되나요?
(ji-yeok-beon-ho-ga eo-tteo-ke doe-na-yo)

I would like to make a collect call.
수신자 부담으로 전화를 좀 걸고 싶은데요.
(su-sin-ja bu-dam-eu-ro jeon-hwa-reul jom geol-go sip-
    eun-de-yo)

Emergency Calls

Hello, is this 119?
여보세요, 거기 119죠?
(yeo-bo-se-yo geo-gi il-il-gu-jyo)

There has been a car accident.
여기 차 사고가 났는데요.
(yeo-gi cha sa-go-ga nan-neun-de-yo)

Please send an ambulance here immediately.
구급차 좀 빨리 보내주시겠어요?
(gu-geup-cha jom ppal-li bo-nae-ju-si-gess-eo-yo)

It seems that the passenger is seriously injured.
사람이 많이 다친 것 같아요.
(sa-ram-i man-i da-chin-geot gat-a-yo)

OK, where is the location?
잘 알겠습니다. 거기 위치가 어디죠?
(jal al-get-seum-ni-da geo-gi wi-chi-ga eo-di-jyo)

I don't know the address.
주소는 잘 모르겠는데요.
(ju-so-neun jal mo-reu-gen-neun-de-yo)

It's near the City Bank in Apgujeong-dong.
압구정동 시티은행에서 가까워요.
(ap-gu-jeong-dong ssi-ti-eun-haeng-e-seo ga-kka-wo-yo)

OK, an ambulance will be there soon.
알겠습니다. 구급차가 곧 도착할 겁니다.
(al-get-seum-ni-da gu-geup-cha-ga got do-cha-kal kkeom-ni-da)

Thank you for your report.
신고해 주셔서 감사합니다.
(sin-go-hae ju-syeo-seo gam-sa-ham-ni-da)

Vocabulary

ambulance	앰뷸런스 (aem-byul-leon-seu)	
	구급차 (gu-geup-cha)	
fire department	소방서 (so-bang-seo)	
fire truck	소방차 (so-bang-cha)	
poison information	독극물 관련 정보 (dok-geung-mul gwal-lyeon jeong-bo)	
police	경찰 (gyeong-chal)	
police department	경찰서 (gyeong-chal-sseo)	
a car accident occurs	차 사고가 나다 (cha sa-go-ga na-da)	
a fire occurs	불이 나다 (bul-i na-da)	
someone is hurt	사람이 다치다 (sa-ram-i da-chi-da)	

2. E-mail and Internet

(1) Cultural Notes

Internet cafés or computer access places are common in most cities. Internet cafés are one of the most frequent hangout places for young people who enjoy online games. Some public libraries or post offices also offer Internet access. Most homes have Internet subscriptions. ADSL and cable service are very common and telephone hook-ups are rare these days.

(2) Model Phrases

Is there a place near here where I can get access to
  computer?
혹시 이 근처에 PC방이 어디 있는지 아세요?
(hok-si i geun-cheo-e pi-ssi-bang-i eo-di in-neun-ji a-se-yo)

  Go straight, and you can find many in front of the
    school.
  좀 내려가시다 보면 학교 앞에 많이 있어요.
  (jom nae-ryeo-ga-si-da bo-myeon hak-gyo ap-e man-i
    iss-eo-yo)

How much do you charge per hour?
이 PC방 한시간에 얼마죠?
(i pi-ssi-bang han-si-gan-e eol-ma-jyo)

  3000 won per hour.
  시간당 3000원인데요.
  (si-gan-dang sam-cheon-won-in-de-yo)

May I check my e-mail here?
여기서 이메일 체크도 할 수 있나요?
(yeo-gi-seo i-me-il che-keu-do hal ssu in-na-yo)

  Sure.
  그럼요.
  (geu-reom-nyo)

3. Copying Services

(1) Cultural Notes

In Korea, you can get copy service at bookstores, photocopy stores, and stationery shops near the schools. Whether self-service or full-service is provided depends on the store. Only photocopy stores offer binding services. Unlike those in the U.S., Korean photocopy stores do not have computers for public use.

(2) Model Phrases

Can I have some copies made here?
여기서 복사 좀 할 수 있나요?
(yeo-gi-seo bok-sa jom hal ssu in-na-yo)

> Sure.
> **네, 그럼요.**
> (ne geu-reom-nyo)

> We do not have a machine. Would you try next door?
> **우리집엔 없는데 옆집에 한번 가 보세요.**
> (u-ri-jib-en eom-neun-de yeop-jib-e han-beon ga
>   bo-se-yo)

> Do you want to make copies yourself, or do you want
>   me to do them for you?
> **복사 직접 하실래요, 아니면 해 드릴까요?**
> (bok-sa jik-jeop ha-sil-lae-yo a-ni-myeon hae
>   deu-ril-kka-yo)

I only have a few pages, so I will do it.
몇 장 안되니까 제가 할게요.
(myeot-jang an-doe-ni-kka je-ga hal-kke-yo)

I have a lot, so would you please do it for me?
분량이 좀 많으니까 좀 해 주시겠어요?
(bul-lyang-i jom man-eu-ni-kka jom hae ju-si-gess-eo-yo)

When do you want me to come back?
언제 찾으러 오면 되나요?
(eon-je chaj-eu-reo o-myeon doe-na-yo)

> Please come back in about 3 hours.
> **한 3시간쯤 있다가 와 보세요.**
> (han se-si-gan jjeum it-da-ga wa bo-se-yo)

How much do you charge per page for copying?
복사 한 장에 얼마씩이에요?
(bok-sa han-jang-e eol-ma-ssig-i-e-yo)

> 100 won per page.
> **한 장에 100원씩이에요.**
> (han-jang-e baeg-won-ssig-i-e-yo)

Would you please bind them after copying?
복사 다 하신 다음에 제본도 좀 해 주시겠어요?
(bok-sa da ha-sin da-eum-e je-bon-do jom hae
　　ju-si-gess-eo-yo)

OK. How would you like your binding done?
그러세요. 제본은 어떻게 해 드릴까요?
(geu-reo-se-yo je-bon-eun eo-tteo-ke hae
　　　deu-ril-kka-yo)

Spiral binding, please.
스프링으로 해 주세요.
(seu-peu-ring-eu-ro hae ju-se-yo)

Vocabulary

to bind	제본하다	(je-bon-ha-da)
copy machine	복사기	(bok-sa-gi)
paper clip	클립	(keul-lip)
to photocopy	복사하다	(bok-sa-ha-da)
stapler	호치키스	(ho-chi-ki-seu)

4. Media

Cultural Notes

Some large hotels and public libraries provide international
newspapers and magazines. Some large bookstores also
have certain English-language magazines. There is an
English-language TV channel, which is mainly watched by
U.S. military personnel. The largest newspaper is the
Choson Daily Newspaper. The *Korea Herald* is the only
daily newspaper published in English. Many newspapers
publish news online.

Lesson 15. Numerals, Numbers and Weights & Measures
수량 단위 (su-ryang dan-wi)

Korean uses two sets of numbers, native Korean numbers and Sino-Korean numbers. Some native Korean numbers have two forms, depending on whether they are followed by a counter or used in isolation.

When you count, you must use different counters. Nouns are classified into many groups depending on shape or kind. Some counters take Sino-Korean numbers, and others take native numbers. Word order in counting is noun + particle + number + counter, as in 사과가 네개 있어요. (sa-gwa-ga ne-gae iss-eo-yo). *There are four apples.*

1. Numeral and Numbers

Cardinal numbers

Number	Sino-Korean	Native Korean
1	일 (il)	하나 (ha-na) (한- [han-])
2	이 (i)	둘 (dul) (두- [du-])
3	삼 (sam)	셋 (set) (세- [se-])
4	사 (sa)	넷 (net) (네- [ne-])
5	오 (o)	다섯 (da-seot)
6	육 (yuk)	여섯 (yeo-seot)
7	칠 (chil)	일곱 (il-gop)
8	팔 (pal)	여덟 (yeo-deol)
9	구 (gu)	아홉 (a-hop)
10	십 (sip)	열 (yeol)
20	이십 (i-sip)	스물 (seu-nul)
		(스무- [seu-mu-])
30	삼십 (sam-sip)	서른 (seo-reun)
40	사십 (sa-sip)	마흔 (ma-heun)
50	오십 (o-sip)	쉰 (swin)
60	육십 (uk-sip)	예순 (ye-sun)
70	칠십 (chil-ssip)	일흔 (il-heun)
80	팔십 (pal-ssip)	여든 (yeo-deun)
90	구십 (gu-sip)	아흔 (a-heun)
100	백 (baek)	백 (baek)

| 1000 | 천 (cheon) | 천 (cheon) |
| 10000 | 만 (man) | 만 (man) |

Examples

17	십칠 (sip-chil)
	열일곱 (yeol-il-gop)
246	이백사십육 (i-baek-sa-sim-nyuk)
	이백마흔여섯 (i-baek-ma-heun-yeo-seot)
3589	삼천오백팔십구
	(sam-cheon-o-baek-pal-ssip-gu)
	삼천오백여든아홉
	(sam-cheon-o-baek-yeo-deun-a-hop)

Counters

With Sino-Korean Numbers

year/month/date	1965-7-28 (July 28, 1965)
	천구백육십오년 칠월 이십팔일
	(cheon-gu-baek yuk-sip o-nyeon chil-wol i-sip-pal-il)
phone number	534-7642	오삼사에 칠육사이
		(o-sam-sa-e chil-lyuk-sa-i)
time (minutes)	30분	삼십분 (sam-sip-bun)
mathematics	2 x 3 = 6	이 곱하기 삼은 육
		(i go-pa-gi sam-eun yuk)
	1/5	오분의 일 (o-bun-ui il)
	0.75	영 칠오
		(yeong-jjeom chil-o)
story, floor	9층	구층 (gu-cheung)
money	50원	오십원 (o-sib-won)
	50불	오십불 (o-sip-bul)

With Native Korean Numbers

time (the hour)	12시	열두시 (yeol-ttu-si)
time (hours)	4시간	네시간 (ne-si-gan)
people	3사람	세사람 (se-sa-ram),
		세명 (se-myeong)
items	10개	열개 (yeol-kkae)
months	5달	다섯달 (da-seot-dal)

bottles	7병	일곱병 (il-gop-byeong)
glasses, cups	1잔	한잔 (han-jan)

Ordinal numbers

	Sino-Korean	Native Korean
first	첫째 (cheot-jjae)	첫번째 (cheot-beon-jjae)
second	둘째 (dul-jjae)	두번째 (du-beon-jjae)
third	셋째 (set-jjae)	세번째 (se-beon-jjae)
fourth	넷째 (net-jjae)	네번째 (ne-beon-jjae)
fifth	다섯째 (da-seot-jjae)	다섯번째 (da-seot-beon-jjae)
sixth	여섯째 (yeo-seot-jjae)	여섯번째 (yeo-seot-beon-jjae)
seventh	일곱째 (il-gop-jjae)	일곱번째 (il-gop-beon-jjae)
eighth	여덜째 (yeo-deol-jjae)	여덜번째 (yeo-deol-ppeon-jjae)
ninth	아홉째 (a-hop-jjae)	아홉번째 (a-hop-beon-jjae)
tenth	열째 (yeol-jjae)	열번째 (yeol-ppeon-jjae)
eleventh		열한번째 (yeol-han-beon-jjae)
twelveth		열두번째 (yeol-ttu-beon-jjae)
nineteenth		열아홉번째 (yeo-a-hop-beon-jjae)
twentieth		스무번째 (seu-mu-beon-jjae)
twenty-first		스물한번째 (seu-mul-han-beon-jjae)
twenty-second		스물두번째 (seu-mul-ttu-beon-jjae)
twenty-ninth		스물아홉번째 (seu-mul-a-hop-beon-jjae)
thirtieth		서른번째 (seo-reun-beon-jjae)

	Sino-Korean	Native Korean
fortieth		마흔번째 (ma-heun-beon-jjae)
fiftieth		쉰번째 (swin-beon-jjae)
sixtieth		예순번째 (ye-sun-beon-jjae)
seventieth		일흔번째 (il-heun-beon-jjae)
eightieth		여든번째 (yeo-deun-beon-jjae)
ninetieth		아흔번째 (a-heun-beon-jjae)
hundredth		백번째 (baek-beon-jjae)

Days

	Sino-Korean	Native-Korean
one day	일일 (il-il)	하루 (ha-ru)
two days	이일 (i-il)	이틀 (i-teul)
three days	삼일 (sam-il)	사흘 (sa-heul)
four days	사일 (sa-il)	나흘 (na-heul)
five days	오일 (o-il)	닷새 (tat-sae)
six days	육일 (yug-il)	엿새 (yeot-sae)
seven days	칠일 (chil-il)	이레 (i-re)
eight days	팔일 (pal-il)	여드레 (yeo-deu-re)
nine days	구일 (gu-il)	아흐레 (a-heu-re)
ten days	십일 (sib-il)	열흘 (yeol-heul)
fifteen days	십오일 (sib-o-il)	열닷새 (yeol-dat-sae) /보름 (bo-reum)
twenty days	이십일 (i-sib-il)	스무날 (seu-mu-nal)

2. Weights and Measures

Weight

1 kilogram = approx. 2.2 pounds
100 gram = approx. 3.5 ounces
1 pound = approx. 455 grams
1 ounce = approx. 28.5 grams

Liquid

1 liter = approx. 1 quart
1 gallon = approx. 3.8 liters
1 pint = approx. 0.47 liters
1 quart = approx. 0.95 liters

Distance

1 kilometer = approx. 0.62 mile
1 meter = approx. 39.3 inches
1 mile = approx. 1.6 kilometers
1 yard = approx. 91.4 centimeters
1 foot = approx. 0.31 meter
1 inch = approx. 2.54 centimeters

Fahrenheit and Celsius conversion

$°C = (°F - 32) \times 5/9$
$°F = (°C \times 9/5) + 32$

Handy approximations

5 centimeters = 2 inches
10 centimeters = 4 inches
30 centimeters = 1 foot
10 kilometers = 6 miles
16 kilometers = 10 miles
0°C = 32°F
16°C = 61°F
30°C = 86°F

Vocabulary

centimeter	센티미터	(sen-ti-mi-teo)
foot	피트	(pi-teu)
gallon	갤런	(gael-leon)
gram	그램	(geu-raem)
inch	인치	(in-chi)
kilogram	킬로그램	(kil-lo-geu-raem)
kilometer	킬로미터	(kil-lo-mi-teo)
liter	리터	(li-teo)
meter	미터	(mi-teo)
mile	마일	(ma-il)

ounce	온스	(on-sseu)
pint	파인트	(pa-in-teu)
pound	파운드	(pa-un-deu)
quart	쿼터	(qwo-teo)
ton	톤	(ton)

REFERENCES

말이 트이는 한국어 1, 1999, Ewha Woman's University Press: Seoul, Korea

말이 트이는 한국어 2, 1999, Ewha Woman's University Press: Seoul, Korea

한국어 1, 1993, Korean University Press: Seoul, Korea

한국어 1, 1994, Yonsei University Press: Seoul, Korea

한국어 2, 1994, Yonsei University Press: Seoul, Korea

한국어 2, 1995, Korean University Press: Seoul, Korea

한국어 3, 1993, Korean University Press: Seoul, Korea

한국어 3, 1994, Yonsei University Press: Seoul, Korea

한국어 회화 1, 1996, Korean University Press: Seoul, Korea

한국어 회화 2, 1996, Korean University Press: Seoul, Korea

한국어 회화 3, 1993, Korean University Press: Seoul, Korea

Integrated Korean: Beginning 1, 2000, University of Hawaii Press: Honolulu, Hawaii

Integrated Korean: Beginning 2, 2000, University of Hawaii Press: Honolulu, Hawaii

Integrated Korean: Intermediate 1, 2001, University of Hawaii Press: Honolulu, Hawaii

Integrated Korean: Intermediate 2, 2001, University of Hawaii Press: Honolulu, Hawaii

Introductory Course in Korean Book 1, 1993, Yonsei University Press: Seoul, Korea

The Revised Romanization of Korean, 2000, Ministry of Culture & Tourism: Seoul, Korea

Korean
Dictionary & Phrasebook

Korean-English
English-Korean

Jeyseon & Kangjin Lee

HIPPOCRENE BOOKS, INC.
New York

Pages 7-9, 11-14, 17-19, and 211-213 feature revisions of
material that originally appeared in *Integrated Korean:
Beginning 1*, by Young Mee Cho, Hyo Sang Lee, Carol
Schultz, Ho-Min Sohn, and Sung-Ock Sohn, © 2000
University of Hawaii Press. Used with permission.

For information, address:
HIPPOCRENE BOOKS, INC.
171 Madison Avenue
New York, NY 10016
www.hippocrenebooks.com

Library of Congress Cataloging-in-Publication Data

Lee, Jeyson.
    Korean dictionary & phrasebook / Jeyseon & Kingjin Lee.
    p. cm.
    Includes bibliographical references.
    ISBN-13: 978-0-7818-1029-6
    ISBN-10: 0-7818-1029-9
    1. Korean language--Dictionaries--English. 2. English
Language--Dictionaries--Korean. 3. Korean language--
Conversation and phrase books--English. I. Title: Korean
dictionary and phrasebook. II. Yi, Kang-jin, 1964- III.
Title.

    PL937.E5L435 2005
    495.7'321--dc22

                                        2005050306